AF674182

ENCYCLOPAEDIA OF EDUCATIONAL TERMS

(In 5 Vol.)

Edited & Compiled by:

Ekta Thani, Rohit Sharma,
Anoop Jain, Mohit Sharma, Kanika K.,
C.H. Judd, & L.B. Earhart

Vol. II

SPORTS PUBLICATION

4264/3, Ansari Road, Darya Ganj, Delhi-2
Ph.: 23290142, 27241050, 27562163 (R)

Published by:

Lokesh Thani

SPORTS PUBLICATIONS

H.O. 4264/3, Ansari Road, Darya Ganj, New Delhi-110002
B.O. WP-474, Ist Floor, Shiv Market, Ashok Vihar, Delhi-52
Phones: 23290142, 27241050,
(R) 27562163, (M) 9868028838
E-mail: sportspublication1@rediffmail.com
Website: *www.sportsbookshouse.com*

I.S.B.N. – 81-87818-68-9

PRINTED IN INDIA 2004

Laser Typeset by:

JAIN MEDIA GRAPHICS

B-4/40-A, Lawrence Road, (Keshav Puram),
New Delhi-110035 Ph.: 27183573, (M) 9811430646

Printed by:

BANDEMATRAM PRESS

Maujpur, Delhi

Price: Rs. 4,200/- (In 5 Vol.)

VOL. II

PART 2

MANAGEMENT

The present study provides all information on all aspects of management, its Classifications and it is especially created for the students as well as for the scholars.

The salient features of this books are:

- A to Z terms that covers many subjects which comes under management.
- Vast definitions are explained with instances where necessary.
- Alphabetically arranged terms from A to Z.

With the rapid unveiling of the aetiological factors and also with the changes in the classifications, the field of management has undergone a frequent amendments and which need a dictionary for its completion.

It has been our aim to provide explanations that are easily understood, whilst maintaining a high academic standard.

It is endeavoured to include the more important terms used at advanced level, but would welcome any comments regarding serious omissions or indeed about the content of any of the entries.

PART 2
MANAGEMENT

a and d rates

refers to the published rates that apply to freight moving to assembly or consolidation points and from distribution points.

a and S Insurance

abbreviation of accident and sickness insurance.

aar

refers to the initials for against all risks, with special reference to freight insurance. Also, refers to the initials for association of American Railroads.

ab

abbreviation of Aktieboleg or Aktiebolag which literally means share company. A limited company organized according to the laws of Sweden.

abandonment

in accounting, it refers to the complete retirement of a fixed asset after it is removed from service. There are several legal applications; abandonment of property means the giving up of all control over it with the intentioning of relinquish all claims to it. Loss of property is involuntary: abandonment is a voluntary act. When used in connection with duty or responsibility, abandonment has been synonymous with repudiation.

abatement—of—rent clause

in a lease, it refers to a provision that the tenant will be released from his obligation to pay rent if the premises are made uninhabitable by such causes as flood or fire.

abandonment stage

it refers to the final stage in the life cycle of a product. The product may have been successful and saturated the market, or it may have failed to find a market, at all—either way, the producers no longer finds it profitable and, therefore, discontinues its manufacture.

abc analysis

a technique which is used to identify those items in a firm's inventory which provide it with the highest sales. The technique is used for planning and control purposes. Items are listed by sales volume and classified into three categories: (a) those that account for the largest percent of sales and must be stocked at all times: (b) those that account for medium levels of sales: (c) those that account for the lowest level of sales. Lower levels of stock may be maintained for the B and C categories.

abc control

also known as selective inventory control. A system of inventory control in which every item carried in stock is assigned a rating of A, B, or C, according to its costliness, with the two-fold aim or of reducing capital investment in inventories and lessening the likelihood of running out of low-cost but did not pay for a TV set she purchased, the defendant might file a counter—claim that the plaintiff's truck damaged her driveway while delivering their cost for a given period. The most expensive items, constituting perhaps 10 per cent of the period's outlay, have been classed A; the next most expensive comprising an additional 20 per cent of the period's expenditures, have been classed B; all others are class C. As they represent a high investment, inventories of A items are kept as low as possible, inventories of B items are also kept low, but with a slightly generator safety margin against depletion; and inventories of C items are much larger and less closely controlled.

abc method

an application of the principle of management by exception by which stock is analysed into categories by value of total annual usage. The object is to focus attention on those groups of stock items which warrant closest control. Also shown as split inventory system.

ability to pay

a wage theory which holds that the wage level must be based on a company's ability to pay. Under this theory , wage levels should increase as profits increase. Those who support this theory rarely recommend the converse, lowering wages as profits decline. Also, a theory of taxation holding that taxes should be based on the taxpayer's ability to pay, the rich paying proportionately more than the poor.

ab initio

Lation, "from the beginning" for example: a person who enters upon the land of another with permission and thereafter abuses the permission becomes a trespasser ab initio; that is, he has nullified the permission and is legally regarded as a trespasser from the time he first entered upon the land.

abnormal cost

a cost which has been incurred in connection with an activity but which would not normally have been expected to be incurred.

above par

as used in the securities market, it refers to a premium price, either paid or quoted, that is higher than the face value of the item.

above the line

the term, in relation to business, refers to promotional expenditure incurred by a concern on the sale of its products or services by means of direct advertising through newspapers, radio, television, posters etc.

above-the line Advertising

any form of advertising for which a commission or fee is payable to a recognized advertising agency operating on behalf of its client(s). Usually press, television radio, cinema, and posters, sometimes referred to as Theme Advertising.

above-the-Line Promotion

term used by marketing men of sales promotion in the form of expenditure on advertising in the press, on television or in other media. The term below-the-line promotion, on the other hand, is used for such forms of sales promotion as reduced price special offers, premiums, and point-of sale displays.

abridged accounts

accounts which, while covering the full financial period to which they relate, are not fully detailed financial statements. They may be used where a company wishes to give information of its financial affairs in a summarised form to those who may not be entitled to or require a full set of accounts, e.g. its employees.

abscond

to disappear, often taking property or money. An employee, for example, may abscond with the contents of the cash box.

absence of demand

a demonstrated lack of interest in a product or service so that a considerable segment of the market either feels no need for the product or service or is unwilling to pay the price asked by the seller.

absenteeism

1. refers to the time lost in industrial establishment by avoidable or unavoidable absence of employees

2. failure of workers to report for work when they are scheduled to work-especially when caused by unwillingness rather than incapacity.

absolute advantage

a country is considered to be at absolute advantage if she, with equal quantities of productive factors of production, can produce more of a given product, than another country.

absolute advantage, of law

the principle that a basis for trade exists between nations or regions when each of them, because of natural or acquired advantages, can provide goods or services that the other wants at a lower cost than each could provide for itself. This law accounts for much of the world's trade.

absolute Cross-Elasticity of Demand

means the absolute change in the quantity of commodity. A demanded which would result from a unit change in the price of B, other factors remaining constant.

absolute Income-elasticity of Demand

the change in the quantity demanded per unit change in income, all prices and determinants held constant.

absolute income-elasticity of demand

the change in the quantity demanded per unit change in income, all prices and determinants held constant.

absolute liability

legal liability for an act that causes harm, even though the doer of the harm is not at fault.

absolute product failure

the failure of a product to recoup in the marketplace the investment made in its development, production, and marketing.

absolute sale

the term used for an agreement between a buyer and a seller in which both parties agree that there will no conditions or restrictions affecting the sales transaction.

absolute thresholds

the point at which sensory stimuli first become discernible. This is important to marketers seeking to discover means of differentiating their product in the marketplace as well as those seeking to create effective advertising messages.

absolute value

synonym magnitude.

absorb

to allocate or apportion an item of overhead to some unit of production or cast centre. Thus if fixed overhead is charged to production on, say, a machine hour rate it is said to have been absorbed on that basis.

absorption accounting

an accounting system in which all costs (fixed or variable, direct or indirect) are "absorbed" by the goods or services produced within the accounting period.

absorption costing

an American term sometimes used to describe historical 'costing or orthodox' costing, i.e. the assignment of all fixed and variable costs to goods and services produced.

abstinence

(1) the conduct of a person who either abstains from the unproductive use of what he can command, or designedly prefers the production of remote to that of immediate results. (2) the sacrifice of the present for the sake of future has been called 'abstinence' by economists. However, this term is misunderstood. Therefore, we may better use the term 'waiting' for it.

abstinence theory of interest

according to this theory, interest gained by saving money in an interest-bearing savings account is a reward for not spending the money on good and services.

abstract of title

a written document used to determine the ownership of a particular of land. It summarizes the material portions of every deed and other transaction that affect the little of that land, thus representing a history of its ownership.

abusive dismissal

when an employee is dismissed in a way which is technically correct according to his contract of employment—for example, by giving the stipulated period of notice—but in such a way that management has abused its power in doing so.

aca

the designatory letters of an associate member of the institute of chartered accountants in many countries.

acca

the designatory letters of an associate member of the chartered association of certified accountants.

accelerated depreciation

depreciation of a fixed asset at a faster rate than with straight-line depreciation—e.g. by using the declining balance method.

accelerating vocational training

training or (usually) retraining which is intended to help adult workers to acquire skills which traditionally have been acquired by apprenticeship in a much shorter period than is usually taken by an apprenticeship. Training programs of this type are usually government sponsored.

acceleration clause

a provision in an agreement for the repayment of a loan by installments that if a specified number of installments are not paid then all the outstanding payments are due immediately.

acceleration principle

the basic relationship between the change in the level of output and the volume of investment spending is known as the acceleration principle. The capital output ratio is known as the accelerator. The theory of investment based on this relationship is known as the acceleratory theory.

accelerator

relatively small change in demand for consumer goods resulting in a comparatively substantial change in demand for capital plant supplying these goods.

accent

in fashion merchandising accent is the particular point of emphasis used by the designer to give the style a point of view.

acceptability

extent of customer approval of package, product, service, as expressed during a survey.

acceptable quality level

in manufacturing, it refers to the level of quality at which components, processes, or finished goods are considered good to be continued without reword, or immediately shippable. The maximum percentage of defectives (or number of defects per 100 units) that will be accepted in the output from a production process.

acceptance

the action of signifying on the face of a bill of exchange that liability is accepted under it. An accepted bill of exchange is likely to be easier to negotiate than one which has not been accepted.

acceptance bank

also, accepting house. An organization that specializes in accepting or guaranteeing domestic and foreign bills of exchange.

acceptance credit

a credit whose terms involves the drawing of time bills needing acceptance either by the bank issuing the crediting or by the customer.

acceptance, sampling

in quality control, this term refers to a process of sampling that forms the basis for accepting or rejecting a product. For example, an inspector 'might inspect 10 items from every lot of 200. From the number or defects found, the number of defects in the entire shipment can, by statistical inference, be estimated.

acceptance test

made early in the progress of a project, etc., with the object of checking that the finished work will be fit for its purpose.

accessible site

a site for a retail establishment that may easily be reached by customers and employees. The driving time and/or distance to the site is short and the store's parking area is easy to enter and leave.

accessorial service

a transportation service in addition to the line haul service, usually at an added cost, such as heating, packing, loading and storage.

accessory equipment

products, usually movable, having a lower cost and shorter life span than installed equipment and which are not incorporated into the finished manufactured product (e.g., tools and office equipment). Although accessory equipment is often charged to the capital budget, it may be treated as an expense item in some organizations.

access right

1. the level of access which is granted to users of a system e.g., read a file only, or write to a file. 2. The right of an owner or his authorized agent to enter or leave his properly without trespassing.

access time

the time required for information to be put into or taken from computer storage.

accident

refers to an event that occurs even though no reasonable person could foresee its occurrence. Due to this, the law holds no person legally responsible for any harm that may result from an accident, unless injury or damage is increased by negligence.

accident book

a book which almost every employer must keep at each work place so that any employee can make a record of any personal injury suffered by him as a result of an accident at work.

accident frequency rate

number of lost-time accidents per 100,000 man-hours worked.

accident industrial

under the notification of accidents and dangerous occurrences regulations 1980 (NADOR) an accident causing death or major injury to an employee, a self-employed person or to a member of the public had to be reported by the responsible person to the appropriate enforcing authority. Normally the responsible person would be the employer or the person controlling the premises in connection with which the incident occurred, such as a mine manager or quarry owner. Similarly the enforcing authority would normally be either the appropriate inspectorate of the health and safety executive (e.g. factory, mines, nuclear, etc.). Or the relevant local authority. Under the regulations major injuries included: the loss of sight of an eye; fracture of the skull, spine or pelvis; amputation of hand or foot; or any injury that put the person concerned into hospital as an in-patient, other than for observation, for more than twenty-four hours. Other injuries to employees were notifiable if they resulted in more than three day's absence from normal work, when the local DHSS office would ask the employer to complete a form relating to a claim for industrial injury benefit of the employee. The regulations also required the responsible person to report a variety of specified dangerous occurrences, such as an explosion or the collapse of a crane.

Changes in the statutory sick pay scheme in 1983 had the effect that a doctor's certificate for an injured person's incapacity for work only became available to employers after seven days' incapacity (industrial injury benefit being abolished), and the number of reported accidents of a less serious nature declined. Faced by an 80 percent reduction in the flow of information about accidents, in 1983 the health and safety executive put out a consultative document proposing new reporting arrangements to replace NADOR. These wove together into one system lost-time accidents, fatalities and major injuries, dangerous occurrences, and illness known to be associated with work-the latter being the only entirely new category compared with NADOR. The proposed system would have the advantage of using a single report-form, which would facilitate computer storage, retrieval and analysis of information.

accident insurance

this is a loosely used term to include personal accident insurance or other forms of insurance in which accident may be a factor, e.g., accidents at sea, accidents on the highway and accidents involving building.

accident prevention

the policy or procedures followed in a workplace to prevent accidents to employees, or at least to reduce the occurrence of accidents. It includes physical aspects—proper maintenance of machinery or the provision of protective shields, and managerial aspects such as effective supervision and training.

accommodation bill

a bill of exchange which has been drawn on and accepted by a reputable party for the purpose of giving value to the bill so that it can be discounted. There is no underlying trading transaction as would normally be the case for a bill exchange.

accommodation note

a note which is signed by one person as the maker, endorser, or accepter on behalf on another whose credit position is not strong enough to be self-supporting. Usually no consideration gets involved. The signer acts as guarantor for the note.

accord and satisfaction

the legal term for a change in contract, meaning that the parties are in agreement regarding the changes and are satisfied with the new document.

account

(1) any document or device whereby a record is kept of flows of value measured in money terms. A business will record all of its transactions in a set of accounts making up its ledger. A cash account, for example, will show all cash received and paid. A fixed asset account will show purchases, sales and depreciation of fixed assets. The term may also apply to a record of dealings between contracting parties. Thus one may have an account with a shop from which one makes regular purchases or an accounts with a bank. (2) a period of time designated by the stock exchange during which all transactions fall to be settled at the same time. All the transactions within an account are due for settlement on settlement day which is the Tuesday next but one after the end of an account.

accountability

refers to the obligation of an employee or a manager to undertake a task or to fulfil an assignment and to bear responsibility for the effects of his or her effort. In government accounting, the designation of the account or the amount of a disbursing officer's liability.

accountancy

the activity of preparing and auditing the financial records and statements of organizations.

accountancy convention

the generally accepted practices of accountants (accountancy). Some of the principal conventions and assumptions are as follows:

(1) the accounting entity. By convention an entity is defined as the unit or organization that is treated as the separate whole for the purpose of accounting control. The entity is not necessarily coextensive with a legal entity. For example the various branches or departments of a firm may be treated as separate entities. A group of companies will generally be treated as an entity for purposes of publication of financial accounts (consolidated accounts).

(2) the going-concern assumption. In preparing financial accounts an assumption is made, where nothing is specifically known to the contrary, that a firm has an indefinitely long existence and will continue in its present kind of business indefinitely. Accordingly valuations are made on the basis that assets will continue to be used for their present purposes and therefore may not reflect market values (valuation of assets).

(3) money values. In preparing accounts accountants have traditionally used historical monetary values, despite their recognition of the fact that 'real' economic values may well be changing and will differ. The impact of inflation has, however, resulted in demands for changes in the measurement process, which, if applied, would alter the application of this convention (changing price levels, accounting for).

(4) objectivity. In order to serve as a basis for accounting measurement, evidence must be easily and clearly verifiable, hence the emphasis by accountants on original costs or certification by experts. Clearly such objectivity may result in the sacrifice of relevance in accounting statements.

accountant

a person trained in accounting who may either be employed by a firm or work independently.

accountant's international study group

a body representative of accountants from a number of countries which considers a variety of topics and issues reports on them.

accountant's return

alternative term for return on capital or book rate of return.

account executive

the manager on the staff of an advertising agency who handles all negotiations with a client and is responsible for the agreed service to him.

account group

sub-unit of an advertising agency, handling a group of clients or accounts. May be fully or partly self-contained.

accounting

the establishment, maintenance, collection and analysis of financial records. It is used to provide data on the financial position of an organization and any changes that have occurred or may occur over time. This is one aspect of the profession (or art) of accountancy.

accounting bases

the various methods of constructing accounting figures which are available. There are, for example, several bases on which depreciation might be determined. From the available accounting bases any business has to make an appropriate selection which become its accounting policies.

accounting concepts

the fundamental framework of ideas which underlie the preparation of accounts. There is no authoritative agreement on what these concepts are or ought to be although some attempts have been made by to codify them.

accounting conventions

accounting conventions are certain fundamental accounting principles that include those customs and traditions which guide the accountants while preparing the financial statements. For example, the convention of conservatism makes the accountant feel the need for making a provision for expected loss but, at the same time, to ignore expected profits.

accounting cycle

the repetitive processing of financial transactions during an accounting "cycle"—typically one month. The basic steps in the accounting cycle are: (1) entering transactions in one or more journals, (2) balancing the journals, (3) posting information from the journals to the general ledger, (4) posting information from the journals to the subsidiary ledger accounts, (5) reconciling and balancing the ledger accounts, (6) preparing financial statements, and (7) using the resulting information to improve operations.

accounting date

a date marking the end of a period for which accounts are prepared. Thus if a business prepares accounts for periods which coincide with the calendar year its accounting date will be 31 March in each year.

accounting department manual

this is a manual which outline the system of accounting, the entries or number of typical transactions in the books and giving sample entries; also outline the duties of the cashier.

accounting equation

a mathematical representation of the basic relationships between parts of a financial statement. For example, the accounting equation for the relationship among assets, liabilities, and fund balance (on a balance sheet) is :A=L+FB Assets=Liabilities+Fund Balances.

accounting information

accounting information is one of the principle sources of data to support an operation research study. Accounting data, however, require careful interpretation and organisation before they can be used safely and efficiently. Businessmen tend to forget that accounting costs are definitions derived in the light of fundamental accounting purpose, and sometimes they tend to confuse accounting figures with "truth". Operations research, using the same raw data, may make other definitions which serve the special needs of the particular study. One of the great stumbling blocks in the organisation and implementation of an operation research study is the disentangling from accounting records of the costs appropriately defined and truly significant to the problem at hand.

accounting models

forms of simulation of a business situation in financial terms. Other forms of model of business situations include computer models and mathematical models.

accounting period

the time interval, e.g. year or month, for which financial transactions or costing data are summarised and reported to management.

accounting policies

the particular accounting bases judged by a business to be the most appropriate to its own circumstances and therefore the ones which it adopts.

accounting principles

accounting principles have been defined as the body of doctrines commonly associated with the theory and procedure of accounting, serving as an explanation of current practices and as a guide for the selection of conventions or procedures where alternatives exist. Rules governing the formation of accounting axioms and the principles derived from them have arisen from common experiences, historical precedents, statements by individuals and professional bodies and regulation of government agencies. In other words, these are guidelines to establish standards for sound accounting practices and procedures in reporting the financial status and periodic performance of a business.

accounting procedure

a clearly defined sequence of actions prescribed for the recording of a particular type of transaction. Each organization is likely to have its own distinctive accounting procedures.

accounting rate of return

a crude arithmetical determination of the return offered by an investment project. It should be contrasted with the theoretically more acceptable internal rate of return. Although an accounting rate of return may be calculated from information concerning project which is completed, it is usually calculated on the basis of the estimated returns from a future project and is thus a method used for investment appraisal.

accounting ratio

any ratio in analyzing an organisation's financial condition. For example, a current ratio is the ratio of current assets to current liabilities.

accounting records

these are records which are maintained according to the needs of the business concern.

accounting standards

short term referring statements of standard accounting practice and financial reporting standards.

accounting system

a consistent way of organising, recording, summarizing, and reporting financial transaction. The minimum requirements for an accounting system include the following: (1) It must provide financial information for management to make policy decisions, prepare budgets and grant proposals, and provide other useful financial reports. (2) Similar transactions must receive consistent accounting treatment. (3) It must be sufficiently flexible to handle hand or machine recorded accounting information without restricting the organisation's accounting pattern. (4) It must be able to show whether or not the organisation is in basic compliance with federal, state, and local laws, rules and regulations, including tax laws and codes. (5) It must have a self-balancing group of accounts, a double entry system, and a general ledger and subsidiary ledgers. (6) It must match revenues and expenses for the same time periods — for example, a month of a year (accrual accounting) — or match cash received and expended for the same periods (cash accounting).

account opener

in bank marketing, an account opener is a gift or premium given to a depositor by the bank as an incentive to open a new account or add to an existing account.

account payable

synonym for creditor commonly used in the USA.

account payee

these words, or their

equivalent, such a'a/c' are frequently added to the crossing of a cheque with the idea of safeguarding it in transmission.

account payee only

words which are written as a crossing to a cheque have the effect that the cheque may be paid only through a bank account in the name of the original payee. Such a cheque cannot be transferred to another person by endorsement.

account receivable

the amount owed to a business by its customers, who are customarily granted anywhere from 10 to 90 days to pay for merchandise already shipped.

account receivable insurance

refers to a fire insurance policy that provides coverage against losses due to the inability to collect outstanding accounts because of destruction records.

account rendered

a term appearing against the opening item on a statement sent by a supplier to a customer. It signified that this amount is brought forward from a previous statement from which full details may be obtained if required.

account sales (a/s)

an account sent by one agent to the consignor showing the total quantity and the amount to be realized after deducting freight, commission, etc.

accounts and audit control

accounts of the public corporations are kept in the forms to be settled in consultation with the Government or the Auditor-General and the audit of their accounts is either done by the Auditor-General of India or by auditors appointed by the Government.

accounts payable

amounts owed to others for goods and services received and assets required.

accounts receivable

amounts due from others for goods furnished and services rendered, usually from customers or clients.

accounts reporting rules

a statement issued jointly by the main accountancy bodies setting out guidelines for accountants who have to report on the profit forecasts contained in company prospectuses.

accretion

an increase in value which takes place over a period of time.

accrual

a liability in respect of goods or services provided to a business in the form of a continuous supply, consumed up to an accounting date but not billed by that date. Common subjects for accruals are electricity, gas and telephone services.

accrual basis

that basis of the preparation of the profit and loss which takes into account not merely amount paid and received but also expenses accrued but not paid and for income accrued but not received. It is the normal basis of the preparation of account for commercial undertakings.

accrual costing

in accounting, the expensing of goods and services as they are consumed.

accrued asset

in accounting, it refers to the interest, commission, or revenue earned but neither received nor past due.

accrued benefits

benefits which have accumulated up to the current point in time. A member of a pension scheme, for example, could refer to the accrued benefits of membership to the scheme.

accrued charges

an accrued charge is the expense incurred by a creditor. For example, the fees chargeable for an audit may appear under this heading when the accounts are printed before the auditor has submitted his account. Rent, rates, electricity charges etc., may also fall under this heading when demands for these are made as in arrears, i.e., the charge for electricity used can only be assessed when the meter is read, which must be after the expense has legally been incurred. Accrued charges should be distinguished from provision for anticipated liabilities, the amount of which cannot be determined at the time an account is being drawn up, or from payments made in advance, i.e., money paid for future benefit. Telephone bills are a useful instance of the application of both accrued charges. They contain both a bill for calls made in the past and a rental charge for the future.

accrued costs

costs which have been incurred in the sense that their associated benefits have been consumer but where no payment has yet taken place because it has not formally become due. The cost of electricity consumed between a billing date and the end of an accounting period is an example of an accrued cost.

accrued dividend

unpaid and undeclared dividend on preferred stock.

accrued income

the cumulative running of interest, usually on a day-to-day basis on a capital asset.

accrued interest

interest which has been earned by money loaned or deposited but which has not yet formally become payable. It the interest on a deposit is payable on, say, 30 June and 21 December in each year, there will be accrued interest at any other date.

accrued revenue

the amount accumulated, upto a specified date, of a continually increasing debt, due to one, which is customarily payable at fixed times.

accumulated depreciation

the total amount of depreciation provided on a field asset from its date of purchase to the present time. The figure will thus, normally, include several years' depreciation.

accumulated dividend

a dividend which has not been paid when due and which has become a liability of the corporation to be paid, presumably, at some future time.

A rapidly growing company may absorb a declining firm because the latter has a large amount of cash (or marketable securities) that is much needed by the growing company. For tax reasons, the owners of the declining company prefer to hold stock rather than to receive a high cash dividend.

A company may have suffered severe losses for years and may have accumulated a large tax credit. If this company absorbs another firm with high profits, the past losses can (within limits) be used to offset profits of the second firm and thereby to avoid paying about half of these profits to the government as income tax.

The combined operations resulting from a merger should have clear economic advantages that were not available when the companies operated independently.

Mergers involve more than identifying a major economic advantage and negotiating a deal. The two enterprises have to be fitted together into a new composite institution. Unless this true amalgamation is done effectively, many of the anticipated benefits may not materialize.

accumulated fund

an item on the balance sheet of a non-profit making organisation representing the net investment in the organisation of its contributing members. Such an organisation does not normally employ the concept of capital which is associated with proprietorial rights and with the earning of profit.

accumulated income

net income which is retained and not paid out in dividends or dissipated by subsequent losses. Also referred to as accumulated earning and accumulated profit.

accumulation

the process of allowing some value to grow. There will be an accumulation of interest in a deposit account where this is not withdrawn. There will be an accumulation of retained profit if a company pays a dividend which is regularly less than the profit.

accumulation plan

refers to an arrangement under which the purchaser of shares in a mutual fund (open-end investment company) agrees to acquire more shares over a given period of time.

accumulation schedule

refers to a table in which computations are provided for the periodic write-up until maturity of the discount relating to an investment or obligation.

accumulation units

units in a unit trust where the income is reinvested in further units rather than being distributed in cash. Many unit trust managers offer their units on an accumulation basis at the option of the holder.

accumulator register

synonymous with accumulator.

achieved penetration

a measure of the number of persons in a potential target market who are actually the purchasers of a product or service.

achievement analysis

examination of stages in the progress of a project, perhaps at project milestones.

achievement motivation test

one of several psychological tests developed of achievement. The most widely-used is the thematic appreciation test (TAT).

achievement tests

tests designed to measure the level of knowledge and proficiency in certain skills already achieved by the applicants, e.g., knowledge of English, Mathematics etc.

acid ratio test

the determination of the ratio of total cash, accounts receivable (debtors) and the market value of marketable investments of a business to its current liabilities.

acquisition

the purchase of a firm or of its assets.

acquisitions and mergers

large stockholders in a closely held company want to convert their assets into marketable securities or cash, frequently in anticipation of high inheritance taxes. Poor health or old age makes them willing to merge at an attractive price.

acquisition budget

funds to be used in acquiring customers through sales promotion activities and advertising.

acquisition cost

the funds which are required to acquire goods or services.

acquisition method

a method of preparing consolidated accounts. The essential feature of the acquisition method of consolidation is that the preacquisition profit of the subsidiary company is unavailable to support dividends which will be credited to the profit and loss account of the holding company, for whom it has the status of capital funds.

across the board

affecting every value equally. An across the board increase in salaries, for example, means that every employee will have a similar proportionate increase. An across the board reduction in prices means that all prices have been reduced.

across-the-broad settlement

agreed pay increase that gives of the employees concerned an equal proportional increase in pay.

act

letters standing for advance corporate tax.

action Ex contractu

legal action to recover damages for the breach of a duty arising out of a contract.

action learning

a management-development activity in which a manager is required to solve an actual problem of an existing organization.

action of the sun

in real estate, it refers to a consideration in the selection of a retail store the shades side of the street is usually more desirable.

action program

in a marketing plan, those, specific steps which are calculated to achieve the plan's objectives.

action research

kind of research to harness an understanding of the group behaviour being studied to the attempted solution of practical problems within an organizational or social setting. It therefore has both an applied and theoretical aspect to it, and often includes monitoring and evaluation research of effectiveness as well.

action skill

refers to the ability to carry out skillfully the behaviour required by a situation—e.g., in some forms to T-group training or sensitivity training.

activating mode

why sound decisions developed and implemented by a good organisation fail to achieve desired results even through the decision are understood and acted on with commitment? Why even the best control systems occasionally fail to spot problems on time or help in pinpointing the causes? May be in this unpredictable and frequently competitive world imperfect planners, organizers and controllers guess wrong or are beaten by competitors. However, just as a we seek to improve the quality of management functions, so too we must focus on achieving optimum performance through what is called activating.

active account

an account, usually with a bank, on which transactions are currently and regularly taking place.

active buyer

in direct marketing any

customer whose last purchase was made within the last 12 months. Also called actives and active customers.

active crops of executives

an organization of executives who are still employed and who have volunteered to offer expertise in many operational aspects of business.

active exporting

activities of firms which vigorously seek export business.

active market

one in which there is a large amount of trading. Where there is substantial interest in a company and thus a great deal of buying and selling of its shares, there may be said to be an active market in those shares.

active member

in direct marketing, particular in such operations as book and record clubs, any member who is currently fulfilling the original commitment or who has already fulfilled that commitment and has made additional purchases in the last 12 months.

active subscriber

a customer who has committed himself/herself to receive regular delivery of magazines, books, stamps, or other goods and/or services for a period of time currently in effect.

activities analysis

one of three techniques identified by drucker to be used in deciding the organization structure appropriate for a company, the other techniques being decision analysis and relations analysis. Activities analysis is used to establish what are the key activities in the company, as distinct from generalized assumptions.

activity

a term used in Project Network Techniques to describe the work required to complete a specified event.

activity-based costing

a method of absorption costing whereby indirect costs are analysed in detail and each element is then associated with the activity from which it arises. This activity becomes the driver for that element of indirect cost. This means that it becomes the basis for changing the indirect expense to production.

activity chart

diagram showing the break-down and composition of a series of operations or a process-plotted against a time scale.

activity-on-arrow network

a network in which the arrows represent activities.

activity on node

method of representing a series of associated activities in critical path scheduling or network analysis. Each activity is by a circle or node instead of an arrow, which is conventionally used. The interrelationships between each activity are shown by lines known as dependencies, as in the diagram to form precedence diagrams.

activity ratio

a management ratio showing what part of budgeted production has been completed.

activity sampling

a work study sampling technique in which a large number of planned instantaneous observations is made over a given period of time of a group of machines, processes or workers. Each observation records what is happening at a given instant, and the percentage of observations recorded for a particular interval of time is taken to be a reflection of the actual percentage of time during which activity or delay occurs. Also known as work sampling, snap reading method, ratio-delay study, random observation method.

activity vector analysis (AVA)

psychological test developed in the USA for use in temperament and personality testing. It has had mixed fortunes and reactions as a personnel selection test.

act of bankruptcy

an action committed by a debtor that a court will recognize as a ground for making a receiving order (the first stage of making the debtor bankrupt).

actual cost

cost data which is based on transactions that have been completed, is contrasted with costs that have been estimated.

actual market volume

sum total of suppliers sales made at a given price or in a given price range to a specific market segment.

actual total loss

an insurance term meaning that the object insured has been completely destroyed or otherwise lost. The full amount of the insured value then becomes payable.

actuarial value

a valuation of contingent liabilities based on probabilities. It is most commonly used in the field of insurance and pension funds.

actuary

an actuary is defined in a Oxford English Dictionary as an expert in statistics, especially one who calculates insurance risks and premiums.

actuating

comprises of practising participation by all affected by the decision or act, leading and challenging others to do their best, motivating members, communicating, developing members to realise full potential, rewarding by recognition and paying for work well done, satisfying the needs of employees through their work efforts and revising actuation efforts in the light of control results.

actuarial value

a valuation of contingent liabilities based on probabilities. It is most commonly used in the field of insurance and pension funds.

acuity

term used to describe someone's ability to discriminate fine detail in using one of the senses. Most often used of vision, though also used of hearing and other senses.

adaptation

advertisement adapted from basic layout and copy to fit different space, shape and size.

adaptive behaviour theory

a theory of evolutionary change in which firms most capable of adapting to changing conditions in the market place are seen as having the best chance of survival.

adaptive control

classical control theory is largely concerned with the problems of minimizing the difference between an actual output value of a system and a fixed reference value (feedback). Adaptive control involves the additional sophistication of having the reference value itself also subject to regulatory control in order to improve the performance of the system in a changing environment. A hypothetical example may best illustrate the significance of adaptive control. The governor of a steam engine is perhaps the best known, and historically the earliest, example of automatic regulation using feedback. The control characteristics of such a device are, however, fixed at the time of its design and manufacture. An adaptive governor would be one with variable characteristics that would, in turn, be controlled by the output of other systems. Thus if the object of an adaptive governor were to minimize the cost of operating a vehicle, the adjustment of the governor would vary in relation to such economic factors as the cost of fuel, the hourly pay of the crew and the rates of depreciation of the machinery at various operating speeds. Thus an adaptive control system of this type would be utilizing a versatile form of self-regulation appropriate to a changing environment.

adaptive control model

a method used by some firms to set the advertising budget and to measure the sales effect of advertising expenditures. The model assumes that the advertising sales response function changes through time due to changing competitive activity, advertising copy, product design, and economic climate.

adaptive forecasting

continual tinkering with a forecasting technique to provide a rapid response to changing relationships.

added hours

in cases where employees work overtime, the amount paid is calculated by adding hours to the normal working week for which the employee is paid. For example, two hours worked at double time would add four hours payment at the standard rate.

added value

an attempt to 'measure' productivity by calculating the additional value given to a product or job by people or machines doing work on it (now used as a basis for some bonus 'incentive' schemes).

additional mark-up

an increase in the original retail price of goods, commonly due to an error in original marking or because the value of the merchandise has increased.

additional premium

a premium charged in respect of an insurance policy where its terms are amended at the request of the insured after the original premium has been paid. The amendment may be of the risk insured against or of the value of the property insured.

additional voluntary contribution

an amount paid by an employee into an approved occupation pension scheme in excess of the amount required under the contract of employment. The purpose of making an additional voluntary contribution is to increase the amount of pension ultimately payable.

add-on service

a service provided by the Direct Marketing Association, which allows customers to request that their names be added to specific mailing lists.

address correction requested

a message printed in the upper left-had corner of the address portion of a piece of mail which authorizes the U.S. Postal Service to provide the known new address of a person no longer at the address of appearing on the mailing. The postal service charges a fee to direct marketers requesting this service.

adequate distribution

distribution of retail products in advance of advertising campaign so that response can be satisfied.

adequate price

price which is just enough to make the employer decide to employ a worker to make the product.

ad hoc

Latin, "for this." Refers to a limited or particular situation. An ad hoc committee is one limited to a specific purpose and may be dismissed on completion of its task. An ad hoc decision means for this purpose only. And ad hoc attorney is one appointed to perform a special task in a particular case.

adjournment

temporary stopping of negotiation, usually to allow time to counsel or think. It can be a device to 'postpone' depression of a problem indefinitely.

adjudication

adjudication refers to the complete processing of one or more claims by an insurance company. Most insurance organizations divide the claims process into the steps of claims receipt and screening (review for completeness), claimant eligibility determination, provider eligibility determination, adjudication, reimbursement determination, utilization review, quality assurance, payment, and records management.

adjudication provisions

while the upward spiralling of wages and process is not looked upon with favour by the government, it is agreed that wages increase should be granted in order to remove anomalies and to restore the level of real wages in cases where the levels were abnormally low. While awarding considerable increases in pay, the industrial courts have contributed to the thinking regarding standardization of wages within industries. They have made use of the family budget enquiries in the areas, the standard per capita requirements of food, clothing, fuel, etc., as recommended by various authorities the size of the average family etc., in deciding the actual quantum of minimum wages.

adjustable peg

a system that permits changes in the par rate of foreign exchange after a nation has had long-run disequilibrium in its balance of payments.

adjust basis

in income taxes, the basis used to compute depreciation or gain or loss on sales of fixed or non-inventory assets

adjusted cost basis

for accounting purposes refers to the value of property equal to the original cost plus improvements less depreciation.

adjusted earned income

taxable income that is earned income.

adjusted earnings statement

a statement of the profit of a business showing adjustments to exclude the amounts which have distorted the overall picture. This usually takes the form of excluding non-typical amounts which, for this reason, are unlikely to recur.

adjuster

in the insurance industry, an employee of an insurance company authorized to study, and make recommendations to his employer relative to, the cause of an event that has resulted in a claim, the amount of the loss, and the extent of the insurance company's liability.

adjusting entry

in accounting, an entry which is made to correct or offset an error, accrual, write off, determent, etc.

adjusting entry

in accounting, an entry, which is made to correct or offset an error, accrual, write off, determent, etc.

adjustment

an amendment to an accounting figure which is basically correct but which needs to allow for some circumstance not recorded in the book-keeping system. Adjustments in accounting are very common.

adjustment allowance

compensation made to a customer to settle a claim or complaint.

administered pricing

prices which are set by the seller rather than by competitive market forces and are designed to meet the seller's objectives (such as return on investment). Prices may be set, or administered, by the manufacturer or other marketing channel members. The seller may hold this set price steady over a period of time, but unless the firm sells directly to• the ultimate consumer, other channel members may make the set price difficult to hold.

administered vertical marketing system

a system in which the channel members, while retaining much of their autonomy, are informally coordinated in their marketing activities by the dominant member of the channel. Dominance is achieved through the exercise of political or economic power rather than through outright ownership.

administration

administration is basically an organizational process concerned with the implementation of objectives and plans and internal operator efficiency. It often connotes bureaucratic structure and behaviour, relatively routine decision making and maintenance of the internal status quo. Entrepreneurship implies more creative external or open systems orientation. It involves innovation, risk taking, and relatively dynamic leadership. The true modern professional manager tends to be both an administrator and an entrepreneur, although in varying degrees.

administration and management

the terms management and administration have been used by different management authorities in a manner that sometimes they seem to be one and the same while at some other time, they diverge.

According to most of the modern writers like Foyal, Koontz, Allen and Perry, there is no real distinction between the two terms. Foyal, for instance, stated : "All undertakings require planning, organisation, command, coordination and control and in order to function properly, all must observe to some general principles. We are no longer confronted with several administrative sciences but with one which can be applied equally well to public and private affairs".

administration cost

all management expenses concerned with directing and controlling an organisation which are not directly related to research, development, production, distribution and selling activities.

administrative accounting

refers to that part of the accounting process generally associated with management.

administrative costs

an important classification of cost within the profit and loss account. It contains costs which directly relate to administration and might include telephone, office salaries and postage. It will be an objective of management to minimize administrative costs subject to maintenance of the quality of the administrative process.

administrative law

the law relating to the discharge of functions of a public nature in government and administration.

administrative management theory

an approach to the study of management, based on the work of Henry Fayol and others in the 1930s which emphasizes the importance of the formal structure and the hierarchy of an organization.

administrative science

the systematic study of administration in all its aspects. It includes both business administration and public administration and attempts to formulate general principles that are applicable to all forms of organization.

administrator

in business, a person who directs, co-ordinates, or controls the activities of subordinates.

administratix

the feminine form of administration.

admission charge

an amount charged for the right to enter some sporting or entertainment event.

admission to listing

the action whereby the shares of a company achieve a stock exchange quotation and are thus able to be bought and sold through the market.

admitted assets

assets of an insurance company that are recognized by a state regulatory or other examining body in determining the company's financial condition.

admos

abbr. Automatic Device for Mechanized Order Selection. Term used to describe machinery used in an integrated warehouse which checks product availability, selects correct quantities of specific goods, records stocks and shortages and in conjunction with conveyor systems passes goods direct to the packing and despatch location.

adoption curve

a distribution curve which graphically represents the diffusion of an innovation as various groups adopt new products. The curve illustrates the number of adopters who have purchased a new product or service during each time periods beginning with the launch date. It takes the shape of a normal statistical distribution in that a small number of people adopt the innovation when it first becomes available and this rate of adoption increases until 50% of the potential users have tried it. After this point has been reached, the number of individuals adopting the product within each time period decreases until there are no potential adopters who have not yet tried the innovation.

adoption process segmentation variables

the stages that each consumer must pass through in the process of becoming a regular user of a product or service. These stages include awareness, interest, evaluation, trial, and adoption. For a new or unconventional product or service (such as home banking by computer) these stages offer a key to segmentation.

adulteration

the act of debasing a commercial commodity or substituting an inferior article for a superior one in order to gain an illegitimate profit. The term is usually applied to the debasement of foods, drugs or cosmetics.

ad valorem

in proportion to value. Thus an ad valorem tax on an article is a tax whose total depends on the value of the article. Value added tax is an example of an ad valorem tax.

ad valorem subsidy

refers to a fixed-percentage subsidy granted to producers of commodities as a form of financial aid or relief from hardships resulting from economic conditions beyond the control of the producers.

advance

any payment made before it falls due, thus representing a loan.

advance against securities

a central bank's assistance to the banking system in a country is made available, in the main, through the alternative facilities of advances from the central bank.

advance bill

an invoice submitted before the goods or services itemized therein have actually been delivered or performed. It is usually requested by buyers for tax purposes or some similar reason.

advance corporate tax

an amount of corporate tax which becomes payable in advance of its otherwise due date as a consequence of the payment by the company of a dividend. Tax legislation requires that this payment is made and it is equal in amount to the tax credit imputed to the dividend.

advance dating

the practice of setting a specific future date, after shipment and after the invoice date, when the terms of sale become applicable. For example, under the terms "2/10, net 30 as of March 1;," a 2% discount will be made for payment within 10 days and the net payment period will be calculated from March 1, regardless of the shipping and/or invoice dates. Advance dating is sometimes used to allow for transportation of merchandise and sometimes to encourage orders in advance of the normal buying season.

advance factory

built by the Government in regions in need of development, the factory then being rented at attractive rates to an industrial firm setting up in the region.

advancement

a payment made by a trustee out of the capital of trust funds to a beneficiary for the purpose of establishing him in life.

advances

amounts of money prepaid in contemplation of goods, services, or other assets to be received at a later date. Advances are ordinarily made only to payees to whom an organisation has an obligation. A common example is the travel advance, which is an amount of money made available to an employee prior to the beginning of a trip, for costs the employee will incur.

adverse selection

the insuring of a group of risks that represents an above-average expectation of loss. Also the tendency of poor risks to seek insurance.

adverse variance

a difference between an actual expense or cost and the amount of a budgeted or standard cost such that its effect is to reduce profit below that planned. If, for example, materials are bought at a price higher than standard this will lead to an adverse variance. All adverse variances of material amount should be investigated so that the source of any loss or inefficiency can be eliminated as early as possible.

advertisement

a form of public announcement intended to promote the sale of a commodity or service, to advance an idea or to bring about some other effect desired by the advertiser.

advertisement department

part of a publishing or other organization in the communications business concerned with selling advertising space or time, either to an agency or direct to a client.

advertisement manager

executive responsible for selling space, airtime, sites and other media facilities to advertisers, as distinct from advertising manager who is responsible for a company's advertising.

advertisement representative

firm dealing in space for local and foreign newspapers, and for magazines sub-contracting their space—selling operation.

advertiser

organization or person on whose behalf an advertisement appears, and who ultimately pays the bill.

advertising

any form of presentation and promotion of ideas, goods or services by an identified sponsor. Involves the use of media such as magazines and newspapers, direct mail, posters, radio, television, circulars, etc.

advertising agency

an individual or organization that is concerned with marketing. It is an expert body which prepares and place advertising for others.

advertising allowance

a sum of money paid by a manufacturer or producer to a reseller (usually a retailer) to compensate the reseller for the cost of locally advertising the producer's product. Such advertising is most generally aimed at the ultimate consumer and is developed at the local level in support of a particular product, line or brand. Also known as coop money.

advertising appeal

the central theme, motif, or idea of an advertisement which tells the potential consumer what the advertised product or service offers and why it should be purchased.

advertising appropriation

the money allocated to advertising in a marketing or sales budget period.

advertising—benefits to society

advertising brings to the greatest number of people actual knowledge concerning useful things, it is essentially a form of education and the progress of civilization depends on education.

advertising budget

sum of money set aside for spending on an advertising

campaign. Sometimes represents total sum available to cover all advertising expenditure including overhead. Alternatively referred to as 'advertising appropriation'.

advertising campaign

a planned program using various media, conducted over a period of time, to sell ideas, goods or services to the public.

advertising-characteristics of

(1) advertising is a paid form of communication. Advertiser has to pay for the space or time hired by him for advertising. (2) it is a mass non-personal communication and persuasion. There is no face-to-face direct contact with the customer. (3) it can be oral, written or visual. (4) it can be done through various media, such as press, samples, audio-visual aids, etc. (5) its purpose is to stimulate demand for goods and services. (6) it is done by an identified sponsor, i.e., it is never anonymous. It is always done on somebody's behalf, called the sponsor.

advertising copy

advertising copy is the name given to the published advertisements issued by a company. The advertising copy should give the message in the briefest, most interesting and forceful manner. The copy must be addressed to the type of people who are exposed to the advertising medium.

advertising coverage

the extent of market or segments which is coverage in an advertising campaign.

advertising goals

those specific purposes which underlie an advertisement or advertising campaign. Most advertising has as its goal the stimulation (within a particular time frame) of some specific and immediate activity on the part of the consumer.

advertising information group

informal international group monitoring treats to advertising freedom and promoting self-regulation.

advertising management

an employee of a firm who provides for some form of advertising, e.g., the press, television, ratio and transport services.

advertising managers

an employee of a firm who supervises the production of the firm's advertisements and decides which media will carry them.

advertising media

all of the channels employed by advertisers to reach their audiences and convey their sales messages. Advertising media include print media (such as newspapers and magazines), broadcast media (radio and television), outdoor (such as billboards such as car cards and posters in stations), and point-of-purchase displays.

advertising message
the creative component of an advertisement or advertising campaign. The function of the message is to carry out the advertising objectives of the product or service.

adverting objectives (advertising goals)
the targets towards which an advertising campaign is directed—for example, increased customer awareness, increased market share, increased sales etc.

advertising platform
the main issues or selling points an advertiser wishes to include in an advertising campaign.

advertising rates
this rates charged by various media for disseminating advertisements.

advertising regulations
conditions imposed upon advertising by media owners, trade associations, or government.

advertising sales manager
the employee of a media organization (newspaper, magazine, television network, etc.) responsible for selling advertising space or time to prospective advertisers. In the broadcast media more commonly called a sales manager.

advertising sales-response and decay model
a model used to measure the response of sales to advertising in an effort to determine the most appropriate advertising budget. The model was developed by M.L. Vidale and H.B. Wolfe and postulates that the change in the rate of sales at a particular time (t) is a function of four factors: (1) the advertising budget, (2) the sales response constant. (3) the saturation level of sales, and (4) the sales decay constant. Vidale and Wolfe developed the following formula to determine the optimum advertising expenditure of any given firm:

$$\frac{dS}{dt} = rA = \frac{M - S}{M} - S$$

where:

S = rate of sales at time t

$\frac{dS}{dt}$ = change in the rate of sales at time t

A= rate of advertising expenditure at time t

r= sales-response constant (defined as the sales generated per advertising dollar when S=O)

M= saturation level of sales.

d= sales-decay constant (defined as the fraction of sales per time unit when A=O).

advertising sales response curve
the graphic representation of the relationship between advertising expenditures on the horizontal axis and the results in sales on the vertical axis. The usual assumption is that sales will increase as advertising expenditures

increase.

advertising schedule

program of planned advertisement insertions, showing detailed cost, timing, nature of media and the bookings to be reserved.

advertising scheme

scheme advertising.

advertising specialties

items of little value (pencils, key rings, ash trays, etc.) which carry the name of the firm or product, its picture, logo, etc., and which are used as giveaways. The objective of such advertising is to create goodwill.

advertising strategy

the overall plan of an advertising campaign.

advertising techniques

any of a number of techniques are used to induce the customer to purchase specific products. Some have a rational basis while others are largely psychological or emotional. Thus, when you buy aspirin, you are to insist on a given brand because it is pure, it dissolves, and it acts more quickly. At other times reliance is placed primarily upon repetition of the brand name so that the consumer will automatically select that particular product.

The manufacturer uses advertising extensively for assisting the salesman in making sales when he calls on his customer. He seeks to familiarize the customer with his products and to create a favorable attitude towards his company before the salesman approaches the customer. Practically all advertising is expected to build institutional goodwill but only in some cases may this be the primary objective.

advertising theme

theme advertising.

advice note

a document sent by a seller to a buyer stating the descriptions, quantity of goods that have been despatched, to him.

advisory, conciliation and arbitration service (ACAS)

this independent body was established under the Employment Protection Act 1974 to help employers, workers and their representatives resolve trade disputes and improve industrial relations. It seeks to discharge these responsibilities through the voluntary co-operation of the parties concerned. Its approach is impartial and confidential and its services are free. The main functions of ACAS are: the provision of conciliation and arbitration in collective disputes; individual conciliation in cases where claims are or may be made to industrial tribunals; and the provision of advisory services. A series of free advisory booklets on basic industrial-relations subjects has been published. There are also three codes of practice, obtainable from HMSO. The service is staffed by about 600 people, has a head office in London, offices in Scotland. Wales and seven English regions, and is publicly funded. The service is directed by a council comprising a full-time chairman (since 1981, Sir Patrick Lowry) and none part-time members, appointed by the Secretary of State for employment. Three members are appointed after consultation with the CBI; three after consultation with the TUC and three are independent. The provision of conciliation, mediation and arbitration in collective disputes is the most publicized aspect of ACAS's work. Conciliation is a voluntary process and agreements are the responsibility of the parties concerned. There is a settlement or progress towards a settlement in approximately 80 percent of cases. Failure to reach a settlement may lead, by agreement, to arbitration or mediation. Arbitrators and mediators are appointed by ACAS from panels of specialists in industrial relations.

advocacy advertising

advertising whose objective is to support a particular belief or course of action on the part of its audience. It is designed to induce or discourage certain specific forms of activity with regard to controversial subjects.

advocate channel

a personal communication channel consisting of company sales people contracting buyers in the target market.

affective component

in attitude research, particularly in the tripartite view or structural approach, the affective component is the individual's overall feelings of like or dislike about a service, product, or similar object. It is the emotional component of attitude formation.

affidavit

a declaration in writing made an oath before a person entitled to administer oaths—a commissioner for oaths, normally a solicitor. It is a criminal offence deliberately to make a false statement in an affidavit.

affiliated company

one under the same ownership,

affiliation

refers to a connection which is existing between a holding or parent company and its subsidiary, or between two corporations or other organization owned or controlled by a third.

affiliation need

a motivational factor, the desire to be associated with, or to be in the presence of, another person or persons. The need to "belong" to a group.

affiliative group

any reference group such as the family, church, school, etc.

to which an individual actually belongs.

affinity card

a credit card issued on a condition that specified amounts are paid by the issuer to a named charity. The card is usually produced in a distinctive style to indicate this and so also gives publicity to the charity concerned when the card is used.

affirmative action

Us term for the hiring, employment and promotion of people previously discriminated against.

affirmative disclosure

a procedure adopted by the Federal Trade Commission in its attempt to regulate advertising. The procedure stipulates that if the information contained in an advertisement is considered insufficient by the commission, it may require a company to disclose some of the limitations of its product or service within its subsequent advertising. This is done so that the consumer may judge the product's (or service's) negative as well as positive-attributes.

affreighment

a contract for transporting goods by sea. Also known as charter party or ocean bill of lading.

after hours dealing

trading in the stock exchange which takes place after the official close of business. Such dealing will not be recorded as part of the transactions of the day on which it actually takes place.

after-look journalizing

in a system in which extensive recovery facilities are required to safeguard against system failure, a journal is made of amendments to files. This term indicates that an entry is made to the journal after each change made to the file concerned.

after market

the market in a security, usually shares, which develops immediately after their original issue. If, for example, shares in a company were the subject of an offer for sale to the public at a price of Rs. 150 per share but were quoted at Re 190 immediately dealings began on the stock exchange it might be said that the after market in the shares had established a useful gain on the issue price.

after-sales services

depending on product or services, after-sales service embraces everything that enables customer to enjoy full benefits of product and to be satisfied in event of complaint. May include spares and parts, repairs, inspection, instructions, advice or guarantee.

after sight

a bill of exchange drawn after sight, payable when it has been accepted and the acceptor has indicated a date of acceptance.

after tax

words which signify that the amount to which they relate has already had tax deducted from it so that there is no more to pay.

against all risks

term used in marine insurance meaning insured against all general accepted risks.

age admitted

words used in a policy of life assurance to signify that the insurer has already seen evidence of the age of the insured, usually a birth certificate, and that no further evidence of his will be required in the event of a claim. Clearly the age of the assured is an important factor in determining the premium in a policy of life assurance.

age allowance

an allowance given against the income of an individual in calculating the amount of income tax due when the taxpayer is over the age of 65. It is given in place of, and is greater than, the personal allowance.

ageing schedule

an analysis of the debtors of a business which shows how old each separate element of debt is. It is useful in assessing the success of credit control and, since bad debts first show up as late debts, in determining the correct amount for the charge for bad debts in the profit and loss accounts.

age life depreciation

refers to a method which is used by real-estate appraisers in estimating depreciation of building, based on expected life.

agency

an agent, in law, is a person who has authority to enter into a contract on behalf of another party, known as their principal. The agent's authority may either have been conferred on them expressly by their principal or its existence may be implied by law. Thus, where someone leads others to believe by words or conduct that a certain person is their agent, they will be responsible for any contractual commitments entered into by this apparent agent, even if the agent acted without any express authority. Where the agent has their principle's express authority, they may, but need not, be acting under a contract with the principal. Where such a contract exists, the agent is under an obligation to the principal to perform the agency transaction and is entitled to claim from the principal the agreed remuneration for their services. In the absence of such a contract the agent refrains from acting on the principal's behalf; if the agent does act for the principal, they are not entitled to remuneration.

Apart from general agents there also exist certain classes of special agent whose authority is generally determined by commercial custom or by statute. These include mercantile agents, estate agents and broker. W.f.f.

agency bills

bills of exchange drawn on and accepted by the branches of foreign banks.

agency shop

a place of employment where all employees doing particular types of work must pay subscriptions to particular trade unions although they may refuse actually to join a union.

agenda

details of business to be transacted at a meeting, made out by the person calling the meeting or the secretary appointed to do so. The agenda is sent out to those invited to attend. It is generally accompanied by an invitation to appoint a proxy if a member cannot attend personally.

agent

someone who transacts business on behalf of other. In law, a person who has the power and authority to put another person (who is called the 'principal' of the agent) into binding legal relationships.

agent middleman

a wholesaling middleman (sometimes called an agent wholesaler or simply an agent) who, acting as a market intermediary, performs a number of wholesaling functions without taking title to the goods he sells and frequently without taking physical possession of the goods.

age of debt

management accountancy term meaning extent of customer credit.

agency catalogue

mail order catalogue distributed to agents who sell to friends and neighbours on credit terms, as with mail order clubs.

aggregate cost method

(also called aggregate method) a projected funding technique that computes pension benefits and costs for an entire plan rather than for its individual participants.

aggregate depreciation

a total amount of depreciation. Where an aggregate is given no analysis is supplied of its components according to assets depreciated or according to periods in which it was charged.

aggregate income

an amount which is lying being between the value of the gross product and net national product. It is another name for national income.

aggregate monetary demand

the total planned expenditure (within an economy) by consumers, firms, government, and foreigners on goods and service which are produced within that economy. Indirect taxes and import components are deducted before calculating the aggregate monetary demand.

aggregate supply

refers to the amount of goods and services produced by all firms in the economy during a given time period in response to demand expectations. In the short run, aggregate supply is a relatively fixed quantity of output, which can, however be increased over the long-term, as population grows and resources are expanded.

aggressive demarketing response to shortages

an approach to actual or anticipated shortage of the raw materials required for production. When companies feel they cannot produce enough goods to meet their customers needs, they may take any or all of the following steps: raise prices sharply; cut product quality and new product development; eliminate weaker customers; reduce customer services; allocate supplies to customers according to their ability to pay; cut marketing budgets for research, advertising, and sales calls; and drop low-profit items in their product lines. Aggressive demarketing in this fashion, however, may have unwanted negative consequences, especially losing the good will of many customers.

aging

an analysis of individual accounts receivable according to three time elapsed after the due or billing dates.

agm

abbreviation of annual general meeting.

agreed procedure

negotiated between management and trade union(s) as the procedure to be followed in attempting to solve any grievance before resorting to strike action. Where a strike is called without first going through the agreed procedure, it is known as an unconstitutional strike or a wildcat strike.

agribusiness

the business functions related to agriculture. Agribusiness includes farming as well as the processing of food and other agricultural products, the manufacture of farm equipment, and the production of ancillary farm goods such as fertilizers.

agricultural co-operation

broadly speaking, it means the application of the co-operative principle to the requirements of the farm-population.

agricultural property relief

a relief given against inheritance tax in respect of property used for agricultural purposes. There are detailed rules determining the conditions under which the relief is available.

aida

a well-known mnemonic, used in training salesmen, to indicate the correct sequence for a selling interview (the initials stand for: attention, interest, desire, action).

aida model aida

is an acronym for attention interest, desire, and action: which represent the desirable qualities found in an advertising or personal selling message; i.e., it should get attention, arouse interest, create desire, and precipitate action. The concept was first propounded by E.K. Strong in 1924.

aided recall

a technique used in psychological testing in which individuals in interviews are promoted to talk about something by reminding them of associated thing. It is particularly used in Market Research.

AIMA

All India Management Association.

aiming

type of psychomotor skill. An individual's ability to perform swiftly and accurately a sequence of movements demanding eye-hand co-ordination.

aio inventory

in psychographic research, a method used to determine consumers' activities, interests, and opinions (AIO) by means of a life-style measurement survey.

air freight

the first type of air freight was mail, which took up relatively little space. As the time progressed producers of goods saw the competitive advantages of being able to fulfil orders particularly those for light-weight goods in a far shorter time by using air transport. The transaction is still greater where the weight-related charges offer a particular advantage. Now, far from seeing cargo as an 'extra' airlines are becoming increasingly conscious of its economic benefits. Sometimes aircraft design planes for 'cargo only'.

Air Freight Decision Tool (AFDT)

a computer model designed to help shippers determine when to use air freight as the preferred mode of transportation.

airmail

a postal service for letters sent abroad by which the letters are carried by air. The service is more expensive than surface mail. Letters to be sent by airmail are identified by a blue sticker in addition to the postage stamps.

airtruck

a coordinated mode of shipping goods which involves the combined use of air freight and truck freight. Its ease of use is made possible through containerization.

AITUC

All India Trade Union Congress.

AJF

Adjusting Journal Entry.

alcohol advertising

an advertising practice which sets out rules to which any advertiser of alcohol must adhere. Advertisements should not be directed at young people or in any way encourage them to start drinking.

algol

an algorithmic procedure-oriented computer language.

algorithm

a systematic sequence of instructions or rules for problem solving.

alienation

the condition of a worker who becomes a mere cog in the production process, spending all day on an assembly line doing the same simple task over and over.

alienation clause

a special type of acceleration clause that requires payment of an entire loan balance upon sale or other transfer or title to real property.

alien corporation

the classification assigned by state governments to a corporation doing business within the boundaries of that state but chartered by a foreign government.

All India Trade Union Congress (AITUC)

this labour organization was founded in 1920 for representing the interests of the workers and to co-ordinate the activities of all workers organizations in the country.

all-in rate

wage rate that incorporates various extras, such as bonus payments in addition to the basic time-related payment scheme.

allocate

to spread a cost systematically over two or more time periods, objects, activities, processes, operations, or products. In government accounting, to transfer an appropriation, or a part thereof, from one agency to another.

allocating skills

the skills used by marketing managers to budget time, money, and personnel for the firm's functions, policies, or programs. Marketing managers use these skills to achieve effective implementation of the firm's marketing strategy.

allocation

the direct association of a particular cost with a specified activity or cost centre. The process of allocation, in which a cost is dealt with intact, should be contrasted with the process of apportionment.

allocation basis

the systematic rules that assign indirect costs to two or more cost centres in order to assure that the full costs for providing health care and facilities are included in determining billing rates. The allocation basis is separate from the determination of billing rates. Market demands may dictate that indirect costs allocated to a given cost centre be reallocated to other cost centres in which higher market demand will permit additional loading of indirect costs.

allocation of overheads

apportioning indirect costs and expenses (e.g. cleaning materials, lighting, heating and depreciation) which cannot be directly identified with particular cost centres (centres).

allocation problems

a company may manufacture a number of different products and they may be a 'best' way of making each. However, the company may have insufficient resources available to make each product in the 'best' way and will therefore have to decide which allocation of resources provides the 'best' way of making all the products taken together. A number of operational research techniques have been developed to solve this problem (mathematical programming), giving an answer that is better than that given by common sense. As well as in production planning, allocation problems also occur when deciding: (1) where to build a new plant; (2) how to allocate workers to jobs; (3) how to plan the distribution of finished products from factories to customers so as to minimize transport costs. M.J.C.M.

allonge

refers to an attachment to a document that provides for endorsements when no space for the purpose remains on the document proper.

allotment

the acquisition, by one or more persons, of newly issued securities; commonly as a result of an administrative decision by which securities are allocated among applicants.

allotment letter

the letter sent by a company to a successful applicant for its shares. It confirms the allotment and states the number of shares. An allotment letter is usually transferable to others and can, therefore, be sold.

allowance

a reduction from list or invoice price made by a manufacturer, wholesaler, or retailer in return for the performance of certain services or activities on the part of the customer or to compensate the customer for some other reason.

allowed time

the time, which, for the purposes of wage payment, is taken to be the normal time for performance of measured work. It consists of the standard time for the job plus a bonus increment and/or a policy allowance.

all risks

a type of insurance which covers the insured for any loss or damage to the property insured howsoever caused. The premium for this type of policy is higher than where the cover is restricted to loss or damage caused by specified risks, e.g. fire or theft.

all times high

this refers to a price, or more probably an index of prices, which has reached the lowest level ever recorded. Thus share prices may be said to be at an all time high when an index of share prices reaches a higher level than any previously recorded.

almoner

a person responsible for the financial control of an institution providing a humanitarian service, such as a hospital or a home for the aged.

alms

amounts of money given to a poor person, usually by an institution.

alph numeric codes

computer codes using letters as well as numerals.

alpha stock

a category of shares traded on the stock exchange. It includes the shares of large companies, which are dealt in every day.

alternate

a person who is appointed to act as a substitute for another person in performing specified duties whenever the other person is unavailable.

alternate standard

work study term for the alternative Standard time when a specified different or alternative method or work is used.

alternating day and night

a two-shift system in which one groups of workers work for a period (e.g., a week, fortnight, or month) on a day shift then for the same period on a night shift.

alternating shift

where shift workers change periodically to a different shift (often weekly or monthly).

alternative director

a director who may act in place of another, e.g. at a meeting of the board of directors, when that other director is unable to be present.

alternative marketing

unconventional marketing strategies, or marketing or unconventional goods or products-outside mainstream marketing. Could be opening up new markets like Sinclair Research and Home Computers, or Barratt Developments and their original ways of marketing houses.

alternative strategies

alternative strategies for the solution of the problem are developed after a decisional problem has been identified. This aspect of decision making generally involves both the question of ends and means.

amalgamation

a merger by agreement of two or more concerns with or into a major organisation.

ambiance

the pervading mood, tone, or atmosphere which characterizes a business establishment or other facility. In its marketing context, ambiance commonly refers to store environments.

amendment

at a formal meeting an amendment may be moved as what the mover of it believes to be an improvement in the action proposed in the motion before the meeting. An amendment should not be a direct negative or merely destructive in intent, and a chairman may also refuse to have it put to the meeting if he judges it to be either irrelevant or frivolous.

amongst matter

position of an advertisement, where it is situated amongst editorial material.

amortization

it is the writing off of assets— the lives of which are determined not be deterioration or absolescence but the expiry of the tenure of ownership. The principal instance would be a leasehold property. A business with a fixed lease of an asset, particularly a building or land, would wish to provide for the renewal of the lease or its replacement with another type of tenure by writing off the cost of the asset over its fixed life and, in addition, probably putting an equal amount each year into a sinking fund which would be invested to provide monies for the eventual replacement or renewal. This manner of writing off an assets is called amortization. It is distinguished from depreciation in that there is generally no deterioration in the performance of the asset during its life.

amortized cost

in accounting the cost of an asset minus the portions written off or depreciated.

analog computer

U.S. usage, see analogue computer.

analogue computer

a computer which calculates by using physical analogues of variables (e.g., distance). It is used primarily for scientific applications in contrast to digital computers.

analogue representation

the representation of a variable by a physical quantity (such as angular position or voltage) which is made proportional to the variable.

analysis

the breakdown of a total figure into its component parts. In accounting, for example, we use the analysis of sales.

Analysis of Variance (ANOVA)

a complicated statistical test used to check if differences

(variance) exist between the means of several samples. It might be used to establish whether the average output of each of half dozen engines varies due to one factor, perhaps operating temperature (one way anova); due to several factors, say temperature and fuel additives (two- way anova): and so on; or whether it varies due to chance sampling error. Anova does not reveal the size of differences, nor does it confirm that the test is correct; variance might be due to some other unidentified factors.

Analytical Marketing System (AMS)

one of four subsystems of a company's marketing information system (MIS), which consists of a statistical bank and a model bank for analyzing marketing data and problems. The statistical bank is essentially a collection of statistical procedures or routines which may be used to extract meaningful information from data. These procedures include routines for calculating averages, measuring dispersion, and cross-tabulation of the data.

and reduced

words which may be required for a period to be added to the name of a company whose capital has been reduced.

annual percentage rate.

the true rate of interest on money lent. The law now requires that all retail lenders of money state in their quotations an annual percentage rate, usually abbreviated to APR.. This is so that all such quotations are on a comparable basis.

annual report and accounts

the annual published report of an organization, containing both a narrative and a financial description of the operation of the organization during the year. The minimum contents of an annual report and accounts for a limited company is prescribed in the Companies Act 1985 and by various Professional standards, Accounting standards.

annual return

a return that a business house is obliged to make annually. Specifically, the details of membership and financial structure that each registered company must send to the Registrar of Companies who makes it available for public inspection.

annuitant

a person who receives an annuity.

annuity

a series of regular payments. The arithmetic for dealing with annuities is used for solving most interest rate problems, such as "should I repay this loan? or "How much should be transferred to a sinking fund".

annuity fund

the fund that is created as a result of an annuity agreement.

annuity method

refers to a method of depreciating an asset.

anomie

a social condition characterized by the absence of a clear and consistent normative structure.

a highly integrated community develops norms which regulate personal behaviour and interpersonal relationship and define the limits of individual aspiration. Within such a community individuals know what is expected of them and their conformity is rewarded with the approval and support of their fellows. The system provides security and emotional support for its members and is conducive to the maintenance of their mental health. Conversely the absence of clear norms leads to individual doubts and anxieties and the loss of supportive social relationships. The term anomie was first introduced in sociology by Emile Durkheium at the end of the nineteenth century. In a classic study (suicide, 1897) he showed, inter-alia, a positive relationship between suicide rates and anomie. More recently the concept has been shown to be related to the incidence of various forms of social deviation and individual stress.

in the industrial organization some degree of anomie may be manifest in the absence of closely knit social groups of their break-up by technological requirements. Consequently the persons so affected may be deprived of meaningful social relationship and, if lacking compensatory job commitment, become alienated. Blauner's 'isolation' category of alienation is closely related to anomie. Alienation; institution; morale; nor; role conflict; socio-technical system.

antedate

to give a document a date before that on which it was actually executed. The intension is to give effect to it retrospectively. This may sometimes be illegal as, for example, when a deed of covenant is antedated so as to obtain a tax benefit.

anthropometry

in work study, the study of human body measurements.

anti-avoidance

a description of measures, usually in the form of legislation, to prevent taxpayers from avoiding the payment of tax by methods which, although technically legal, were not intended in the drafting of the original legislation.

anticipation stock

raw materials, parts or finished goods purchased or manufactured in advance of expected demand or in anticipation of rising costs and prices.

anticipatory repudiation

a breach of contract occurring when a buyer of real estate informs the seller before closing escrow that he does not plan to fulfil the transaction.

anticipatory socialization

where someone is eager to enter a new role, they may anticipate the situation by adopting the attitudes and interests associated with it, e.g., someone about to become a student, or a manager, or a parent for the first time.

anti-dumping tariff

a tax levied against imported goods which are being dumped (sold at prices below those in the home market) on the domestic market.

anti-inflation

description of a policy adopted by the government with the object of preventing or reducing inflation.

appliance credibility

customer acceptance that company is good at making its product. If company is well-known for making, say lawn mowers, appliance credibility is likely to apply if company produces a lawn raker, but less likely if it diversities into making, say, a foot-pump for motor-car tyres.

application

an offer by an investor to subscribe for a specified number of shares in a company. The offer must be made on the prescribed form which is issued only with a prospectus.

appraisal

assessment of performance and/or progress in the exercise of a given responsibility or in the development of personal and technical competence.

appraise

to value. Thus an expert might appraise an asset in order to give an authoritative opinion as to its value.

appreciated property

items of property that have increased in value since their acquisition. Typical examples include art, stocks and bonds, and real estate. Historically, it has been more advantageous to donate appreciated property to tax-exempt organisations that to give cash, because the taxpayer obtains both a deduction for the full amount of the gift and also escapes the capital gains tax that would be incurred if the donated property were sold (except for gifts to private foundations). Therefore, it has been more advantageous to donate appreciated property than to sell it and give the proceeds there from to a tax-exempt organisation.

appreciation

an increase in value. The opposite of depreciation.

apprenticeship, contract of

a contract of apprenticeship does not today differ

significantly from other contracts of employment. Apprentices are merely a special type of employee differing from other employees in that the consideration for their services is represented by the employer's duty to teach them the basic skills of the trade or profession concerned. Although many apprentices are infants (under eighteen years of age), an adult could equally well be apprenticed. The apprenticeship agreement, unlike other contracts of employment, must be made in writing and is often made in the formal manner as a deed. Although it may be desirable to make an infant apprentice's parent or guardian a party to the contract, it is not essential that they should be associated with it. Since, however, in earlier days the employer occupied a quasi-parental position vis-a-vis the apprentice, even today it is not possible for an employer to sue the apprentice for breach of contract, but if the apprentice's parent or guardian were a party to the contract the employer could sue them. Although apprentices are treated as employees by the employment-protection legislation, apprentices who are not kept on a qualified employees at the end of their apprenticeship will not be entitled to a redundancy payment nor (ordinarily) to compensation for unfair dismissal. Young persons engaged on work experience and youth training programmes sponsored by the Manpower Services Commission are not normally regarded as either apprentices or as employees and so are outside the scope of the employment-protection legislation, though not of the health and safety legislation.

apprenticeship training

this method of training is in vogue in those trades, crafts and technical fields in which a long period is required for gaining proficiency. Apprenticeship training aims at providing necessary background, practical knowledge and necessary experience to the worker. It is very useful for complex crafts and trades. It combines classroom instructions, demonstrations and on the job training. A trainee, serving as an apprentice has to work in direct association and under the direct supervision of his masters.

approach

the first few minutes of the contact between a salesperson and a potential customer. Approach is the stage in the sales presentation which is designed to gain and hold the prospect's attention. It includes the following three steps: (1) salesperson introduces himself/herself to the prospect: (2) salesperson "sells" himself/herself, the product, and the company to the prospect: (3) salesperson gets and holds the prospect's attention and interest. During the approach, the salesperson draws out the prospect to determine his/her needs. This information will later be used to convince the prospect of the advantages of the salesperson's product or service. There are many different approaches, including the benefit approach (which emphasizes the benefit to the prospect of doing business with the salesperson), the curiosity approach (in which the salesperson bases his/her presentation on the approach (an eye-opening show or demonstration which often involves the prospect), and the factual approach (which uses an interesting fact about the product or service to capture the prospect's attention).

appropriation

an amount set aside out of profits for a specific purpose.

approve

to sanction officially; to accept as satisfactory; to ratify.

apr

letters standing for annual percentage rate.

apt

a programming language developed in USA and used for the production of tape for controlling numerically controlled machine tools.

aptitude

fitness, natural ability, readiness to learn-usually used to describe potential ability-to learn specific skills, for example, mechanical skills.

aptitude test

a test of a person's ability to learn a task or of potential ability to perform a task.

arbitrage

this relates to deliberate switching of funds between markets in order to maximize net gains on short term investments. Dealings may be in currencies, commodities or bills of exchange. A person may buy a quantity of rice or a currency three months forward and then invest in another commodity or currency. He will do so if he receives a higher return on his immediate investment than has to pay on his forward transaction. Arbitrage is different from pure speculation. It can be conducted on a genuine basis and can help the smooth running of international or national trade and commerce, by making funds available in the right place at the right time.

It is the process of buying a thing in one market and selling it at the same time in another market in order to take advantage of price differences. The arbitration must be agreed initially in the contract as it cannot be imposed afterwards. Some advantages are: simplicity, speed, economy, and the avoidance of publicity. There is, of course, no guarantee of justice or impartiality on the part of the arbitrator. Contracts of arbitration may be oral or may be in writing in accordance with the Arbitration Act of the country concerned. The arbitrator need not be named but the parties must sign, though signatures may be dispensed with where the contract is obvious from the behaviour of the parties. An agreement to refer a matter to arbitration does not, however, prevent either party taking legal proceedings. A court may, however, insist on the arbitration. Costs of arbitration will be apportioned by the arbitrator. Where there is more than one arbitrator, an umpire is appointed. His decision is final if the arbitrators fails to agree (known as umpirage).

The term may imply taking advantage of the existence of two or more different market prices for some commodity by entering into contracts simultaneously to buy and sell it (or to borrow money at a low rate of interest and lend it at a high rate). When only two market prices are involved the operation is called 'simple' or 'one-point' arbitrage; if there or more market prices (and contracts) are involved the operation is called 'compound' or 'two-point', 'three-point', arbitrage.

arbitrary approach

a method for allocating a firm's promotional budget in which the amount spent on promotion for a particular time period is the result of deriving an executive decision rather than from scientific analysis. Also known as arbitrary allocation.

arbitration

in negotiations, the process by which both parties to a dispute agree to submit the dispute to a third party for a binding decision.

arbitration, commercial

a method of settling commercial disputes by referring them for adjudication to a nominated person or group of persons who will decide the issue by means of an arbitration award after having given both sides an opportunity to present their respective cases. Reference of a dispute to arbitration has generally to be made in writing and is governed in the UK by the provisions of the Arbitration Acts 1950-79. Valid arbitration awards are enforceable in much the same way as judgments of a court of law.

Commercial arbitration is often preferred to judicial proceedings in a court of law for the following reasons:

(i) the arbitrator or arbitrators may be selected by the parties to the dispute from among persons who combine knowledge of the law with knowledge of the particular commercial or technical problems that are involved in the dispute. Arbitrators, unlike judges, may use their practical experience of commerce in reaching their award.

(ii) arbitration proceedings may be conducted privately and not necessarily in open court. This is particularly useful where some confidential information is likely to be disclosed in the course of the proceedings.

(iii) arbitration proceedings may be held where and when the parties wish and some of the delay of the law may thus be avoided. Previously much of the time saved could be lost when the award was subsequently challenged in the courts, but the Arbitration Act 1979 severely restricted the right to apply for judicial review of arbitration awards. In some cases the parties may exclude this altogether and the award will be final.

(iv) it is doubtful whether arbitration is much less costly than court proceedings, but some economics may be made in the number of expert witnesses who have to be called.

The Arbitration Act 1975 enables arbitration agreements with an international element to be recognized and enforced in the United Kingdom.

arbitration, industrial

the settlement of a trade dispute, i.e. one concerning wages and other conditions of employment, by the award of an independent third party, who may be either an individual or an arbitration board or tribunal. Industrial arbitration must not be confused with Commercial arbitration. While the latter is governed by the Arbitration Acts 1950—79, these Acts do not apply to industrial arbitration proceedings.

The awards of an industrial arbitrator are normally today only legally enforceable if adopted by the parties and embodied in individual contracts of employment. However, the statutory Central Arbitration Committee (known as the Industrial Arbitration Board before 1976, and before 1971 as the industrial court) can in certain circumstances make an award that becomes binding by being incorporated in the employment contracts, concerned, e.g., where a recognized union complains of an employer's failure to supply information to its bargaining representatives under he Employment Protection Act 1975 (→ Disclosure of Information).

The 1975 Act also provides that where a trade dispute exists or is apprehended, the Advisory, Conciliation and Arbitration Service may refer the dispute, if all parties to the dispute so agree and, generally speaking, agreed disputes procedures have been exhausted, to an arbitrator or to the Central Arbitration Committee → Collective Bargaining; Lockout; Strike.

arbitrator

a person chosen by the parties to a dispute to suggest a way of settling the dispute. An arbitrator is usually chosen because he is independent of the disputants and because they think he will apply principles of fairness and practicality, rather than legal rules, in formulating his suggested solution (which is usually called an 'award). It is usual for disputants to agree to be bound by any award their chosen arbitrator makes.

area manager

normally a manager responsible for controlling a number of salesmen or other personnel with decentralised responsibilities operating in a given geographical territory.

area sampling

a method of probability sampling in which the stratified sample is made on the basis of geography rather than by demographics or other population characteristics. Geographic areas (such as city blocks) serve as the segments or primary units.

arithmetic ability (Ar)

personnel selection and vocational guidance test devised as part of the engineering apprentice test-battery of the National Institute of Industrial Psychology in the U.K.

arm's length policy

a practice in transfer pricing in which the home or parent company charges foreign subsidiaries the same price it charges firms who are not part of the organization.

arrangement

debtor's plan for the settlement of unsecured debts or the extension of time over which repayments will be made.

array

a statistical term for an orderly grouping of values according to magnitude, usually from the smallest to the largest, e.g. 1,8,15,23,54,80.

art

in advertising, art is the illustration appearing in an advertisement (photographs, drawings, charts, graphs, etc.) as well as the layout of the visual components of the ad.

articles of incorporation

synonym for certificate of incorporation.

article of partnership

a legal document that covers all items agreed upon by the partners in a business and which each partner has signed.

artificial person

an enterprise, business firm, or organization that has powers, either granted by law or by custom, that resemble those of a natural person.

artificial trading area

that geographic area specified

by a firm as the territory in which it will conduct its business.

artificial transaction

a transaction which has of itself no commercial justification but which has been undertaken purely to gain some benefit deriving from the form of the transaction.

artisan's lien

a legal claim against another's property as security by a person who has invested labour upon, or added value to such property and who has not been reimbursed for the value of the labour and materials.

artists' medium

material used by artist for his particular visual expression, e.g., pencil, ink, paint photography.

ASCH phenomenon

named after a study conducted by S.E. Asch (published 1958) in which he demonstrated the influence groups have upon individual choice making.

As is goods

condition of sale that a buyer will accept delivery of goods ordered as they come and without warranty.

a shares

shares in a company which are in every respect like its ordinary shares except that they do not carry a vote.

asking price

the price at which a good or a security is offered for sale. In some circumstances, such as in local retailing, asking price is taken to indicate willingness on the part of the seller to negotiate the final selling price to some level below the asking price.

aspirational group

any group to which an individual would like to belong (such as a little leaguer wishing to become a professional baseball player). For marketing, the implication is that the desire to emulate the chosen group influence consumer buying decisions.

assay

a process by which the purity of a precious metal is determined and certified.

assembling

the process of developing an inventory of homogeneous product, such as agricultural produce, from the small lots of a number of small producers so that they may be handled economically further along the marketing channel.

assembly lines (flow or production lines)

assembly and flow lines are the chief methods of production used for high-quantity standardized items. The operations necessary for completion of the job are located at successive stations on the lines, an approximately equal amount of work being undertaken at each station. This method of production has the following characteristics: (i) minimum distance moved by product, hence minimum handling and minimum space are required; (ii) job specialization, hence little training is necessary and a high level of performance is possible; (iii) minimum work in progress, hence minimum production time; (iv) inflexibility, hence dependence upon continued, stable, quantity demand for a standardized product; (v) maximum resource utilization. Even with complete line balancing, i.e. equal standard times at each station, underutilization of resources may occur because of the variability of operation times resulting from human error, faulty material, etc. (system loss). Too rigorous pacing of work may also result in the production of defective or incomplete work. → Assembly line balancing; system loss; pacing. Production planning for this type of production is comparatively complex because of its inflexibility. A continuous supply of raw material and sub assemblies is essential and the output rate is effectively fixed:

$$\text{out rate/hr} = \frac{1}{\text{cycle time (hr)}}$$

however, production control is comparatively simple.

Job simplification has been a continuing trend since the beginning of industrial engineering, and assembly-line work incorporates many of the traditional concepts of work design. Recently, however, there has been a counter trend, i.e. → Job Enlargement, based on the theory that over-simplification of work affects the needs of the individual and leads to diminishing economic returns. Perhaps the two principles of assembly-line work that are most questionable are the principles of work simplification and → pacing. Assembly lines differ a great deal in the extent to which these principles are adopted. Cycle times vary from a few seconds to several hours, and similarly situations where work is rigorously paced often exist alongside assembly lines incorporating large buffer stocks. Assembly-line manufacture is normally in anticipation of demand, i.e., for stock, unlike jobbing manufacture, which is in response to demand, i.e. direct to customer order.

assented stock

a security whose holders have agreed to some course of action so that the agreement is binding on a purchaser of the security. An example would be where a covertible debenture has been presented for conversion into equity.

assessment

a procedure to identify ability carried out on individuals as part of the processes of recruitment and selection; a procedure carried out on property or profits to determine tax liability.

asset

the financial accounting standards board (FASB) has defined an asset as a "probable future economic benefit obtained or controlled by a particular enterprise as a result of past transaction" (1979). Simply stated, an asset is any item owned (such as cash, receivables, inventory, equipment, land, buildings, and good-will) whether tangible or intangible).

asset conversion

a means of internally financing a firm's projects by liquidating one form of asset to employ elsewhere within the firm or repay a liability.

asset cover

the extent to which a share is represented by valuable assets.

asset turnover

the ratio of net sales to average assets for a defined fiscal period. The ratio expresses financial activity in an analysis of return on investment.

assigned mailing date

in direct marketing, the date on which a list user must mail a particular purchased list, by virtue of a prior agreement between the list owner and the user. The user may not mail that list on any other date except with the specific authorization of the list owner.

Assignment

the transfer from one party to another of the right or interest in real property, or of the little to and interest in an item of personal property; for example, ownership of a patent or receivable may be assigned or transferred.

assignment analysis

a method of job evaluation developed for professional and technical jobs in which the assignments that the job holder carries out are graded according to complexity, experience required and so on.

associate broker

a licensed natural or legal person who acts for another in a real estate or related transaction.

association

a group of individuals united voluntarily for achieving a determinate purpose/s and held together by mutually determined code of procedure and rules.

association advertising

a form of horizontal cooperative advertising performed for trade associations (such as the Floria Citrus Growers Association) to promote primary demand for a class of products (such as Florids a organges).

association advertising format

a type of advertisement that conveys its message by establishing a relationship between an event, an activity, or an image and the product being promoted.

association of direct marketing agencies (ADMA)

a professional organization of firms engaged in multimedia direct marketing ADMA sponsors seminars and workshops. Its headquarters are in Brooklyn, Massachusetts.

assorting

the process of developing a heterogeneous inventory of products for the convenience of customers. The function is usually performed by wholesalers or retailers in order to supply an assortment of products such as hardware, drugs, grocery items, etc. The convenience factor may motivate sellers to stock related items not directly associated with their principal line of goods. For example, a lawn mower dealer may sell grass seed and other related gardening items.

assortment

(1) a mix of similar and or complementary products designed to provide benefits to a specific market. (2) in retailing, the range of choice within a particular classification of goods, such as style, colour, size, and price.

assumed liability

the assumption of the payment of an obligation incurred by another.

assumption fee

the fee charged for processing papers when a buyer assumes a loan from a seller (for example, assumes a mortgage).

assurance

indemnity against the financial consequences of some inevitable event such as death. The term insurance is applied to indemnity against the consequences of events which may not occur, e.g. destruction of a property by fire.

assured

a beneficiary of an insurance policy; a person who would be indemnified by another against a risk of loss.

atmosphere

qualitative or subjective value of a medium or publication for advertising purposes.

atmospherics

the environmental factors consciously designed to create a certain mood, develop a particular image, and/or stimulate sales. These factors include layout, architecture, colour scheme, and other sensory stimuli.

atomistic competition

a condition in the marketplace in which there are so many competitors that no one seller can influence the price of the product or commodity they all make or produce. This condition exists in farm commodity production and in the women's ready-to-wear industry.

attachment

the appropriation of assets for the purpose of satisfying a

judgment involving a claim of debt.

attachment of earnings

the court order made on an employer to deduct money payable to the court at specified periods direct from the employee's (debitor's) wages or salary.

attainable standard

a particular basis for setting a standard cost. Its feature is that standards are set so as to represent a realistic but not impossible challenge to attainment.

attachment of earnings

the consequence of a court order whereby a portion of a person's wages or salary can be deducted before payment and applied in settlement of an obligation to a third person.

attainment test

or achievement test. Type of psychological test that measures knowledge in a particular area or attainment in a particular kind of skill rather than potential or aptitude.

attendance allowance

a social security benefit payable to those who are bound to attend on an invalid.

attendance at stocktaking

this will usually be undertaken as part of an audit. An auditor might be though to have been negligent if there was not attendance at the stocktaking.

attendance bonus

an addition to normal wages which an employer promises to give to any of his employees who achieve a certain standard of time keeping or lack of absence from work.

attendance pay

a bonus paid for good attendance or time keeping.

attention value

extent to which and advertisement can secure the initial attention of a reader, sometimes expressed in quantitative form in Starch or other page-traffic studies.

attention value

extent to which an advertisement has been noticed and remembered by respondents.

attitude

a person's knowledge and positive or negative cognitive evaluations about an object such as a product or service. Attitudes are learned, enduring, and made up of three components: (1) knowledge: (2) effect: and (3) action tendency.

attitude survey

the systematic collection of attitudinal data, usually for the purpose of predicting behaviour, testing reactions to specific phenomena, or ascertaining the relationship between attitudes and other variables. The data may be collected in a variety of ways but the most common are probably interviews, questionnaires, → Attitude Scales, and for the more sophisticated, the use of projective techniques. As techniques of attitude scaling and measurement have developed, so the use of attitude surveys has increased, and opinion polling is now an established profession. Attitude surveys are a valuable research tool in the hands of the trained psychologist or sociologist, but despite an apparent simplicity, the design and conduct of such a survey contain many pitfalls. It is necessary to be absolutely clear what data are needed and how they can best be collected; what population is to be studied and what kind and size of sample is to be drawn; how the questions should be phrased and by whom, and where the questioning should be carried out; what statistical analysis is appropriate and what inferences may properly be drawn. Additionally it must be borne in mind that attitudes are often ephemeral and subject to considerable influence from perhaps temporary circumstances.

attributable profit

the part of the total profit currently estimated on arise over the duration of a long-term contract which fairly reflects profit arising from the work done to date.

attribute mapping

in new product planning a statistical means of analyzing a market in an effort to find openings for new products. Existing products are positioned on a chart called an attribute space with each position being determined by the product's characteristics. Open spaces indicate gaps into which new products may be introduced. Also known as market position analysis.

auction company

an agent and middleman selling by the auction method; i.e., customers may examine the product before engaging in competitive bidding for its purchase, commonly employed in the sale of agricultural products, such as fruit, tobacco, livestock, etc. The auction company receives a commission from the seller of the merchandise based on the final sales price. Also known as auction houses.

audience

(1) the total number of individuals reached by an advertisement or other promotion. For example, the number of viewers seeing a particular television commercial or seeing a particular print advertisement in a magazine or newspaper. (2) the target group at which a promotional message is aimed. For example, marketers may gear their advertisements to appeal to a particular segment of the population, such as "supplies." Also called target audience.

audience profile

the characteristics of the audience reached by an advertising medium (print or broadcast) or a particular station, newspaper, or magazine, etc. It includes both demographic and psychographic characteristics. Generally presented as a percentage figure which may be compared to the population as a whole. Also known as audience composite, and audience composition.

audience share

the percentage of the total listening or viewing audience, i.e., those with their sets actually turned on, which are turned to a particular program data specific time.

audience study

survey research aimed at learning who the audience is for an advertising medium and how it reacts to the advertising message.

audit

an audit may also be said to be such examination of books, accounts and vouchers of a business, as will enable the auditor to report, whether he is satisfied that the balance-sheet is properly drawn up so as to give a true and fair view of the state of affairs of the business and that the profit or loss for the financial period, according to the best of the information and explanations given to him and as shown by the books; and if not, to report in what respect he is not satisfied.

audit brief

a description of the scope of scale of an audit. The audit brief for some forms of organisation, e.g. a limited company, is laid down by statute.

auditing

the principal function of an auditor (when appointed for the purpose of the audit of a limited company) is to certify that a company's annual accounts show a 'true and fair view' of the company's affairs. The auditor is also required to certify that proper books of account have been kept and that the annual accounts are in accord with the books. The meaning of the terms 'true and fair' and proper books is not obvious but accountants acting as auditors have generally interpreted these terms to mean that the books and accounts are in accordance with currently accepted principles of accountancy → Accounts Conventions). However, auditing practice does not consist only of the application of accounting principles. At least as important is the comparison of the books and accounts with independent evidence to verify the transactions entered into by the company and its present financial status in terms of the values of assets and liabilities. The verification process consists mainly of the examination of documents such as invoice, receipts, contracts, documents of title, etc. as well as an investigation of the company's administrative system in order to determine whether it is such as to encourage fraud, embezzlement or defalcations. Owing to the size of the task, it is generally accepted practice that auditors should carry out intelligent test checks of the company's system of accounting and administration and original documents rather than carry out an exhaustive check. The use of statistical methods of sampling for this purpose is growing. An internal audit, by employees of the organization, is frequently used to complement the work of the external auditor.

auditing guidelines

statements issued by the professional accountancy bodies which are intended to prescribe the principles and practices which members are expected to follow in their conduct of an audit.

auditor

a qualified examiner of financial accounts; also, reviewer of an organisation's operations, an agent who performs a monitoring and feedback function.

audit trail

a notation accompanying a transaction entry or posting that refers to its source records or documents.

audit year

the year covered in an annual or balance-sheet audit; usually the fiscal year.

augmented product

the core product together with its attendant benefits and services.

authenticate

recognised method or symbol of verification for a process or output, such as credit or claim status, or use of a signature stamp in claims filing, to denote anthorship of an entry made in a patient's medical record by means of a written signature, identifiable initials computer key, or a personally used rubber stamp.

authorised capital

total value of a company's share capital as registered or formally approved for the time being, not all of which need have been issued.

authoritarian leadership

a style of management in which the leader plays a strong, directive role in setting group goals and in planning and directing the activities of the members of the group. The authoritarian leader delegates few of the functions of leadership to the members of the group.

autiority

the power attaching to a job or function which enables the job holder to undertake and discharge his duties and responsibilities and make decisions appropriate thereto.

autocracy

a type of power structure in which one individual-an autocreate has power over all others.

autocratic control

tight personal control of a company of department by the chairman or a manager. Also known as Caesar management.

autocratic management

synonym for authoritarian management.

automated warehouse

a warehouse which is controlled by a central computer and which utilizes sophisticated electronic materials handling systems. Automated warehouses require far fewer employees than traditional warehouses, thus reducing labour costs. They tend to be single-storied structures.

automatic check

any facility, software or hardware, for automatically carrying out a check for the absence of specific errors.

automatic guided vehicle

load-carrying vehicle (e.g. truck, pallet) that is self-propelled and capable of following a predetermined or selected path e.g. by following wires buried in the ground, wires or lines on the ground, or by means of remote control. Such vehicles are used in automated factories to transport parts from and to storage areas or production machines.

automatic programming

the use of an automatic data processing system to perform some stages of the work directly involved in preparing a computer programme. Also ,known as automatic holding.

automatic reorder

an inventory system in which supplies of staple merchandise are monitored and replenished only when they have been reduced to a predetermined minimum. At that minimum point a reorder procedure is activated.

automatic saving

if a person's net income is too large to spend, the unspent income is called automatic saving.

automatic teller machine (ATM)

it is a robot which dispenses cash and, income cases, deals with certain other basic banking transactions of a kind which traditionally would have been handled by cashier to teller over bank counter.

automatic test equipment (ATE)

automatic test equipment. Equipment, usually computer-based, which carries out testing of components and products automatically. It is extensively used in the electronics industries.

automatic vending

a form of non-store, non-personal retailing of goods and services through coin operated, self-service machines. Merchandise most commonly sold by this method includes cigarettes, candy, soft drinks, and hot beverages. Services provided by automatic vending machines include telephone calls via pay phones and banking services via automatic tellers.

automation

the replacement of human labour by more or less automatically-run machinery, particularly electronically controlled equipment.

automatization

replacement and/or extension of human control by machine.

automobile information disclosure act (1958)

federal consumer legislation which prohibited automobile dealers from inflating the factory prices of new cars.

autonomous work groups

a pattern of work organization which gives a group of workers considerable scope and responsibility for planning and carrying out production. It is an important element in Socio-Technical Systems.

autonomy

the property of self-determination in individuals or in an organization. It can refer specifically to the degree to which an individual or group is free to make decision without having to refer to others.

auxiliar capital

alternatively it can be called instrumental capital. Goods that aid labour in production such as tools, machines, railways, docks, ships etc., and raw materials of all kinds.

auxiliary dimensions of a product

features of a product other than the product itself, which add to the product's attractiveness, usefulness, and consumer appeal. For example, packaging, warrantee, repair services, and brand names are all examples of auxiliary dimensions of a product which may influence the consumer to select it over other products or other brands of the same product.

auxiliary functions

apart from the basic functions an office performs the following auxiliary or administrative functions. Also:

Managerial function. An office has to be managed effectively. Therefore, the managerial functions of planning, organizing, directing and controlling are performed in every office.

Personnel function. In a small enterprise, the office is expected to recruit, select and train the personnel. But in large organization, this task is entrusted to the personnel department. In such cases, the office supplies information about staff absenteeism and turnover to facilitate proper selection and training of employees. It also helps the personnel department in developing an appropriate promotion policy and incentive schemes.

Safety function. An office performs the task of safeguarding the assets of the organisation. It protects important documents relating to assets against theft, fire, etc. It arranges for suitable insurance cover to safeguard the fixed asset like plant and machinery, furniture and fixtures, etc. It maintains proper records of stock, debtors, cash, stationery and other assets.

Purchase function. Every office procures the right type of furniture, machines and equipment for carrying out its tasks. It designs office forms. It also purchases office stationery and issues the same to different departments according to their requirements.

System and routines function. An office develops appropriate procedures and practices for efficient performance of tasks. It also creates proper checks and balances to regulate day-to-day operations.

Cost control function. A modern office assists in controlling costs. It employs time and labour-saving devices, utilizes well-designed systems and procedures and work study methods to cut down waste and expenses.

Public relations function. An office keeps continuous liaison with the public to build up a favourable image of the enterprise. It provides good reception services, consumer education campaigns, necessary information to government agencies, etc. It also keeps the management informed about public opinion.

available market

the available market for a product or service consists of all the potential customers who can afford the product or service, who have access to it, and who have exhibited an interest in using or owning it.

available to promise

the uncommitted portion of a company's inventory or planned production, usually calculated from the Master Production Schedule.

availability

in industrial psychology, availability reflects the perceived limitations of the environment. It is determined by the accessibility of goals that can satisfy a given need, as perceived by the individual.

available quantity

in materials requirements planning (MRP), the available quantity of a given part is equal to the sum of the onhand quantities in all stock locations.

average

normally synonymous with arithmetic mean. 2. In broader sense it may refer to any measure of central tendency of a series of quantities.

average cost

the average cost of producing goods, also referred to as the unit cost. It is customary, in the accounting world, to distinguish average fixed cost from average variable cost. There is also an important difference between the short-term average and the long-term average. The average cost of producing a single batch of goods or of one month's production, may be very different from the average taken over a long period. This distinction is important in price fixing especially under free competition, for although a company cannot fix prices below the long-term average on a permanent basis, it can bring them down to the short-term average and below if any competitive advantage is to be gained.

average fixed cost

the total fixed cost divided by the quantity of goods produced. A fixed cost is one that remains constant regardless of changes in sales volumes.

average revenue

the total revenue (income generated by sales, etc.) divided by the quantity of goods required to produce that revenue. The average revenue line is the demand curve facing the firm.

average salary

alternative term for pensionable salary in calculations for an average salary pension scheme.

average stock

the amount which represents the midpoint between the highest and lowest inventory levels for a given period. The average stock is calculated by adding each month's opening stock figure plus the closing stock figure of the last month. The sum is then divided by the number of months being considered. For example: average stock (January-December)=opening stock of each+December closing stock) ÷ 13.

average variable cost

the total variable cost divided by the quantity of goods produced. A variable cost is one that changes as sales volume changes (for example, delivery costs).

avoidable cost

a cost which may be avoided by the discontinuance of a particular activity.

award

the documentation, or the content, of a decision made by an external court, commission or trinal; also of a committee jointly established by trade unions and employers to examine conditions of employment; a pay increase.

awareness

the initial stage in the consumer adoption process during which the buyer becomes aware of the product but has gathered little information about it.

awareness survey

similar to attitude survey and opinion poll, and awareness survey studies respondents' familiarity with the subject. Periodic surveys measure the shift in awareness over time. Methods or evaluating PR program aimed at improving awareness.

back cover

in advertising, the back cover of a magazine usually available at premium rates for advertising. Special rates apply to both inside and outside back covers.

back duty

tax relating to a period in the past which was unpaid then because fraudulent or erroneous returns were made.

backed note

an authority, endorsed by broker, the master of ship arranging the loading of goods for shipment.

back haul

reshipping freight over the route it has just completed. This may occur when shipping goods to a customer located between the warehouse and the plant.

backhaul allowance

refers to a practice reduction given to customers who pick up their own merchandise at the manufacturer's or distributor's warehouse, thus saving the seller the cost of delivery.

backlog

the total of a business's unfilled orders at any one time.

back order

the portion of a customer's order that has not been shipped against an accepted order that is in backlog.

back selling

promotional efforts of secondary suppliers who supply components, ingredients and other materials which are incorporated in the production of products but may not be known to or be identifiable by the final buyer.

backstep analysis

an analystical technique for diagramming a problem, its causes, and its consequences; used to help decide what a program can and should do to abate a problem, and to establish that a true problem is being attacked rather than the symptoms of such a problem.

backward channel

a marketing channel running backward from the consumer to the middleman and, on occasion, back to the manufacturer or producer. The recycling of aluminum cans, the return of empty soft drink bottles, and the collection of waste materials are examples of backward channel activities. Also referred to as reverse distribution.

backward integration

efforts on the part of a firm to

buy or gain control of its supplier companies. For example, a large retail organization may own its own manufacturing facilities and operate its own distribution system.

backward invention

a product planning strategy in international marketing in which firms doing business in developing countries modify (and sometimes simplify) their products so that they may be more appealing in the domestic market.

backward market segmentation

a means of identifying segments of a population on the basis of some kind of common behaviour, e.g., the use of particular products or services or the viewing of particular television programs.

backward pass

in project network techniques the calculation of latest event times, or of latest start times of activities and earliest start times of activities.

bad debts

accounts going out of business and still owing money to suppliers. Also an item in financial accounts referring to actual amount of monies so lost, or written off.

bad title

a defective legal document used as evidence of lawful ownership of land.

bailee

a person who is entrusted with the possession of goods and, by a warehouse receipt, bill of lading, or other document of title, acknowledges such possession and contracts to deliver those goods.

bailment

a transfer of possession of goods without the passing of title, as on consignment for safekeeping, repair, or sale.

bailer

a person who gives possession over some of his property to another person during bailment.

bait and switch merchandising

the promotion of a product (the bait) at a very low price for the purpose of luring customers into a store. The retailer, who has no intention of selling the bait, attempts to sell the customer a more expensive item (the switch).

balance budget

a budget in which receipts equal the outlays of expenditure.

balance stock

in retailing, a balanced stock is an assortment of merchandise with sufficient breadth and depth to meet the demand of target customers while maintaining a reasonable investment in inventory. Also called model stock or ideal stock.

balance-due

the quantity of material or parts ordered on a purchase order or requisitioned on a work order but not yet received.

balance economy

an economy which aims at stabilization of employment at a high level.

balance of payments

the difference between the payment a country makes to other countries and those it receives over a certain period of time.

balance of trade

the relationship between the values of a country's imports and exports. A trade deficit exists when imports exceed exports. A trade surplus exists when exports exceed imports.

balance sheet

a classified financial statement showing a firm's assets, liabilities and net worth at a particular moment in time.

band chart

a chart in which the difference between two curves is emphasized by shading in or colouring the space between them.

banded pack

a form of sales promotion in which consumers are offered two or more packages of a product, or a package of a product plus another product from the same manufacturer, attached together (usually by a band of tape printed with details of the offer), at a reduced price.

banding

the rationalizing of pay structures and the substitution of a defined number of pay brackets or bands for a wide variety of separate rates. Job evaluation techniques are often used to establish which jobs should be placed within each band. The term 'broad banding' is sometimes used where a large range of jobs is placed within each band.

bank

banks provide means by which capital is transferred from those who cannot profitably use it to those who can use it most productively for the benefit of the society as a whole. Banks provide with channels to invest savings without any risk and at a good rate of interest. They advance loans to businessmen of credit, provide facilities for making remittances at home and abroad and settle credit payments. The system of banking and finance not only bring about the distribution of goods among the consumers but also enables modern productive processes to go on. Where the manufacturing process is very long it becomes necessary that throughout its course the producer should not fall short of money.

bank charges

the amount charged by bankers from their customers for services rendered in operating a current account. They cover not only the handling of cheques but also the provision of other services such as meeting standing orders. These include interest on overdrafts and a national commission. Practices vary between banks but generally the person with a small account will pay more; this is justified by the claim that they involve much work and little profit. Many banks waive charges where customers keep a minimum balance in their accounts.

banker's commercial credits

of considerable importance in international trade. An exporter who has agreed to supply goods to a foreign customer will wish to have some guarantee of being paid when the goods are delivered. The exporter may insist, therefore, as part of the deal that a reputable British bank should undertake to pay for the goods. The buyer will then have to approach his own bank to arrange the opening of such credit for him. The importer's bank, if satisfied as to the customer's credit rating, will then contact its agents or correspondent bank in Britain, asking that they should open an irrevocable documentary credit in the exporter's favour, accepting responsibility for reimbursing the British Bank in due course. The exporter will then be informed by the British bank of their willingness to honour drafts → Negotiable Instruments, up to a stated maximum amount, provided that these drafts are accompanied by the appropriate shipping documents. Unless these documents are produced in the exact form stipulated in the bank's letter of confirmation to the exporter, the bank will not be obliged to accept the draft. The documents will then be forwarded by the bank to the instructing bank in the importer's country, who will reimburse them and hold the documents until the importer has paid the amount involved and the charges incurred. The documents in question are those at are needed to claim the goods from the carrier who has been conveying them to the importer's country.

bank holiday

any legal holiday or other special occasion when banks remain closed, usually but not always along with most other businesses.

bank note

a kind of paper currency that is, in effect, the promissory note of a bank. Such notes promise to pay the bearer on demand the amount stated on the face of the note. Bank notes are now issued by the central banks. In the 19th century, almost all banks issued notes (even now in some countries, e.g., France and Scotland).

bank overdrafts

bank overdraft is granted when the customer has a current account in the bank. Under an overdraft arrangement, a depositor is allowed to draw by a cheque more than the deposited amount to his credit, but upto a specified limit. Interest is charged on the exact amount overdrawn by the customer. The rate of interest on it is always higher than that charged on the loans. This facility is given by banks on the security of some assets or on the personal security of the customer. It is a short period arrangement.

bankrupt (noun)

a person who is bankrupt.

bankruptcy

the state or condition of being unable to pay one's debts. The debtor may be an individual or corporation and the bankruptcy proceeding may be voluntary (initiated by the debtor) or involuntary (initiated by creditors).

bankruptcy notice

a notice requiring a judgment debtor to pay his debt within a certain period or given a satisfactory guarantee that the debt will be paid. Failure by a debtor to comply with such a notice is an act of bankruptcy.

banner

relating to an advertisement headline stretching across open space. Also large board or piece of fabric held or towed aloft bearing some slogan or symbol.

bar

the direct exchange of goods or services between the parties involved in a commercial employed. In international marketing barter is regarded as a type of counter trade.

bar chart

a graphical method of illustrating statistical information. It takes the form of a diagram in which quantities or frequencies are expressed as columns of different height.

bargain (verb)

1. to negotiate the terms and conditions of a contract.

2. to engage in collective bargaining.

bargaining structure

ground rules established in a company to facilitate bargaining between management and trade unions.

baseline

an on-line statistical reporting system service computer-based service provides demographic data on a local, state, regional, or national basis. It includes a marketing module.

base period

in economic and business research, a base period is a year or span of years used as a reference point and to which current data is compared.

base stock method

a method of inventory valuation in which a minimum amount of goods (the so-called base stock), carried at all times, is valued at its long-term normal price; while the goods carried in excess of this minimum are valued according to some other method.

basic

an introductory computer

language that combines Algol, Cobol and Fortran.

basic data

the results obtained from any control procedure are not better than the accuracy of the information fed into the system. Inaccurate costs, standard times, inventory counts, or any one of the other items of basic data upon which the system operates will result in poor performance.

basic functions of office

an office performs the following basic functions:

Collecting information. It is the main function of an office to collect and receive information. An office has to collect information from various internal and external sources. The internal information refers to letters, circulars, bills, reports, memos, etc. received from different departments of the same organisation. The external information includes the information received from customers, dealers, suppliers, government agencies, trade associations, etc.

Recording information. The information collected from various sources must be properly recorded for the purpose of future reference. Recording should be done in such a way that the information can be made available to managers quickly and easily.

Compiling information. Mere recording of information will not serve the purpose. The information collected by the office is in raw form. Therefore, it must be systematically arranged and analyzed. The information becomes meaningful after it is compiled in the form of reports, charts, bills, financial statements, etc. Certain statistical operations like tabulations, calculations, etc. are performed to compile information.

Furnishing information. An office serves as a clearing house of valuable information. The office provides the information whenever it is required by the management. For example, the office provides information concerning sales turnover, stock position, cash position, staff attendance, etc.

basic product

or industrial product, product marketed not to the pubic or consumer, but to industry as a component or constituent part in other products.

basic rate

the minimum wage rate for a job excluding any allowances such as overtime premium or bonus. Used as a nominal rate from which other rates (e.g., overtime rates) are calculated. Also called 'base rate' or 'basic wage rate'. It is also the minimum wage rate for a job agreed in a national agreement but subject to local increase.

basic workweek

the number of hours in a normal workweek. Premium payments or compensatory time off must usually be made for time worked in excess of the basic workweek.

basing-point pricing

a pricing strategy in which the cost of goods has two components: (1) their cost at the point of production plus. (2) the cost of transporting them from a designated center (the basing point), which may be different from the point of manufacture.

basing point system

a system of delivered pricing in which the price quoted by the seller is the factory price plus the cost of shipping from one or more places called basing points, from which the goods may or may not be actually shipped.

batch costing

process or activity of allocating costs to a batch of identical items of production, treated as a single unit.

batch production

productive activity, of which the output over a period of time, consists of numerous small batches of different products and in which any production facility is involved, at different times, in work connected with various products.

battery

a collection of test which have a similar purpose or are to be administered one after another at a single session.

battle of the brands

the competitive struggle at the retail level between national brands on the one hand and middleman and retailer brands on the other. More recently, generic or "no-name" products have joined the competition.

bayesian analysis

statistical techniques which use and establish probability curves to help in decision-making by exploring potential outcomes of different options.

Banyan statistics

a type of statistical analysis for management decision making, developed for translating subjective forecasts into mathematical probability curves. In many typical business situations there are no normal statistical probabilities because alternatives are unknown or have not been tried before. Bayesian statistics use the best estimate of a given circumstance as if it were a firm probability.

bazaar

although associated with markets and oriental bazaars, the term has Western usage meaning a variety store like Wool-worth. Also applied to groupings of traders under one roof, e.g., coin, stamp, antique dealers.

beanstalk

a stack of trays or shelves used for displaying products at the point of sale.

bearer

the person in physical

possession of a negotiable instrument payable to the bearer. In such a case, title (legal ownership) is defined by physical possession.

bearer share

a share, ownership of which is evidenced by a bearer security. Also the bearer security, usually called a share warrant, that evidences ownership of such a share.

bed and breakfast deal

sale of an asset followed by an immediate repurchase of the same asset, order to establish that its capital value has changed at a time when it is most advantageous to report the change for the purposes of capital gains tax.

behavioral engineering

a part of learning theory which holds that people behave in direct relation to what they believe will be the consequences of their acts. Behavioral engineering has been applied in limited forms in marketing, having more uses in personnel management. Also known as behavioral technology, applied behavioral analysis, and Skinnerian psychology.

behavioral research

research into human behaviour, single or in groups, particularly in connection, with consuming or buying habits but also concerned with wider aspects of social and organizational conduct.

behaviorism

in an advertising context, an application of the stimulus-response theory of learning in which a stimulus (an advertising message) is repeated often enough to produce the desired response (the purchase of a product or service).

behaviour study

market research statistical technique for assessing the behaviour pattern and the opportunities existing in a particular market.

belief

a thought or understanding held by a person about a thing or occurrence.

below the line advertising

this is a form of sale promotion which uses outlets such as direct mail, special discounts and point-of-sail offers as opposed to the mass media used in above the line advertising.

below-the-line promotion

marketing term for sales promotion in such forms as reduced price special offers, premiums and point-of-sale displays. The term above-the-line promotion, on the other hand, is used of sales promotion in the form of expenditure on advertising in the press, on television or in other media.

benefit approach

a technique used by salespersons in the first few

minutes of contact with a prospect. The salesperson attempts to focus the prospect's thoughts directly on the benefit to be derived from the goods or service being sold. The benefit should be concrete and specific, such as a monetary savings.

benefit, direct

also indirect benefit, a result closely related to a specific project or programme in a cause-and-effect manner.

benefit market segmentation

a market segmentation technique which attempts to identify the benefits consumers seek in a product or class of products and divide the consumer market accordingly.

beravement pay

pay given to an employee while he is given leave because a close relative of his has died.

bernreuter personality inventory

psychological inventory developed in the USA of use in temperament and personality tests.

bed brand rating

based on consumer opinions of the best product for particular purposes, counterpart for brand share as revealed by retail audit research. Given high brand recall, the two results should be similar.

bid

(1) an offer to buy, as in a public auction. (2) an offer to perform a task or supply goods made by a vendor at a price which he feels will be competitive and acceptable to the buyer.

bid price

a term associated with unit trusts. Units are quoted at two prices: the bid price, which is the sum that the management company will pay for units held by third parties; and the offer price, which is the figure at which they will sell. The offer price is higher than the bid price so that when people buy units they must, if they are not to lose on the investment, retain them until they have risen to a point above the bid price. For this reason unit trusts are seen as a long term rather than a short term investment.

big early, little late method

a method of developing media advertising schedules in which the beginning of the campaign is regarded as most significant and thus allocated the largest amount of money.

bilateral trade

a relationship of balancing trade between two countries. Under bilateral trade, the trade between two countries, strictly speaking must eventually balance.

bilateral trade agreement

agreement between two countries to extend to each other specific privileges in their international trade which are not extended to other countries.

bill

a statement of items and charges made for services rendered, products purchased or rented, or accommodations used; also, a draft of a law for consideration by a legislative committee or body.

bill broker

bill brokers are merchants whose traditional business is the buying and selling of bills. They are more usually referred to nowadays as discount houses.

bill of entry

a bill of entry is a document prepared by the importer for the purpose of paying the custom duties. It is prepared in triplicate and contains full information regarding the goods due to arrive.

bill of exchange

a bill of exchange is an unconditional order, drawn by one person against a second person, ordering the second person to pay a specified sum of money to the first person, or to a third person named in the bill, or to the bearer, such payment to be made on the presentation of the bill or after a specified period of time named in the bill has elapsed.

bill of lading

a list identifying all goods or property within a shipment, which serves as an inventory, provides directions for shipment, and acknowledges their transfer and receipt.

bill of materials (bill of requirements)

a list of the component parts of a product, usually arranged in a 'structured' manner so that different 'levels' are identified, e.g. the final product level, below which there are the major subassemblies, then the component level, and so on. Bills of material are used in inventory control, production scheduling, and in purchasing → Materials Requirement Planning.

bill of sight

it is banking term used in internal and external trade. The bill of sight is presented by the supplier to the buyer for payment on presentation. It is also applicable where an importer is not able to give full details of his cargo. He completes a bill of sight. The cargo is then inspected by customs authorities. The importer then completes the entry, and the completion is known as perfecting the sight.

binary scale

this is used to represent numbers in a computer rather than the familiar decimal scale. The latter, a 'ten-state' scale, uses the arabic digits 0-9 inclusive, and is based on power of 10 (that is, 1, 10, 100, etc.). The conventional method of writing a decimal number is really a shorthand notation for expressing the coefficients and successive power of 10. For example the decimal number

329 is really

$3 \times 10^2 + 2 \times 10^1 + 9 \times 10^0$

the choice of a basis of 10 is arbitrary and was probably originally determined by the number of digits on two hands, which would provide a convenient basis for counting. Other scales are in common use, for example, a duo-decimal scale (12) to convert inches to feet, and a tertiary scale (3) to convert feet to yards. The binary scale is used to convert pints into quarts.

Electronic circuits represents digits, and hence numbers, in a computer by adopting alternative configurations or states for each digit. It is much more convenient to design 'two-state' rather than 'ten-state' circuits, so in a computer the binary rather than the conventional decimal scale is used to represent numbers. Further, a computer makes decisions that require alternative to be formulated logically. These formulations must be expressed electronically and a two-valued, or binary, logic is preferable to a ten-valued or decimal one.

bin card

a record of usage of a stock-keeping unit that is kept near the place of storage. It normally records the quantity and date of each movement of stock in or out of the store.

bionics

refers to the studio the functions and characteristics of living systems in relation to the development of hardware designed to operate in a similar manner.

birdyback

a coordinated transportation arrangement in which both air and ground modes of transportation are used. For example, goods would be shipped partly by airplane and partly by truck.

black

to declare that one will not handle certain goods-especially as part of a trade-union campaign against a firm that used, manufactured, processed or transported the goods.

black box

a term used by marketing researchers to describe the consumer's mind and to indicate that what goes on inside their mind is largely hidden from the researcher's view.

black capitalism

an effort begun in the late 1960s to increase the ownership and control of business by black people. Its objective is to improve the job market, the ghetto economy, and condition and status of the black community.

black economy

the informal sector of the economy where work is done but no record of its is officially available and on which on tax is paid.

backleg

a worker who does not support

union action: for example by working when others are on striker, by refusing to join a union by accepting employment in place of a union members who is on strike or by working for less than union rates.

blacklist (noun)

list (especially one circulated among a group of people or firms) of people who are not to be employed or of people or firms who are not to be given credit.

black market

trade in products, commodities, currencies, etc. which is in violation of the law; e.g. tax laws, regulations governing rates of exchange, price ceilings, etc.

blank application

candidates who qualify the preliminary interview, are given the application form for filling in facts. The blank application provides a written record of the qualifications, experience, etc. of candidates.

blank cheque

a cheque where no sum of money is stated. The holder can fill in the amount himself. Blank cheques are often used in latter transactions where the price of the goods to be purchased is not known. The buyer may send a blank cheque but write, e.g., 'Not to exceed Rs... on it. The bank will heed this instruction.

blanket agreement

collective agreement resulting from industry wide bargaining or national bargaining.

blanket mailing

indiscriminate, mass mailing of a news release, an abuse of press relations to be discouraged, Examples: mailing of managerial appointment story to all national newspapers when perhaps only two or three print such announcements, or mailing of agricultural story to entire farming press when it is relevant to only a section.

blanket order

a pre-season order placed with a vendor to be delivered in a number of late shipments.

blind advertisement

and advertisement which is anonymous, i.e., it omits the name of the sponsor as in 'situations vacant' where the company does not wish to disclose its identity and uses a box number or similar device instead.

blind test

a form of market researching which consumers are asked to test in product which has all-identifying markings removed—often in comparison with other similar competing products which are also disguised.

blink-meter

used in advertising research to measure the frequency of a person's blinking, so giving indications of interest or arousal.

block diagram

a schematic drawing of operations in the sequence in which they are performed. Block diagrams are used in the planning, development and analysis of business operations, manual systems, computer systems, and computer programmes.

blocked accounts

non-resident funds which cannot be transferred freely.

blocked currency

a currency of country is said to be blocked when the government of that country creates categories of its currency that can be used only for purchases within the country.

blocked need satisfaction

when the satisfaction of a need is blocked, a reduction in the strength of the need may result.

blue chip

the term used to describe the ordinary shares of long established, large and reputable companies. Such shares are generally regarded as being a good long-term investment; more generally the term may be used of anything that is highly regarded for its reliability and performance.

blue chip investment

an investment which, though not gilt-edged, is considered to be safe, so that there is little likelihood of losing capital or income. It can be generally in the form of well-known companies.

body copy

main copy in advertisement, as opposed to headlines or illustration.

boiler room

a facility from which telephone salespeople make solicitations.

bolt-on promotion

ready made promotion e.g., scratch-card games, which can be linked to a product in a sales promotion exercise.

bona fide sale

a transaction in which the seller acts in good faith regarding the terms of the sale.

bonded block loading

an effective and secure method of loading freight; the items are stacked in the manner of overlapping "bricks".

bonded warehouse

a warehouse in which goods may be stored without customs duty or excise duty being paid until they are withdrawn from the warehouse. The proprietors of the warehouse enter into a bond to guarantee that duty will be paid when necessary on the goods they store.

bonding of salesman

buying indemnity against possible loss arising from negligence of dishonesty through employment of salesmen.

bond note

a term used in shipping with reference to export of goods. Dutiable goods must be put in bond. A bond note is issued indicating that the necessary formalities have been observed. The note acts as authority for recovering the goods from the warehouse and exporting them.

bond in insert

an insert that is attached publication.

bonus account

a savings account that pays a higher than normal rate of interest.

bonus earnings

earnings over and above merely paid rate or basic salary.

bonus formula

the formal provisions in an incentive bonus plan that determine the total funds available for bonus purposes in a given year. Individual bonus awards are made from this total pool.

bonus increment

in payment systems, an addition to standard time which is used as an incentive.

bonus pack

a promotional package in which the customer is offered more than the regular amount for the regular price.

bonus payment

an incentive payment to salesmen for above–the–norm achievement; often ex-gratia rather than contractual.

bonus share

shares of a company that are organization's financial transactions that allows a clear picture of its financial situation to be obtained at any time, i.e., by reference to its 'books'.

bonus stock

common stock offered as a bonus, either to the underwriter of the issue as additional incentive, or to buyers of bonds or preferred stock in the same company.

book inventory

a perpetual system of inventory maintained by adding the value of incoming goods to the value of previous inventory and then subtracting the value of sales, mark-downs, and discounts.

book keeping

keeping the financial records (books) of a business or other economic unit, recording all the transactions in which it engages. Book-keeping is a branch of accounting.

book of account

the records of a firm's financial records.

book value

it may also be stated as the worth of something as recorded on an organization's balance sheet, rather than its worth as established by the market; also, an organizations' net worth, or its clearly proven assets minus its liabilities.

born salesman

sales or other personnel attributed with natural qualities that result in superior selling achievement.

borrowing time

where under a payment–by–results scheme a worker uses time allocated for one task to push ahead with or complete another task.

bottom up approach

an approach to planning or decision making which is based upon consultation with those at the bottom of an organizational hierarchy—as opposed to top-down approaches in which instructions and decisions come down from the top.

bottom up planning

planning initiated by employees near the bottom of the organizational ladder. Unit objectives and the resources required to attain them are set forth and subsequently transmitted up the organization for evaluation and approval at the decision-making level.

bottom up theory

a theory of fashion adoption in which young, lower-income persons are seen as the innovators of new styles. Fashion then spreads upward through the various social classes, although in order of adoption the next group may be members of the confident, secure, upper class. The new fashion is then likely to spread widely throughout the population.

boutique

organization providing a specialized advertising service rather than a full range of facilities. Usually associated with creative services.

boutique agency

an advertising agency that specializes in writing and designing advertising material and thus focuses on the creative and art aspects of the advertising campaign.

boutique merchandising

a form of store organization in which related merchandise from a number of departments is brought together in one shop to meet special customer demand.

boycott

a refusal to participate in something on grounds of principle. For example, refusing to use a particular service or buy a product because the firm involved in its supply is in breach of an agreement, or practises some form of discrimination.

box-jenkins techniques

type of exponential smoothing techniques which, with computer aid, are used to improve forecasting and to take into account variations from earlier forecasts.

branch

a geographically detached unit of a firm which is still an integral part of the business. Branches of companies frequently restrict their activities to the selling function.

branching network

in project networks a condition in which the network branches to a series of optional routes. The choice of which route to take depends on information obtained when that point is reached in the project and cannot be planned in advance: it is felt upto the discretion of the project manager as to which course will be most suitable.

branch store

in department or other large stores, the smaller retail units owned and operated by the parent store and generally located in the suburbs or in metropolitan area shopping centres.

brand

a particular product, or line of products, offered for sale by a single producer or manufacturer and made easily distinguishable from other similar products by a unique identifying name and/ or symbol.

brand extension

the practice of marketing new products under well-known brand names in an effort to capitalize on the positive image the parent brand has in the consumer's mind.

brand extension strategy

a marketing strategy in which a firm uses one of its established brand names on a modified product; i.e. a new line, or on an entirely new product.

brand familiarity

the customer's ability to recognize and accept a particular brand of products. Brand familiarity is often divided into five levels: (1) brand rejection: (2) brand non-recognition: (3) brand recognition: (4) brand preference; and (5) brand insistence.

brand image

that perception of a product formed in the mind of the consumer which is the result of the symbols and meanings associated with a particular brand.

branding

branding is the act of affixing a name or a design or some words or letters to the products in order to distinguish it from the products of others. It is usually done to make the manufacturer's name familiar among the public. The primary purpose of brands and trade marks is to furnish a means of identification so that repeat demand may be centred upon a product whose use has resulted in satisfaction and goodwill.

brand insistence

an extreme form of brand loyalty in which the customer will search extensively for the desired product or brand and accept no substitute. Consumers who are brand insistent are known as "hard core loyals." Consumers who share their loyalty between two or three brands are said to be "soft core loyals," and those who shift from favouring one brand to another are called "shifting loyals". The least brand insistent consumers, those with no loyalty to any brand, are known as "brand switchers."

brand leader
a term used in marketing to describe a brand or a product that appears to the most prominent one in its field to consumers, and is marketed accordingly—unlike a follower in the market or a new product.

brand loyalty
a situation where consumers remain loyal to a particular brand of good or services even if it costs more than its competitors.

brand mark
that part of a brand consisting of the signs, colours, symbols, and designs; i.e. those elements which are not words, and are closely identified with the product. Brand marks; e.g. the red tab on the back pocket of Levi Strauss jeans, may also be a part of the firm's trademark.

brand marketing
a strategy in which each of a firm's products is marketed independently, generally under the direction of a brand manager.

brand name
that part of brand consisting of the actual letters or words; i.e., that part which can actually be vocalized, which comprises the name of the product or service as distinct from other identifying signs, symbols, and designs incorporated into the overall design.

brand name bias
a tendency on the part of persons being questioned about product use to name a widely advertised brand despite the fact that they may never have bought it.

brand position
a product's niche in the marketplace. The term "position" refers to the product's relationship to competing brands and is generally measured in terms of how the consumer perceives the various attributes of the brand, i.e., brand position depends on consumer attitudes.

brand preference
in the process of brand acceptance, a middle stage in which the consumer will choose a particular brand over its competitors because of previous favourable experience with the product.

brand recognition
a stage in brand acceptance in which consumer remember having heard about or seen a product, even if they have not yet tried it. Such recognition is a company's first objective for a newly introduced product.

brand rejection
customers' refusal to buy a particular brand of goods because of its poor image or because of previous bad experiences with the brand. Remedies for brand rejection are: (1) change the brand's current image: (2) change the product: (3) change the target segment.

brand strategy
the plan employed to create, introduce, and promote a particular brand. Strategies involved include picking a name, selecting an image to project, positioning the product in the marketplace, etc.

brand switcher
a consumer who shows no loyalty to any brand and who looks instead for the brand that is readily available, is on sale, or is novel. Consumers often maintain brand loyalty for certain items while displaying a willingness to accept substitutes for others.

breach of contract
the failure to perform or fulfil the terms of a contract.

breach of warranty
a violation of the guarantee or representation of the contents, performance, condition, quality, or endurance of a product or service. A breach of warranty does not necessarily entail fraudulent misrepresentation.

breakaway union
a new trade union formed by a group of dissident members who have withdrawn from an existing trade union. Secession from a trade union and the formation of a breakaway occurs when a section, having lost confidence in the union and developed different goals, becomes large enough and active enough to form an independent body. White the rights of worker to join unions of their own choice need to be respected, the right to break away and form a new union has always been condemned as likely to undermine the strength of the parent union, to encourage discontented members to seek a solution outside the union rather than internally through the democratic process, and to weaken the unity of the trade-union movement. The formation of a Broadway union is the most serious crime in the trade-union calendar.

The larger, more complex, more centralized unions with a heterogeneous membership can better withstand external stresses because of their numerical strength, but are more vulnerable to internal stress than the smaller, more homogeneous and less centralized unions. Thus the Transport and General Workers' Union has suffered breakaways in the form of the National Amalgamated Stevedores' and Dockers' Union and in the National Passenger Workers' Union; and the Aeronautical Engineers' Association is a breakaway from the former Amalgamated Engineering Union. Breakaway unionism may come about through the enhanced status of a membership group, now acquiring a feeling of exclusiveness. For example, for their now high-status workers the National Association of

Signalmen aims to provide an organization similar to the footplatemen's and salaried staffs' unions, and separate from the National Union of Railwaymen, which is formally responsible for the organization of signalmen.

The official policy of the → TUC is to refuse to affiliate a new union if there is already one in existence organizing the type of worker concerned. Employers are reluctant to incur the ire of powerful, established unions by dealing with breakaways; indeed an employer may not bargain with a breakaway even if it represents a majority of those employed by the firm.

public policy has tended to discriminate against breakaway unions and their formation in the civil service has compelled the government, as an employer, to define its policy towards them. Following the report of the Terrington Committee (Cmd. 8470) the government will not recognize for bargaining purposes any new union unless it can prove that existing associations have failed and were unable to look after the interests of those concerned. In practice this is extremely difficult.

break bulk center

a central distribution point where large shipments of goods (such as carload and/or truck load quantities) are broken down into smaller quantities and shipped to customers closer to the final market.

break down approach

a method used to allocate a firm's advertising budget. In the break-down approach, the firm begins with a pre-determined total budget, which is then allocated by the person or department in charge of promotions to particular lines of merchandise offered by the firm.

break even analysis

a mathematical analysis in which the fixed and variable costs of production are compared to projected revenue in an effort to reveal the break-even point; i.e. that point at which expenses and revenues are balanced.

break even chart

a chart on which two curves are plotted: the expected sales revenues from the production of various quantities of a product and the costs (fixed and variable) of producing those quantities. The curves intersect at the break even point.

break even point

the sales volume at which income (or revenues) equals total costs; for example, the number of tickets that must be sold to a fund-raising event before a profit is realized.

breakthrough opportunity

a marketing situation which enables an innovative firm to establish a new marketing strategy, develop and market a new product, or create a new marketing mix.

brightness

the intensity level of both a physical stimulus and the corresponding subjective sensation is sometimes referred to as brightness. The relation between these objective and subjective levels is not a simple one. The ambiguity in meaning is removed by the use of the term luminance to describe the stimulus level and luminosity for the subjective level. The amount of light radiated by a source is termed luminous flux. The unit in which this is measured is the lumen. (Approximately 1,200 lumens are radiated by a 100-watt tungsten bulb). Luminous intensity in a given direction is measured in candelas, which express the luminous flux divided by the solid angle of radiation. The illumination of a surface is defined by the luminous flux per unit area falling upon it. Thus units of illumination are lumens/m^2 (also called lux). The luminance emitted by a surface is a function of both the incident light and the reflecting characteristics of the surface, and is measured in candelas/m^2.

brightness contrast provides a measure of the difference between the luminance of a viewed object (e.g., a letter on a road sign) and the luminance of the background (e.g., the field area of a sign). The contrast is expressed as where B_1 is the higher luminance and B_2 the lower. Visual performance is facilitated by high values of contrast.

Luminosity, or apparent brightness, depends not only upon luminance but also upon such factors as colour, contrast and state of adaptation of the eye. → Colour; Illumination; Vision.

broad line strategy (full line strategy)

in strategic management, a strategy based on having a high variety within a product line.

broken lot

goods offered for sale in smaller than normal quantity. Include damaged packed goods where some contents have been lost or removed.

broker

a mercantile agent who, in the nature of his business, makes contracts in regard to shares, goods or property. He needs not carry the goods or documents of ownership. There are also specialized brokers, e.g., in stock exchange, commodity markets, and even insurance or in services. A broker is not bound by any personal liability unless custom dictates. He has implied authority to sell on normal credit terms, receive payment, and do other things consonant with his trade.

He is a person who arranges

transactions between the other people, and receives a commission (usually a percentage of the value of the transaction) for doing so, e.g., a commodity broker, an insurance broker, a money broker, a ship broker or a stock broker.

brokerage

commission charged by a broker. Synonym for broking.

brokerae allowance

a discount paid to buyers, particularly large organizations such as grocery chains, for performing the broker functions. These organizations request the broker's commission in the form of a price reduction. The practice is technically a violation of the Robinson-Patman Act.

Brown–Spearman formula

method of validating an intelligence test. Particularly when its length has been increased and the validity of the extended test needs to be checked.

budget

the term is derived from the old English word Bougette the sack or pouch from which the Chancellor of the Exchequer extracted his papers presenting to parliament the government's financial programme for the ensuring fiscal year. It has been defined as the "document containing a preliminary approved plan or public revenues and expenditures." The term budget refers to anticipated revenue and proposed expenditure by a government in the budget (i.e., next financial year). The central budget is presented by the Union Finance Minister to the parliament a few days before the commencement of new fiscal year.

budgetary training

budget training should be focused on the underlying problems not on the superficial difficulties. In line with the major problems the following specific suggestions seem appropriate: budget training should be focused to help the finance staff perceive the human implications of the budgetary system. The training should help show the finance staff the effects of pressure upon people. Thorough discussions seem necessary to understand the advantages and disadvantages of applying such pressure. The training should include discussions concerning the effects of success and failure. The accounting staff should be helped to perceive their difficult position.

budget as a means of control

the question whether budgets are a means of control does not yield a straightforward answer because budgets perform more than one function. They perform three : (1) They present the objectives, plans and programmes of the organisation and express them in financial terms. (2) They report the progress of actual performance against these predetermined objectives, plans and programmes. (3) Like organisation charts, delegations of authority, procedures and job descriptions they define the assignments which have flowed down from the chief executive.

budget based institution

an organization that is required to prepare, and work to, a budget.

budget control techniques

among the techniques of financial control from the internal management point of view one of the most important is the budgetary control and standard costs higher business control and financial models setting out predetermined factor relationships so that the actual operations remain on track and under constant review.

budget, current services

a budget that projects estimated outlays for the upcoming fiscal year at the same programme level (i.e., same quantity and quality of programme—not the same funding level) as the fiscal year in progress. The estimates take into account the budget impact of anticipated changes in economic conditions (such as unemployment or inflation); beneficiary-levels, pay increases, and benefit changes.

budget determination

consideration and decision-making on the size of a subject.

budget, full-employment

the receipts, outlays, and surpluses or deficits that would occur if an economy were continually operating at full capacity (traditionally defined as a certain small-percentage unemployment rate in the civilian labour force).

budgeting

the preparation of an accounting instrument that holds officials responsible for the expenditure of a body of funds with which they have been entrusted. Budgets also hold organizations accountable in the aggregate. The very concept of a budget implies that there is a ceiling or a spending limitation on an organisation, which requires organization to live within their means.

budgeting capital

a budget process that deals with planning for large expenditures for capital items. Capital expenditures are typically made for long term investments that yield returns for years after they are completed; they typically cover five-to-ten-year periods and are updated yearly. The items included in capital budgets may be financed by borrowing, capital funds drives, savings, grants, etc. A capital budget distinguishes capital or investment expenditures from current or operating expenditures.

budgeting, short term

an accounting budget is a short-term (annual) plan of action made in terms of physical resources and their monetary equivalents. If it is to be a business plan, a budget must necessarily begin with a financial objective, e.g., a specified rate of return on capital or the maximization of sales revenue given a minimum specified rate of return on capital invested. The complete plan of action is then prepared in terms of subsidiary operation budgets for sales, production, selling and distribution, administration and finance, so as to arrive at a budgeted manufacturing, trading and profit-and-loss account, showing how the historical accounts should turn out if all matters go according to plan. The implications for cash flows, changes in stocks, debtors and creditors are then calculated and given a separately determined figure for additions to fixed assets→ (Capital Budgeting). A budgeted→ Balance Sheet can also be prepared, showing the expected financial position at the end of the budgeting period. Theoretically the budgeting process should consist of the formulation of various alternative plans of action, from which the 'best' in terms of achievement of objectives is selected. However, in practice, such is the present state of the methods of budgeting, the only budget that is fully written down is usually the one that is to be accepted. In the future mathematical programming methods may help to improve this aspect of budgeting. It is important to stress the control functions of the short-term budget, as well as those of planning. Provided that the budget plan is fully worked out in substantive and physical terms as well as financial terms, a budget provides a specification of activities and target for all levels of management and therefore also acts as a management control device.

budget operating

a short-term plan for managing the resources used to execute a programme. "Short-term" can mean anything from a few weeks to a few year. Usually, an operating budget is developed for each fiscal year, and changes are made in it as necessary.

budget period

the length of time during which a budget is effective. For most organizations, the operating budget period is one year.

budget preparation of

the process of preparing a firm's budget is much the same in all businesses.

budget surplus

the amount by which budget receipts exceed budget outlays for any given period.

buffer stock

stock maintained as cushion

against unforeseen fluctuations in the demand or scarcity of any commodity specially with regard to food–grains, cotton, sugar, tea etc.

bug

a error or fault in the software which causes a computer program to malfunction.

build schedule

statement and record of the modifications made to a project as it progresses, listing all drawings and other documentation. May be based on the original product drawing list.

build up approach

a method used to allocate a firm's advertising budget. In the build up approach, the firm begins by ascertaining the advertising needs of each line of goods offered by the firm, as determined by the person in charge of each line.

bulk checking

the process of checking arriving merchandise by comparing the package markings against the invoice or packing list without actually opening the packaging to verify contents.

bulk goods

(1) goods, such as coal, grain, or gravel which are sold and delivered in loose or unpacked form. (2) any large shipment of one item.

bumper strike

now largely outdated type of industrial action in which strikers are directly supported financially by similar workers in other factories.

bundle of benefits concept

a theory that customers purchase not only the goods offered by a firm, but also the advantages and capabilities those goods are expected to provide. The real value of the merchandise, therefore, resides in what the goods can do for the consumer, and not in the goods themselves.

bundle of service concept

a theory in support of leasing rather than purchasing industrial equipment. The theory takes into account the comparative costs of leasing and buying, including the service and maintenance costs inherent in purchased equipment. According to the budle of services concept, leased equipment is more cost effective.

burden cosk

as indirect cost.

bureaucracy

the term is usually applied to a system of government the control of which is so completely in the hands of officials that their power jeopardizes the liberties of ordinary citizens.

bureaucratic management

a style of management based on the principles of bureaucracy, emphasizing rules, procedures and hierarchical authority.

bureau de change

this is a shop or sometimes merely a counter where one type of currency may be exchanged for another. It is primarily a service for tourists.

burn in

a form of test, used particularly in the electronics industry, which allows a component or system to run for a sustained period in order to ensure its reliability and adherence to required performance specifications.

business

activities comprising buying and selling goods, manufacturing goods or providing services in order to make a profit. Also an enterprise engaged in such activities. The term usually excludes activities relating only to primary production, operation of nationalized industries and the activities of non-profit-making organizations. An industry is also a particular type of business activity.

business administration

the science and art of conducting an enterprise with a maximum efficiency and minimum cost.

business analysis

in new product development, efforts made to estimate the profitability of new products before large amounts of money have been spent on their development.

business care advertisements

small advertisements resembling business cards in directories of services published in newspapers and magazines.

business corporation

joint-stock company.

business criterion

as commercial criterion (management technique in public administration).

business cycle

a recurring sequence of changes in business activity. Beginning with the period of prosperity, business activity declines until a low point, called a depression, is reached. A period of recovery then follows when business conditions become more and more active until prosperity is again restored and a cycle is thus completed.

business domain

that sector of a market which a firm targets as its business environment. It may be defined in terms of a line of products, a particular group of customers, or some other combination of market factors.

business insurance

insurance coverage written to provide benefits to a business rather than an individual. Types of business coverage include casualty, liability, and loss of services of key employees, partners, or owners.

business motivation

an integral part of any analysis of the firm is a definition of the goal(s) of the firm. Whilst information on demand and cost functions and market structures may be available, goals need to be defined so that the information may be effectively used. It is also true that adequate definition of the goals may conceivably alter the information required to achieve them.

Traditionally economists have approached the firm from an optimizing standpoint and, at its simplest, the goal of the firm has been taken as the maximizing of profits. It should be stressed, however, that for a long time the firm was not really the centre of interest for economists, but was merely a convenient building block in an elaborate theoretical structure that determined prices and hence allocated resources.

With the growth of oligopoly as a market structure and the division between ownership and control in the modern large corporation, the traditional theory has come under increasing criticism. This has been reinforced by various surveys that have questioned businessmen about their goals. One critic has argued that the nature of the modern corporation is such that the maximization of sales receipts is a much more plausible goal. This is partly because the professional managers are concerned with the competitive position of the company, and partly because they are naturally concerned with their own rewards. Both of these, it is argued, are more closely geared to absolute sales receipts than profits. Of course, the shareholders are not entirely neglected and so this goal is subject to a minimum profit constraint to provide satisfactory dividends and funds for capital investment. Another critic has argued that the main goal is the growth of gross assets. Management is again free to pursue this goal because of the demise of shareholder power and the growing significance of undistributed business profits. However, again a constraint is introduced by the wish to avoid loss of employment, that is, the need to avoid being taken over by a predator who sees undervalued assets.

Both these approaches are developed from an optimizing standpoint. Over against these are goals that have been developed from a satisfaction standpoint. Their roots are in psychology rather than classical economic theory, and in particular in the view that the motive to act stems from drives, and action terminates when the drives are satisfied. The term 'satisfaction' means being satisfied with some standard of achievement below the maximum possible. Hence the goals that would follow from this approach are achieving a particular level of profit, market share, or sales.

business name

name under which a person or organization trades and, under most legal systems, has to register. May be related to a trade mark.

business policy

a general rule or set of rules laid down to guide executives in making their decisions. They are therefore statements of the type, 'When faced with a situation of the type X, always choose course of action A, rather than B or C.'

Policy statements are usually broad and far-reaching in their effect on the company and it may require only a comparatively few such statements to define the character of a company completely. To achieve this complete delineation, policy statements must be made covering three aspects of a company: its objectives, the means by which it intends to achieve these, and the constraints upon it. Policy decisions are more often made as a result of moral, political, aesthetic or personal considerations than as the result of logical or scientific analysis, and are usually made by the owners or the directors of a company rather than by executives at the lower or middle levels.

The subject of business policy had received little systematic thought until recent years when management techniques for use in this area began to be devised (Corporate Planning; Decision Theory; Company Models). Of these the first is probably the only technique that attempts to systematize all areas of policy, while the latter two tend to be more useful in the area known as strategy (Strategy; Tactics). There is in fact considerable confusion as to the distinction between policy and strategy but it may be said that policy decisions refer more often to the character or nature that the company wishes to adopt, while strategy refers to the means to be employed in bringing about these desired characteristics.

The three areas of the company in which policy decisions are required are considered under → Objectives; Means; Constraints, but the following is relevant here. The nature or character of a company-and indeed of every organization of every type-is made up of two elements; the purpose of the organization and how it choose to go about the task of fulfilling it; this in turn can logically be split into two elements; those actions that it will take to achieve its objectives (i.e., means) and those that it will not take even though they may have helped it to achieve its objectives (i.e., constraints).

The decision as to its objectives must be the first to be taken, for unless these are known, no appropriate strategy can be selected to achieve them. Normally the founders of the company state explicitly or implicitly what the purpose of the company is (and the pursuit of profit must be the main or perhaps the sole purpose of any company), and this decision is unlikely ever to be changed radically, for any major change made to the fundamental objectives of a company may so alter its character that it ceases to be a company as such and becomes instead a charity or a nationalized organization or some other type of organization not having the pursuit of profit as one of its fundamental objectives. It may be possible for changes to be made in some of the less fundamental objectives of a company, but there must be some doubt as to whether an objective that can be altered frequently is an objective at all. In general, the more precisely the objectives are defined, the more accurately can strategy be devised to achieve them, and the more precisely can the progress of a company towards its objectives be judged.

business unionism

trade unionism viewed as a business, with the leader's job to sell his members' labour at the highest obtainable price. Business unionism is a concept that originated in the USA where trade unionism is concerned almost exclusively with larger wage packets, shorter working hours, better fringe benefits, etc., i.e. with the protection and improvement of the economic position of members rather than with political and social reform. In Britain there has been a mixture of both; throughout the twentieth century many trade unions have supported the Labour Party, financial and otherwise. At the same time, British unions have moved nearer to the business union form.

In so far as it may be said to operate in Britain, business unionism is associated with the changing structure of the trade union movement. New techniques, services and skills have changed the work force, with increasing emphasis on white-collar and female employment. White collar unions are a twentieth-century phenomenon, and, reflecting the changing political attitudes of their members, are on the whole more interested in business unionism than political commitment to the labour party. (Trade Union-Politics).

buyback

a product or service buyback agreement involves the sale of a product (or service) which in turn produces other products or services, e.g., the sale of industrial production facilities.

buyclasses

the three types of industrial

buying; (1) the straight rebuy. (2) the modified rebuy, and (3) new task buying.

buyer

a manager with responsibility for purchasing within a firm.

buyer behaviour (consumer behaviour)

a branch of marketing involving the study of why consumers purchase particular items and what influence their choices.

buyer credit

a method of financing exports in which a bank in the exporter's country loans money to foreign buyers for purchases from the exporter. Such a deal is usually set up on the exporter's initiative and the money is in practice paid direct to the exporter.

buyer for export

in international marketing, a middleman who buys goods in the domestic market outright and then sells them overseas.

buyer seller dyad

in personal selling, the buyer-seller dyad is the relationship between a salesperson and a customer, which strongly emphasizes personal, individual attention on the part of the salesperson.

buyer's market

a situation in which the supply of goods is high so that a seller finds it difficult to sell his entire stock at a price that yields him a good profit.

buy-in

a business arrangement by which an individual secures a financial or ownership interest in a partnership or organisation. The buy-in is often used by physicians to become members of group practices.

buying

in marketing, the term "buying" commonly refers to the purchase of goods at the wholesale level for resale at the retail level.

buying allowance

a reduction in price on specific goods offered by a producer or manufacturer to a purchaser as an incentive to buy.

buying and assembling

buying refers to the purchase of raw materials for use in production and the purchase of finished products for sale. Efficient buying is essential for success in selling.

Assembling being after the goods are purchased. It implies gathering of products purchased from different manufacturers at some central place.

buying behaviour

way in which a buyer behaves when deciding whether or not to buy a product or service and the factor that determine the behaviour. These include rational and emotional factors, the life style of the purchaser and the particular product life cycle.

buying centre

in industrial marketing the

buying centre is made up of those persons who are responsible for purchase decision-making in an organization. They may be the actual users of the products and services, purchasing officers, persons with influence over buying decisions (sales-persons, executives, etc.) gatekeepers; etc.

buying committee

in large retail organizations, especially those which handle large numbers of staple products, the buying committee assists individual buyers in making decisions regarding specific merchandise.

buying group

Group of associated buyers, e.g., farmers, retailers, horticultural societies, buying in bulk and selling at low price to members.

buying-in

the practice of hiring expert help as required by an organization rather than employing such experts on its staff.

buying point

manufacturer's outlets such as central buyer of groups and chains, wholesalers and hypermarkets.

buying power

(1) an organization's capacity to buy large amount of merchandise, thereby commanding price concessions on the part of suppliers. (2) an individual's capacity to purchase goods or services; i.e., personal income less taxes and other non-tax financial obligations plus available consumer credit. (3) the aggregate disposable income for persons living in a particular area or having some common characteristics; i.e. the money income available for purchasing goods and services.

buying signals

indirect indications of a prospect's growing interest in the product being presented.

buying syndicate

collective negotiating and buying group.

buzz group

a form of Brainstorming group used in management problem-solving.

by-laws

standing rules for the governance and regulation of an organisation's affairs.

by-product

a product made by a manufacturer or processor on a much smaller scale than another product of his but using the same materials and initially at least, with the same operations or processes.

bye turnman

person employed in casual labour.

C

a high level programming language which was developed at Bell Laboratories for writing systems software.

cable transfer

in foreign trade, a bank draft, transmitted by cable or telegraph instead of main. The correspondent bank then notifies the payee of the remittance's arrival.

calendars

a below-the-line medium which serves as a permanent advertisement in a prominent place, and also promotes good-will. The advertiser may use his own pictures and bring his own calendars.

call analysis

a technique used in marketing to measure the performance of different salesmen by examining the frequency and effectiveness (e.g. conversion of enquiries to orders) of calls made to customers.

call frequency

frequency with which salesmen visit or contact customers. Distinguished from conventional journal cycle by customer categorizing into groups of varying priority.

call frequency schedule

salesman's journey plan.

calling cycle

average period of time between salesmen's or maintenance engineer's calls on customers.

call-off-system

arrangement for buying manufactured parts for use in assemblies by which the purchaser places a firm order for a specific quantity of the parts to be manufactured over, say, the next year on the basis that required quantities will be delivered as and when the manufacturer needs them.

call report

summary, usually in writing, of visit by salesman to a customer, account executive to client, or similar business meeting.

campaign plan

a direct mail promotion which extends over a period of time and which is designed to arouse and build interest in an upcoming event or new product. The final mailing is the actual announcement of the event or product. Also known as a teaser campaign

cancel order

a market or limited price order given to a securities broker, to be executed in whole or in part as soon as it is represented in the trading arena. The portion not so executed is to be treated as cancelled.

canned presentation

a standardized sales talk memorized by members of the sales force and delivered to customers verbatim.

canvasser

sales representative or selling agent calling direct on users or consumers. Cold canvassing is the term used to describe a salesman's uninvited (often the first) call on a prospect.

canvassing

door to door or telephone sales technique that involves the solicitation of orders for merchandise which will be delivered at some time in the future.

capacity cost

the cost of operating a plant or unit at full capacity.

capacity of firms

the amount of land, buildings, plant and machinery and other fixed capital of a firm.

capital

in accounting, capital is the term for the total financial assets of an organization whether in the form of money, property, goods or equipment. It represents the organization stock of wealth as opposed to its income. The organization human resources may be represented in the form of human asset accounting; in economics capital is traditionally one of the three major factors necessary for production along with labour and land.

capital accumulation

an increase in man made equipment such as machine tools, buildings and other structures and stocks of goods used for or capable of being used for the goods and services.

capital account

the section of the statement of a country's balance of payments that records all payments not in the current account. An account recording the contributions by partners to the capital in a partnership.

capital allocation

planning holds out some hope for capital allocation decisions. The traditional method of allocating scarce capital resources on the basis of past and current returns on investment has its drawbacks. The chief is the unrealistic implication that relatively divisional returns will remain constant in the future.

capital commitments

specifically capital expenditure contracted for but not yet paid.

capital credit

the present acquisition of long-term productive facility such as land, buildings, and machinery against promises of enterprisers to pay in the future.

capital depreciation

the decline in value of capital assets (assets of a permanent or fixed nature, goods, and plant) over time and with use. The rate and amount of depreciation may be calculated by a variety of different methods (such as the straight-line, sum-of-the-digits, and declining-balance methods) which often yield quite different results.

capital equipment

an umbrella name for the several different kinds of equipment used to produce products or services, such as machinery, office equipment, test equipment etc.

capital expenditure

it is that outlay which benefits several accounting period. It is a long term asset (called fixed asset) and its useful life is estimated by experts for spreading the cost over this life-period. The amount allocated and expired in an accounting year in an expense: termed 'depreciation'. The rest is the cost-residue (or unexpired cost) and carried forward as an asset for future expansion.

capital financing

the acquisition and use of funds for purchasing, improving and expanding capital assets such as buildings and non-disposable equipment contrasted with the financing of operations and maintenance.

capital intensive industries

these are those industries where the amount of fixed capital used in production is high, both absolutely and as an amount per person employed, Capital-intensive industries are those which depend more on the machines involved in production than on the people employed to work them, i.e., industries where the cost of capital constitutes the major cost factor and outweighs the cost of labour. The ultimate in capital-intensive industry is a fully automated factory.

capitalisation

the term 'capitalisation' is derived from the word 'capital'. While capital represents total investment in a business or the total wealth or resources of a company, capitalisation refers to the sum of the par value or face value of the long term securities, shares and debentures and free reserves. Capitalisation is the process of determining long term capital requirements of a business and obtaining capital for it from various different sources of funds.

capitalism

an economic system characterized by the private ownership of a society resources; by competition in the pursuit of financial gain; and by support for the ideal of a free market in goods and services.

capitalization ratio

the total of fixed assets (after depreciation) divided by net worth; one of many ratios that are sometimes used in measuring quantitatively the effectiveness of an entrepreneurial effort.

capitalized value

the capital equivalent of an annual payment. Capital values are determined by the rate of interest and the rent produced.

capital profit

a profit or surplus arising from the transfer (for cash or kind) of an asset other than the one normally bought for resale in the course of business. A capital profit is also called capital gain when a personal asset (e.g., a house or some land or a car) is sold for a price exceeding that at which it was purchased. With limited companies the term has an additional significance. Capital profits made by companies are quite different from ordinary revenue or trading profits and are treated separately in the company's accounts.

capital reconciliation statement

statement of sources and application of funds.

capital redemption reserve

account representing the nominal value of shares that have been redeemed in so far as the redemption was not paid for by the proceeds of a new issue of shares and is not a payment out of capital.

capital structure

the term 'Capital Structure' refers to the constitution or composition or make-up of the amount of long term funds of a business. It involves the form and proportion of various securities to be issued to secure the total capital of a business. It includes both owned as well as owed funds or ownership securities as well as creditorship securities.

capitalist industry

an industry in which the material instruments of production are owned or hired by private persons and are operated at their orders with a view to selling at a profit, the goods or services that they help to produce.

capital turnover ratio

this ratio measures the relationship between the sales and the capital employed in business, i.e.,

$$\text{Sales Capital Turnover} = \frac{\text{Sales}}{\text{Capital Employed}}$$

refers to the permanent capital or long term funds invested in business. It includes the owners' equity and long term liabilities. This ratio measures the efficiency in the use of capital employed in business. The higher the capital turnover, the greater is the efficiency with which capital is utilized. A more rigorous test can be obtained by using cost of goods sold in place of sales.

Cost of goods sold=opening stock+purchases+manufacturing expenses-closing stock.

capitation tax

fixed rate tax on every person in a class or geographic location.

captive market

customers, commonly at the retail level, who have little choice about where they shop. For example, the customers of retail or service establishments in hotels or airports where alternative or competitive businesses are relatively inaccessible, constitute a captive market.

captive product pricing

a pricing strategy used by makers of products which require supplies, accessories, or ancillary equipment for operation. The principal product is moderately priced while the supplies and accessories are given substantial markups.

carbon-copy theory

in personal selling a theory that new salesperson are best trained by memorizing the techniques of a master salesperson.

card steward

trade union official or shop steward having responsibility for collecting trade union dues.

carload freight rate (c.l)

a reduced rail shipping rate allowed to large freight shipments which make up a full carload.

carry over

carry over transaction. In Indian terminology it is called Budla. It is also called contango, carrying over, give-on and continuation.

carryover effect

any effect that present marketing expenditures, such as advertising expenditures or new package design, may have on future sales. When a time period has elapsed between the expenditure and the visible results of that expenditure, it is known as a delayed response effect.

cartage

the fee charged by carriers for hauling freight. The term is used primarily in connection with trucking. When short distances are involved, the term "drayage" is often used instead.

cartel

an association, often international, of firms in the same industry, established to limit competition by allocating markets among its members, regulating prices, and other means.

cascaded systems

in production, multiple operations in which the input of each stage is the output of a preceding stage.

case method of teaching

teaching based on an actual problem faced by a business. Students are required to gather additional information and to form an opinion concerning the action that should be taken.

cash and carry

an epithet applied to a manufacturer's or wholesaler's collection of goods for sale to the general public; cash and carry is a kind of retailer's supermarket.

cash audit

an examination of cash transactions, recorded as cash receipts and disbursements, and cash in banks and on hand.

cash book

a journal in which cash receipts, disbursements, or both are recorded.

cash budgets

a statement of the estimated totals of cash that will be received and paid by a firm during each of a number of future periods. If a significant surplus is forecast for a month then plans can be made to invest it; if a deficit is forecast then arrangements must be made to borrow the necessary cash.

cash cow

in large business enterprises, cash cows are units which enjoy high earnings but often have low growth potential. Because they generate large amounts of cash, these units are often "milked" to support other divisions of the enterprise, thus the term cash cow.

cash credit

a cash credit is an arrangement by which the banks agree to lend money upto a specified limit. The bank places a certain amount to the credit of the customer. The customer draws the money as and when he needs. Interest is charged only on the amount actually utilized by him and not on the limit granted. Cash credit is usually granted on a bond or certain other securities.

cash discount

a reduction from invoice price granted to a buyer of goods for prompt payment of his bill. For example, if the terms of the bill are 2/10. Net 30, the buyer may deduct 2% from the billed amount if paid within 10 days, otherwise the full amount is due in 30 days.

cash flow

the amount of cash flowing into and out of an organization; the amount if cash required to finance operating expenses or further production over a given period of time.

cash flow analysis

an analysis of the timing of the movement of money into and out of an organisation.

cash flow statement

a statement of a firm's actual or projected cash inflows and cash outflows measured at suitable intervals over a period.

cash forecast

schedule of the estimated cash flow through a business for a period of time. It takes account of money required for wages and salaries and the approximate dates for major items such as capital expenditure.

cash in advance (CIA)

a term of sale requiring payment to the seller before goods are transferred to the purchaser. No credit is extended and no risk is assumed by the seller. Also called cash before delivery.

cash labour

workers not employed on a regular basis, but only as and when work is available. The casual labour system has been operated in certain industries where the availability and throughput of work have been uncertain.

cash management

the general strategy of managing the short-term timing of cash receipts, disbursements, and investments so as to maximize the use of an organisation's liquid assets; more particularly, maximizing returns on short-term investments and/or minimizing the costs of short-term borrowing.

cash sale

in business law, a transaction in which the title to goods passes when the buyer pays the seller, as opposed to a conditional sale, in which the seller retains title.

cash terms

an agreement to pay cash for purchased goods, usually within a specified period of time.

cash with order

a term of sale requiring that a payment sufficient to cover the cost of the merchandise and delivery accompany the customer's order.

casting vote

may be made by the chairman of a meeting when there is a tie in voting. The chairman may use his casting vote irrespective of whether he has earlier used his ordinary, 'deliberative' vote.

casual

describing an employee or a job that is irregular in some way, in that it is occasional, temporary, or part time. Casual workers usually do not accrue seniority, and often they do not share in benefits such as pension plans.

casual exporting

activities of firms which engage in some export business but who do not actively seek it. Also known as accidental exporting.

casual work

work, or opportunity for employment, that occurs intermittently.

catalogue marketing

selling direct from mail order catalogue.

catalog retailing

a form of selling in which the retailer provides the consumer with a merchandise catalog by either mailing it to his home or by making it available in a facility maintained by the retailer for that purpose. The consumer may submit his order by mail or by telephone or may fill out an order in the retailer's catalog store. Merchandise ordered is delivered by mail or parcel service.

catalog showroom

a warehouse showroom where catalog selling and in-store retailing are brought together. Merchandise is presented in catalogs which the customer consults before giving his order to a clerk; who has the merchandise brought in from the warehouse.

category analysis

market research technique for checking whether market conditions and opportunities are propitious for the development of a product.

cause marketing

the application of marketing principles to political, social, educational, charitable, cultural, and religious causes, etc. in an effort to change people's attitudes and, ultimately, their behaviour. Not to be confused with cause related marketing.

caveat emptor

a Latin term meaning "let the buyer beware." Intended as a warning to buyers, it implies that purchases are made at the customer's own risk, the seller assuming no responsibility and offering no guarantees.

cease and desist order

an order, often emanating from a court of administrative agency, which prohibits the continuance of a particular activity, e.g., the Federal Trade Commission may order a company to cease and desist from a particular marketing practice which has been judged deceptive.

ceiling price

the highest price obtainable or permissible in the sale of particular goods or services. It is the price to change above which is an offence.

celebrity marketing

a form of person marketing in which the promotion of entertainers, sports figures, etc. is undertaken by managers, publicity directors, or agencies such as the William Morris Agency. In celebrity marketing, the goals of the marketing campaign are to create, maintain, or alter attitudes toward a particular celebrity or group of celebrities through media appearances, press coverage, and other publicity.

celebrity testimonial

a type of promotion in which big name personalities are used to praise or recommend a particular product, service idea, or institution.

cell organization

a form of organization based on grouping activities and workers together into a cell concerned with one particular product or sub-assembly.

cellular radio

a form of mobile communication in which radio telephones are linked to a computer system which constantly changes frequency so that the signal remains strong despite moving around of the equipment.

census

in marketing research, a census is a complete canvas of every member of a population (or universe) under study, as opposed to sampling. Also known as a population survey.

census of production

a method of calculating national income. According to it, an attempt is made to find out the total net value of all goods and services produced in a given year. Its another name is Inventory method.

central area shopping

buying in shopping areas or centres with large thresholds of customers.

Central Bank

a bank which specializes in the transaction of government business and which advises on and implements the government's monetary policy.

central buying

in large retail organizations, the concentration of the authority and responsibility for merchandise selection and purchase for a chain of stores or the branch stores of a department store in the hands of the headquarters staff rather than in the individual units. The central buying function is generally located in the flagship store.

Centralized Data Bank for Public Enterprises

PESB is maintaining about all Public Sector personnel, practically the personnel drawing Rs. 2500 per month or above. This Bank maintains a list of suitable candidates for the top level managerial posts which may be drawn from various Government Departments, Defence Services, State Governments etc., and also person from the Private Sector, particularly specialists in the industries concerned, willing to serve in the Public Sector. The Biodata of each personnel is duly maintained in the Data Bank.

Central Market

a geographical area containing a large concentration of suppliers. The central market may be a merchandise mart or simply a cluster of suppliers in the same section of a city.

Central Processing Unit (CPU)

the principle component of a computer which controls its operations of input, data transfer, arithmetic/logic, and output as instructed by an applications programme; the part of a computer that contains facilities for control, memory, and calculation; a hardware device that receives and stores instructions, and receives, stores, transfers, processes, and edits data.

cents-off deal

a form of price promotion is which particular consumer products are marked down and prominently labelled to indicate the number of cents reduction, the implication being that the reduction is from the regular retail price – a common practice in the grocery business.

certificate of origin

in international trade and particularly since the creation of the European Economic Community any article exported must have attached to it a certificate of origin. This states the country from which the goods are deemed to have originated—although in the course of production they may have been partly processed in various countries. The identification of the true country of origin is made necessary because tariff laws differ from one country to another.

certificate of value

a statement in a transfer or conveyance that the consideration being received is less than a certain amount so that conveyance duty is either not payable or is payable at a reduced rate.

chain prospecting

a method used by salespersons to gather new leads by obtaining additional names from current prospects. When the current prospect is a satisfied customer, the leads are called referral leads. Also called the endless chain method.

chain stores

sometimes when a retail shop becomes popular, the retailer finds it profitable to open new branches in the city. All these branches deal in the same commodities and are chained together as they are one of a group of retail stores of essentially the same type, centrally owned and controlled. Chain stores may be defined as retail selling organisation with a number of branches which are centrally owned and controlled. All the branches are operated on very similar lines. The purchases are centrally made, and thus, economics in buying are secured. A chain store system represents centralized buying combined with decentralized selling. The chain store may be a 'variety store' when it deals in a wide variety of goods, or it may be a specialized store when it specialises in a limited range of goods or it may be a fixed price chain store when the price of goods sold is fixed and varies between narrow limits.

chairperson

the presiding officer of an organisation, committee, task force, or meeting."Chairperson" (or "chair") generally has replaced the term "chairman".

channel conflict

in marketing, channel conflict is dissonance between two or more members at different levels of the channel (thus, vertical conflict). It is commonly found when one member of the channel, e.g., a dominant manufacturer, attempts to control the entire distribution system.

channel cooperation

the positive interaction between all members of a channel of distribution, resulting in increased sales and profits for all participants. In general, it is up to the channel captain to win the voluntary cooperation of other channel members.

channel fit

in product marketing, channel fit refers to the degree to which a new product fits into existing channels of distribution. A product is said to have good channel fit when it is simply added to an existing line and does not require the opening up of another channel; e.g., a product which can be sold through the same wholesalers and retailers who handle the company's other products.

channel interdependency

a relationship among members of a channel of distribution in which the activities of one member may, to a considerable degree, influence the activities of others.

channel number

the number of different marketing channels employed by a marketer. The number of different channels varies if the company is selling to entirely different markets or to different market segments.

channel of distribution

specific means of channelling goods from their point of origin to their point of sale or consumption, e.g., wholesale to retail distribution or manufacturer to mail order concern.

channel power

the capacity to make other members of a channel of distribution conform to one's wishes. The member who exerts this power is called the channel captain or channel leader.

channel strategy

choice of channels of distribution. Whether a company should sell direct to consumer or retailer, through wholesales or factors back own brands, export through agents, or manufacture and sell abroad.

channel vision

a firm's view of the allocation of marketing functions among the members of a channel of distribution and its recognition of places in the channel where there are opportunities for improvement.

characteristics of government undertaking

there are certain features, peculiar to government undertakings and their management:

(1) There is a tendency to pioneer into fields to industrial activity which are comparatively new. (2) The policy of progressive march to socialism. (3) Government undertakings are usually set up on a large scale. They involve huge capital investment and are time-bound in respect of implementation of their targets. (4) Social achievement rather than profit maximization. (5) The executives of public firms are accountable to Parliament. They are directly influenced by the policy of the government, its evolvement and development on the basis of Policy Resolutions announced by the Ministers on the floor of Parliament. (6) Finance for public sector undertakings derived from government treasury after a number of formalities have been fulfilled and the projects scrutinised even before they are put into action, or gone through experimentation of any kind. (7) The bigger and larger objectives of the public sector are fulfilled over a longer time as compared with the simple profitability motive of the

private sector.

chargehand

an employee who to some extent, does the same work as others in a group of workers but is given some supervisory duties as well.

charisma

capability, or a person to influence a wide range of the behaviour of other people (or to persuade the people to accept a wide range of his views) especially when the capability seems to be an innate capacity.

charity promotions

sales promotion schemes in which contributions to a charity are offered instead of consumer benefits. Should have right appeal, be easy to understand, and support a worthwhile cause.

chart

a diagrammatic way of expressing information, e.g., bar chart, histogram, pictogram and pie chart.

charter

a document issued by a legislature or other government authority granting certain rights and privileges to a bank or corporation, and also imposing certain restrictions on it.

chartist

in investment, an analyst who forecasts securities prices from charts of past prices and price movements.

cheap money

money is said to be cheap when credit is easily obtainable and interest rates are reasonably low. Governments sometimes deliberately foster a cheap money policy with the intention of promoting a high level of investment.

checking copy

copy of a publication sent to an advertiser or an advertising agency to show that an advertisement appeared as specified. (Also known as a voucher copy).

checking references

generally the references given by the applicant are contracted to investigate the candidate's past employment, personal reputation and character. However, references may not give their frank opinions unless they are persuaded to do so by promising that all information will be treated as strictly confidential.

check list

comprehensive categorization of actions to be taken in order to achieve a given effect with maximum efficiency.

check off agreement

an agreement between employers and trade unions that the former will deduct union dues directly from employees' wages on behalf of the latter.

cheque

a bill of exchange drawn on a banker payable on demand, a common way of settling debts. Cheques may be open (bearer) or crossed. An open cheque is payable over the counter provided it is in order. A crossed cheque has to be paid into a bank account only.

cheque-writing machines

cheque writing machines as used in big offices are required to issue numerous cheques regularly. Handwritten or typewritten cheques are exposed to possible frauds. The contents of the cheque may be wittily altered and the crossing lines may also be erased. The alternations and the erasion may go unnoticed by the bankers and then the wrong persons are likely to encash the bills. In order to prevent the tempering of cheques, big business houses use cheque-writing machines. Cheque-writing machines shred the contents into the very texture of the cheque and then fill them with an indelible ink. Any alteration subsequently made with fraudulent intention is easily distinguished. Thus, the chances of frauds are minimized. Moreover, cheque-writing machines save time because large number of cheques can be written quickly with their help. Officers may also use cheque-signing machines.

chief executive

a member of an organization who has authority over all other members in determining the conduct of the organization.

child labour

the employment of children under a particular legal age.

Chinese marketing

a form of faulty reasoning (based largely on wishful thinking) in which a market is viewed as containing an unrealistically large number of potential customers. The underlying assumption is that the bigger the target market the better.

choice criteria

those critical attributes employed by a purchaser when evaluating merchandise offered for sale. Among criteria commonly used are convenience of retail outlet, price, quality, etc.

chronic unemployment

long-term unemployment, that is lasting six months or longer. It is caused by a variety of factors, among them structural changes in the economy (structural unemployment), technologic changes (technological unemployment), or a slowdown in the economy as whole (cyclical unemployment).

chunking

the process of grouping items of information into units, or 'chunks' as an aid to memorizing them.

circulating capital goods

a capital good that is destroyed in the course of use by a single use. Coal and similarly expendable fuels are examples.

circulation

in the print media, circulation refers to the number of copies of a single issue of a magazine or newspaper which are offered for sale or distributed free. Because circulation implies that someone has looked at the publication, the figure for circulation will always be lower than the actual number printed, as a certain percentage of each issue never reaches a reader.

circulation manager

publisher's executive responsible for promoting sales of copies to wholesale and retail trade.

civilian labour force

the total working population of a nation. It consists of all non-monetary personnel 14 years of age or more, who are either gainfully employed or are unemployed but seeking a job.

civil service

an organized system of rules, procedures, and an appeals mechanism for government employees that addresses the definition and classification of government jobs, recruitment for them, and personnel selection, compensation, evaluation, promotion, benefits, and retirement, and the review of adverse personnel actions.

claimant (insurance)

an individual asserting eligibility as a beneficiary of an insurance policy or contract and who is presenting a demand for payment.

class

a group of members of a registered company whose interests in the company are in some way different from those of other members.

class conflict

the conflict between the working class interest in high wages, and the employing class, interested in low wages.

classical functionalism

a strategy in which marketing functions (classically there are eight: buying, selling, transporting, storing, standardizing and grading, financing, risk bearing, and collecting and disseminating marketing information) are viewed as discrete tasks: i.e., they are not integrated into a comprehensive marketing program.

classification merchandising

in retailing, classification merchandising is the practice of planning the breadth of an assortment on the basis of related types or classifications of merchandise. Data reporting is then controlled by these classifications. The theory behind this practice is that small, homogeneous classes of merchandise are preferable for purpose of control.

classified advertisement

an advertisement in a section of a newspaper or magazine that contains many advertisements, all set of the same simple style, grouped according to a classification scheme devised by the publisher.

class rate

the standard rate, established by government regulation, for shipping various commodities. These rates were originally established to guarantee fair prices to all users of both common and contract carriers and to avoid the abuse of railroad shipping prevalent in the 19th century. Class rate are established for shipping certain categories of goods between two geographical points, with distance and weight determining the rate.

clerical work improvement programme

a technique for work measurement in offices based on predetermined motion time systems.

client

person or organization, for whom a service is performed, such as advertising, market research or public relations. Some times used to refer to customer.

clock card

a card on which a particular employee's starting and finishing times are stamped by a device connected to a clock, each day or each shift. (Also known as a time card).

close company

company controlled by five or fewer shareholders and in which the public holds less than 35 per cent of the equity.

closed corporation

a corporation in which only a limited number of persons hold stock, and the stock is not offered for public sale.

closed mortgage

a mortgage that cannot be paid off before maturity.

closed shop

a situation in which all the members of an organization must belong to the appropriate trade union. After legislation passed in the 1980s this is no longer formally possible in the United Kingdom.

closeout

an offering of selected discontinued goods by the vendor to the retailer at reduced prices. This merchandise has been discontinued because of slow sales, a broken assortment, overstock, the need to make space for a new season, etc.

close rate

the number of actual sales made by a salesperson divided by the number of calls made to potential customers. This is one factor used in the evaluation of salespersons, since it indicates the proportion of successful sales or closings.

closing price

it is the price at which shares are quoted at the close of any day's stock exchange dealings. The prices can be found in the daily official list of the stock exchange. Two prices are given for any share. This is because stock jobbers and brokers quote two prices: one for buying and one for selling.

closing the sale

salesman technique in requesting his order from a buyer (and securing it).

closure

method of terminating discussion on an item at a meeting or conference, usually at the chairman's discretion or according to the rules of procedure or standing orders of the organization concerned.

cluster sampling

a sampling procedure used when the population is widely dispersed geographically but where representative groups ('cluster') can be identified. A random sample is taken from each cluster.

clutter

in advertising, clutter (the crowding together of advertising messages in the print and electronic media) results in a loss of advertising effectiveness. Advertisers may avoid clutter by buying more time or reserving more space in the media used. They may also pay a premium for positioning their advertisements in such a way as to avoid clutter.

codes of practice

laid down conditions under which business should be conducted in a particular area of activity.

codetermination

the policy of giving labour unions representation on a company's board of directors to an extent equal to that of the stockholders.

coding

in market research data analysis, the translation of gathered information into a form (usually numerical) which can be more readily analyzed.

coding frame

pattern of likely answers which can be coded on questionnaire (or afterwards from open-ended answers) so that individual answers may be aggregated into limited number of categories.

coercive power

coercive power is based on one person perception of another's ability to punish him. The strength of coercive power is proportional not necessarily to the ability to punish but to the degree to which he perceives ability to punish.

coercion

the use of power to get people to do something they should not otherwise do. Typical of authoritarian management.

cognition

a general term which includes all the psychological processes by which people become aware of, and gain knowledge about the world.

cognitive component

in attitude research, particularly in the tripartite view or structural approach, the cognitive component is the knowledge and beliefs a consumer has about a product or service, including evaluative beliefs. It is the intellectual component of attitudes.

cognitive processes

those mental activities which involve thought and reasoning as for example, learning and judging.

coincident techniques

technique in market research interviewing in which a consumer or user is asked about somethings that is happening or something that he is doing at the time of the interview.

cold call

a visit or telephone call be a salesman to a previously unapproached (cold) potential customer.

cold canvassing

door-to-door or telephone solicitation of order for merchandise without the benefit of leads or prior appointments.

cold storage warehous

a refrigerated warehouse that provides controlled, low temperatures for the storage and preservation of perishable foods such as fruits and vegetables.

collateral agreement

it is an agreement of contract coupled to and referred in an existing agreement or contract. If the initial contract is void, the collateral agreement may not necessarily become void: much depends on whether the second contract restates the void agreement. However, when the initial contract stops to be in force, the collateral agreement may also cease to be legal.

collateral security

security for a debt given by someone other than the debtor. An extra security for a debt given by a debtor in addition to a major security that in some circumstances might be considered sufficient. A security for a debt that consists of right over property, as opposed to personal guarantees.

collective agreement

a collective bargaining contract agreed upon by management and a union, describing wages, working conditions, and other matters of mutual interest.

collective bargaining

an industrial relations process in which employers or their representatives negotiate with employees or their (trade union) representatives on the level of wages and the conditions of employment of a group of employees as whole, rather than for individuals.

collusion

the coming together of two or more parties in a secret understanding or agreement to the detriment of one or more other parties. Restraint of trade agreements commonly involve collusion.

colour coding

identification of subject by colour. Can be applied to

packaging so that associated products can be linked by a common colour as with certain razors and their particular blades.

colour vision test

a test to check for the existence of and the extent of colour blindness.

combination

a selection made from a set of items is regarded as a combination if the order of items within the selection is immaterial.

combination house

a middleman organization which serves the wholesale, retail, and institutional markets.

combination offer

a form of consumer fraud involving the sale of a product at a low price tied to the purchase of a continuing service. The sale of food freezers tied to the purchase of frozen foods is a notorious example as the food is frequently of inferior quality.

combo store

(1) an outgrowth of supermarket, the combo store has a significantly larger share of floor space devoted to higher margin general merchandise. The combo store, although retaining many aspects of the supermarket is in fact, an incipient full-line discount store. (2) an outgrowth of the large drugstore in which general merchandise is combined with drugs and health and beauty care products. Sometimes called a combination store.

commando or pioneer salling

intensive selling into new markets, often with an entirely new product and sometimes by a specially employed sales force instead of or augmenting existing personnel.

commando sales team

sales force introduced over and above normal staffing for the purposes of a particular sales promotion campaign.

command through sanction

when the staff is no influential as to lead to demotion and removal of opponents, in such situations though staff's request may be called 'advice', line people know that this is advice which it is perilous to ignore.

commercial apprentice

young man or woman indentured or otherwise contracted to an employer to learn commercial skills usually in conjunction with appropriate further education.

commercial bribery

the illegal attempt to influence business decision-making by offering gifts or favours to the person charged with making the decision.

commercial credit

the debt or promises to pay of enterprisers or businessmen incurred or given in the present acquisition of goods to be used in productive operations.

commercial ribbon

linear developed shopping areas which occupy main roads, or discrete shopping streets.

commissary store

(1) a store operated by the military (and commonly staffed by civilian employees) for the benefit of military personnel and their dependents. (2) a store operated by a large employer for the benefit of its employees.

Commissary stores generally sell food products and other supplies at prices substantially below those on the open market. Also known as company stores.

commission agent

agent paid on a commission basis for the business be obtains, the principal then dealing with the customer.

commission merchant

an agent middleman who although he often has physical control over the goods he sells, does not take title to them. Commission merchants most commonly represent the sellers of such agricultural products as grain, livestock, and produce, which are usually accepted on consignment. They have the authority to negotiate prices and terms of sale on behalf of their principal and may arrange delivery, extend credit, make collections, etc. In this respect the commission merchant has more freedom than the broker.

committee

a group of people appointed by an organization to take responsibility for a particular task of function on behalf of the organization as a whole. The committee may or may not be given executive power. It may be a permanent standing committee or a temporary ad hoc committee.

committee buying

purchasing activities collectively performed by a group of buyers on behalf of a multi-unit operation.

committee on public accounts

in a democratic form of government, the executive and the legislature have their well-defined prerogatives and spheres of responsibility. It is the responsibility of the executive to formulate demands for money and to initiate necessary fiscal measures to finance its plans and policies, while it is the prerogative of the legislature to exercise control over taxation, to grant supplies for public expenditure and to control issues and appropriations.

commodity

synonym for primary product, especially a primary product for which an organized market exists. Synonym for goods.

commodity approach to marketing

an approach to the study of marketing in which the movement of goods from producer to consumer is viewed as key to understanding the marketing process.

commodity exchange

a nonprofit organization which provides members with a place in which commodities are traded, either among themselves or for others, on a commission basis. The exchange does not engage in buying or selling, but does make and enforce rules and may adjust disputes among member–traders.

commodity market

the market in which commodities are bought and sold. The other types of market based on the subject of transaction are factor market, money market, capital market, bullion market, stock exchange etc.

commodity rate

an allowable deviation from the class rate charged by shippers to their customers. The reduced commodity rate may be awarded to the customer for regular use or for the size of the quantity shipped. However, the commodity rate is still subject to government regulation.

common carrier

carrier prepared to transport goods of any description for anyone willing to hire its services.

common cost

cost incurred generally and not readily attributable to particular activities or departments.

common market

an association of countries who have reduced or eliminated the trade barriers which existed between them and are parties that share a common external tariff agreement. In addition, common markets generally provide for the free flow of labour and capital; from country to country.

common ownership

principle that everyone who works permanently for an enterprise should have a proprietary share in it.

common stock

shares of ownership in a corporation that depend for their worth on the value of the corporation.

communication

the process of transmitting or exchanging information, ideas, beliefs and opinions mainly by the use of language—though non-verbal communication can also be important in certain situations. Transmission of information may be by formal communication or informal communication.

communication adaptation

a strategy employed in international trade in which a company exports the same products that it manufactures for the domestic market but changes the advertising and other promotional messages which accompany them in the foreign market.

communication network

a method or form or pattern of

communication. The two most frequently studied kinds of networks are wheel-shaped and circle-shaped. The wheel network facilitates quick and accurate communication but is less equipped to handle complexity and change. The circle network adapts well to complexity and change in communication and seems to involve and satisfy its members better. These networks are often discussed in the comparison of a mechanistic organization and an organic organization.

communication process

a process consisting of five components: (1) a source (or sender), (2) an encoding process in which the message is put into a transmittable form, (3) transmission of the message, (4) a decoding process at which time the message is translated into a comprehensible form, and (5) the reception of the message at its destination.

communication skill

effective communication is the medium through which managerial understanding is created. Information, ideas and views are exchanged by the use of verbal and written expression. Orderly construction and direct expression in communication will go a long way in presenting and analyzing problems in a business situation.

communicator credibility

in social psychology this term describes the extent to which the communicator of message is believable. It is thought to be related to wether the communicator is perceived as expert and trustworthy or not.

community health services

diagnostic, therapeutic, and preventive health services provided for individuals in the community.

Companies (Amendment) Act, 1960

this amending act was enacted on the recommendations of Shastri Committee which was appointed by the Government on 15th May, 1957, to review the Act and point out the defects and to give suggestions. Under this Act some restrictions were imposed on management of companies, managerial remuneration and private companies. By adding Section 43A a new class of companies, 'Deemed to be Public Companies' was introduced.

Companies (Amendment) Act, 1965

this was the third major amending act based mainly on the recommendations of Dapthary-Shastri Committee. It amends fifty Sections and added several new Sections, via, 68-A, 233-B, 250-A, 294-A, 394-A, 396-A, 511-A, 635-A, 637-B, and 640-B. Some of the more important changes introduced by this Act are (i) by amending Section 13, the Act provided that the Objects Clause in the

Memorandum of Association of any company must be divided into two sub-clauses: (a) the main objects and (b) other projects, (ii) by adding Sub-section (1A) to Section 108, restrictions on the period of currency of blank transfers were imposed, and (iii) by amending Section 410, 'Advisory Commission' attached to the 'Company Law Board' was to be replaced by an 'Advisory Committee.'

Companies (Amendment) Act, 1969

this act prohibited companies from contributing any amount to any political party or for any political purpose, and abolished the institution of Managing Agents and Secretaries and Treasurers with effect from 3rd April, 1970.

company

broadly, any group of people voluntarily united for performing jointly any activity, business, or commercial enterprise. Synonymous with firm. Partnerships and corporations are also considered to be companies.

Companies (Amendment) Act, 1974

under this amendment the Central Government was given more legislative powers: (a) to prescribe in consultation with the Reserve Bank of India the limits upto which, the manner in which, and the conditions subject to which, deposits may be invited or accepted by a company (New Section 58A). (b) to make rules to regulate declaration of dividends by a company out of the accumulated profits earned by it in previous years and transferred by it to reserves (New Section 205 A(3)). (c) to prescribe provisions of the Companies Act with which a foreign company must comply, in relation to the business carried on by it in India, if fifty percent or more of its paid up share capital is held by Indians and/or companies registered in India (Section 591-2). (d) some of the powers of quasi-judicial nature which had so far been exercised by the Courts, were transferred to the Company Law Board. In order to enable the Company Law Board to discharge its enlarged functions, the Board was clothed with the powers of a civil court to enforce the attendance of witness and production of documents, etc., and also to provide for punishment for its contempt. (e) the scope of Section 43A was widened whereby some private companies satisfying certain conditions shall be deemed to be public companies in certain circumstances and shall be made subject to the discipline applicable to public companies.

(f) To prevent the companies from accepting deposits from the public by circumventing the directives issued by the Reserve Bank, it was made obligatory for companies to disclose their financial position to the public before accepting such deposits through an advertisement in the prescribed form.

(g) The Act introduced eight new Sections 108A to 108H with a view to preventing the regulating 'take over' of shares in a company by a 'group' or 'combine' having the common intension of acquiring control over that company.

(h) A curb was put on auditors taking up auditing work of too many companies.

(i) The Central Government has given the power to appoint as many directors as it thought necessary on the Board of Directors of a company in the public interest. Prior to the Amendment Act, the Government could appoint only two directors which was found to be inadequate to control the affairs of mismanaged companies.

(j) The Act provided preventive measures against the practice of former Managing Agents continuing to control companies in one garb or the other.

(k) It was made compulsory for companies having a paid-up share capital of rupees twenty-five lakhs or more to have a whole-time secretory.

(l) The Act included many important amendments relating to restriction on beaming transactions, transfers of unpaid dividend to special dividend account, sole selling agency, inspection of books of accounts, cost audit, appointment or reappointment of managing or wholetime directors and fixation of their remuneration, etc.

company — articles of association

registration of the articles is the second step in the course of incorporation of a company. A private company, a company limited by guarantee and unlimited companies should prepare their own articles and file them with the registrar. A public company limited by shares, however, may register its own articles or adopt all or any of the regulations contained in Table A attached to the First Schedule of the Act.

company bargaining

collective bargaining in quest of a company agreement.

Company Director

the member of the board of directors appointed to run a company by its shareholders. A director may or may not be a shareholder himself.

company model

computerized model of the overall operation and activities of a company or organization.

Company Secretary

the term 'Secretary' has been derived from the Latin word 'Secretaries' which stands for a notary, scribe or confidential writer. In fact, the term has been used for a person who keeps the secrets of any venture, public or private. Presently the term 'Secretary' is used to signify an officer who is entrusted with confidential matters by his employer or who conducts correspondence, keeps records and transacts other business for a person or an organisation. Whenever the question of defining the secretary comes to our mind, immediately we get the picture of a person of integrity, intelligence and personality, moving with grace and discharging his duties to the administration, shareholders, directors and the company law authorities, with unprecedented accuracy and efficiency.

comparative marketing

in international marketing, the study of the differences and similarities between various national systems regarding supply and demand as well as distribution.

comparison shopping

a retail trade practice in which one retailer obtains information about his competitor's activities by sending a comparison shopper to the store. Comparison shopping may be carried on by the outside agency organized for that purpose or by the store's own comparison department.

compensation

payment for injury, damage or loss. The term is also used, particularly in the United States, for the remuneration of salary and fringe benefits.

compensation deal

in international marketing a form of counter-trade in which payments are partly in the form of currency and partly in the form of goods.

competition

the attempt to do better than others supplying goods and services in the same market. Fostering competition is one of the basic principles of capitalism, which was first formulated in the eighteenth century by Adam Smith.

competitive advantage

anything that gives an organization an edge over the competitors in its market.

competitive advertising

advertising which features specific brands rather than broad product categories and which is intended to motivate the consumer to buy the particular product.

competitive environment

to any company in the market place, the competitive environment is the sum total of other firms marketing products similar to or substitutable for the company's own. For example, to a marketer of sugar, the competitive environment would include all other companies marketing sugar as well as those marketing artificial sweeteners.

competitive market

a competitive market is easily defined only for a perfect market or perfectly competitive market; it is then a market in which the individual buyer or seller does not influence the price by his purchases or sales. Alternatively stated, the elasticity of supply facing any buyer is infinite, and the elasticity of demand facing any seller is infinite.

competitor's advertising method

basing advertising appropriation on what rival firms are spending. May be used when a firm is uncertain of the likely cost of promoting its product, and judges by expenditures of other firms or when it desires to match another firm's competitive activity.

complementary product

a product which is accessory to or which in some way supplements another product as, for example, software supplements a computer.

complete segmentation

a form of market segmentation in which each potential customer is treated as an individual rather than as part of an aggregation because each is seen as identifiably distinct from all others.

compliance

the act of following instructions, orders, or prescribed pattern of behaviour.

compliance agency

generally, any government agency that administers laws/ or regulations.

components

book debts and bills receivable which arise out of credit sales should be considered. Average debtors can be arrived at by adding opening and closing balance of book debts and bills receivable and then dividing the result by two. The receivables turnover ratio, when calculated in terms of days, is known as average collection period ratio.

composite demand

the total demand for a given good or service from all sources, even though it involves a variety of uses. For example, low-carbon steel sheets are used in a wide range of manufactured products, including automobiles, refrigerators, office furniture, etc.

compositive organisation mind

the cooperative action that takes place within the hierarchical structure involves highly complex and subtle executive interrelationships. A decision is frequently little more than a formal expression of the results of cooperative activity.

compound interest

interest paid on a principal sum and the interest already collected by that sum.

compound trading
retailing which aims at widening range of merchandise carried, either of related or unrelated goods, plus extension of customer services, e.g., garden centres, petrol stations.

comptroller
traditional form of the term controller, from the French verb comptroller, to check off.

compulsion
an overwhelming unconscious need to engage in some behaviour that is usually contrary to one's conscious wishes. Being made to obey statutory requirement or a legal obligation.

compulsory winding up
a winding up of a company ordered by a court. (Also called 'compulsory liquidation'.

computed-aided design
a process in which a designer interacts with in computer system to produce a design, from the original idea to the finished product, by electronic manipulation and the use of a visual display unit rather than pencil and paper. Closely associated with computer aided manufacturing.

computer-aided engineering
the process that links computer aided design with computer-aided manufacturing, for example in the manufacture of tools or machine under computer numerical control.

computer hardware
mechanical, magnetic, electrical, and electronic equipment that comprises a computer system (or part of a computer system), including the mainframe or central processing unit, input and output devices that communicate with the mainframe or central processing unit, and data storage devices.

computer-integrated manufacturing
the ultimate form of automation in which every aspect of manufacturing form the initial design to the delivery of the finished product, is both controlled and co-ordinated by computer.

computer literacy
the ability to use computer language.

computer numerical control
the control of machines by computer using numerical information.

computer package
this refers to the software required for a particular application.

computer program
a set of instructions to a computer, written in a computer language, that tells it to perform a particular task. The spelling of 'program' is usually American, in recognition of the American predominance in this field.

computer simulation
a simulation , exercises conducted by computer, e.g., to

produce the realistic experience of flying in the training of airline pilots.

computer training

a method of training in which the medium of instruction, with which the individual interacts, is the computer or computer terminal.

conative component

in attitude research, particularly in the tripartite view or structural approach, the conative component is the readiness of an individual to purchase a particular product or service or take some other action. It is the active component of attitude.

concealed surplus (of labour)

manpower surplus concealed by labour hoarding.

concentration market

geographical, industrial and purchasing market concentrations. Important factor in industrial market research which may be required to record changes within market, and a chief difference between industrial and consumer market research.

concept testing

an early stage in the product development process, concept testing attempts to determine consumer reaction to new product concepts before large amounts of money are committed to their production. Typically, potential customers are shown pictures of proposed products and are asked to react to them.

conditional sale agreement

an agreement for the sale of goods or land under which the purchase price or part of it is payable by installments and the property in the goods or lands is to stay with the seller until conditions specified in agreement are satisfied.

conditional sales contract

a retail instalment contract which requires the buyers to pay monthly payments to a retailer or other creditor. The retailer retains title of ownership until all payments have been made, so that merchandise may be repossessed whenever the buyer fails to meet the terms of the contract.

conditions of employment

issues such as wages, benefits, hours of work etc., usually covered in an employee's Contract of Employment.

confined merchandise

in retailing, merchandise sold by a producer or distributor to a limited number of stores so that, in effect, each retailer has exclusive resale rights in his trading area.

conglomerate

a business organization, usually comprising a group of companies, with diverse and often unrelated financial interests but sometimes trading under the one name.

conglomerate merger

a merger of two or more

corporations in unrelated industries, such as a cosmetics manufacturer and a children's clothing manufacturer. The two firms need not be on the same level of the channel of distribution.

cognitive ergonomics

a form of ergonomics in which factors of congestion are more important than physical factors.

connect time

the time during which a remote computer terminal is in use on a time-sharing computer system.

conscious parallelism

identical or similar actions taken by two or more firms in the market especially regarding price changes, which may be seen as collusion.

consignment

merchandise shipped by a producer to a distributor or retailer with the understanding that the producer retains title to the goods until they are sold. Consignment sales offer the producer the opportunity to control its terms of resale and help overcome dealer resistance to the product.

consignment account

special accounts must be kept by both a seller (or principal) and his agent to record the rule ownership. When goods are distributed through agents, the ownership remaining vested in the seller, the transaction is said to be on consignment.

consignment distributor

distributor who pays for the goods he has bought only as he re-sells them.

consignment note

document listing the goods that are supplied (by the consignor to the consignee) with the particular order.

consignment selling

goods sent to distributors who take possession by title remains with manufacturer until consignment is paid for.

consolidation of capital

this applies to a limited company. Shares are consolidated when the nominal value of the shares is raised by stating that thereafter Rs. 10 shares shall become Rs. 20 shares in order to consolidate the shareholding by shareholders. This can be done by an ordinary resolution at a general meeting, or some way as the memorandum of association requires. Share capital may also be subdivided in the reserve procedure to diversify shareholding.

consortia

in international marketing, a partnership arrangement similar to the joint venture with the exception that it typically involves a large number of participants and functions in a market in which it was not previously involved. Consortia helps to bring together financing and spread risk among more participants.

consortium

large contracts are often tendered for by a consortium (i.e., a group) of companies or firms none of which is competent to fulfil the contract alone. It is generally a rare combination for the purpose of bringing together a number of quite different operative skills or area of specialized knowledge under one organisation.

constituent company

subsidiary company which belongs to a parent or group of companies. The accounts are normally consolidated with the other organizations which make up the whole company.

constraint

a prior limit on the solution that will be acceptable to a problem.

constructive dismissal

legal term for situation where an employee leaves his employment on the face of it of his own accord, but in reality because the employer has made the employment intolerable. Under most legal systems this constitutes unfair dismissal.

consumer acceptance test

market research term for making a product or service available under controlled conditions in order to discover how far it is acceptable to consumers.

consumer advertising

loosely relating to all advertising of goods or services to the mass market of individuals or families. Used in contrast to industrial or capital goods advertising.

consumer advocate

one who speaks for or represents the interest of the consuming public, particularly with respect to social, economic, and ecological matters.

consumer behaviour

the actions of consumers in the marketplace and the underlying motives for those actions. Marketers expect that by understanding what causes consumers to buy particular goods and services they will be able to determine which products are needed in the market place, which are obsolete, and how best to present those goods to the consumer.

consumer credit

the ability of individual consumers to obtain money, goods, or revenues on the strength of their promise to pay at some specified time in the future, generally in installments. Such purchases are thus referred to as being on "time".

consumer durable

consumer goods designed for long-term use, such as washing machine, refrigerators or hi-fi systems as opposed to consumer disposable, designed for one time or short-term use, such as food-stuffs.

consumer goods

goods that are usually bought by individuals for consumption or personal use by themselves or by members of their households but not for incorporation in, or assistance in manufacturing other goods.

consumerism

a movement that looks after interests of the consumer in the market-place by trying to have the safety, quality and informational content of consumer goods and services improved. It can be traced back to the effort of Ralph Nader in the early 1960s to publicize serious safety hazards in the manufacture of American cars.

consumer market

the market for consumer goods.

consumer motivation

the driving force in an individual that impels him to act in the marketplace. It may be positive or negative depending on how he perceives his needs and goals.

consumer panel

in marketing research, a group of individuals brought together for the purpose of determining consumer preferences with regard to products or ideas. The panel members are interviewed collectively and their expressed opinions are tabulated for use in new product development etc.

consumer perceived risk

a consumer's perception of the possible effects, mostly negative, of an incorrect purchase decision. Includes functional risk, physical risk, financial risk, social risk, and psychological risk.

consumer promotion

sales promotion aimed directly at the consumer or ultimate customer through cut-price offers, trading stamps etc. Promotions aimed at distribution are known as trade promotions.

consumer research

the study of the ultimate consumer to determine the factors that influence purchase decisions involving time, money, and effort in the consumption of goods and services. Consumer behaviour includes the related studies of demography, sociology, anthropology, and psychology. Marketers look to consumer research to help them identify their target markets and determine how to market their goods and/or services to those target markets most efficiently.

consumer satisfaction

satisfaction of a consumer want is an essential part of the marketing operation. Fundamentally, a person buys (acquires) a product or service for the satisfaction it will provide.

consumer stimulants

various promotions and incentives employed to attract the consumer and to stimulate demand. Consumer stimulants may take the form of free samples delivered to the home, cents–off deals and premiums offered at retail, contests and sweepstakes, and other promotional activities.

consumer surplus

the difference, as perceived by a consumer, between the value of a purchase and the price he pays for it. A consumer surplus exists if the customer feels he is getting more than his money's worth and if he would be willing to pay a some what higher price for the same goods.

container

large metal box in which goods are packed in bulk for shipment by road or rail to container port. Also means of containing or packing goods; e.g., bottle, jar, tube, carton, box, aerosol, etc.

content label

a tag or label affixed in conformance with the requirements of the federal wool, fur, or textile fiber products acts intended to protect the consumer against the misbranding mislabeling, and false advertising of furs and other textile products.

contest

a sales promotion device in which the participant competes for prizes by submitting an entry which requires a degree of skill or judgment to prepare, e.g., a statement or jingle. Unlike games and sweepstakes, the element for pure chance is eliminated in contests.

contingency planning

the process of developing a series of alternative plans for achieving an objective. Different alternative plans may be implemented according to future events, opportunities, or barriers.

contigency theory of leadership

any theory of leadership which emphasizes the need for flexibility in dealing with any given situation. The complexity of the modern organization means that effective leadership is contingent upon a great many factors: what may be successful in one context may not be successful in another.

continuity

in advertising, the flow of advertising messages over a period of time. In some respects continuity is like a schedule or plan in that it provides some control over the spacing and frequency of ads.

continuous demand

the need and/or desire for goods or services which remains stable for a prolonged time period.

continuous innovation

a continuing process by which new products are developed and introduced into the marketplace. Rather than representing some new departure, these new products commonly were already in production and have been slightly altered or improved.

continuous process

a method of production that

enable the uninterrupted flow of materials and parts into a processing operation and of completed and products cut of the operation.

continuous production

a production system in which the production units are organized and sequenced according to the essential steps of a manufacturing process. The routing of the job is fixed, and changes in setups are seldom required.

contract

a formal binding agreement between two or more parties, presenting pledges of tasks, acts, processes, products, or resources to be provided by one party in exchange for a consideration (money or other goods) from another party.

contract farming

a contractual arrangement between farmers and middleman or manufacturers in which the farmer receives supplies and/or working capital and the manufacturers or middlemen agree to purchase the farmer's crop, sometimes at a guaranteed price.

contract guarantee

general term covering performance, repayment and tender guarantees.

contractor

an organisation or person who takes on work from another organisation but generally retains control over his or her own work. Usually, contract work must meet negotiated standards and be done within a specific period of time. Other stipulation also govern the work.

contract warehouse

a storage facilitate which combines public and private warehousing services. It is like a public warehouse in that it serves a variety of customers. It differs from a public warehouse, however, in that the arrangements are long term rather than on a month by month basis.

contracyclical pricing

a pricing strategy which runs counter to the usual economic cycle in that during periods of prosperity the firm increases production and reduces prices (because of the high level of demand), and during an economic downturn, reduces production and increases prices (because of reduced demand).

contribution

in marketing cost analysis and break-even analysis, contribution generally means the sum of money generated by sales after variable costs have been substracted. The term may also be applied to the amount of money a unit in a firm contributes toward discharging the firm's overall fixed costs.

contribution pricing

a pricing strategy in which, under special conditions (e.g., the promise of a very larger order). A firm sets the price of its product lower than that which would cover the full cost of production. Contribution pricing covers the variable costs associated with the production of the specific product and makes a contribution toward meeting the firm's overall fixed costs even though prices at this level may not contributed to the firm's overall profits.

contributory pension scheme

a form of pension scheme which involves employees paying a fixed proportion of the income into a scheme to which their employer also contributes.

contribution margin ratio

the ratio of contribution from selling a given quantity of a product to the sales revenue made by selling that quantity.

control

the aspect of management concerned with the comparison of actual versus planned performance, as well as the development and implementation of procedures to correct substandard performance. Control, which is inherent to all levels of management, is a feedback process that should ideally communicate only unexpected situations.

control audit

an examination and evaluation of the results of a marketing plan. A control audit is designed to help identify and correct any deviations from the plan and to monitor the plan's progress.

control chart

synonym for quantity control chart.

control departments

control departments include personnel, credit, budgeting, accounting and auditing and such departments typically have full authority to see that their particular functions are properly carried out everywhere in the organisation.

control function

control function includes those activities designed to compel events to conform to plans or to recognize deviations therefrom. It is thus the measurement and corrective function. It involves the establishment of control standards and the gathering of information required for evaluating performance, and provides the inputs for subsequent planning.

controlled brand

a brand of merchandise owned by its manufacturer whose distribution is restricted to a limited number of distributors, generally selected because they are (1) not large enough to support a private brand of their own, and (2) are not in direct competition with one another.

controlled circulation journal magazine

a periodical publication that is sent free of charge to individuals selected because of their job title, business or profession and which consists largely of advertisement.

controlling

controlling in management is the measuring and correcting of activities of subordinates to ensure that actions conform to plans; shows where negative deviations exist, and, by putting in motion actions to correct deviations, helps assure accomplishment of plans.

control process

one of the main jobs of a manager is to give responsibility and authority to assistants who are capable of using it but still for himself the means of assuring that performance is satisfactory.

control question

in a questionnaire, that which seeks to check consistency of answers given and efficiency, even honesty, of interview. Control questions generally have known answers, or the likely proportion of certain answers is known. Validity of all other answers is checked. Alternative forms of control may be postcard checks to verify answers or to seek additional information.

control system

a subsystem, of an open system, in which activity is directed towards maintaining or affecting in a prescribed way, the value of some parameter of the output of the system. The parameter so effected is called the 'controlled condition'.

convenience sample

a method of non-probability sampling in which the researcher interviews those members of the population most readily available. For example, "man-in-the-street" interviews are a form of convenience sample.

conventional channel

a channel of distribution which is loosely organized (as compared to a vertical marketing system) and in which the members are largely autonomous. Most consumer goods follow a conventional channel from manufacturer to wholesaler to retailer to ultimate consumer.

conversion training

retaining for occupation that is slightly rather than radically different from previous occupation. Cf. booster training, refresher training, retraining, updating training.

convertible loan stock

occasionally companies issue loan stock, with a right to convert this stock into ordinary shares or preference shares at some stated time in the future. This is known as convertible loan stock. The term is also applied to stock issued by the Government, which the holder has the right to convert into new stock instead of obtaining repayment.

conveyance

the transfer of title to land from one person to another:

the instrument that effects and records the transfer.

cooling–off laws

local laws which allow customers a period of time (usually three days) in which to reconsider a purchase, and if they so choose, to cancel the commitment. These laws have been passed to protect consumers from deceptive or high-pressure practices employed by telephone and door-to-door salespeople.

cooling-off period

a period during which a trade union is forbidden to call a strike or an employer is forbidden to enforce a lockout.

co-operative

a group of producers or purchasers who set up a trading organization, the profit from which is shared out among the members of the group.

co-operative advertising

a strategy in which advertising costs are shared by seller and reseller (commonly manufacturer and retailer). Ads are run at the local level by the retailer and part of the cost is reimbursed by the manufacturer upon receipt of verification that the ads were actually run. This arrangement, because it involves more than one level of the market, is called vertical cooperative advertising. When the cooperative effort is at one level of the market (as with two or more retailers sharing advertising costs) it is called horizontal cooperative advertising. Also known as vertical advertising, dealer-cooperative advertising, and manufacturer's cooperative advertising.

co-operative banks

cooperative banks are banks organized on cooperative lines. They encourage thrift, accept money on deposits and extend loans to the members at a relatively reasonable rate of interest. Cooperative Banks are primarily intended to help agriculturists by providing loans at low rates of interest and on easy terms. They are organized both at State as well as District level.

co-operative international marketing organization

a cooperative group composed of several domestic manufacturers who have come together to market their goods abroad. The cooperative organization is partly under the administrative control of its members firms. This type of international marketing middleman is used frequently by producers of primary products such as fruits, nuts, grains, etc.

co-operative society

a cooperative society is an economic enterprise set up by economically weak individuals to eliminate middle men, competition, waste and to bring the producer and consumer together. It is a voluntary association with unrestricted membership and collectively owned funds. It implies association of individuals on equal terms to fulfil their economic needs to promote thrift and self-help among themselves.

co-opt

to invite someone to join an established group of people (e.g., a committee) in order, for example, for the group to benefit from his special experience or to attempt to silence his criticism of the group.

co-opting

inviting someone to join an already established group because of some particular quality or skill, the need for which may not have been foreseen when the group was set up.

coordinating departments

typically give advice, but such advice is usually followed by the like groups so that essentially such departments do turn out to have authority. Typical departments might be order and distribution departments as well as a production planning department.

co-ordination

the process of integrating all the parts and function of an organization.

co-ordination system

Ferguson gives a model coordination system which not only improves the information flow among departments but also changes the organizational structure to improve communication channels and enhance accountability, increasing or decreasing the centralization of authority as per need of each situation, analyzing at the same time the timing requirements among the functions performed by various departments.

co-ownership

shared ownership and usually control of an enterprise by employees.

copartnership

an arrangement by which all those who work in a firm share to some extent in the profits, capital and control of the firm. The share of profits or capital is in addition to the normal wages paid in the firm's industry.

copy

in advertising, copy refers to the words (either written or spoken) which express the message in an advertising pieces or commercial.

copying machines

copying machines are used to obtain a limited number of copies of the same letter, statements or documents that may be needed for office records, reference or for general notification. The appliances commonly used for taking out a few copies are: (1) typewriter (2) press copying (3) roller copier (4) photostat (5) electrostate (6) laser composing.

copy platform
main copy theme of an advertisement.

copy test
test of advertising copy, either before or after publication aiming to discover readers' comprehension, interest, brand preference, company image etc.

copy right
a grant of property rights to a writer or artist which protects his work from unauthorized sale, reproduction, display, performance, etc.

copy thrust
in advertising and promotion, copy thrust refers to the message to be communicated by the written copy and the accompanying illustrations. It flows directly from the objectives of the promotion, whether it is intended to inform the customer of a sale, or to persuade the customer that the product is worthwhile, etc.

core group
a central group of workers in an organization operating some form of flexible manning who have long term security of employment and constitute the permanent core, as opposed to peripheral workers who are taken on and laid off as and when required.

core time
particular periods in flexible working hours during which all employees must be in attendance. Outside this core time employees are free to choose their working hours.

cornering the market
a firm or company is said to corner a market when it obtains a virtual monopoly over particular goods or services. It is then able to dictate its own price. In the past this sometimes happened in the market of raw materials.

corporate licensing
the use of a firm's name to enhance the saleability of a product.

corporate plan
a document that maps out the future work and development of an organization over a period of years in the light of its resources and the environment in which it operates. The plan is concerned with the long-term objectives of the organization and the strategy used to achieve them.

corporate vertical marketing system
a system in which a large corporation controls two or more levels of a marketing channel. For example, a manufacturer may own the distribution facilities for his product as well as the retail outlets through which it is sold.

corrective advertising
correction of a false or misleading claim in earlier advertising. Corrective advertising can be a major item in advertising budgets.

correlation analysis
in market factor analysis, a

procedure which makes it possible to translate the behaviour of variables in the marketing environment into estimates of future sales. Correlation analysis involves the sophisticated manipulation of market factor statistics in an effort to project potential sales for a product or service.

correlation coefficient

in statistics this is measure (denoted by the letter Ö) of the extent to which two variables are correlated. It can range from zero correlation to perfect positive correlation (1.00), where the variables are always associated in the same way, or perfect negative correlation (-100), where the variables are always associated but in different ways.

cost

(i) the amount spent on producing or manufacturing a commodity. Cost usually refers to money, but may be used in a broader context to include time and effort, etc., (2) the price a vender charges a retailer for goods. (3) in retailing, any money expended to bring merchandise into a store, including the wholesale price of the merchandise, freight, charges, etc.

cost accountant

an accountant or accounts officer whose job concerns the fixing of monies due for work done in manufacturing a product (i.e., reckoning the cost of material and labour consumed) but who is increasingly called upon the estimate to probable unit cost of a manufacturing process so that the price to the buyer can be determined by the company for the purpose of making a tender.

cost accounting

planning, decision-making and control are the basic managerial functions. The cost accounting system provides the necessary tools such as standard costing, budgetary control, inventory control, marginal costing, and differential costing etc., for carrying out such functions efficiently. Hence, cost accounting is considered as a necessary adjunct of management accounting.

cost benefit analysis

any information has a cost of production although it is well nigh difficult to assess what it is. A cost benefit analysis of information may therefore become necessary in may cases.

cost centre

a unit whose direct costs can be ascertained and to which fixed costs can be allocated in the pursuit of effective financial control. This unit may be a department, a place, a person or even a machine. Contrast with profit centre.

cost effectiveness

a measure of the extent to which money has been effectively spent on something. It is found by seeing whether the benefits that have resulted could have been obtained with a lower expenditure.

cost ledger

a subsidiary ledger for the accumulation of accounts used in computing of summarizing the cost of goods manufactured or of services produced.

cost of goods purchased

the net price paid to the vendor for merchandise, plus the price and for transportation and delivery. In calculating the net cost of delivered purchases, cash discounts are subtracted from the above amount. In calculating the net cost of purchases, cash discounts are subtracted from the original invoice price, without consideration of transportation and delivery fees.

cost–oriented audit

an examination and evaluation of the results of a marketing plan from the point of view of costs and costs-effectiveness.

cost plus pricing

a method for determining selling price based on the cost of manufacture (to the producer) or cost of acquisition (to the distributor or retailer) in which a standard markup is added to the cost figure.

cost reduction plan

a form of payment-by-result scheme where cost savings above an agreed level are shared between the employer and the employee in agreed proportions.

count and recount offers

salesmen count stocks of their product held by wholesale retail customers, then recount on next call, and pay bonus on stocks sold in meantime.

counter marketing

efforts aimed at eliminating entirely the demand for a product, service, or idea. Countermarketing is generally carried out by parties who find the product in question undesirable or unwholesome.

counter-segmentation

a strategy in which the number of market segments targeted by a company are reduced, generally through the elimination of products which have been serving narrow segments of the population.

counter trade

international business in which some payments are made in the form of goods rather than currency. Counter trade includes four types of transaction: barter, compensation deals, counter purchase, and buyback.

coupon

a printed certificate employed by producers, distributors, or retailers as a sales promotion device. The coupon is redeemable by the customer for specified goods or services at a reduced price.

cover

outer faces of a magazine usually available for advertising purpose, i.e., front, back, inside front and inside back cover.

coverage

the extent to which a medium reaches an audience. In the electronic media coverage includes the number of homes reached by the station's signal. In the print media coverage refers to the ratio of circulation to the total number of individuals, families, or organizations in a geographic area. Sometimes called penetration.

covered time

time spent on work for which a bonus or piece work scheme exists but where it is not used. Instead of payment by result, payment is on a daywork or other time related payment scheme.

cow

expression used to describe products whose performance is past their best but which remain profitable. They are 'milked' i.e. provide a source of funds for new product development.

coworker

someone that a person works with who is neither his superior nor a subordinate.

craft union

an labour union whose membership is limited to people who work at the same craft.

creative conflict

concept developed by Mary Parker Follett that if opposing views can be integrated rather than simply resolved by compromise, conflict can be used as a means of achieving progress. Virtually as constructive conflict.

creative group

collection of individuals specializing in the development of creative ideas, particularly for the origination of advertising campaigns.

credit

although generally used as an adjective (credit card, credit note, etc.) the word credit has a more precise meaning in the business world where it is considered as the opposite of cash. Transactions are made on a 'credit' basis where no cash changes hands. The introduction and acceptance of credit in business transaction has been the principal cause of great expansion in trade and industry over the past hundred years.

credit bureau

an agency that acts as a clearinghouse by collecting and maintaining credit information about individuals or firms and by providing it to members or subscribers.

credit card

a card issued to an individual which identifies him and permits him to obtain goods or services on credit. Credit cards are either two-party or three-party. A two-party card is issued by a retailer and may be used only to purchase goods from that retailer.

credit manager

executive responsible for determining customers credit ratings as part of the credit control function.

credit note

a document issued by a vendor giving credit to the debtor for, say, goods returned, or overcharges acknowledged on an invoice.

credit rating

a person's credit refers to an assessment of his creditworthiness i.e., to what extent (both in terms of time and money) he may be allowed credit for amounts due. Credit ratings are temporary, and are discussed between banks, insurance authorities and potential vendors with the knowledge and agreement of the person in question.

credit screening criteria

in mail order or direct response marketing, adoption of some charge such as enrolment fee to help test customer reliability.

credit squeeze

the government control of credit, aimed at making credit more difficult and expensive to obtain, by imposing high interest rates, restrictions on hire purchase and back lending, and similar measures. The goal is to damp down demand in order to reduce the risk of inflation.

credit union

a cooperative financial institution chartered by a state or by the federal government which serves the members of a homogeneous group (the employees of a firm, the members of a union etc.) Credit unions resemble savings and loan institutions in the services they provide to their members.

crippled leap-frog test

a variation of leap-frog testing in which the test arithmetic is carried out in only one part of store, not on different locations.

crisis management

the form of management adopted in an emergency or an exceptional situation which focuses all the resources of the organization on getting through a temporary period of difficulty leaving more fundamental or longer-term issue aside. There is a great temptation for this state of affairs to degenerate is not management by crisis.

criterion behaviour

term used particularly in programmed learning, but also in some other areas of training, for a detailed specification of what is expected of a trainee/ student after training or a defined part of it.

criterion group

specially selected group of employees to whom psychological tests etc., are administered, to assist in making an evaluation of the tests.

criterion test

test to measure terminal behaviour of a trainee/student after training and thus to establish extent to which he/she has achieved criterion behaviour and objectives of training. Can also be a test before training to identity individual's training needs.

cross–branding

a form of brand promotion calculated to enhance an existing product by drawing on the brand strength of one or more of its ingredients or constituents. For example, advertising for a food product may include reference to a well-known and respected ingredient in an effort to trade on the ingredient's brand equity.

cross branding promotion

form of sales promotion when one manufacturers pack refers to a brand from another manufacturer, usually as some kind of premium or money off offer. Such packing often handled by a contract packer.

crossed cheque

a cheque may be either an open cheque or a crossed cheque. Crossing is an indication appearing on the face of the cheque that it should be paid only through a banker; it is usually done by drawing two parallel lines on the face of the cheque. Crossing has been evolved to avoid wrongful persons from obtaining payment on it.

cross elasticity

a concept which relates the change in price of one product to a change in demand for another product. Cross elasticity may be positive, the increase in price for product. A may generate increased demand for product B (which may now be a cheaper alternative), or it may be negative—reducing demand for product B (because demand for product B is dependent on sales of product A). Also known as price cross elasticity.

crosswalk

a diagram showing the relationship between items in programme budgets and those in budgets that have been prepared for departments or other budget centres of an organization.

culture

from a marketing standpoint, culture most directly relates to the way people behave in the marketplace. Culture is, as anthropologist A.L. Kroller has stated, "a set of patterns, of and for behaviour, prevalent among a group..." which includes the group's laws, customs, norms, and institutions.

cumulative audience

aggregate of persons or home reached by successive issues or broadcasts; synonym for cumulative reach.

cumulative reach

number of people in a target audience reached without duplication by a given promotional schedule over a particular period of time.

cumulative voting

a system of voting for the directors of a corporation that enables a shareholder to multiply the number of his or her shares by the number of directorates being voted on and cast the total for one director or a selected group of directors.

curiosity approach

a technique used by a salesperson in the first few minutes of contact with a prospect. The salesperson presents the prospect with an unexpected question or gadget to arouse the prospect's immediate interest and curiosity.

current account

an account with a bank where the customer makes demand deposits and asks for repayment of the deposits by drawing cheques.

current assets

the broad categories of current assets include such items as cash (including fixed deposits with banks) sundry debtors, bills receivable, marketable securities, inventories, advances recoverable and prepaid expenses. Generally, the term 'current assets' may be used to designate any asset which is reasonably expected to be released in cash, or consumed during the normal operating cycle of the business.

current demand

present willingness in the market to pay the ruling price for goods.

current liabilities

these are obligations which are normally paid within a period of one year out of the current assets or by creating current liabilities. At the most these are to be paid within the period of business cycle, normally a few years. Current liabilities include short-term borrowings from banks including overdrafts, sundry creditors, bills payable and provision for taxes, etc., due for the current year.

current maturity

the portion of a long-term obligation that is to be retired during the next twelve months; usually classified as a current liability.

current ratio

the current assets (for example, cash and accounts receivable) of an organisation or person divided by current liabilities (for example, accounts payable). The current ratio is a common measure of an originations' liquidity.

current value accounting

an accounting approach that reports assets at their present replacement cost rather than at their original purchase price.

curriculum vitae

a summary of a person's life given by him when applying for a job. It usually contains date of birth, education qualifications and previous jobs.

customer

person or organization actually making the purchasing decision not necessarily the consumer or user. Legally a party to a contract for the sale of goods.

customer-contractor principle

a term used in the public sector to describe research commissioned or sponsored by a government department from a publicly-funded research council. The research council is the contractor, or middlemen, for the funds which it awards to professional researchers, and the government department is the end user or customer for the research findings.

customer loyalty

pattern of repeated purchasing—by a person, household or firm—from one supplier, or of repeated purchasing of the goods of one producer (brand loyalty, or institutional brand preference).

customer profile

total list or estimate of all customers divided into pertinent categories, e.g., age-groups, with each group expressed in percentages of the total.

customer service level

in physical distribution, the customer service level is a measure of a firm's ability to deliver what the customer wants quickly and dependably. A higher service level may be desirable in highly competitive environments (such as pure competition or oligopoly) where it may allow the firm to increase its market share without changing its products, prices, or promotions. An increase in the customer service level, however, may increase total costs, since it may require additional distribution points, warehousing facilities and inventory costs.

customer services

as a business activity, customer service may be regarded as either an attribute of the product itself or as a part of the selling process. As the industrial level, customer services generally involve the installation, repair, and maintenance of the vendor's product, but prompt deliveries, accuracy in filling orders, and the availability of merchandise are also regarded as significant services. In retailing, services include delivery, gift wrap, credit, and other activities performed by the retailer for the customer's convenience which are not directly related to the sale of a specific product within the store.

custom marketing

a form of marketing in which the target customers are completely segmented, i.e., each customer is so distinct from all others that he must be treated as an individual. A unique marketing mix is developed for each customer.

custom quotas
the practice of allowing a certain amount of commodity (being imported) at a favourable duty and after that point charging normal duty.

customs union
an association of countries which have agreed to reduce or eliminate the trade barriers existing between them and who have, in addition, agreed to levy a tariff on goods imported from countries outside the union.

cut-price merchandise
goods subjected to cut prices. May or may not refer to goods of inferior quality.

cybernetic
from a Greek term meaning something like 'steersman' introduced in 1984 by Norbert Wiener, an American computer engineer. It is usually defined briefly as the study of regulatory mechanisms (like thermostats). Out of this field come the analogy of the brain as a computer and the model of psychological processes, as systems of message with their own built-in feedback.

cycle of advertising development
four stages; moving strategy definition (what to say and to whom); creative development (how to say it); communication assessment (have we said it); and campaign evaluation (what was the effect of what we said?).

cyclical unemployment
unemployment caused by a downturn in the business cycle, specifically by lack of demand for labor.

daf
trade terms under which the seller make the goods available at the frontier of the buyer's country.

damages
a sum of money claimed or awarded as compensation for loss or harm suffered by a person or by his property or reputation

dangerous occupations
all those that present hazards to the health or life of workers.

dangle
an arrow in an activity-on-arrow network, that has no preceding or succeeding event or activity at one end.

database
also data bank, information stored in a computer system so that any particular item or set of items can be extracted or organized as needed. Databases typically are structured for query-type use as well as for generating repetitive reports.

data flow chart
a diagram of the sequence of operations, both manual and automatic, involved in processing data. A data flow chart identifies the particular items of data at each stage and is normally used to describe a complete data processing system.

data processing

there are manual, mechanical or electronic data processing systems. By means of these raw information is collected, recorded, organized and analysed and converted into a form where it may conveniently be used or stored. A broad term for the manipulation of data in a desired manner; classifying, sorting, entering or extracting data from a machine or computer; calculating results; preparing reports, performing other operations.

data protection

legislation has been introduced to comply with the terms of the Council of Europe Convention for the protection of Individual with Regard to the Automatic Processing of Personal Data. The Data Protection Act 1984 provides for the introduction of a Data Protection Register to maintain a register of data-users and of persons who run computer bureaux concerned with personal data in both the public and private sectors. The provisions apply to automatically processed information, mainly that stored in computers, and do not cover records stored in manual files.

The Act introduces a series of criminal sanctions for failing to register etc., and gives the Registrar enforcement powers to ensure compliance with the eight 'data-protection principles' set out in schedule 1 of the Act, which broadly correspond to the convention's requirements. These are:

(i) the information to be contained in personal data shall be obtained, and personal data shall be processed, fairly and lawfully.

(ii) personal data shall be held only for one or more specified and lawful purposes.

(iii) personal data held for any purpose or purposes shall not be used or disclosed in any manner incompatible with that purpose or those purposes.

(iv) personal data held for any purpose or purposes shall be adequate, relevant and not excessive in relation to that purpose or those purposes.

(v) personal data shall be accurate and, where necessary, kept up-to-date.

(vi) personal data held for any purpose or purposes shall not be kept for longer than is necessary for that purpose or those purposes.

(vii) an individual shall be entitled, (a) at reasonable intervals and without undue delay or expense, (i) to be informed by any data-user whether they hold personal data of which that individual is the subject; and (ii) to have access to any such data held by a data-user; and (b) where appropriate, to have such data corrected or erased.

(viii) appropriate security measures shall be taken against unauthorized access to, or alternation, disclosure or destruction of, personal data and against accidental loss or destruction of personal data.

The Act also provides civil remedies for data-subjects. These include a right of access to personal data, compensation for loss occasioned by inaccurate data and an order that the data be rectified or erased. Certain exemption apply to information such as tax and criminal records.

The data protection tribunal will hear appeals from data-users and computer bureaux against refusal of registration and enforcement orders.

There are transitional provisions to allow for the implementation of the Act in stages, beginning with the appointment of the Registrar in 1984, and there will be a two-year period after registration has begun, in November 1985, before data-subjects acquire their right of access.

data reduction

refers to the selection and editing of operands to derive facts from large volumes or raw data.

date of deed

a deed takes effect from the date of its delivery and not necessarily from the date on which it is stated to have been executed.

dating

on invoices, dating refers to the time period during which discounts may be taken by a reseller customer (typically a retailer) as well as to the date on which the total dollar amount on the invoice becomes due.

day book

day book is a book wherein all the transactions of a business for a particular day are recorded. Day book is prepared on a daily basis. It may also be called Waste Book. This is prepared in the order to avoid dependence on memory of the businessman.

day release

arrangement under which employers give their employees a period off work (typically one day a week) without loss of pay in order that they can attend a course of further education.

daywork

1. synonym for time work. 2. work that is performed mainly during the hours of daylight. 3. synonym for casual work.

dead rent

a fixed annual sum paid for a mine or a quarry in addition to payment of royalties which vary in amount.

dead time

a term used in payment by results schemes. It refers to the time people spend waiting around during work hours before they can actually start a piece of work.

dealer

an individual or firm which sells merchandise without altering it. The term is most frequently applied to retailers, e.g., automobile dealer, but is sometimes used synonymously with wholesaler or distributor.

debenture

a corporation's obligation to pay money (usually in the form of a note or a bond) that is not secured (blacked up) by any specific property. The common use of the word is only for long-term bonds.

debit and credit

conventionally, the left side of an account is called the debit side (abbreviated Dr.) and the right side thereof is called the credit side (abbreviated Cr.) Amounts entered on the left (debit) side are termed debits and the account is said to be debited; and the amounts recorded on the right (credit) side are termed credits and the account is said to be credited. The difference between the total debits and the total credits is the account balance. But where the sums of debits and credits equalize, the amount is said to be in balance.

debt

a debt is money owed by one person or firm to another. It may carry interest covering the period during which it is due but not paid, although common business usage allows an agreement. It also applies for obligation of goods and services.

debt limitation

a plan designed to restrict current expenditures of governments to a limited amount in excess of current revenue collection by establishing the maximum amount of debt which may be incurred.

debt management

the process of managing the national debt, i.e., arranging for the payment of interest and the refinancing of maturing bonds.

debtor

the person or organisation that owed goods, services or money. The person or organisation to whom it is due is known as the creditor.

debtors to sales ratio

debtors expressed as a percentage of sales.

debt ratio

a comparison of total debts to total assets; an accounting ratio used to evaluate the risk of increased debt to or opportunity for expansion or development of an organisation.

debt service ratio

this ratio relates the fixed interest charges to the income earned by the business. It is also known as Interest Coverage Ratio. It indicates whether the business has earned sufficient profits to pay periodically the interest charges.

decasualization

process by which the workers in an industry are switched from a casual labour system to regular employment.

decay curve

in product development, a decay curve is a graphic representation of the survival rate of new product ideas. As each item is subjected to screening and analysis, development, and testing more and more products are dropped from further consideration until only a small percentage ever reach the commercialization stage.

decentralisation

some of the psychological reasons for decentralisation in a business remain as compelling as ever. For instance, decentralised organizations probably provide a good training ground for the top manager. They make better use of the 'whole man'; they encourage more active cooperation. But though interest in these advantages should be very great indeed, it is counterbalanced by interest in the possibilities of effective top management control over the work done by the middle echelons.

decentring

the process of continuing to perceive a situation in a way that changing circumstances have rendered ineffective. A psychological version of culture lag.

deception

to provoke spontaneous and revealing responses under motivational depth interviewing research, respondents may be deliberately deceived by given information. Challenges them to refute statements and so expose attitudes.

deceptive packaging

the packaging of products offered for sale in a manner calculated to deceive the purchaser, e.g., large boxes only partially filled with merchandise.

deceptive pricing

pricing tactics which are calculated to deceive or confuse the purchaser. Included are all misrepresentations of credit terms as well as the use of fraudulent reference prices and other deceptive markdown practices.

deceptive promotion

a promotional practice calculated to deceive or mislead the consumer. The misrepresentation of price or performance is common in deceptive promotions.

decision

a kind of flow chart used to summarize a possible sequence of decisions in which alternative choices are open at each stage and where each alternative is dependent on choices already made.

decision analysis

one of three techniques suggested by Peter Drucker to help a work organization decide on its most appropriate organizational structure. This technique is to establish what the key decisions to be made in the organization actually are as opposed to unquestioned assumptions about what they are. The other two techniques are activities analysis and relations analysis.

decision dynamics training

management development technique developed by Strathclyde university using videotapes and simulation exercise with the emphasis on examining the overall operations of the decision making group rather than a detailed examination of self or others.

decision-maker

anyone charged with the formal responsibility for making decisions in an organization. Usually applied to senior management people.

decision-making

process of being made aware of a course of action, idea, product or service, gathering information about it, undertaking a test or trial and finally adopting it. Can be applied to introduction of a new product or to buying in general and is not unlike AIDA in advertising.

decision-making in business

though business is wider than decision-making yet the decision-making is the essence of business. According to P.F. Drucker, "whatever a manager does, he does through making decisions". It is deeply embedded in the management process and is the only vehicle for carrying managerial workload. It permeates through all managerial functions. All matters relating to planning, organisation, direction and control are settled by managers through decisions which are executed into practice by operators of the enterprise.

decision making in industry

decision- making in industry is made simpler if management sets the boundaries within which the business is to operate. These boundaries are established by defining the objectives which should be generally understood whether implicitly or, preferably, explicitly. Writing them down can help to clarify them still further. One of the values of so defining objectives is that it will distinguish them from management beliefs which may be shown to have no present purpose. The objective may include the kind of products to be manufactured; the type of market to be aimed at; the ethics governing the relations with customer, employees, and the community; and the rate of profit to be sought. Less frequently they may also include other factors such as the location of the plant(s), the desirable size of the company, or an approximate yield on the company's share in relation to the market average which may be aimed at as an indication of market prestige.

decision making process

this process begins with planning decisions setting forth previously non-existent behavioural norms which are communicated to subordinate managerial, or non-managerial personnel. Performance information is relayed back to the superior who may make motivational decisions if behaviour is not in accord with the norms of planning decisions.

decision making skill

adequate conceptual understanding is required for taking sound decisions. With the development of intellectual, communication and organizational understanding skills, the manager reaches that stage of awareness when he can take effective decisions. The decisions so made will have to be carried out at the working level and hence the most difficult task is to see that such decisions are carried out at the proper time by the right people.

decision making—three level of

three traditional levels of decision-making in organizations: (a) the institutional level for strategic planning, i.e., those concerned with general company objectives and broad problems of the position of the organisation in its environment. (b) the managerial level which focuses on the gathering, coordinating, and allocating of resources for the organisation, e.g., planning budgets, formulating personnel practices, and deciding on routine capital expenditures; and (c) the technical level, involving the acquisition and utilization of technical knowledge for operational controls, e.g. production scheduling, inventory controls, and decisions concerning the measurement of worker's efficiency. Although some descriptions regarding the levels of decision-making are more restrictive, here we will argue that all three basic levels involve boundary spanning activities.

decision rule

any rule set-up to help make decisions in the face of uncertainty.

decision symbol

a graphic symbol in flow chart or decision analysis, indicating the need to make a judgement about a course of action.

decision theory

various mathematical techniques—such as game theory risk analysis and sensitivity analysis—which are used in forecasting to explore the likely outcomes of different decision options.

decision tree

in marketing planning a method of graphically depicting a series of alternative course of action the shape of a tree with each branch of the tree representing a possible decision along with its projected outcome. Decision trees aid managers in visually understanding an array of alternatives.

declaratory judgement

a judicial decision defining the rights and duties of parties to a dispute, but excluding payment of damages or an order compelling one of the parties to take a specific action.

declining balance

a method of calculating depreciation of a fixed asset in which the amount of depreciation is a fixed percentage of the previous year's depreciated value. (Also known as 'diminishing balance').

declining block pricing

the pricing of a service (e.g., electricity) so that its unit price decreases as the level of its consumption increases.

decreasing variation

in statistical analysis, the principle that the reliability of a sample increases as the square root of the number(n) in the sample increases. A sample of n=100 is twice as reliable as a sample of n=25 because the square root of the former is twice the square root of the latter.

deed of trust

a document that creates a trust; also, a document by which an organisation or person transfers ownership of land to an independent trustee for holding until a debt on the land (a mortgage) is paid off.

defective

a unit of production which is some way does not conform with specified requirements.

defective investment

any investment, domestic or foreign, undertaken principally to insure against loss rather than to make a profit.

defensive pricing

a strategy in which a company prices its products so as to protect (or defend) established products or market share e.g., a new product may be introduced at a price higher than another of the firm's products so as not to cannibalize it.

deferred annuity

an annuity that does not start until after a specified period or until the annuitant reaches a specified age.

deferred compensation

a portion of current earnings withheld until a later time (usually retirement) when the receiver is likely to be in a lower income-tax bracket.

deferred rebate

a rebate or discount on a purchase which is accumulated for a specified period to encourage customers to remain with a particular supplier. Also it is called aggregated rebate.

deferred shares

these are shares which rank for dividend and return of capital after all other classes of shares have received a fixed rate of divident or have been paid out in the case of winding-up of the company.

deficit

the result of an expenditure in excess of income, a lack or inadequate amount of something.

defined contribution plan

a pension plan that obligates the employer to contribute money to a pension fund according to a formula (such as a specified percentage of earnings). The benefits of the plan are not fixed, but depend on the amount of employer contributions and earnings of the pension fund.

definition of management

E.F.L. Brech defines management as a social process entailing responsibility for the effective (or efficient) planning and regulation of the operation of an enterprise, such responsibility involving (a) judgment and decision in determining plans and using data to control performance and progress against plans; (b) the guidance, integration, inspiration, and supervision of the personnel comprising the enterprise and carrying out its operation.

deflationary unemployment

the unemployment which results from a general insufficiency of jobs. It is often called involuntary unemployment.

deflator

present price level divided by price level at some past date is termed as deflator.

defraud

to cheat another or to withhold wrongfully that which belongs to another; to deprive one of some right by deceitful means.

defunct company

a company that has been struck off the official register of companies because it has ceased to function. This may arise after a winding up or where, after proper formalities have been completed.

degree of control

means how close a control needs to be maintained. Is it necèssary to record production every hour, day or week? Must an accurate inventory count be made of all parts at all stages in their processing? It is obvious that there is a point of diminishing returns where the value of such controls no longer justifies the cost of their accumulation.

delayed quotation bidding

a pricing strategy employed in the industrial market in which the final price of the product or service is not set until the item is either complete and/or delivered. Delayed quotation bidding is most common in large projects involving extensive development time.

delayed response

reaction to marketing initiative at a later time but often within the expected period of time.

delegation

the act of passing authority and responsibility for a task onto other usually subordinates in the organization; a group of people with the authority and responsibility for representing a large group.

delivered price

a price quotation at wholesale or retail level which includes the cost of delivery. This price strategy is also known as freight allowed pricing.

demand

the concept demand has two components. On the one hand, purchasers must have a need or desire for the product or service offered for sale and, on the o

ther hand, must be willing and able to pay the price asked by the seller. This condition (in which the buyer can actually fulfill his needs) is known as effective demand.

demand backward pricing

a method of setting prices which starts with what is considered an acceptance final (retail) price and works backward to what a producer can actually charge. The producer determines how much may be spent on producing the item by starting with this acceptable final price and subtracting both the margins which channel members typically expect and the average or planned marketing expenses.

demand cure

a diagram used to show how much of a certain product is likely to be bought at certain prices. A rise in price for example usually leads to a fall in demand.

demand deposit

a sum of money deposited by someone in a bank on condition that he can withdraw it on demand.

demand elasticity

responsiveness of sales or demand to relatively small changes in price. A product is said to be 'elastic' when a small change in price greatly affects demand.

demand expansibility

demand for a product or service which can be increased through the use of advertising alone. No change in price or any other variable is necessary to affect the change.

demand function

relationship between demand and the determinants of demand such as price, substitute products, income, or credit facilities.

demand inflation

inflation caused by an increase in demand that cannot be met, with the result that prices rise. Cost inflation is caused by an increase in costs.

demand information

refersal of traditional supply of information, such as news, with individual demanding what he wants from. View data, teletext, electronic newspapers. Active participants replacing passive participants.

demand pull

resultant of demand stimulants applied in marketing works in conjunction, for example, with sales push.

demarcation dispute

a dispute between trade unions over which union's members should perform a job.

demarketing

a marketing strategy calculated to reduce rather than increase demand for a product or service. Demarketing efforts are usually confined to periods of product shortage, e.g., American oil companies discouraged gasoline consumption during the Arab oil boycott. Sometimes called creative demarketing.

democratic management

(democratic leadership) a style of management which is based upon consultation and participation in the decision-making process-as opposed to authoritarian management in which a single manager takes all decisions.

democratic planning

when planning is adopted under a democratic type of government, it is called democratic planning.

demographic segmentation

a method of market segmentation based on geographic location (such as world or national region, population density, city size, etc.) or shared socio-economic characteristics (such as age, sex, religion, education, income, etc.).

demographic targeting

aiming messages at specific sections of the public, and ability of de-massified TV to reach numerous delivery systems.

demographics

categorization of people according to age, sex, income. Occupation, geographical distribution, so that; in marketing, market segments may be determined.

demography

the study of population of human beings, including vital and social statistics.

demonetize

to declare something to be no longer legal tender.

demonstration

showing the product or service in action. Sometimes used to refer to an artificial situation where audiovisual equipment is used instead of the actual product/service itself.

demonstration advertising

a form of advertising in which the attributes of a product are actually demonstrated and which frequently emphasizes the competitive strength of the product.

demonstration effect

the stimulation of consumer demand through advertising, displays of greater varieties of goods, and similar means. Such actions may increase consumer purchases even when consumer income has remained stable propensity to consumer, both on an individual or family level and on an international level.

demotion

assignment of an employee to a job of lower status, responsibility, or pay. There are three basic kinds of demotions: (1) voluntary demotion, usually the result of a reduction in force, (2) involuntary demotion, which results from a worker's inability to perform adequately on the job, and (3) disciplinary demotion, which usually takes place after an employee has been repeatedly warned to stop some kind of misconduct or disruptive behaviour.

demotion payment

made to an employee to compensate for being demoted.

denigration

advertisements should not unfairly attack or discredit other products, advertisers or advertisements directly or by implication.

department of employment

this large government department has wide-ranging responsibilities, its chief task being to promote the efficient use of manpower in a socially responsible way.

The title Department of Employment was adopted in 1970, following an alternation in the functions of the earlier Department of Employment and Productivity curtailing its responsibilities for government policy on productivity, prices and incomes (Price and Income Policy). Its earliest origins can be traced to 1909, when, as a result of the first Trade Board Act, the Board of Trade set up sixty-two labour exchanges with the purpose of bringing together employers and unemployed workers. Other developments which have affected DE activities include the establishment of the Ministry of Labour in 1917 and of the Ministry of National Insurance in 1945. In 1974 there was a major reorganization that split the DE from the → Manpower Services Commission (MSC) and the independent → Advisory, Conciliation and Arbitration Services (ACAS).

The Secretary of State for Employment is responsible for manpower policy, for the manpower aspects of regional policy and regional economic planning, and has senior representatives in each regional centre. Other responsibilities include promoting the policy of equal employment opportunity for workers, regardless of race, colour, origin or sex, and redundancy payments policy.

The Secretary of State also has powers to provide temporary employment for unemployed people and to finance schemes such as Community Industry, under which socially useful tasks are carried out by unemployed young people. These powers can be delegated to the MSC. The payment of unemployment benefit and supplementary benefit to people is carried out by the DE as the agent of the Department of Health and Social Security. The Secretary of State for Employment is also responsible for the Government's dealing with the MSC, ACAS and HSC and answers to parliament for their work.

The department consists of a London headquarters and a number of regional offices, each headed by a controller responsible for the execution of DE policy in that area through employment exchanges, sub-offices, branch employment offices and local agencies. Regional offices ensure compliance with orders made under the Wages Councils Acts. There are also several Factory Inspectorate divisions.

The department's manpower policy is based on the maintenance of a high and stable level of employment and its basic objective is to make the best use of the labour and skills in the economy. It publishes statistical and other information in its monthly journal, the Employment Gazette, and sponsors research. A National Joint Advisory Council consisting of representatives of the → Confederation of British Industry and the → Trade Union Congress meets periodically to advise the Secretary to the DE on broad policy questions. Present policy emphasizes the need to increase labour mobility.

departmental store

a departmental store may be described as a large retail establishment having in the same building a number of departments each of which confines its activities to one particular kind of trade and forms a complete unit in itself and is controlled.

departmental undertaking

a departmentally managed undertaking managed by the officials of the government under the charge of the Secretary of the Ministry concerned. Such organizations do not enjoy any legal entity. They are managed by civil servants who are government employees and who work under the control of a Minister.

departmentation

departmentation means divisionalization of work, the desire to obtain organization units to manaeable size and to utilize managerial ability. An organization structure and design are shaped significantly by the departmentation followed. The chief means of departmentation include by (1) function (2) product (3) territory

(4) customer (5) process (6) task force and (7) matrix. An organiser is free to use any means of departmentation in constructing an organization structure.

departmentation by matrix

this is one of the important newer concepts of organization featuring not only departmentation on a highly technical basis, but on a management basis as well. The supervision is dual technical from the technical chief and administrative from the administrative chief. This concept uses a matrix. In this groups A,B,C,D, and E represent five different technical skills.

dependency arrow

synonym for sequence arrow.

deposit account

an account with a bank from which deposits are repayable only to the depositor, who is required to give notice in advance if he requires repayment.

deposition

testimony in a law case given under oath, particularly as a written statement by a witness for use in court.

depreciation

in accounting this is a financial measure of the reduction in value of fixed capital assets over time e.g., the wear and tear of equipment.

depreciation, method of calculation of

there are several methods of calculating depreciation for the purpose of charging to costs. The methods are based on the following principles: (a) time factor, (b) usage function, (c) depreciation should include an element of maintenance costs, (d) besides providing for wear and tear, obsolescence etc. depreciation should also include an element of interest on the investment in the asset.

deprivation question

technique used in group depth interviewing, respondents asked which product they would miss most if it were no longer on sale.

depth interview

informal conversation between interviewer and respondent but with underlying cross-examination following clear cut objectives. Intended to discover facts which might not emerge from direct questioning.

depth interview of focussed interview

interviewing technique without a questionnaire, respondent being asked open-ended questions. Unstructured or non-directive interview.

deregulation

the systematic discontinuance of laws and regulations which once controlled business activities but have subsequently been deemed undesirable.

derived demand

market demand for a product

which can be traced to the demand for another product. Most derived demand is, finally, traceable to consumer demand.

descriptive research

market research calculated to yield information about a particular problem, e.g., how consumers behave under specific marketplace conditions or how one can identify the users of a given product.

descriptive statistics

statistics that summarise or describe a set of measurement, e.g., measures of central tendency.

design factor

term used particularly in market research to indicate the level of efficiency and reliability of a sample used for a survey.

de-skilling

modifying methods of performing a job to reduce the level of skill or skills demanded.

desk training

on the job commercial and clerical training.

determining dimensions

the needs and preferences of the customer which affect the purchase of a specific product type or specific brand in the marketplace. Such factors as a product's value as a status symbol, color of the product, demographic characteristics of the customer, behavioural needs, attitudes, the degree of a customer's urgency for satisfaction of his/her needs, and brand name are examples determining dimensions.

determining the resources

for artistic programming we must recognize the need for facilities, materials and supplies and personnel. Next we should appraise the availability of these necessary resources.

If any of them is not available we should set up another project designed to obtain this resource.

devaluation

this term is used with reference to currencies and their value on the international exchange. It is reduction of the official rate at which the currency of a country is exchanged for other currencies thereby lowering is value. It had the effect of making imported goods dearer and its own exports cheaper in overseas markets. Strictly speaking it applies only to currencies with a rate of exchange that is fixed in terms either of gold or some other currency of international repute. When an exchange rate is fixed it can only be changed by devaluation or revaluation of currencies by one of the countries concerned or by mutual agreement. It is also an action by the government of a country to change the peg for its currency in terms of the currency of another country so that in future a unit of currency will be exchanged for fewer units of currency of the other country.

development

the planned promotion of understanding, participation, and support among potential donors, of all varieties. Usually, development is used broadly and is considered to consist of three major, distinct groups of activities that must be coordinated if it is to be effective: planning, public relations, and fund-raising.

development area

area of unemployment and depression towards which government attempts to attract industry, using devices such as investment grants and tax concessions.

development director

a person who manges a development programme in larger organisation.

development of more resources

marketing promotes the development of economic resources of a country and puts it on the road to faster economic development. The revenues generated by business houses are invested in exploiting more and more economic resources of the country.

deviation

generally speaking a departure from the norm whether social, psychological or statistical. In statistics it refers to the difference of a given score from the mean.

dexterity

manipulative ability achieved through good coordination of motor and perceptual skills.

dexterity tests

tests designed to determine an individual's capacity to coordinate the use of different parts of the body.

diadic

paired comparison test involving informants reporting on two products or advertisement one against the other.

diagonal intergration

in this, auxiliary goods or services required for the main process or production in an industrial concern are provided inside that organisation.

difference between authority and responsibility

authority and responsibility are closely interrelated but they differ from each other in the following respects.

Meaning. Authority is the legal right of the superior to command his subordinates while responsibility is the obligation of a subordinate to perform the duties assigned to him by his superior.

Origin. Authority arises either from a formal contract or from legal provisions. It is attached to, a particular position, and tends, therefore, to be impersonalised. On the other hand, responsibility arises from a superior-subordinate relationship. When a subordinate receives authority from his superior, he becomes responsible to the latter. Responsibility is attached to a particular person and it is, therefore, personalised.

Delegation. Authority can be delegated by a superior to his subordinate. But responsibility is absolute and can be never be delegated. When a superior delegates his authority to a subordinate, he continues to be responsible to his own superior.

Continuity. Authority usually has a longer life than responsibility. Responsibility generally comes to an end after the assigned duty is performed.

Termination. Authority may be terminated by a notice. Responsibility cannot, however, be so terminated.

Despite the above differences, authority and responsibility are closely interrelated. They are the two wheels of the management cycle and management cannot be successful unless both move together.

differential

a difference between wage rates to total remuneration of different individuals or groups of employees, which is part of a planned or negotiated pay structure.

differential aptitude test

actually a battery involving eight different tests of aptitudes like verbal reasoning and spatial relations. The test is used to assess educational and vocational performance.

differentiated marketing

a marketing strategy in which a manufacturer produces a number of related products, each with a narrow segment of the total market as its target. The manufacturer attempts to build sales by addressing various segments of the market individually rather than by marketing a single product for all customers.

differentiation

in organizational structure, differentiation is the structuring of jobs in such a way as to allow for specialization of functions and provide greater efficiency within the organization. The larger the organization, the greater the opportunity for differentiation. In large companies, the marketing task may be differentiated into such specialized units as commercial research, advertising and promotion, application development, sales, and customer service.

digital computer

the type of computer most frequently used in business, including health care management. In contrast, analog computers tend to be used most frequently in scientific, mathematical, and aerospace applications.

dilutee

term, often pejorative, for a worker who has undergone shortened training and often experiences difficulty in gaining trade union acceptance as a semi skilled worker on the grounds that this would dilute the level of skill in the work place.

dimension

measurable quantity, used in marketing research to compared responses at different levels or in regard to platforms.

dimensions of management

management touches and influences the core of nearly every human being. Management makes us aware of our potentials, show the way toward better accomplishment, reduces obstacles, and causes us to achieve goals that we probably would not otherwise attain.

diminishing returns

in economics this is the point beyond which any additional input of resources will result in a less than proportionate increase in output. This idea has been borrowed by psychology where it describes an improvement that gets progressively smaller with each succeeding increment. For example, it is used in the study of learning and memory where after a large gain at the beginning extra practice begins to provide less and less gain.

direct competitor

a firm competing head-to-head with another firm, generally offering potential customers similar or identical products or services.

direct cost

a business cost that is directly related to producing a product or service.

direct distribution

depends on number of stages in channel of distribution. Own shops have direct from maker distribution compared with, say, ironmongery or stationery items, or fruit and vegetables where it is indirect.

direct expenses

all costs directly attributable to a product, a project, or an accounting centre.

direct export

a method of exporting goods in which the domestic firm handles its own exporting, independent of any international marketing middleman. Direct export may be achieved through the use of a domestic based export department or division within the firm, an overseas sales branch or subsidiary, travelling export sales representatives, or through foreign-based distributors or agents.

directing

directing in management involves guiding and leading subordinates, whether they be managers or non-managers. Although this concept is very simple, the methods of directing may be of extraordinary complexity. The superior manager should calculate in his subordinates â keen appreciation of enterprise traditions, history, objectives and policies.

direction

direction is that part of the management process which actuates the members of an organisation to work efficiently and effectively for the attainment of desired objectives. It is concerned with influencing, guiding, supervising and inspiring the subordinates to accomplish predetermined objectives.

direct negative

amendment to a motion proposing the direct opposite of the intention of the motion. The meeting or conference chairman should not accept a direct negative. The obvious course for anyone seeking to propose a direct negative is to vote against the motion itself.

direct labour

those members of the work force directly engaged in producing goods or services, as opposed to those carrying out supporting activities such as maintenance or staff function.

direct labour costs

the costs associated with those members of the work force directly involved in the production of goods and services.

direct mail

selective advertising medium using mailing lists and the postal services.

direct mail advertising

a form of below the line advertising where communications are sent directly to customers or potential customers by mail.

direct mail selling

sending specially prepared sales literature through the mail to specially selected prospective purchasers of a product or service, inviting them to place orders directly instead of through shops.

direct marketing

marketing via direct mail, telephone retailing, mail order retailing, catalog retailing, mail order ads and inserts (preprints) in magazines, door-to-door retailing, and such electronic media as two-way cable television. Direct marketing efforts are calculated to elicit a direct response on the part of potential customers.

director

a member of a board of directors, the body which—under an organisation's constitution by-laws—controls and governs the affairs of the organisation.

director's report

a document which must be submitted by every limited company with its annual accounts. It must contain certain information required in the Companies Act. It must report on the state of the company's affairs and give details of : (1) dividends recommended, (2) the names of directors, (3) the principal activities of the company and its subsidiaries, (4) any substantial difference between the market value and the book value of land, or interest in land held by the company, (5) significant alterations in fixed assets, (6) any proposed transfers to reserves, (7) details of shares and debentures issued during the year, (8) any interest that a director has in a contract with the company, (9) each director's interests in shares and debentures as shown in the register of the company, (10) an analysis of turnover, (11) an analysis of profit or loss before tax, distinguishing between the various types of businesses carried on by the company and its subsidiaries.

direct sale
a sale made by a manufacturer direct to a consumer and not through a retailer or other intermediary.

direct sell
a type of advertising message which focuses on a single unique product benefit and hammers it home to the target audience through constant repetition. This approach is often used in conjunction with product demonstrations such as the superior absorbency of certain paper towels, the extra strength relief of a pain reliever, and the inability of coffee drinkers to distinguish between fresh brewed coffee and certain instants. Not to be confused with direct selling.

direct selling
selling without the use of a retail outlet, distributor broker or wholesaler or any other form of middleman.

direct taxation
taxation levied directly on the citizens of a state and paid directly by them to the revenue authorities either personally or through an employer. This is unlike indirect taxation that is not dependent on a person's wealth, but on the goods that he buys. Instances of non-direct taxes are : Value Added Tax, Customs and Excise Duty, etc.

direct worker
an employee whose work is directly concerned with the production of his employer's products. (Also known as a direct).

disbursement list
a printed list containing the identity and quantity of parts and assemblies to be withdrawn from stock and dispatched to the starting point of manufacture or assembly on a given day.

disciplinary action
any action short of dismissal taken by an employer against an employee for violation of policy.

disciplinary fine
a fine that a union or professional association may levy against a member for violating a provision of its by-laws.

disclosure of information

the antecedents are early profit-sharing schemes and formal Joint Consultation within works councils. The Industrial Relations Act 1971 provided that employers of more than 350 persons should make an annual written statement to all employees, and placed upon them a duty to disclose to representatives of recognized registered unions all information within their possession relating to their undertakings', in order not to impede trade unions in carrying out collective bargaining and in accordance with good industrial-relations practice. Following the repeal of this Act, a number of the disclosure clauses were reintroduced and extended in subsequent legislation. In particular the Employment Protection Act 1975 included some significant changes regarding enforcement (allowing trade unions, for example, to make complaints to the Central Arbitration Committee), while the Industry Act of the same year made a number of provisions for information sharing within planning agreements. There is now no legal obligation on employers to make annual statements to employees on disclosure (although there is to make a statement of participation), but none-the-less the practice has continued to flourish. Indeed, despite a falling off in the number of companies newly adopting employee reporting at the end of the 1970s, 42 percent of firms report this practice (80 percent of those with more than 1,000 employees). There are discrepancies in managers' and trade unionists' accounts of the information actually given (consistently on pay and conditions of service, manpower requirements and the financial position of the company, managements were found to take the more favourable view of what had actually been provided). Moreover, there is little doubt that codes on disclosure of information have had only a circumscribed impact upon actual practice. But disclosure of information is an important element in the changing policies of managements in the 1970s and it is clear that supportive legislation significantly encouraged its general expansion. Again, in the 1980s disclosure of information received a further impetus as a consequence of the rise of the new technologies and the emergent problems which managements face in ensuring that they are successfully implemented.

discount

a reduction from list or marked price similar to an allowance granted by a seller to a buyer. Discounts are most commonly granted to induce the buyer to pay for his purchases quickly (cash discount), to buy substantial amounts of merchandise (quantity discounts), to perform certain middleman functions in the distribution channel (trade discount), or to place order during the time of year when business is slow (seasonal discount).

discounting of bills

banks discount bills of exchange. The bank purchases them at their present worth. The bill is purchased by the bank at the face value less the interest at the current rate till the time when the bill falls due. This is known as discounting of bills. This is a form of lending to the business community. Discounting of bills facilitates modern business transactions in a big way.

discount store

a retail establishment which operates on very low margins in order to offer merchandise at prices well below the recognized market level. The discount store emphasizes self-services. Typically volume oriented, it is distinguished primarily by its emphasis on price and value.

discovery method

method of teaching in which work is arranged and topics chosen so that trainee/pupil learns for himself rather than learning directly from the instructor/teacher. Sometimes known as heuristic method.

discrepancy of assortment

the difference between the lines made by the producer and the assortment wanted by the consumer. Wholesalers and retailers compensate for this discrepancy by putting together an appropriate product mix for their customers.

discretionary content

the discretionary content of a task that has been assigned to someone consists of the aspects of the task that are expected to be carried out according to plans or decisions made by that person using his own judgment.

discretionary income

that portion of a person's earnings which remains after taxes have been paid, contracted payments made, and the necessities of life purchased. The individual has a certain amount of discretion as to how the balance shall be spent. Such expenditures are called discretionary expenditures.

discriminating protection

the policy of protecting the goods produced by a few select domestic infant industries from the 'invasion' of foreign goods, through either banning of such importations or levying prohibitive protective tariffs.

discrimination

in employment different treatment of workers based on race, sex, age, religion, ethnic or national background, or union membership (or nonmembership), concerning hiring, wages, promotions, training programs, or any other terms and conditions of employment.

discriminatory pricing

the sale of goods or services at different prices to different customers. Pricing is discriminatory when it is calculated to give one party an unfair advantage over another.

discussion group

motivational research technique in which assembled group of respondents answers questions put by psychologist. Motivational research.

diseconomies of scale

the disadvantages resulting from a large as opposed to a small-scale of operations in an organization. They include difficulties of co-ordination, communication and adaptability to changing circumstances.

disigned decay

managacture and marketing of disposable, e.g. nappies, handkerchiefs, bottles.

dismiss

to carry out the dismissal of an employee.

dismissal

action by an employer to end an employee' contract of employment.

dismissal of employee (law)

dismissal law is complex, partly because the common-law rules (i.e., those made by judges) and a variety of statutory provision overlap. A dismissal may be wrongful or unfair or for redundancy; occasionally it may be all of these, sometimes none of them.

At common law, all employees who are dismissed without the proper notice to which they are entitled (or in breach of an agreed procedure that is contractually binding on their employer) may sue for wrongful dismissal. This action for damage will be heard in the ordinary courts. It is the absence of due notice that renders a dismissal wrongful and accordingly employees cannot sue at common law where they have been dismissed on full notice, even if the employer has no good reason for giving them notice. Nor can employees complain where they are sacked summarily (i.e., without notice) if they are themselves guilty of serious contractual misconduct, such as theft or wilful refusal to obey a lawful and reasonable order. The usual remedy for wrongful dismissal is damage, limited to the sum the employees would have earned net during the pericd of notice that they should have been given. The fact that this amount may not adequately compensate an employee for any period of unemployment following dismissal will not increase the damage. Employees cannot ordinarily prevent their employer from dismissing them wrongfully, nor can they obtain reinstatement once the dismissal has been affected.

The right to terminate employment by giving proper notice is one that the courts will ordinarily imply into a contract of employment unless, for example, the contract is for a fixed term. What amounts to proper notice is primarily a matter to be settled by the parties themselves at the outset of the contract. In default of this, the common law requires 'reasonable' notice (which may be fixed by reference to what is customary in the trade or occupation), subject to the minimum periods of notice prescribed by s. 49 of the Employment Protection (consolidation) Act 1978. The Act provides that where an employee has been continuously employed for between four weeks and two years, one week's notice is the minimum. Thereafter he or she is entitled to an additional week's notice for every year of service up to a maximum of twelve week's notice after twelve or more years. These periods are minima and so may be increased, but not reduced, by agreement between the parties. Employees, however, may agree to accept wages in lieu of the appropriate notice. As indicated earlier, they forfeit their right to notice or to accept wages in lieu where they are guilty of serious misconduct.

Because of the inadequacies of the common-law action for wrongful dismissal, a quite separate right to complain to an Industrial Tribunal of unfair dismissal has been in existence since 1972. An employee must have been employed for two years prior to dismissal in order to claim the dismissal was unfair. A dismissal that is wrongful is not necessarily also unfair, nor vice versa.

dismissal wage

a type of wage guarantees.

display

the impersonal, visual presentation of goods or ideas. Display is frequently employed in the retail trade in store windows and interiors to facilitate customer examination and selection of merchandise.

display advertisement

a printed advertisement which forms part of a newspaper, magazine, book or similar publication which has been especially designed with the intention of attracting the attention of readers.

disposable income

earnings which remain after income and other taxes and mandatory payments have been deducted. Roughly equivalent to "take home pay."

dispute

traditionally, industrial relations disputes in general have been known as trade disputes, with the term industrial dispute becoming more common in modern items. Disputes involving inter-union rivalry may be demarcation disputes, jurisdictional disputes or recognition disputes.

dispute benefit

or strike pay. Paid by trade unions to workers on strike to compensate for loss of their normal wages.

disputes procedures

procedure agreed between employers, or employers' associations, and trade unions for resolving industrial disputes.

dissociative groups

type of reference group brought together for the purpose of examining consumer buying motives.

dissolution of company

a company is dissolved when winding-up proceedings have come to an end (winding up), or when the register of companies has struck the company's name off the register as defunct.

dissolution of partnership

the death, bankruptcy, or retirement of a partner dissolves the firm, and if the remaining partners continue in business a new partnership is created.

distress merchandise

merchandise that has been reduced in price to increase the probability of sale.

distributed practice

a technique of learning in which the lessons or periods of practice are spread out as widely as the available time permits. This is a much more effective method of learning in most cases than massed practice with which it is usually contrasted.

distribution

a marketing term for a retailer who deals in the wares of certain specified manufacturers, having perhaps the sole agency for an area. He buys and sells on his own account and is not therefore an agent for a single manufacturer.

distribution check

survey taken at retail outlets to measure levels of distribution being achieved.

distribution cost analysis

an analysis of the costs incurred, both direct and indirect, in selling a company's products. Such a study is calculated to reveal which salespeople are most productive, which products are most profitable, and other data useful in managing the marketing effort.

distribution network

the wholesalers, retailers and other firms in an economy that do not manufacture or produce goods but participate in the process of changing the ownership of goods from producer to consumer.

distribution planning

determining the optimum methods of distribution and

preparing and implementing programmes to put these methods into effect. This will involve a selecting the best channels of distribution.

distribution standards

in customer service, standards of performance with respect to response time, delivery time, accuracy in order filling, depth of inventory, etc.

distribution strategy

the decision to market goods through a particular channel to achieve the most economic or cost-effective result.

distribution structure

the sum of all the distribution channels existing in an industry.

distributor

firm which buys and sells on its own account but which deals in the goods of certain specified manufacturers. Common in trades where special representation, stocking and service facilities are required, e.g., motor transport.

diversification

diversification in marketing may take a number of forms. A firm may introduce new products into existing markets or it may introduce existing products into new markets. In a complete departure, it may introduce new products into new markets. Some diversification is accomplished through mergers and acquisitions. The object of diversification is almost always expansion with a concurrent increase in profits.

diversion in transit

a practice in rail transportation in which the final destination of goods is determined after they have left the shipping point. As long as the route involves no backtracking, the shipper receives the regular carload rate from the railroad. This practice allows producers of goods, especially perishables, to move them in the general direction of their markets before a final destination is known.

divestment

action or process, undertaken by a firm, of transferring ownership and control of part of its activities to another firm.

dividend

an insured person's share in unexpanded funds, allocated by an insurance company to its policyholders. The dividend may be used by an insurance company to its policyholders. The dividened may be used by the recipient to increase the amount of his or her insurance, shorten the period of payment for the insurance, reduce the premium due, or provide cash income. Also, it is the company's profit paid to the shareholders. The amount payable depends on the number of shares held. Unlike interest, dividends are optional payments made at the discretion of the director—though failure to pay dividends will have an adverse effect on the market value of the shares as nobody will be interested in making non-earning investment.

dividend policy

dividend policy is concerned with the division of net profit after taxes between payments to shareholders and retentions for reinvestment ostensibly on behalf of the shareholders.

From the legal viewpoint, dividends may generally be paid out of the balance of the past profits. It is not essential that profits should have been made in the company's accounting year to which the dividend relates.

Clearly there are a great number of factors which influence dividend policy, including the immediate cash position, the timing of capital repayments for redeemable debentures and preference shares, the financing requirements for growth of assets, profit expectations, future plans for capital raising and therefore the degree of need to please existing and potential investors.

A different, more analytical approach to the question of dividend policy is that of exploring the impact of dividend policy on shareholders' wealth in order to arrive at some optimal rate of dividend payment. The importance to the company of a consideration of this approach is evident, since a high retention rate, although providing a source of financial merit, adversely affects the price of its shares and therefore its attractiveness for the investor.

division of labour

most of the organizations are based on the classical theory of division of labour with division of specialisation as rigid hierarchical positions, rigid and close control and supervision and distinct hierarchy of authority.

document

any form or voucher containing details of some transaction.

documents against payments

these documents are similar to the documents against acceptance but their bill is a sight bill and the importer must pay immediately upon receiving the documents.

documentary credit

banks give facilities to customers enabling them to open credits in favour of persons inland or overseas, so that these persons can obtain credit more promptly on tendering the relevant documents.

dogs

products liked by management but probably uneconomic and should be dropped.

dollar gap

adverse balance of payments in a country with a dollar currency.

domestic

in business, any transaction within a state or a nation, as opposed to one involving two or more states or countries.

domestication

a process in which foreign businesses are forced to give up control of their operations by the government of the host country. The final step in the domestication process is the outright ownership of the corporation's property by nationals.

domestic-based export agent

an independent international marketing middleman used in indirect export. The domestic based export agent negotiates foreign purchases for the domestic manufacturer and receives compensation in the form of a commission. Trading companies are one form of domestic based export agents.

domestic based export merchant

an independent international marketing middleman used in indirect export. The domestic based export merchant buys the manufacturer's product and sells it abroad.

domestic exports

exports of goods or commodities produced within the country of origin.

domestic gold standard

the modern gold standard serves two functions. In the first place it is a method of controlling the volume of the currency. The second function of the gold standard is it to preserve the stability of exchange rates.

domicile

the declared legal home or principal residence of an individual.

donated services

services provided by personnel who receive partial or no compensation; those contributed services which, if not contributed, would have to be paid for in order to operate a programme.

donor

a person who provides a gift or charitable contribution of money, stocks, property, or something else of value to an individual or organisation.

dormant parner

a partner who plays an inactive role in the management of a business and who is not known to the public as having an interest in the enterprise.

double barrelled question

single question actually posing two questions simultaneously. When answered there is doubt as to completeness of the answer.

double decker

two outdoor advertising panels sited one above the other.

double employment

holding of two jobs by one person. This happens, for example, in moonlighting.

double entry book-keeping

the normal method of book-keeping or accounting in an

organization where total credits equal total debits because every transaction is recorded twice, as a credit to one account and a debit to another.

double factoral terms of trade

net barter terms of trade divided by the relative change in productivity in the exports of a given country and in the foreign industries producing its imports.

double front

twin poster sites arranged to utilize both sides of the front of a bus or other commercial vehicle. Usually each a-single sheet' or smaller.

double page spread

two facing pages in a magazine or newspaper, used in advertising as if they were one single sheet, i.e., the design carries right across the gutter in the centre.

double pricing

where a product carries two prices, either actually or by implication, offering to sell to consumers (the technique is used mostly in consumer goods) at the lower of the two prices.

double search

marketplace activity characterized by consumers looking for products they need and producers looking for customers—each is searching for the other.

double tariff

tariff that distinguishes either between autonomous and conventional duties, or between maximum and minimum duties.

double time

payment of wages at twice day rate or time rate, most usually for certain overtime or working special hours.

downer

short strike or stoppage intended to draw attention to a particular grievance. It usually involves workers in 'downing tools' but not leaving the factory premises. A 'downer' is a form of demonstration strike.

down payment

a partial payment of the total purchase price rendered by a buyer to a seller at the time of purchase, with the understanding that the rest will be paid later, according to the terms of their agreement.

downstairs merger

a merger in which a parent corporation becomes a subsidiary.

down time

period during which a machine is not operative due to mechanical failure, machine adjustment, non-availability of materials, labout of maintenance work.

dramatic approach

a technique used by a salesperson in the first few minutes of contact with a prospect. The salesperson presents an eye-opening demonstration of how the good or service works. Often the prospect may be involved in the demonstration.

drawback

it is a rebate for duty paid by an exporter to the customs authorities on imported materials used in the manufacture of exported goods. Drawback is not paid if goods are kept in a banded warehouse for re-export. Goods, imported for repair are exempted from payment of duty.

drop shipment

(1) a shipment of goods arranged by a limited-service wholesaler called a drop shipper. (2) In retailing, the term refers to merchandise shipped by a manufacturer to the individual branch stores of a chain or department store organization rather than to warehouse or distribution center.

drop shipper

a limited-service wholesaler who, although he takes title to the goods he sells, never actually has them in his possession. Drop shippers commonly sell bulk products like sand and gravel, coal, or building materials. They receive orders from customers and then find a suitable manufacturer or supplier who ships the goods directly to the customer. The supplier bills the drop shipper who, in turn, bills the customer. Also known as a desk jobber or drop shipment wholesaler.

drugstore

a retail establishment which traditionally was a place where drugs and medicines were prepared and dispensed according to a physician's written prescription. As drugstore evolved, they added proprietary drugs, health and beauty aids, medical supplies, books and magazines, cigars and cigarettes, small appliances, etc., to the mix of products they stocked.

drum

large cylindrical metal container mainly used for bulk packaging of liquids.

dual adaptation

a strategy employed in international marketing in which the product offered for export is different from the domestic product and which is promoted differently in the foreign market.

dual distribution

the use of more than one channel of distribution to reach customers at different levels of the marketplace. For example, a manufacturer may sell to large customers directly, but to smaller ones through a wholesaler. Or he may sell through his own retail outlets while, at the same time, selling through other retailers. Conflict may arise when more than one channel is used to reach the same market segment. Also called multiple channels and multichannel marketing.

dual membership agreement

agreement between two trade unions for one of them to

represent certain of the other's members in particular situations.

dual prices

a system in which a goods is simultaneously sold at two different prices within a given area.

due date

in purchasing, the expected date or receipt for a part; in manufacturing, the expected completion date of a part.

dues

fees that must be periodically paid by association and union members in order for them to remain in good standing. Dues payments are used to finance the activities of an association or union.

dummy activity

used in critical path planning and network analysis to indicate events not connected in the network by one activity but nevertheless having an essential relationship in time. A dummy activity is shown as a dotted arrow.

dumping

sale of the same product in different markets at different prices.

duopoly

a market in which only two firms compete or which is dominated by two firms.

duopsony

the condition that exists when two buyers control the demand for goods and services offered by many producers.

duplication

(an advertising) extent to which the audience of one medium or vehicle overlaps that of another.

durable consumer goods

non-perishable consumer goods like residential house, furniture etc. which can be used over a fairly long period of time. Such goods are to be distinguished from semi-durable goods.

durable goods

tangible capital or consumer goods having a relatively long useful life (sometimes arbitrarily put at three years.).

dutch auction

an unuusual form of auction in which the auctioneer starts the bidding at very high price and then reduces the price until he receives a bid.

dynamically continuous innovation

the development of products which are either completely new or which are substantially altered versions of existing products. Innovation of this type is generally attributable to changes in the life-styles and expectations of consumers, and may bring with it considerable description in consumption patterns.

dynamic analysis (dynamics)

the study of the behaviour of systems, single market or whole economies in disequilibrium situations.

dynamics

the analysis of economic change over time and the processes of adjustment to change. Necessarily such study involves analyzing changes that have occurred in the past.

dynamic theory

different from other theories about the development of personality, and concerned with contemporary manifestations of personality in interaction with the environment.

EAM

abbreviation of electrical accounting machines.

earliest event time

in network analysis, the earliest time at which an event in a network can take place.

earliest start time of an activity

(or earliest start date of an activity or earliest start). The earliest possible time at which an activity in an activity-on-node network can be started.

early majority

in the diffusion process, the early majority constitutes those consumers in the mass market who have relatively high social status and who are receptive to innovation. The early majority adopts new products and services at an above average rate.

early shift

1. the earlier shift during a day in a double day-shift system.
2. the morning shift in a three-shift system.

earned income

it is the part of a person's income which is obtained as a result of the application of labour either as an employee or as a self-employed person.

earned premium

a portion of a premium payment for which the protection specified in an insurance policy has already been given. For example, 75 percent of an insurance company's premium is earned premium after a period of nine months of the 12– month contract term of the insurance policy has elapsed.

earning concept

a concept in accounting for recognizing income in the operating statement of a non-profit organisation. Under the earnings concept (in contrast with, e.g., the stewardship concept), income is recognized in an operating statement only after it has been earned; because they are restricted, and therefore not available for general use; moneys or funds from restricted donations and endowment gifts are excluded from the operating statement until they are spent.

earning drifts

extent to which wages or earnings rise above national rates through the influence of such factors as local rates, overtime, workplace bargaining, payment by-result schemes bargaining creep, etc. Also known as wage drift.

earnings relationships

relationships between the levels of earnings of the different work or groups occupations in a factory or plant.

easement

a formal grant or privilege to use a parcel of land adjacent to an owned parcel. The use is typically for a special purpose such as a road, highway entrance, irrigation ditch, or other need that is not in conflict with the manner in which the land owner uses his or her major property.

ecology

the study of the general and specific relationship of the human species with its general and specific environment.

econometric analysis

in casual research, econometric analysis is the attempt to project sales or other activities by constructing an econometric model and simulating a future outcome. The model uses two or more regression or similar analysis to simulate future events on the basis of past relationships.

econometrics

the branch of economics that deals with the mathematical or statistical relationships between economic variables.

economic activity

the production and distribution of goods and services. Also, the contribution of persons to the production and distribution of useful goods and services.

economic and monetary union

one of the basic elements necessary in setting up a common market.

economic dynamics

analysis of economic systems, through time, and particularly in relation to behaviour of markets, firms and the national economy in general.

economic environment

the conditions under which man conducts struggle to satisfy his wants.

economic forecasting

the use of changes in the national and international business climate to predict the effects of those changes on specific industries.

economic man

in economic theory, an ideal human being who behaves in totally rational fashion, who is perfectly informed and whose economic motivation when making decisions is towards maximizing utility.

economic needs

those customer needs which are concerned with making the best use of limited resources (from the customer's own point of view). These needs include convenience of product use, efficiency of product operation or use, dependability of the product, reliability of service, durability, improvement of earnings, improvement of productivity of property, and economy of purchase or use.

Economic needs govern how and why customers select certain product features over others.

economic of scale

the advantage resulting from a larger, as opposed to a small, scale of operation in an organization. They include lower unit costs, greater purchasing power by buying in bulk, opportunities for training, etc.

economic order quantity (EOQ)

the optimum size of an order, calculated to minimize carrying and procurement costs, especially the cost of frequent re-ordering, while maintaining sufficient quantities to meet the average level of demand. An EOQ model is the technique use to balance the cost of holding inventory against the costs involved in placing orders.

economic organization

the way in which an economy is organized, that is, who owns or controls the means of production and distribution of goods and services.

economic planning

a totality of arrangements decided upon in order to carry out a project concerned with economic activity.

economic sanction

when the government of one nation, or of many acting in concert, want to make a token objection to the policies of another, then a common tactic is adopted to disrupt the economy of the offending nation by the imposition of boycotts and embargoes on trade with that country.

economic system

the manner in which an economy is organized to utilize scarce resources to produce goods and service and to distribute them for consumption. The economic system of any given society will reflect that society's goals and the nature of its political institutions. Nevertheless, all economic systems must develop some method to decide what and how much is to be produced and distributed as well as by whom, when, and to whom. Planned economic systems are those in which government planners decide what and how much is to be produced and distributed by whom, when, and to whom. Socialist and communist economic systems function in this manner. In market–directed economic systems, such as capitalism, the individual decisions of producers and consumers make the decisions for the economy as a whole. In a pure market directed economy, also known as a free-market economy, consumers determine a society's production by their choices in the marketplace without government intervention.

economy pack

several products, wrapped

together and sold at a lower price than if each were sold separately, to provide a saving to the consumer. The economy pack most often comes directly from the producer, but middleman organizations sometimes repackage merchandise to create an economy pack.

economy size

a large quantity of a product, such as detergent, sold in a single large package to provide the consumer with a lower per unit price.

editorial advertisement

advertisement designed in the form of a piece of editorial matter. Such advertisements must, however, be clearly labelled 'advertisement'.

editorial publicity

space in ajournal or newspaper in which a product, service, or company is discussed or publicized at the discretion of the editor.

educational technology

organized design and implementation of learning systems taking advantage of modern visual aids and communications and teaching methods. A systems approach to the teacher learning process.

effective substitution

the policy of promoting managers only when they have subordinates able to take their place. To accomplish this end, managers are forced to delegate authority. Moreover this policy removes a major cause of hoarding authority the desire of a manager to gain indispensability by making sure that his duties cannot be handled by any of his subordinates.

effective supervision

supervisor's skill in supervising his subordinates as a group is important to successful performance. The greater his skill in using group method of supervision, greater are the productivity and job satisfaction of his subordinates. Proper frequency of work group meeting as well as the attitudes of the superior toward the ideas of subordinates promote harmonious group action and group supervision.

efficient-market hypothesis (EMH)

the theory of efficient markets appears to have its origin in work by the Frenchman Bachelier in 1900. Focusing its attention on the question 'Do stock prices behave randomly? The theory gained considerable impetus in 1953 when work by Kendall suggested that prices did indeed behave randomly. This was a seminal proposition (embodied in the so-called random-walk hypothesis) because it implied that non-random patterns of price behaviour could arise only from imperfections in the pricing mechanism of the market.

According to the EMH, correct

prices, i.e., those having 'true' values, will only arise when the market place is sufficiently competitive and participants are working with all of the relevant information available. Changes from equilibrium prices will only occur when new information becomes available. Thus, three levels of efficiency are now judged to be appropriate in the consideration of stock-market pricing, namely, weak, semi-strong and strong. The weak form states that current prices reflect all information contained in earlier prices; the semi-strong form requires prices to capture all other published information, e.g. dividend announcements, as well as past prices; the strong form places further requirements on the quality, quantity and interpretation of all information considered relevant to the price-formulating process.

effort scale

in consumer behavior studies, the effort scale is an attempt to graphically represent the amount of time and effort consumers are prepared to expend in shopping for a particular product.

ego involved products

products in which the consumer feels he has an emotional or psychological stake. Most designer merchandise, which in some way satisfies a need, may be regarded as ego-involved.

egoistic needs

industrial psychologist's term for the personal sources of job satisfaction other than remuneration. These include self-respect, the respect of others, sense of achievement, status, prestige, etc.

elasticity

the adaptability of a market and its ability to respond to a change in price. Elasticity is calculated as the percent change in the quantity demanded divided by the percent change in price.

elasticity method

a system of basing a firm's advertising appropriation on supply and demand curves. The average cost of any additional expenditure is compared with the average return on increased profit, indicating the point beyond which advertising is uneconomic.

elasticity of demand

a measure of the sensitivity of demand for a product or service to change in either its price (price elasticity) or in the income of the people demanding the product of service (income elasticity). Price elasticity is the ratio of the percentage change in demand to a percentage change in price.

elasticity of expectations

the ratio that exists between the predicted future percent change in price and the most recent current change in price.

elasticity of supply

an economic concept that relates the supply of goods to their market price; i.e., as the price of goods advances, producers are inclined to respond by producing more, thus increasing the supply in the marketplace. If, however, supply does not respond to an increase in price it is regarded as inelastic.

election polls

opinion polls, using either quota or random surveys, to predict likely results of an election. Accuracy of finding may depend on size and kind of sample, questions asked and closeness to the event.

electronic computers

a more modern approach to programmed decisional problems resulted from the second industrial revolution in U.K., the U.S. and Japan. Electronic computers have made possible the practical application of complex mathematical and comprehensive analogue models to help solve decisional problems. Somewhat less dramatic is the use of computer to make many a routine "decision" involved in the informational processing that occurs within accounting finance marketing production and purchasing departments.

electronic funds transfer (EFT)

in retailing, the use of automated electronic equipment, such as computer terminals, to move money directly from the customer's account to the retailer's account at the point of sale or service.

electronic mail

communication based on computer networks which allows users to send and receive, store and forward messages sent between terminals and to obtain hard copy for their records if necessary.

electronic retailing

the use of electronically transmitted information to facilitate consumer shopping without the need to enter a store. Electronic retailing is a form of direct marketing in which telephone lines connected to home computers, television sets equipped with special decoders, and interactive cable television are employed to transmit information to the consumer. The potential buyer views a "menu" combining text and still graphics which includes all merchandise being offered for sale. If the consumer decides to purchase, a number is entered on a keyboard (or, in some systems, a telephone call is made to a central location) and the item is ordered.

embargo

the most strigent form of trade restriction or quota under which specific products are barred from entering a country.

embezzle

the act of stealing money or property entrusted to him or her by that employee.

embezzlement

the fraudulent appropriation of property (personal or real) that has been entrusted to another person's care. For example, the taking of money from a bank by an employee or trustee with concealment of this act by the falsification of accounting records.

emergency

a situation or condition that has a high probability of having consequences that are disabling or immediately life threatening; situation that requires immediate intervention to assist a person with potentially disabling or life-threatening conditions.

emergency goods

products purchased only when the need is very great.

emolument

the return from personal labour received or accrued in the form of compensation, such as a salary, wage, fee, commission, award, price concession, or other personal benefit.

emotional appeal

product advertising appealing to emotional desires rather than logic, economy or utility.

empathy

the ability to put oneself in another's place. In marketing, this allows the perceptive marketer to anticipate a customer's reaction to appeals and campaigns.

empirical school of management

the empirical is based upon the premise that if we study the experience of successful managers, or the mistakes made in management, or if we attempt to solve management problems, we will somehow understand and learn to apply the most effective kinds of management techniques. That by finding out what worked or did not work in individual circumstances, the student or the practitioner will be able to do the same in comparable situations.

employed person (or employee)

one who works for an employer, as opposed to a self-employed person working on his own account, or an unemployed person seeking employment, or a non-employed person neither in employment nor seeking it.

employee benefit

any of the non-wage forms of employee compensation may include paid sick leave, holidays and vacations, group medical and dental insurance retirement programs, etc.

employee booklets

the bigger companies publish booklets containing company information. These booklets are supplied mainly to the new employee and also to other. The purpose of providing **a** booklet about the company is to satisfy the natural desire of he new employee to know the highlights of the company. They are usually very well-written and attractive. It is essential to ensure that informal oral communication supplements the booklet in any programme of indication.

employee contribution

the money individual employees pay to participate in company benefit plans, especially common in the areas of insurance, pension, and saving plans.

employee development

a program designed to upgrade employees through training. The program may aim to improve the performance of employees at their present jobs or to qualify them for advancement within the organization.

employee handbook

a book, given by an employer to all his employees, that gives information on employer-employees, relations.

employee orientation

a period in which all new employees are familiarized with the policies, history, and operations of the business as well as the responsibilities of their particular jobs. The employees are also introduced to employee benefits and opportunities for advancement during the orientation period.

employee ownership

a situation in which the people who work for an organization own some, or even all, of its shares. Figures vary from country-to-country but most employees own no share in the organization for which they work.

employee profile

following a job analysis, this is a descriptive list of the background experience and ability considered necessary for the performance of the job.

employee relations

relations between an employer and his employees regarded as individuals rather than as members of unions.

employee relations index

assessment of the quality of employee and personal relations by noting trends in such factors as labour turnover, absenteeism, safety, medical needs, use made of suggestion schemes, grievance.

employee share ownership plan

a loan scheme to help employees buy some or all of the shares in their company.

employer's association

an organization of employers within an industry or an economy. It is the organization which engages with trade unions by representing its members in collective bargaining and matters of employment, as well as lobbying on behalf of its members' interests.

employers' liability

employers have a legal duty to take all reasonable steps to protect the safety of the persons employed by them. This includes providing employees with reasonably safe premises tc work in, reasonably safe tools, materials and appliances to work with and a reasonably safe system of work. If an employer should be in breach of this duty and this breach were to lead to an employee sustaining injuries, the employer will be liable in damages to the employee concerned. The duty is not, however, absolute: employers are not responsible for all accidents but only for those that they should reasonably have anticipated and prevented by taking appropriate measures. However, an employer's breach of some of the older Health and Safety Legislation (e.g. the duty to fence dangerous machinery under section 14 of the Factories Act 1961) may involve absolute liability in damages. The employers' liability (compulsory insurance) Act 1969 requires employers (other than nationalized industries, the police and local authorities) to take out insurance against this potential liability to pay damage. It is a criminal offence to fail to effect such insurance and to fail to display the certificate of insurance at the place of work.

Employees also have a duty to take reasonable precautions for their own safety and if they should fail to do so, the employer, who has also been in breach of his duties, may offer the defence of contributory negligence. If contributory negligence by the employee is proved, the court will divide the loss suffered between the employee/plaintiff and the employer/defendant in proportion to their respective degrees of negligence.

employment

one of the central problems of macro-economics is the determination of the level of output in the economy and hence the level of employment. The prevailing climate of opinion before the publication of Lor Keynes's The General Theory of Employment, Interest and Money in 1936 was that there would be a tendency towards full employment in an economy because of wage-price flexibility. This was manifestly untrue in the 1930s and Keynes's book changed the approach of economists so that full employment was seen as a possible outcome for the economy, but not the only outcome.

The essence of the Keynesian approach is a blending together of consumption demand and investment demand as determinants of the aggregate level of output, and hence employment. Consumption demand depends mainly upon the level of income, whilst investment demand depends upon profit expectations, the rate of interest and the rate of change of output (Consumption Function; Investment in the Economy). Thus the equilibrium level of output, and hence employment, will occur when the demands upon the economic system balance the supply of goods from the system. This need not occur at the level of output corresponding to full employment.

employment act 1980

this was the first of the main pieces of industrial-relations legislation introduced by the Conservative Government after winning the general election in 1979. It covered trade union ballots, codes of practice, exclusion from trade union membership (Closed Shop), unfair dismissal, maternity rights, action short of dismissal relating to trade union membership, (Picketing, secondary industrial action and coercive recruitment tactics.

Section I empowers the Secretary of State to make, by regulations, a scheme to be administered by the Certification Officer providing for payment towards expenditure incurred by independent trade unions in conducting secret ballots. Section 2 places an obligation on employers with more than twenty workers to comply with a request from a trade union recognized by them to provide a place on their premises where members of the trade union may vote in a secret ballot. Section 3 enables the Secretary of State to issue codes of practice containing practical guidance for promoting the improvement of industrial relations. Such codes are admissable as evidence in industrial-tribunal or court proceedings and may be taken into account by tribunals or courts in determining questions to which they are relevant. They do not, in themselves, render anyone liable to proceedings. Section 4 gives a person who is, or seeks to be, in employment where there is a union membership agreement (a Closed Shop) the right not to be unreasonably excluded or expelled from a trade union. This new right is additional to present common-law rights. Complaints of infringement of the right are heard by industrial tribunals, which are required to consider the matter on its merits and not just on the particular union rules that apply. Section 5 enables a person whose complaint of unreasonable exclusion or expulsion is declared to be well-founded, and who is admitted or re-admitted to membership of the union, to apply to the industrial tribunal for compensation for any loss sustained. Section 6 provides that, in deciding whether or not an employer has carried out a dismissal fairly, an industrial tribunal should take into account the size and administrative resources of the employer. Section 7 enlarges the grounds upon which dismissal for non-membership of a trade union is to be regarded as unfair where there is a union membership agreement (closed shop). The enlarged grounds are:

(i) where the employee genuinely objects to membership of any union or a particular union on grounds of conscience or other deeply held personal conviction. (ii) where the employee has belonged to the class of employee covered by the closed-shop agreement since before it took effect and has not subsequently been a member of a union specified in the agreement. (iii) (in the case of agreements coming into effect after section 7 is brought into operation) where the agreement is not approved in a secret ballot in which at least 80 percent of those covered support it.

Section 11 makes changes to the procedure laid down in the Employment Protection (Consolidation) Act 1978 by which a woman may claim the right to return to work after having a baby. Section 15 provides a general right (qualified where a closed shop operates) for employees not to have action short of dismissal taken against them by their employer to compel them to join a union. Where a closed shop operates, those categories of employees who are protected by section 7 from unfair dismissal for not being a member of a trade union as specified in the closed-shop agreement will also have the right not to have action short of dismissal taken against them by their employer to compel them to belong to a union. Section 16 limits lawful picketing to:

(i) a person picketing at or near his or her own place of work. (ii) a trade union official accompanying a member of that union who is picketing at or near his or her own place of work and whom the official represents.

Section 17 is primarily concerned with other forms of secondary action such as backing sympathetic strikes. It provides that there shall be immunity for the organization of secondary action only where the principal purpose of that action is to interfere with the supply of goods or services during the dispute between the employer in dispute and a first supplier or customer whose employee are taking the action, and where it is reasonably likely to achieve that purpose.

employment interview

it is a dialogue between the employer and the prospective employee for determining the ability of the candidate or suitability of the candidate for the job. Strauss and Sayless observes, "the objective of the interview is to measure the applicant against the specific requirements of the job and to decide whether these will be a good fit".

employment medical advisory service, the (EMAS)

as the operational arm of the Medical Division of the Health and Safety Executive this provides national advice on the medical aspects of employment problems to employers, employee, trade unions, doctors and others. Workers in hazardous occupations are examined medically and surveys are made of employment hazards. Doctors in the EMAS co-operate with school medical officers and careers officers in helping to solve the employment problems of handicapped school-leavers.

employment orientation

a manager is supposed to create increment job opportunities for the weaker sections of the population within the confines of his responsibility. He must endeavour to become increasingly conscious of the potential of his workers and help them to improve their skills through vocational guidance, practical training etc.

employment protection act 1975

the Labout Government of the day introduced a new legal framework for British industrial relations with its repeal of the Industrial Relation Act 1971. The provisions of the Trade Union and Labour Relations Act 1974 and the passage of the Employment Protection Act. The emphasis of legal regulation changed from that of the 1971 Act, but the principle of legal regulation remained. It was accepted that the law could be a force for greater order in industrial relations. The new provisions restricted the use of bargaining power by trade unions much less, and other aspects of industrial relations became more closely regulated than before. N.H.C., amended by M.J.F.P.

employment rate

usually expressed as a percentage of total population, and sometimes as percentage of labour force.

employment test

test of questions or exercises or other means of measuring a person's suitability for a particular job, or for working in a particular occupation or a particular organization.

encumbrance

a claim, charge, or liability on property, such as alien or mortgage, that lowers the property's value.

end of month terms

in the dating of invoices, an agreement indicating that cash discounts and net credit periods begin at the end of the month, the goods were shipped.

Invoices dated on the 25th of the month or later are generally treated as if dated on the first day of the next month.

endorse

in finance, to execute a legal signature on a document authorizing a financial agreement or financial exchange.

endorsee

the person designated in an endorsement as the one to whom the endorser is transferring the right to receive money.

endorsement

the signing of a negotiable instrument, such as a cheque, so that the instrument and the rights it stands for are transferred to another person.

endowment

it is a term used with reference to assurance policies. An endowment assurance is one where the holder of the policy, by paying a certain annual premium, is entitled to a fixed sum at the end of a stated period.

engel's laws

a 19th century theory of spending behaviour developed by Ernst Engel, a German statistician. Engel postulated that as a family's income increases, it spends a smaller percentage of that income on food, about the same percentage of that income on housing and household operations, and a larger percentage of that income on other (less essential) items. This theory was a precursor to Maslow's hierarchy.

enhancement

a condition in which a new product is introduced into the marketplace and which increases the sales rates of one or more other products in the company's line. The opposite of cannibalization.

enterprise

a business undertaking. Unless otherwise qualifies, the entirely of an organization rather than unit or subdivision.

entrepot

a commercial center which receives and redistributes goods and which is free of import duty and/or maintains bonded warehouses. London, Amsterdam, and Rotterdam's Europort are examples of entrepots.

entry

the act of making or entering a formal record by writing it down; for example, to make an entry in an accounting journal.

environment

refers to surrounding conditions of an activity, particularly in marketing, the social and psychological conditions.

environmental opportunity

in a marketing context, a part of the business environment in which there is an unmet need for products or services which a company may exploit.

equal pay

pay is the same for men and women who perform the same or similar work.

equilibrium point

in supply and demand, the point at which the quantity and the price of goods or service that sellers are willing to offer equals the quantity and price that buyers are willing to pay for that good or service. Graphically, the equilibrium point may be represented as the point at which the supply curve and the demand curve intersect. The price of a particular goods or service so determined is known as the equilibrium price.

equilibrium price

the price at which the supply curve for goods and its demand curve intersect.

equitable

fair, reasonable, and evenhanded.

equitable payment

the remuneration which would be generally considered fair (at a particular time and in particular country) for employees with a particular time-span of discretion.

equity

represents the interest of the owner(s) in the business. This is equal to the excess of assets over liabilities, and is designed as capital or more appropriately 'proprietorship'.

equity share

a company share with no restriction either on the amount of dividend or the share of surplus on winding up that may be paid to the holder.

equity theory

a method of explaining employee motivation which assumes that individuals must see a relationship between the amount of work they perform (input) and the rewards they obtain (outcome).

ergonomics

the aspect of technology that is concerned with the application of biological and engineering data to problems related to human beings and the machine. Also known as biotechnology.

errors and omissions excepted (E.& O.E)

these initials are often included at the end of an invoice, retaining the person issuing the invoice from clerical errors.

escalator cards

advertisements, placed alongside underground escalators.

escalator clause

in pricing practice, a clause in an agreement which permits a producer or manufacturer to increase his prices based on a specified formulae such as the cost-of-living index.

escheat

an old legal term giving right to the grant of land or interest in land granted to anyone by retaining the land if the tenant dies leaving no heir.

escrow (escrow agreement)
any arangement in which a bond, deed or other document is adopted by two parties and given to a third for safekeeping to be surrendered only when some condition emerges.

estate duty
it is the tax levied by the state on a deceased person's property. It is a sort of wealth tax. The provisions for assessing the amount payable and the persons who are to pay it are some-what complex. Wealth chargeable to duty includes sums of money or other assets given away prior to death as gift.

estate planning
the making of plans for a person's property for its disposition at his or her death (for example, to a charitable organisation), and for gaining the maximum legal benefit from that property by best using the laws of wills, trusts, insurance, property, and taxes.

estimated liability
the projected costs to be incurred for uncertain, variable obligations such as repairs under warranty.

estimated work
work for which standard times have been set without using work measurement (e.g. they have been based on practical experience or previous production records).

estimating
(i) analytical estimating (in work measurement). A method used to determine basic times for jobs for which it has not been possible to compile sufficient data to obtain a synthetic timing → Work Measurement; Synthetic Timing). It is the most inaccurate and inconsistent work-measurement technique, relying almost entirely on the ability, experience and knowledge of the estimator.

One the job method has been established and agreed, basic times at standard rating are given to each job element. The same principles are used for breaking the job into elements as in direct → Time Study but normally larger elements are used.

The estimator will use available, perhaps incomplete, synthetic data where possible, and working conditions will be considered in arriving at the estimated basic times. Allowances are added to produce standard time.

The method is frequently used in maintenance work and other one-off jobs.

(ii) cost estimating. This is necessary to predict the cost of manufacture of a product or component, in order to establish a sales price prior to manufacture, tendering, etc. Using information from component drawings, material lists, specifications of materials, quality and performance, production quantities and rates, an estimate in sufficient detail is constructed, or is obtained by adjusting estimates or actual costs for previous similar jobs → Costing Systems.

ethical shopper

a customer who feels obligated to patronize small stores or local business to help them stay in business and is willing to sacrifice the potential price and assortment benefits available in larger stores or chains in order to do so.

ethics

a system of behaviours, expectation, and morals comprising standards of conduct for a population or profession.

ethnic market

a group of customers defined by race, country of origin, language, etc.

ethnocentricism

the belief that one's own cultural values are, or should be, the norm. Ethnocentricism is exemplified in the self-reference criteria in which one's values are taken as a reference point for all others.

evaluated data

evaluated data is highly useful for a specific problem and for a certain individual at a certain time to achieve a definite goal. As problems vary from person-to-person or change as time passes, the value of information differs. That is the value of information is not detached and permanent in itself.

evaluation technique

one element in an evaluation design, usually the basic evaluation research approach that is to be used. For example, a two-group before-and-after comparison, or a single group time series.

evaluative criteria

in consumer behavior, those aspects of a product or service which a consumer considers during the process of weighing alternative course of action.

even line pricing

a method of ascribing whole number selling prices to merchandise, to give the impression of high-end retailing. For example, a retailer using even-line pricing would charge $ 100 for an item rather than $ 99.55.

events

non-personal communications such as news conferences, grand openings, etc. designed to communicate particular messages to target audience.

evidence

verifiable information, physical objects, documents, and opinions about an alleged claim, often submitted as part of a claimant's application. Evidence is employed in proving a claim ranging from a claim for health insurance payment to a court trial.

exception rate

a freight rate charged by shippers to their customers.

The exception rate is a deviation from the class rate allowed under special circumstances, though still subject to government regulation. It may be either higher or lower than the class rate and applies to both contract and common carriers. In general, lower exception rates may be charged to encourage competition or otherwise aid the shipping industry. Higher rates are allowed for special services, such as express or overnight deliver.

exception report

in a marketing information system, a report to an executive of some circumstance or occurrence in the system which exceeds predetermined levels. For example, a manager may not be concerned with the level of sales as long as they do not increase or decrease by more than a pre-established percentage. If they exceed these limits he is automatically sent an exception report.

exchange control

action taken by the government of a country to regulate or restrict international settlements by residents of the country.

exchange functions

the buying and selling activities in the marketing process which result in the exchange of title to goods or services. Exchange is regarded as one of the basic marketing functions.

exchange rate

the price of one country's currency expressed in terms of another country's currency or gold. For example, a U.S. dollar is worth a certain number of British pounds sterling, Canadian dollars, French francs, Japanese yen, etc. The exchange rate is not a constant, and fluctuates on a daily basis as currencies are traded in international money markets.

excise duty

a tax charged on goods produced or manufactured on licences; on betting and gaming.

exclusion clauses

clauses in contracts designed to exclude or limit rights that would otherwise accrue to the other party. In the past such clauses have been used to deprive a weaker contracting party of rights such as those implied by the terms of the Sale of Goods Act 1979; provided that such clauses were correctly incorporated into the contract they were very effective. Exclusion clauses are now subject to the Unfair Contract Terms Act 1977. In addition to dealing with the implied terms → Sale of Goods), this Act provides that all notices or contract terms that exclude liability for death or personal injury are void, although no penalty attaches to their continued use. All clauses excluding liability for other loss or damage are subject to the 'reasonableness test'. When business use a standard form contract or enter into a contract with a consumer (i.e. someone dealing other than in the course of business), any attempt to exclude or limit liability for breach of contract or to claim to be entitled to perform the contract substantially differently, or not at all, is also subject to the test.

The requirement of reasonableness is satisfied if the term is a fair and reasonable one to be included, having regard to the circumstances known or contemplated by the parties at the time the contract was made. Such factors as the relative bargaining strength of the parties and the frequency of use of such clauses will be important in determining this question, but it is for the person seeking to rely on the clause to show reasonableness. Relatively few cases establishing the exact scope of the test have been heard.

Exclusion of liability is only regulated if it is liability occasioned during the course of a business, but contracts of insurance and certain other categories of contract are not subject to the Act.

exclusive distribution

a form of distribution in which a product or service is offered for sale to only one distributor or retailer in a particular territory. The manufacturer or producer thus gives the exclusive right to resale to a single organization.

exclusives

merchandise produced for one or a limited number of resellers.

ex dock (named port of importation)

a term of sale indicating that the quoted price includes the cost of the goods and all costs necessary to bring the goods to the named port, Includes duty, if any.

executive

any person whose function is to administer or manage the affairs of a business or other organization. Executives are generally expected to provide leadership by directing motivating, and guiding the work of individual employees and departments and causing others to follow their lead.

executive director

the director of a company who is also a full time employee of the company.

executive order

a rule or regulation issued by a chief administrative authority.

exempt carrier

a form of transportation (rail, highway, river, etc.) which has been granted an exemption from certain regulations by the localities in which it operates when certain specified products are being moved. For example, a barge line may be exempt from all local laws except for those governing safety when it is transporting a commodity like wheat.

exit interview
an interview with an employee who is leaving an organization to find out the person's reason for leaving and his or her perception of the organization.

expected price
the level at which the customer expects a product or service to be priced; i.e., expected price represents what the customer thinks a product or service is worth.

expected value
a concept used in selecting alternative courses of action. The expected value of an alternative is an average of all the conceivable consequences of that alternative with each consequence being assigned a probability percentage. When applied to the marketing of new products, the expected value concept facilities the sorting out of the many probabilities existing in the market place.

expenditure
a relinquishment by a firm of money or some other asset or an incurrence of liability in exchange for a benefit received or to be received.

expense item
any short-lived goods or service which may be charge off as it is used, usually in the year of purchase.

experience curve pricing
a strategy used in pricing manufactured goods in which the selling price is calculated on the basis of projected costs at the time of production rather than on costs prevailing during the planning stages.

experiment
a technique for gathering primary data in which variables are manipulated in such a way that cause and effect relationships become apparent. Experiments provide a basis for small - scale trial runs before the firm totally commits itself to a course of action.

experimental gaming
a method of research which utilizes a simulated environment to observe behaviour.

expiration date
the time established in a contract or by a collective bargaining agreement for the contract or agreement to terminate; for example, the date that an insurance policy terminates.

explicit costs
expenditures such as wages, utilities, supplies, etc., which are clearly stated and readily observable. They appear on the accounting record as costs and are charged against the operation of the business.

export
(1) to send or transport goods to another country or countries especially for the purpose of sales. (2) an export is any item sent to another country or countries.

export broker
an agent middleman involved

in international trade, performing the functions of a broker for domestic firms exporting their goods to foreign markets. The export broker brings buyers and sellers together and essentially provides information to each of them, connecting the needs of the buyers to the available goods of the supplier.

export incentives

these are inducement subsidies given by the state to promote exports. They may be in the form of grants or cash subsides to exporting industries, additional crediting facilities, tax exemptions, duty drawbacks, import licences, etc.

export management company

an independent international marketing middleman which manages a company's export activities in indirect exporting and is paid a set fee.

export sales representative

in direct export, the export sales representative is a domestic-based salesperson sent abroad at intervals to find foreign customers for the producer.

exposure

the degree to which an advertising message is actually perceived by members of the target audience. For an ad. to be exposed it must be more than simply seen—it must be noticed to an extent that there is some measurable impact.

extended product

those tangible and intangible elements which accompany a product or service. Included are warranties, service contracts, supplies, and such intanrgibles as the status and prestige associated with ownership of the product.

extensive market opportunities

opportunities in the market-place for new growth which generally involve a company in activities not previously part of its marketing effort. For example, a company may develop an entirely new product line to appeal to its existing customers.

extensive problem solving

in consumer behaviour, extensive problem solving is the effort taken to understand one's need and how to satisfy them. This is particularly applicable when a need is completely new to the individual consumer.

external communication

communicating with the public outside the corporation is a difficult task. The problem for the public relations manager is to convince the public that the corporation is indeed being responsive. Critic on the outside intend to question a corporation's sincerity.

external recruitment

in external recruitment, the enterprise seeks suitable candidates from outside. The commonly used methods for external recruitment are:

(a) press advertisement.

(b) employment agencies.

(c) campus recruitment.

(d) recommendations.

(e) labour contractors.

(f) notice at factory gate.

(g) casual callers.

external sources of recruitment

external recruitment means the sources through which the personnel management seeks suitable candidates from outside the concern. Selection of the source of recruitment depends on the policy of each individual firm, nature of work, labour supply position, government regulations, etc.

external Vs. internal financial analysis

this method of classification is based on the materials used for the analysis, or on the persons interested in the analysis. External analysis is done by people outside the firm. In the matter of analysis of financial statements, investors, credit agencies, government agencies, shareholders, etc., are outsiders external parties to the firm. An external analyst usually has only the published information to rely upon.

fabricating parts

manufactured components which become part of a larger finished product; e.g., an automobile or coat buttons. Despite the fact that fabricating parts are incorporated into another product, they do not change form.

facilitating marketing function

any activity which assists marketers in the performance of the universal marketing functions. Facilitating marketing functions include standardization, grading, risk taking, financing, and the gathering of market information.

factor analysis

this important and powerful statistical technique provides a method of examining a set of data in order to establish the underlying pattern of organization that brings about certain relations between groups of measurements. An example is provided in the context of intelligence testing. Scores may be obtained on a battery of tests administered to a group of subjects. Inter-correlation coefficients → Correlation and Regression, indicate the degree of association between all pairs of tests in the total battery. Further analysis yields factor loading, i.e. measures of the extent to which the observed degrees of association might due to the existence of a fairly small number of causative factors. This statistical technique has proved invaluable in the testing of hypotheses concerning the nature of human → Personality.

factor endowment

in the international marketing theory called comparative advantage, the advantage rests, at least in part, on factor endowment; i.e., resources such as labour, land, natural resources, capital etc. which provide the advantage in the first place.

factoring

the sale of the accounts receivable of business to a financial institution, e.g., a bank or factor. The buying institution purchases the accounts at a discounted rate but assumes all losses resulting from uncollectable debts. The business profits from this arrangement by having access to ready cash

factory inspector

HM Inspectors of Factories were first appointed in 1833 and now work in the executive of the Health and Safety Commission. Their principal duty is to see that the provisions of the health and safety legislation are carried out. To achieve this, inspectors have wide powers, including the right of entry to examine and investigate industrial premises. They can issue notices to order the improvement of hazardous health and safety conditions within a limited period of time, and to prohibit work where they consider there is imminent danger of serious injury or disease. An appeal against the issue of an Improvement or a Prohibition Notice can be made to an industrial tribunal. Authorized inspectors may also institute a prosecution alleging a specific breach of the law.

Inspectors are supported by groups of specialists whose primary function is to prove rapid technical advice, and who are concerned to help employers adopt the best-known practices for the health, Safety and Welfare of employees.

factory outlet

originally a manufacturer owned store located at the factory site through which unwanted inventory (overruns, closeouts, irregulars, etc.) could be unloaded at greatly reduced prices without offering competition to the manufacturer's retail customers. Now these stores commonly sell in-season first quality merchandise of more than one manufacturer and are often located in factory outlet malls which compete directly with traditional retailers.

factory positioned ware house

a facility in which goods may be stored. The factory-positioned warehouse is located near the place of manufacture and may be used to store raw materials and fabricating parts to be used in production, or to store finished goods waiting to be shipped

fact sheet

an informational document used in media relations and development. A fact sheet provides a concise statement about an organisation or a project.

facsimile

an exact copy; for example, facsimile signatures are mechanically imprinted signatures on checks, stock certificates, and bonds.

fad

a style or product that is accepted quickly by large numbers of consumers but which enjoys short-lived popularity and passes into oblivion in a relatively short time.

faltering demand

that point in the product life cycle when demand for a product or service begins to wane, i.e., when purchasers have less need and/or desire for the product.

family brand

a line of products offered for sale by a single producer all of which carry the company's brand name, logo, or similar identifying design. Also known as family packaging or as a blanket brand.

farm products

raw materials produced by farmers, such as action, hogs, eggs, and milk. These are unprocessed goods that are handled as little as needed to move them to the next step in the production process. They become part of a physical good when they are processed in the form of textiles, frozen or canned foods, etc. This is in contrast to produce, which refers to fresh fruits and vegetables sold at retails.

fashion

those styles (clothing, automobiles, etc.) which are currently most popular are said to be in fashion, i.e., they are widely accepted by consumers at one or more levels of the market. Since styles constantly change in response to consumer demand for the new, it may be said that fashion is, in fact, change—that, fashion is not something so much as it is an ongoing process.

fashion cycle

a theory, similar to the product life cycle, in which styles are seen to appear and rise in popularity, flourish, peak, and finally decline and disappear. The cycle may be seen as having three stage: (1) the introductory or distinctiveness stage (in which some consumers seek and are willing to pay for products different from those accepted by the majority, (i.e., new and innovative fashions); (2) the acceptance or emulation stage (in which a particular style catches on due to the desire of other consumers to imitate the original users; and (3) the regression or economic emulation stage (in which many consumers desire the fashion and manufacturer mass produce the product at low cost. This continues until the market passes through the growth and maturity stages and rapidly moves into sales decline).

fatigue

in ergonomics this is a terms that includes both the subjective feeling of tiredness that worker may report and the objectively observed decrease in his or her level of performance of a task. The issue of finding the most efficient and effective system of work and rest period is of particular importance in matters of safety, e.g., with airline pilots or junior hospital doctors.

Fayol, Henri

(1841-1925) one of the pioneers of management thought and Classical Organization Theory.

Born in France in 1841, Fayol became a mining engineer and eventually managing director of a metallurgical and coal combine. From his experience as a chief executive, he developed a framework for a unifying doctrine of administration, which he believed would hold good for business, public service and wherever the art of management had to be exercised. He believed there were basic principles of management that could and should be taught. In attempting to set up efficient business procedures, Fayol produced a theoretical model that appears mechanistic, but he noted that personal qualities could be of enormous significance and seems to have been aware of an informal structure existing alongside the formal ones– Formal Organization. He compared the Organization to the animal, using the expression corps social (or body corporate) to mean all those engaged in any given corporate activity. This mode of thinking in biological terms continues and forms one of the sources of the modern study of Cybernetics.

Fayol declared that in conducting an undertaking towards an objective, technical activities needed to be supplemented by managerial activity, and to manage is to forecast and plan, to organize, to command, to co-ordinate and to control'. Here he clearly influenced Lyndall F. Urwick in Britain.

Gouvernerc'est prevoir (to govern is to foresee): in giving prominence to foresight as the first characteristic of sound administration, Fayol laid stress on the judgement and intelligent anticipation that are prerequisite to the success of the whole management process. Observing that long-term planning and development studies were often neglected by the busy executive, Fayol proposed a staff of specialized assistants to senior management.

Fayol's central theme in his discussion of organization is the hierarchie. This was translated into English as 'scalar chain', an expression that has taken root in management writings. To indicate that a formal plan could and should be constructed, Fayol emphasized his concept of the organization chart, suggesting that each position on the chart be accompanied by a job description→ Job Analysis. And that lists be prepared showing the value of each employee. Here lay the foundation for his scheme of Management Development. Fayol indicated that each superior should normally have a 'span of control' comprising no more than four or five immediate subordinates, a concept that has sometimes been attributed to his compatriot, Graicunas.

Managers, he alleged, should develop initiative by allowing subordinates 'the maximum share of activity consistent with their position and capability, even at the cost of some mistakes... Freedom to use initiative was a source of job satisfaction. General control could be maintained by a periodic management audit. In dealing with subordinates Fayol emphasized the need to be fair and equitable. Union agreement must be clear and as fair as possible. He deprecated national bargaining and frequent state intervention in industrial relations and favoured plant agreement. Collective Bargaining.

Preparation was necessary for those posts requiring managerial ability. Specialized expertise in engineering or accounting was inadequate preparation and might even be a hindrance. Though there was a dearth of management theory, managerial ability could be developed in the same way as technical ability, first in educational institutions, later in the workshop or other appropriate place.

Fayol's work in France, a country with a long tradition of administration, was complementary to that of Taylor in the USA, where the notion of 'coming up the hard way' has always been revered. Taylor worked primarily on the operative level, from the bottom of the hierarchy upwards, while Fayol concentrated on the senior manager and worked downwards. While Fayol was less clear than Max Weber, his principles of management are akin to the characteristics of the formal organization, or Bureaucracy, laid down by the latter, although it is extremely unlikely that Weber's work was known to him.

federation

the banding together of organizations to form a unit for some common object while remaining independent in internal affairs.

Federated groupings are typical of employers and of trade unions in Britain. Employers' federations may be associations of employers in an industry formed either to manage collective bargaining with trade unions or to deal with trade matters on behalf of members. Alternatively, they may be multi-functional. Employers' Associations. The major federation formed to represent British employers as a whole is the-Confederation of British Industry. Among trade unions, federations are one device for achieving inter-union decision-making; others include the Bridlington Rules–Trade Union-Jurisdiction, agreements on 'closer working', and amalgamation–Trade Union-Structure).

The Webbs, in Industrial Democracy, envisaged the development of a complex of trade union federations within each of which it would be difficult to decide where sovereignty lay. In practice the retention of sovereignty by member unions of a federation has been marked, with few exceptions. Normally there are difficulties in communication with affiliated membership, particularly when joint negotiations run into difficulties. There are other difficulties in connection with policy-formulation, finance and administration. The largest union federation is the Confederation of Shipbuilding and Engineering Unions; other important federations exist in carpets and textiles, the Civil Service, entertainment and broadcasting, furnitute, insurance and banking, metal manufacture, the Post Office and sea transport.

Particularly when the collective-bargaining unit is an industrial one, trade unions pursue varying degrees of co-ordinated action in their external relations and the borderline between regular meetings of union representatives who sit together on national negotiating bodies and more formal federations is an uncertain one. A very large number of Joint Industrial Council have multiple union representation. The federal principle has also been at work on the internal structure of unions where the basis for arriving at amalgamation has involved a degree of internal autonomy and continued identity to the original unions, or where the union is so large that separate 'trade groups' are established, as in the Transport and General Workers' Union.

The major federal organization representing British trade unions is the Trades Union Congress, but there is a small body of a somewhat similar kind, the General Federation of Trade Unions, formed in 1899 because of dissatisfaction with

TUC policy. The original intention was to create an organization that would draw all unions together for joint industrial action and to build up a central strike fund. Its originators wanted the General Federation to have authority lacking in the TUC. In the event only a number of smaller unions joined the body, which retains its support from those that feel lost among the big battalions. There are a number of international federations of trade unions, each of which has come together to exchange information and ideas on common problems within an industry. Some of these are developing policies for dealing with the multinational company.

feedback

a term borrowed from cubernetics where it refers to the direct relationship of the input of a system to its output. The concept of a return flow of output information which can be used to regulate future input is now widely used in programmed learning and the development of teaching machines.

feedback theory

decision points are founded on a theory of discrimination, e.g., short or long term, recurring or irreversible, technical or human, financial or non financial, etc. Similarly control points are grounded in feedback theory, e.g., controllable vs. non-controllable, variances, responsibility centres, etc.

fellow

an individual in a senior class of membership of a professional institute.

fertility rate

the birth rate expressed as the number of children per woman.

fibreboard

two or more sheets of paperboard pasted together to form a stronger, thicker material. Usually a combination of kraft and chipboard.

fidelity guarantee

one person may guarantee the integrity or fidelity of another, e.g., in a contract of employment. Since insurance companies may offer fidelity policies agreeing to make good misappropriations if any incurred by employees.

fidelity policy

a contract of guarantee insurance under which the insurer indemnifies the assured against losses caused by dishonesty of one or more of the assured's employees.

fiduciary

a steward of funds who assures their payment for the purposes intended; a paying agent who acts under given rules and procedures on behalf of the funding source; relating to or founded upon a trust or confidence.

field research

an important part of market

research. It involves the collections of data about products or advertising from actual or potential customers, usually by means of interview or questionnaire. The opposite of desk research.

field salesman

one who works away from base.

field sales manager

executive responsible for organization, direction, control motivation and training of the field selling force in whole or in part.

field warehouser

a specialized public warehouse organization which provides cash for goods on hand. The field warehouser holds some of a manufacturer's finished goods as its own property. In exchange, it issues warehouse receipts to the manufacturer. The warehouse receipts may be used as collateral to borrow money.

fighting brand

an individual brand used to meet the competition while the company's other, higher quality, better known, and more expensive brand is protected.

filler

pre-pared advertisement by publisher used to fill the gap left in a page after make-up.

filter question

or strip question. Market research term for a question which an interviewer only puts to an informant if it is made relevant by the answer given to the previous question.

final approval

after a candidate has been selected, he is formally appointed by issuing him an appointment letter or by making a service agreement with him Generally, the candidates are appointed on probation of one or two years. No selection procedure is foolproof and the best way to judge a person is by observing him working on the job. Candidates who give satisfactory performance during the probationary period are made permanent.

final dividend

the final payment of dividend paid by a company in respect of its profits for a financial year.

final goods

the finished articles which are the end products of production.

finance

the management of public revenues; the conduct or transaction of money matters generally and particularly those affecting the public as in the field of banking and investment.

finance ministry

ministry of finance is charged with the responsibilities of raising the resources for the overall expenditure of the Government of India. Thus, it is an agency which exists more for other Ministries and Departments than for itself. It has to see to the desirability of the demands of other departments, taking into consideration interest of the tax-payers.

finance ministry and public enterprises

finance ministry has a great control over the public enterprises. In the first place, it is represented on the Board of Directors of all the corporations and companies. Secondly, for certain Corporations, it also sends a Financial Adviser, for example, DVC, whose approval is necessary on all financial transactions. If the managing director differs from the financial adviser, then the matter has to be referred to the finance ministry and very often the finance ministry goes by the advice of its own officer rather than that of the director.

financial accounting-limitation of

(i) it fails to provide the required information. Most of the business expenditures incurred today may bring benefits to the business only in future period. Or, the expenditure may be incurred simply to sell the name of the business without any expectation of immediate return. (ii) financial accounting has always been concerned with figures, treating them as single, simple and silent items without any appreciation of the fact that they represent a chair of purposeful and pertinent events. (iii) it fails to meet the information needs of different levels of management. The company form of organisation has brought into existence different levels of management—top management, middle level management, and lower level management. The information needs of these different levels of management vary widely with regard to subject-matter and amount of detail. (iv) it provides only historical information. (v) it considers only quantifiable information. (vi) it provides only elementary information in consolidated form.

financial analysis

a general term referring to the process of extracting and studying information in financial statements for use in management decision-making. For example, financial analysis typically involves the use of ratios, comparisons with prior periods and with the budget, and other such procedures.

financial gearing

the use of debt capital by a firm. When a company has a debt capital, any change in its net profit (measured without deducting payments of interest on debt capital, payment of corporate income tax and payments of preference dividends) is magnified (or 'geard') and produces a larger change in the EPS of the company.

financial leverage

the ratio of a person's or organisation's total debts to

total assets. Other measures of financial leverage (such as those comparing cash inflows to committed cash outflows) are used for particular purposes or because of individual preference.

financial management

financial management is concerned with the proper management of funds. It involves managerial decisions that result in the procurement and utilizations of long term and short term finances. It deals with planning, organising, directing and controlling the financial activities of an enterprise. The scope of financial management is very wide. It is not restricted to raising of capital funds because it also covers other aspects of financing. Financial management covers the following areas of decision-making.

financial planning. A careful estimate has to be made of the total funds required in the business. While estimating the funds needed in the enterprise, both fixed capital and working capital requirements should be considered. Financial needs of business are determined, keeping in view the sales and production budgets of the enterprise.

Financing Decision. Once the amount of funds required is estimated, the sources of funds are identified. The cost and risk involved in each source are analysed and the most appropriate source of funds is selected. The amounts of funds to be collected from each source are determined. This is the problem of capital structure. A proper balance should be maintained between fixed and non fixed cost bearing securities.

Investment Decision. This implies the allocation of available funds among fixed and current assets. Investment in fixed assets is called capital budgeting. Every proposal for investment is analysed in view of the cost and expected profits. Investment in current assets is known as working capital. It depends upon the inventory and credit policies of the enterprise.

Dividend Decision. It involves the distribution of net profit in the form of dividends. The total amount of net profits is allocated into two categories—(i) dividends, and (ii) retained earnings. Retained earnings are reinvested in business.

Thus, financial management is an integral part of overall management. In addition to raising of funds, it involves decisions regarding the acquisition and distribution of assets, proper utilization of funds, distribution of surplus, etc.

financial planning

financial planning is an important part of the overall planning of any business enterprise. It is concerned with the determination of the financial objectives, financial policies and financial procedures of an organisation. Financial planning lays down guidelines for the procurement, administration and disbursement of funds. It is needed in all types of organizations. The objective of financial planning is to minimise the cost of funds without sacrificing safety of the enterprise. Sound financial planning helps eliminate idle funds as well as shortage of funds.

The scope of financial planning is very wide. It consists of the following functions:

(a) determining the amount of capital required.

(b) designing the capital structure, i.e., the proportion between different types of securities.

(c) formulating financial policies concerning borrowing, leading, cash control and other areas of financial management.

a sound financial plan must contain the following features:

Simplicity: The financial plan should create a simple financial structure so that it is easy to manage. It is not always necessary to issue all types of securities in the beginning.

Foresight: All fianancial requirements should be forecasted systematically. The financial plan should maintain the desired level of liquidity in the enterprise.

Economy: The cost of raising funds should be minimum. Proper ratio between debt (borrowed funds) and equity (ownership funds) should be maintained.

Flexibility: The financial plan should be adjustable. A rigid plan reduces the scope for financial adjustments and initiative. Only a dynamic financial plan can enable the enterprises to finance its expansion programmes easily.

Optimum use of funds: There should be no idle funds in the enterprise. A proper balance must be maintained, between fixed capital and working capital.

Provision for contingencies: A sound financial plan should make adequate provision for contingencies which may occur in future.

financial ratios

the series of ratios used to measure a company's productivity, solvency, liquidity, and other items on the company's balance sheet. The ratios indicate trends in these financial areas and provide a means of comparing companies within an industry. The financial ratios are grouped into two types: (1) those that summarize an aspect of the business operation for a period of time (generally one year) and (2) those that summarize an aspect of the company's financial position of a given moment in time.

financial report

fortnightly confidential new letter containing comment and analysis on world wide financial matters.

financial statement

as balance sheet.

financial statement analysis

it is a study of relationship among the various financial factors in a business as disclosed by a single set of statements, and a study of the trend of these factors as shown in a series of statements. By establishing a strategic relationship between the items of a balance sheet and income statement and other operative data, the financial analysis (as it is simply called) unveils the meaning and significance of such items.

financial statements

financial statements are summarized periodical reports of financial and operative data accumulated by the firm in its books of Accounts the general ledger. The individual business transactions are recorded in the books of original entry. The impact of these transactions on the financial position and progress of the enterprise is recorded and presented by the financial statement. By nature therefore they are the end products of financial accounting. They are overall general purpose entity statements. They are periodical statements and the period for which they relate is known as Accounting period, usually of one year duration. As a matter of fact business are living and continuing organisms. The accounting period clocks the stream of business events somewhat arbitrarily into small periods.

financial year

the twelve months chosen by an organization as its accounting period.

financing function

a facilitating marketing function by which funding is provided to manufacture, transport, sell, buy, and store products.

financing of business

financing of business involves activities which are connected with the procurement and the utilisation of funds. It is the process of estimating the financial requirements of a business and raising and using those funds for the business. It deals with the arrangement of adequate amount of capital to achieve the objective of the enterprise. It is concerned with estimation of financial requirements, relative proportion of different sources of funds, investment decisions and business policies regarding dividends, granting of credit and collection of receivables, etc. It ensures profitability, solvency, liquidity and stability to the business. Finance is the activity concerned with the planning, raising, controlling and administering of the funds used in business'—Gruthman and Daougall. It consists of the raising, providing and managing of all the money, capital or funds of any kind to be used in connection with the business.

'Business finance is that business activity which is concerned with the acquisition and conservation of capital funds in meeting the financing needs and overall objectives of business enterprise.'—Wheeler. In a modern money using economy, finance may be defined as the provision of money at the time it is wanted.

finder

a person, acting as an individual or as an enterprise, who brings together a buyer and a seller and earns a fee for the service.

fine control sensitivity

type of psychomotor skill. An individual's ability to make delicately controlled muscular adjustments, particularly where larger muscle groups are involved.

fink

a derogatory word, used as either a noun or a verb, to describe a member of a labour who reports to his employer on the activities of the union and his fellow employees. It was the practice to expel from the union any person behaving in such a way as to be identified as a fink.

firm quotation

quoted price and/or conditions which will remain unchanged, subject to previously defined criteria.

first in system, first served

a rule used in decision-making for production scheduling that is based on the due dates for orders waiting in line. The order that has the earliest planned due date will be assigned first.

first line

a term used, particularly of supervisory or maintenance management personnel, to describe those who are directly connected with the responsibility for keeping production running on the shop floor.

first line supervisor

the supervisor responsible for the management of production workers on the shop floor. The term refers to anyone at the level above chargehand and is most often synonymous with the term foreman.

fiscal

of, or relating to, taxation or government expenditure.

fiscal management

administration of the financial affairs of a care organisation or professional practice, including planning, conducting financial operations, exercising controls, and reporting. Activities within fiscal management include resources planning and development, budgeting, accounting, purchasing, billing investing, and collecting.

fiscal policy
the fiscal policy of a government is the name given to the taxation and expenditure policies by which it seeks to influence the working of the economy. Such a policy can obviously affect all the main components of expenditure and income in the country–□ National Income Accounts). The objectives of fiscal policy may be many. Initially fiscal policy was largely determined by the Government's budget, the aim begin to ensure that sufficient income was raised to meet expenditure in the same financial year. However, in the modern economy there are additional objectives such as the desire to preserve a balance between demand and utilization of resources, the desire for a reasonable rate of growth and the desire to improve the balance of payments. Fiscal policy can play a part in the realization of all these objectives. → Forecasting for the Economy, Short-term; Growth in the Economy (Determinants). The main sectors of the economy are the personal sector, business sector, government sector and foreign sector → National Income Accounts). Dealing firstly with the personal sector, the various fiscal measures available are changes in income-tax rates and allowances, changes in value added tax and customs-and-excise duties, and lastly, changes in social-security contributions and payments. In the UK value added tax can be varied by up to 25 percent of its existing level between budgets and custom-and-excise duties by up to 10 percent. In both cases this is subject to parliamentary approval.

The business sector of the economy is affected by investment incentives and also changes in corporation tax and allowances. With regard to investment incentives, country-wide taxation allowances are available on capital expenditure, and in the Development Areas this is supplemented by cash grants of 15 percent on new plant and buildings.

If fiscal policy is the responsibility of the Government, what can the Government do about its own income and expenditure plans? The key areas on the income side have already been mentioned, but on the expenditure side we find that capital-investment programmes are often an item to be considered. In the past a cut in the investment programmes of the nationalized industries was a favourite way of controlling the economy, but in recent years the emphasis has moved towards the control of government expenditure in such areas as health, education and housing. This is to help the Government's avowed aim of lowering the proportion of public expenditure to gross domestic product.

The foreign sector of the economy is affected directly by changes in tariffs, taxes and subsidies and also, indirectly, by many of the measures that have been mentioned previously. For example, as fiscal policy dampens down the growth of the home economy, so the growth of imports may slow down and exports rise.

In recent years much greater stress has also been placed upon the monetary implications of government expenditures and revenues. In particular a serious attempt has been made to lower the public sector borrowing requirement (PSBR), both in absolute terms and as a percentage of the gross domestic product. The PSBR is the amount by which the revenue of public sector organizations (central and local government and nationalized industries) falls short of expenditure. This must be financed by sales of government stock to the non-bank private sector, increases in currency, borrowing from overseas or bank lending to the public sector. The effects of such financing are likely to be inflationary if new currency comes into circulation, and increased sales of government stocks may drive up interest rates, causing difficulties for company investment. It has been argued by some economists that the size of the PSBR may drain resources, both financial and physical, from the private sector.

In the 1985 Budget the following projections were produced for the PSBR: 1984/5 estimate, £10-5 billion (3.25 percent of GDP); 1985/6 forecast, £7 billion (2 percent of GDP0) – Forecasting for the Economy, Short-term; Monetary Policy.

fiscal year

a financial year. A fiscal year consists of twelve consecutive months which may start and end at any time during the calendar year.

fixed assets

those business assets which are purchased for continued use in manufacture (e.g., land, machine, etc.). They are written off against profits over their anticipated life by charging an annual amount calculated to eliminate the original cost over that period.

fixed costs

in the manufacturing process costs are incurred out only in the provision of the necessary labour and basic materials but also in a wide range of services and ancillary expenses, e.g., rent, rates, depreciation of machinery, interest on borrowed capital.

fixing responsibility

if we are programming a company normal operation the

existing organization structure will already have determined who is to perform each activity. But if the programme covers an unusual event merging with another company for instance, we should give careful attention to deciding who is accountable for each step. These special assignments may create a temporary set of authorizations and obligations.

fixed sum per unit approach

a method of computing a promotional budget by allocating a fixed amount of money for each unit produced or sold.

flanker product

a new product related to an already established companion product and bearing the same brand name. For example, a new hair conditioner bearing the same name as an established shampoo would be an appropriate flanker product, as would a shaving cream with the same name as an established brand of razors. The introduction of flanker products may be used to help boost the sales of the mature product.

flat benefit plan

a pension plan whose benefits are unrelated to the beneficiary's earnings. Such a plan might provide a stipulated amount of money per month per year of the beneficiary's service.

flea market

a market, held either outdoors or indoors, where numerous merchants at separate stalls sell old or used household antiques and curios. Prices are usually subject to bargaining.

flexible budgeting

in financial planning and accounting, adjusting fixed and variable cost to match the level of operations.

flexible manufacturing system

an arrangement of computer controlled machine tools and transport and handing systems which operates as an integrated system under the supervisory control of a larger computer.

flexible pricing

a variable pricing policy which allows for bargaining between buyer and seller as well as for the adjustment of prices to conform to peaks and slumps in the normal business cycle. Flexible prices are commonly found in the industrial market but occur at the retail level in the used car, appliance markets, etc.

flexible spending account (FSA)

an employee benefit in the form of an account with a maximum amount set aside by the employer for medical, legal and other services that the employee and (sometimes) his or her dependents may need.

flexible working time (ewt)

synonymous with flexible working hours.

flexi-time

a flexible work schedule in which workers can, within a prescribed band of time in the morning and afternoon, start and finish their workday at their own discretion as long as they complete the total number of hours required for a given work period, usually a month.

floating capital

financial resources that are readily available for meeting current expenditures.

floating currency

a currency is said to float when it is allowed to find its own level in relation to other world currencies.

floating labour

part of the national or regional workforce (usually unskilled) which has no stable employment but which moves around both in terms of job category and geographical location on a short-term basis.

floating policy

a supplemental insurance policy that covers items that frequently move (change location) or vary in quantity.

floor trader

also, competitive trader; registered trader. A member of a stock exchange who trades for his or her own account rather than for customers.

floorwalker

store security officer, usually mixing with customers and attempting to spot shoplifters.

floppy

a small, inexpensive flexible plastic disk for the storage of and random access to computer data. It is used most frequently in microcomputers and minicomputers.

flow

the term 'flow' refers to change or transfer, and therefore, the flow of funds means transfer of economic values from one asset to another, from one liability to another, from one asset to a liability or vice versa, or a combination of these.

flow chart

a graphic representation of an analysis of or solution to a problem that uses symbols to indicate various operations, equipment, and data flow.

flow of information

whether oral or written communication consists of flow of information that people need and want if they are to get the job done right through team work. It is for the manager supervisor of employee to make himself understood and to find out what other person means. To do it effectively it is necessary to know efficient ways of communicating as well as the difficulties in getting his ideas clearly.

flow process chart

it is a graphic presentation of the sequence of all operations occurring during a process or procedure to indicate the time required and distance moved in the process. A flow process chart is also known as work simplification chart because it helps in simplifying office systems and routines. This chart makes use of the following standardized symbols to depict the flow of work under a specific system or routine.

flow production (continuous production)

continuous production in which raw materials are fed in at one end of the process and finished products emerge at the other having passed through in an uninterrupted flow through the process.

fluctuating demand

in industrial marketing, the volatile demand for industrial goods and services, particularly for new plants, and equipment. This demand is generally regarded as less stable than the demand for consumer goods and service.

flyback timing

a method of timing a job using a stopwatch in time study in which the hands of the stopwatch are returned to zero at the end of each element of the job. (Also called 'snapback timing').

flying pickets

groups of individuals which can at short notice be sent to any location to picket a place a work. Normally used to reinforce local picket so as to bring more pressure to bear on the management.

fob (free on board) factory

a shipping agreement in which the seller of goods places them on a carrier at the factory site at no charge to the buyer (thus "free on board"). The buyer assumes title to the goods as soon as they are board the carrier and pays the freight from the factory to destination.

focused interview

somewhat misleading term, used particularly in market research, for an interview in which the interviewer seeks to obtain answers to particular questions without specifically asking them.

follow up

sales contact, telephone call or letter sometimes but not always as a result of an expression of interest by a prospect and usually after his/her receipt of an initial promotional piece, e.g., a direct mail shot.

fonts

boxes which rest on bars and from which cans and bottles of beer are dispened.

food broker

a manufacturer's agent who specializes in the distribution of grocery items. Food brokers call on grocery wholesalers and large retailers on behalf of their clients and are directly involved in marketing strategy, planning and promotion of the goods they carry.

food stamp program

a program of public assistance to low-income families, which through state and local welfare agencies provides food coupons for needy persons.

force closure

collection of a debt (usually a mortgage) by seizing and selling the debtor's property or security.

forecasting

predicting future business conditions and the state of the economy on the basis of various statistics describing past and current conditions, particularly those selected as indicators.

forecasting for the economy, short-term

since the Second World War the British Government, in common with many other, has accepted considerable responsibility for the running and performance of the economy. This stems from a desire to avoid the waste of resources and potential output and the misery of the 1930s. This responsibility means that the modern Government must ascertain the direction in which the economy is moving and taken appropriate action if it appears that difficulties might arise. Thus it is necessary for the Government to know if demand is likely to outstrip production overall or in certain sectors, for appropriate action can then be taken before price rises begin or wage demands are made. Similarly corrective action can be taken if it appears that resources will be under-utilized. The purpose of short-term forecasting procedures is to ensure that this knowledge is available so that corrective action may be introduced through fiscal or monetary measures.

Forecasting exercises have been carried out in Whitehall for the last forty-five years and present practice in the Treasury is to use both formal methods (including econometric models) and informal ones (including business surveys and institution). Since the passing of the 1975 Industry Act, these forecasts must be published at least twice a year; they are now published with each Budget and again later in the year. The forecasts extend about fifteen months ahead and contain, in addition to the table of constant price GDP and its components, forecasts of retail prices, public-sector borrowing and the balance of payments on current account, all assuming a continuation of existing policies. Formal methods involve the use of the Treasury model, which consists of some 700 economic relationship determining the main economic variable, many of which interact with each other. However, this does not preclude the use of judgement where formal and informal methods differ.

Forecasting of categories of aggregate demand, such as consumers' expenditure and public expenditure (both current and capital), can be either functional or autonomous. For example, consumers' expenditure is functionally derived from a knowledge of its previous relationship with personal disposable income and other variables, whilst public expenditure is autonomous, because it is deduced from the plan and programmes laid down by the government. The various approaches for the other categories of aggregate demand are as follows. Exports are closely dependent upon world production and relative prices. Fixed investment by business is derived from anticipations data, interest rates and modified accelerator relationships→ Investment in the Economy. House-building data is obtained from data on housing starts and permits or licences, the average time taken to build and Building Society advances. Investment in stocks, in principle, is determined by the concept of a normal relationship between stocks and total sales. If each of these categories is forecast for the next period (be it a quarter or year), then we will almost have total final demand. However, since consumers' expenditure is closely related to personal disposable income (Consumption Function), this cannot be known until total demand is known.

One way of proceedings at this point is to take a plausible figure for consumption, thus obtaining total final demand, and then deduct the forecasts for imports and indirect taxes to give a forecast for gross domestic product (National Income Accounts). From this we must now work out the implications of the future level of GDP for employment, given the general expectations about labour productivity. When this is combined with a forecast of average earnings, transfers, salaries and dividends and taxation, we have arrived at our required figure of personal disposable income, which will yield a figure for consumers' expenditure. If this fails to agree with our initial plausible assumption, then the process is repeated until consistency is achieved.

Besides publishing the forecasts, the Treasury is required by the Industry Act to analyses from time to time the errors in the forecasts. The reference article below contains a report of an analysis of the early forecasts. The general conclusion is that errors increase the further ahead the forecast looks, and that whilst there is no clear evidence of bias, there is some tendency to overstate the growth of exports, understate the growth in consumers' expenditure and, when forecasting twelve months or more ahead, to underestimate the rise in prices. Fiscal Policy; Monetary Policy.

foreign based export agent in direct export, a foreign

company which sells the goods on behalf of the exporting company. The agent may have either exclusive or general rights to represent the exporter in that country.

foreign corporation

a corporation organised and chartered in a state or a country different from that in which its status or performance is being considered.

foreigners

private work undertaken by artisans for the customers of their employers with or without the employer's approval or knowledge.

foreign trade

trade with foreign countries. It implies buying and selling of goods between one country and the other countries beyond its national borders. Mutual advantage is the basis of all internal trade. Theory of comparative costs gives rise to trade between different countries. Every country tries to produce those goods which it can produce at a cost which is not higher than that at which it can obtain them from other countries. It will obtain all these goods from other countries which it cannot profitably produce at home, and will give in exchange those things in which it has got an advantage over other countries. It is always carried on wholesale basis.

foreign trade zone (FTZ)

a city (frequently a seaport) designated by a country which may receive foreign goods to store and further process them without the importer paying import duties unless the goods actually enter the country. Foreign trade zones facilitate international trade in that exporters can ship from the zone where large quantities of goods are stored to other countries without being involved in the country's trade restrictions—the zone is, infact, an enclave free of these regulations. Also known as a free trade zone or free port.

foreman

in manufacturing, construction, and similar industries, a person in direct charge of production workers, generally considered a member of middle management.

foreshift

the morning shift in a three-shift system.

forefeitures

funds relinquished by a terminating employee in a qualified profit-sharing or thrift plan.

formal agreement

express undertaking between the various business unit concerning trade conditions or prices, insofar as they do not mean any collective control of the quantity of output to be marketed.

formal channels of communication

the existence of formal

channels help to a considerable extent the free flow of information. In the absence of formal channels rumour is likely to predominate. It is common experience that rumours contain distortion, misrepresentation and exaggeration of fact. Quite often rumours are floated out of fear, anger and jealousy. It is essential to size down rumours to facts. An additional barrier to free flow of information is lack of time and pressure of work.

formal group

a group set up by the management of an organization with written mandate and a well-defined purpose. Usually compared with an informal group.

formal organisation

it refers to the structure of jobs and position with clearly defined functions and relationship. In formal organizations, every subordinate must obey his superior, whether he likes it or not. As such everybody becomes responsible for the performance of a given task.

forms of departmentalisation

three major forms of departmentalisation are the functional form, the divisional form, and the matrix structure. In the functional form the governing principle is that all personnel that can contribute to the accomplishment of a specific function are located together. Thus, in a manufacturing corporation that is functionally departmentalised, all personnel concerned with the marketing function—such as sales and media persons, marketing and sales managers, market researchers, etc.—are grouped together.

forms of public enterprises by management

(a) departmental corporations.

(b) public corporations.

(c) joint stock companies.

(d) joint sector undertakings.

(f) the contract system.

formula pension

the category of pension covering most salaried employees, under which a rate formula is applied to individual earnings to calculate the employee's pension.

formula pricing

a pricing strategy in which final price is established through the use of a formula e.g., price may be set at three times cost without consideration of any other variables or with competitive conditions in the marketplace.

form utility

the usefulness (or consumer satisfaction) derived from the physical transformation that raw materials undergo in processing or manufacture. Form utility may be regarded as the economic utility derived from the actual physical product.

fortran (formula translation)

a system of words and symbols used in science and technology to instruct a computer in its task of information processing.

forward integration

a marketing system in which a producer or manufacturer owns or controls the distribution channels (up to, and sometimes including, trail outlets) through which his product passes on its way to the ultimate consumer.

forward market segmentation

a means of identifying segments of a population using such attributes as race, nationality, age, education, psychological traits, life-style characteristics, etc. The underlying assumption is that groups, or market segments, which share certain attributes will react homogeneously to marketing efforts.

foul weather pricing

a pricing strategy in which a company charges so little for its product that it is sold at no profit or, in extreme cases, production costs are not even met. This strategy is employed on the short-term in an effort to keep a company in business during times off economic crisis.

foundation

a non-profit organization set up for charitable or other benevolent purposes, such as supporting scientific research, artistic endeavour, educational institutions, etc.

fractionation

charging separately for several services or components of a service that were previously subject to a single charge or not billed at all. The usual effect is to increase the total charge.

fragmentation

more sophisticated market segmentation when segments are sub-segmented in a highly competitive market and news source of sales are sought.

franchising

manufacturer's products, or to operate a service in which the manufacturer has a monopoly of equipment or supplies, e.g., washing machines and launderettes.

franco domicile

price including free delivery to customer's address.

freedom of association

right of workers to organize themselves in a trade union or similar representative body.

free enterprise

production of goods and provision of services by private individuals and corporations owned by private individuals for profits in which individual producers act according to own judgement and not under the direction or influence of government; thus the government provides no subsidies or price controls.

free good

a good which, at a given time and place is either in such abundance that anyone can obtain it without cost (e.g., air) or is incapable of being sold (e.g., sunshine).

free interview

Harry Henry's name for depth interview.

free market

the term may be used in relation to the purchase and sale of any commodity where there is complete freedom to deal.

free trade

unrestricted international trade either with no customs duties or with customs duties that are used only to create revenue and not to exclude imports.

free trade area

a group of trading countries, normally inspired by geographical proximity, sometimes join to create an area of free trade by scrapping tariff barriers between themselves. By doing this they hope, through the pooling of knowledge and the growth in mutual understanding to increase not only mutual trade but also the internal efficiency and economic expansion of each individual country.

free trade association

an association of countries that agrees to reduce or eliminate the trade barriers which exist between them.

freight

the money paid by a character to a ship-owner in consideration of the latter letting the space within the ship. The fee charged for carrying goods.

freight absorption

the practice of a seller's paying part or all of the freight charges for goods sold.

freight forwarder

a transportation intermediary who consolidates the small shipment of a number of manufacturers into carload or truckload lots to take advantage of the lower rates offered by common carriers.

freight prepaid

this expression means the seller will pay transportation charges to the carrier and the buyer will remit the full amount of the invoice without deduction for freight charges.

frequency-distribution

the concept of frequency-distribution curves is fundamental to statistics. The shape of such curves, that is, the pattern of variability they display, can vary widely, but some distributions occur very often. Three commonly occurring distribution are:

(i) normal distribution. Many present day goods are manufactured by mass-production methods on machines that repetitively produce almost identical items. However, owing to uncontrollable variations in the quality of the processed materials and the settings of the processing machines, no two units are exactly identical. Thus, if we operate a manufacturing process that produces one-inch-diameter ball bearings, we cannot expect every bearing to have a diameter of exactly one inch. Rather, we can expect to produce quantities of the bearings with a mean (Measures of Location) diameter of one inch, but although some individual bearings will have one-inch diameters, others will have diameters slightly below or above this value. If we plot a histogram (with sufficiently small class intervals) of the diameters of the bearing, we shall generate a distribution curve of diameters with mean values of one inch and the variation about this mean. Such a curve would be a normal distribution.

Hence a normal distribution curve is produced when we plot measures that are subject to variation, for a variety of causes, about some mean value. Another example is the distribution curve for the heights of Cup Final spectators since men's heights are determined by numerous factors in their heredity and environment.

(ii) binomial distribution. Suppose that instead of manufacturing ball bearings we are making transistors. Our manufacturing process is a very inefficient one and each transistor has a 30 percent chance of being defective and therefore a 'reject'. Suppose that the transistors are made in batches of ten, so that one average three in each transistors are made in batches of ten, so that on average three in each batch are rejects. However, just as the diameters of ball bearings discussed above varied about an average diameter of one inch, similarly the number of rejects in successive batches of transistors will vary about an average of three. This follows because each transistor has a 30 percent change of being defective, so, purely by chance, some batches will contain anything from none to ten rejects. Using the laws of probability, we can calculate the probability of obtaining 0,0,2, etc. rejects in a batch.

fringe benefit

a reward beyond the basic pay for the job. Example can range from subsidized meals and travel to pensions, holidays and sickness benefits.

fringe market

that segment of a firm's customers who are outside the firm's core market: i.e., who patronize the firm on an occasional basis.

frustration

in human behaviour, the blocking or thwarting of goal

attainment, defined in terms of the condition of the individual rather than in terms of the external environment. Frustration may take different forms of expression, including aggression against unrelated persons or objects.

fudge

mistake.

fulfilment house

specialist firm which handles response to mailing, sales promotion offers, direct response marketing sales and other postal responses to advertising.

full cost model

method of determining price by calculating direct costs, adding percentages for average expected overheads and profits.

full cost pricing

a relatively rigid pricing strategy in which all the variable and fixed costs of a product or service are covered by its sale price.

full coverage

insurance that pays for every rupee of a loss with no maximum and no deductible amount.

full demand

a condition in the marketplace in which purchasers want and are willing to pay for all the products which are being produced.

full liability

a liability of a sole person or company, not shared with others.

full line forcing

a trade practice in which a manufacturer forces wholesalers and retailers to buy his entire line of merchandise (including the less saleable items) if they are to sell any of his products.

full line strategy

synonym for broad-line strategy.

full service agency

advertising agency offering clients a wide range of activities and expertise over and above the normal creative and/or media facilities.

functional account

a functional account is one which indicates the purpose for which the expenditure was made. In marketing such accounts may include marketing research, sales and sales promotional activities, order processing, shipping, warehousing, bookkeeping, etc. Sometimes referred to as a marketing function account.

functional and social equilibrium

the qualities of the superior play an important part in determining the kind of functional and social equilibrium that will be achieved in superior subordinate relationships. Many subordinates have experienced similar problems in working for and with superiors. They may consider the boss to be somewhat less than efficient or even a little touched in the head but they rarely suggest that he changes his work habits. If the boss likes to work early in the morning or late into the night may subordinates are inclined to adjust their schedules.

functional approach to marketing

an approach to the study of marketing in which such functions as sales, distribution, advertising, etc, are viewed as a key to understanding the marketing process. The investigator studies how each of these functions works and from these findings generalizes about the larger marketing picture.

functional authority

the authority that is associated with a particular job.

functional division of work

the main principles in allocation of office work are specialisation, correlation, and business connection. The functions are allocated to different persons according to their suitability. Different activities concerned with the administration of the business are grouped together under a department. Efforts are also made to co-ordinate the work of several departments. The work of control and co-ordination is vested in the top authorities like Board of Directors, General Manager, Secretary, etc.

functional organization

organization into departments according to function.

functional specialists—difference

in studying differentiation it is useful to focus on the functional specialists differences in outlook in terms of orientation toward goals; orientation toward time; perception of the formality of organization.

functions of financial management

(i) to estimate the total capital requirements of the enterprise, both for short term and long term needs, for fixed assets as well as current assets.

(ii) to plan about the most economical capital structure for the enterprise. He has to decide about the financial mix, i.e., the ratio of proportion in which funds be raised from various sources. In other words, a proper ratio between equity and debt is to be determined.

(iii) to see that the funds procured from various sources are properly and efficiently used. These funds should be invested in various assets in order to secure optimum return on investment.

(iv) to administer the income of the business and its allocation.

(v) to exercise control and evaluate the financial performance of the enterprise so that the various financial decisions yield maximum benefits.

(vi) to identify and raise funds

from different sources. Such as issue of shares, issue of debentures, public deposits, loans from financial institutions, etc. The finance manager will decide about the most economical source of funds.

(vii) to manage the cash for payment to creditors, purchases, wages to the workers and to meet day-to-day expenses of the business.

fund

1. to provide for a financial obligation by borrowing money for a specific period. 2. to provide for a future financial obligation by setting aside money and lending it to earn interest; to create a sinking fund.

funded debt

a debt that does not have to be repaid, especially one represented by an irredeemable security.

funds flow analysis

it is an invaluable analytical tool for a financial manager or a creditor for evaluating the employment of funds by a firm, and in determining the sources for such funds. In addition to studying past flows, the analyst can evaluate future flows by means of a funds-statement based upon forecasts. Such a statement provides an efficient method for the financial manager to assess the growth of the firm and its resulting financial needs, and to determine the best way to finance those needs. In particular, funds flow analysis is very useful in planning intermediate, and long-term financing.

funds–flow statement

a summery of the way in which the net current assets of a firm have changed over a period. (Also called a statement of source and application of funds).

fund for multinational management education

aims to bring about greater understanding of role of private enterprise in economic development.

funds, unrestricted

money donated, granted or received from general revenues that can be expended at the discretion of the administration or the governing board.

funnel technique

method of interviewing which directs open-ended questioning without topic of investigation. More disciplined depth interview.

further education

that part of the national system of education which is concerned with the full-time education of those who have left secondary school but have not yet moved into higher education at the universities. In the 1980s a government policy of reducing public expenditure, widespread youth unemployment policy of reducing public expenditure, widespread youth unemployment and the effects of an earlier decline in the birth rate all stimulated major changes in the financing and content of further education in Britain.

Advanced further education, more commonly described as public sector higher education (PSHE) took place in some thirty polytechnics and seventy or so colleges and institutes of further education, concentrating on academic qualifications beyond GCE A level, such as a degree, or upon vocational qualifications like those of the accountancy and banking professions, or the higher certificates and diplomas of the Business and Technician Education Council (BTEC). Because of the high cost of advanced course, the cost of PSHE was pooled amongst all the local authorities, each authority being assessed for a contribution to the 'pool' on the basis of its school population and non-domestic rateable value by central government. In recent years these institutions have provided an increasing number of part-time courses leading to degrees.

Non-advanced further education (NAFE) was provided by local education authorities and funded by the Rate Support Grant from central government and from local rates. It took place mostly in colleges of further education. These tended to offer; (i) traditional vocational course leading to BTEC certificates and diplomas for the qualifications of the City and Guilds of London Institute; (2) academic course leading to GCE 'O' and 'A' level qualifications; (3) an increasing number of pre-vocational courses in response to initiatives from the manpower services commission, which introduced the Youth Training Scheme (YTS) in 1983. This offered a one-year full time programme of work experience, linked with further education and a certificate of training. In 1984 the Government allocated the MSC considerable funds to enable it to purchase more work-related NAFE for school leavers, provided by local education authorities, complicating yet again the funding process of further education.

The MSC was also closely involved in the establishment of the Open Tech, initially in association with the Technician Education Council (TEC, which later became BTEC). The Open Tech programme was set up to extend opportunities for adult training and retaining using a distance (or 'open') learning approach, the emphasis at first being upon the knowledge and skills required by technicians. The production of suitable material to meet the needs of such students was funded by the MSC, which created an Open Tech Unit for this purpose. Tec and the Business Education

Centre (BEC) had already entered the field, TEC running distance learning schemes and BEC directing private study and correspondence courses. Other institutions, such as Henley-The Management College, operated variants of the distance learning model where students studies mostly at home, but were supported by a network of tutors available for consultation or by a series of short residential courses.

The further education sector has traditionally provided a wide range of recreational and cultural courses through adult education centres and institutes, these courses being held mainly in the evenings. Other courses, usually of a cultural nature, are offered to adults by institutions outside the further education sector, such as the extra-mural departments of universities and the Workers' Educational Association.

futures

forward sales or forward purchases, often by speculators who have no intention of taking up or providing the goods personality.

future market

an organised market for buying and selling futures contracts.

future movement

somewhat fragmented futurist movement recognizing that intellectual approaches are necessary to face up to dramatic changes in future development.

galloping inflation

slow price increase are one thing. But when each increase in price becomes the signal for an increase in wages and costs, which again sends prices up still further, we may be in the midst of a malignant, galloping hyper inflation.

gaming

the manipulation of a process or system, usually in an unethical or illegal manner for the purpose of unwarranted gain or advantage.

gaming, scientific

application of business game and other simulation and decision-making techniques, usually with computer assistance, in industry, commerce, government, public service, etc.

gantt chart

a device which displays in a graphic form various production data which are essential to managerial operations.

gap analysis

methodical tabulation of all known consumer wants of a particular product category, together with a cross-listing of the features of existing products which satisfy those wants. Such a chart shows up any gaps which exist and thus provides a pointer as to where new products might find an unfulfilled demand.

garnishment

any legal or equitable procedure through which earnings of any individual are required to be withheld for the payment of any debt. Most garnishments are made by court order.

gatekeeper

an individual in an organization who acts as an informal communication focus, collecting information from a variety of sources external to the company on passing it on to individuals within the company to whom it will be relevant.

gazumping

backing out of a proposed sale of property because another buyer has offered more for it.

geared incentive scheme

payment by results scheme in which incentive payments go up in stages rather than directly in proportion to output.

gearing of capital

after the ascertainment of the total needs of the industry, planning of capital structure involves the selection of the different modes or raising the total amount. Determination of some proper ratio between any two or more methods of raising capital is called gearing of capital, i.e., the ratio of the fixed income securities to the total capitals.

general clerical test

three party psychological test developed in the USA and measuring verbal, numerical and clerical skills. The test takes about 30 minutes.

general contractor

a person or firm whose contracts include several types of skilled work in the construction field.

general electric strategic planning approach

a company-wide approach to marketing planning which takes a number of factors (market growth, competition, market share, profitability, margins, technology, etc.) into account in order to set corporate strategies and objectives.

general expense

an administrative expense, not identified with a specific process, product, or service generated by the operation of the facility. Also known as burden.

general inflation

the inflation that accompanies full employment of all other resources.

general legacy

a general legacy should be distinguished from a specific legacy and a demonstrative legacy. A general legacy is a gift by will out of the personal estate of the testator but is not necessarily and particular part of the estate. General legacies are usually, but not necessarily, pecuniary legacies.

general line wholesaler

a full-service wholesaler who carries one or two lines of merchandise in full assortments and who, for the most part, supplies single line retailers: e.g., a general line hardware wholesaler will have as his customers hardware stores.

general management

1. the work performed by general managers.
2. the general managers within an organization.

general manager

the manager responsible for the whole range of administration in an organization and not just a specific function.

general meeting

a meeting which may be attended by all the members of an association and which gives them some opportunity to control the association's affairs.

general merchandise wholesaler

a full service wholesaler who maintains a broad inventory of a number of unrelated products (such as non-perishable groceries, plumbing supplies, hardware, soft goods, etc.)

general partner

an active member of a partnership who has unlimited liability for the actions of the partners.

general planning

planning may be general as well as detailed. General planning concerns itself with major issues only. It lays down only the broad outlines of future development.

general product manager

the executive who functions as the supervisor of a number of product managers and who, in addition, is responsible for coordinating their plans and programs and for submission to the firm's marketing manager.

general staff assistants

some companies use a general staff which is an adaptation of army practice. This is in reality a group of staff assistants functioning at a high level. These staff assistants usually serve as advisors to top management in specified areas. The general staff is used in addition to the regular company specialized staff.

general store

a type of retailing institution that usually sells a limited selection of a wide range of goods.

general union

trade union whose membership is drawn from all kinds of workers as opposed to the more specialized membership of, for example, a craft union.

generic brand

something of a misnomer inasmuch as a brand is a product made distinguishable from other similar products by a unique identifying name and generics lack just such a name. In common usage, generic brand refers to unbranded products.

generic name

the letters or words used to describe a particular kind or

type of product, i.e., a product's common name as distinct from its brand name. Generics are common in the pharmaceutical industry where drugs are sold under their common chemical name as well as under brand name.

generic product advertising
advertising which features a product type without identifying a brand name for company. This type of advertising is undertaken to stimulate primary demand for a class or products.

generic term
in marketing, applied to brand name which have come to be adopted as the general descriptive term for a product, often as the result of extensive promotion, e.g., Hoover, Biro. Linoleum.

geocentrism
a form of organization found in some multinational marketing firms in which the marketing effort focuses on the whole world rather than on any particular nation or region. No single national market is preferred over others. Employees including management personnel are hired from diverse backgrounds and nationalities.

geographic division of authority
in marketing management a form of organization in which line authority is organized along geographic lines i.e., management is set up on a regional basis often in an effort to promote better supervision.

geographic pricing
occurs when the price for the same product or service varies according to the class of store, retailer or shopping area, whether within one town, or from one part of the country to another, or in different countries, e.g. motorcars.

German inflation
the German inflation had a very bad reputation. Prices rose with staggering rapidity, until at one time they were one million times the prewar level. This was inflation without recovery with a vergence. Overnight, every from of property and income lost its real value. Hundreds of thousands of families were ruined. It wiped out the German middle class and made the Nazi revolution possible.

gerontology
study of the social, psychological, biological, and health aspects of the aging and the aging process.

gestation period
length of time which elapse between an initial inquiry for a product and the placing of an order. More often applied to capital goods where it can amount to several years.

ghosting
1. providing an inner view of a package or product by cutting away part of the exterior.
2. shadow on television film.

giffen's paradox

a situation in which consumers by less of the goods when its price falls and more of the good if its price rises.

gift

a class of public revenue. Voluntary contribution from non-governmental donor generally for specified purpose.

gift deed

an instrument that transfers the title to real estate for which the consideration is love and affection, rather than material consideration.

gift voucher

special incentive to purchase, usually involving money-off against purchase of qualifying brand or providing an opportunity for a special purchase.

giles-archer lantern tests

form of colour vision test in which the subject is presented with a number of lights of different colours and different degrees of brightness.

gilt edged securities

the term is used to describe stocks and bonds issued by the government and quoted on the stock exchange. Theoretically they are non-risk investments at it is assumed that the state will never retreat on its debts. In fact, the low capital risk makes the market value of such securities totally dependent on prevailing interest rates, and consequently, an investor may be forced to sell them at a price lower than the one paid for initially. These are government stocks, and marketable loans raised for public corporations where repayment is guaranteed by the government.

glare

three deleterious effects result glare; reduction in visual performance, discomfort and increase in visual fatigue. Glare may be induced directly from a light source, or by reflection.

Several methods of glare reduction are available: (i) removal of light source from direct line of sight; (ii) reduction of brightness of source, e.g. by using large numbers of low-intensity sources instead of fewer, brither ones; (iii) use of screens and visors; (vi) avoidance of highly reflective surface e.g., high-gloss paint, polished metal.

The extent of existing glare be assessed using the glare index. This may be calculated from data describing the luminances of a light source and of the background, the angle subtended at they eye by the source, and the position of the source in relation to the viewer.

gnatt chart

a chart widely used for monitoring the progress in relation to the target and time horizon in industry for production planning and plant utilization.

goal

something an individual or organization aims to

accomplish.

goal obsession

term used in T-group training for too great concern with goals and too little concern with existing behaviour patterns.

goal orientated research

research of practical application as distinct from research for its own sake.

goffman model

a view of consumer bahaviour based on the sociology of Irving Goffman in which the consumer is seen as a role player and the goods he is shopping for are seen as props in a play. The buyer is thus viewed as a player in a drama of his own making.

going private

the process of buying back publicly held stock in order to convert a publicly held company to a private firm.

going rate pricing

a "collective wisdom" approach to pricing strategy in which a firm bases the prices of its products less on what it costs to make them and more on what their competitors are charging or on what the firm believes its customers may be willing to pay.

golden handcuffs

a payment made to an employee as an inducement to him to remain with organization because of his value to it.

golden handshake

a provision in a preliminary agreement for merger with a target firm that gives the acquiring firm an option to purchase the shares or assets of the target or to receive a substantial bonus if the proposed take over does not occur.

golden hello

a payment made to induce a prospective employee to join a firm.

golden rule fallacy

fallacious view in some T-group training that there is a right way for all people to interact in all situations.

gold standard

a country on the gold standard agrees, by definition, to convert its currency freely into gold through its central bank.

go no-go gage or go not-go gage

in manufacturing, a type of limit gage utilized to measure the dimensions of a mechanical part to determine whether or not the part is within allowable limits.

good

material or physical objects, either natural or man-made, used to satisfy human needs or desires.

goods in consignment

an arrangement whereby an agent takes possession of goods but no title to them.

goods on consignment

goods sent to an agent for sale. The agent has possession but not the title, though he may be able to give a good title to a bonafide purchaser, even when acting outside his authority. The goods are usually returnable by the agent who works for a commission. The venture is normally made for a limited period only.

goods received note

a document issued by a firm on receipt of a delivery which sets out what goods and how many items have been delivered.

goodwill

the likelihood that customers will return to the same supplier. Also an estimate of the value of goodwill of the supplier. The standing of an enterprise as a successful business house.

goodwill (in law)

goodwill has been defined as 'the benefit arising from connection or reputation' of an existing business. While it clearly has a monetary value it is not at all easy to quantify this. Lawyers have distinguished between 'cat goodwill' and 'dog goodwill'. The former is goodwill attached to premises that occupy a convenient and valuable site for particular business purposes, while the latter is goodwill that is based on the special knowledge or skill of the people running a business. The difference is important when it comes to disposing of the goodwill. Cat goodwill can only be sold with the premises, while dog goodwill is either not saleable at all or, if saleable, implies that some know-how or other information is being sold with the tangible assets of a business.

A new partner admitted to a– Partnership will be required to make a payment to the existing partners for a share in the goodwill. When a partnership is dissolved and the assets of the firm are sold, goodwill is generally disposed of as one of the assets and the purchaser of it will have a sole right to it. If, however, no provision is made for the sale of the goodwill, any of the former partners could use the goodwill of the firm's business (e.g. to the extent of using the former firm's name), provided always that in doing so they do not imply that their former copartners are associated with them in their new enterprise.

goon

slang for a person hired to break up meetings, damage property, and otherwise threaten or terrorize individuals or groups.

go-slow

action by employees, involving doing less work than normal without actually stopping work, which is taken to bring pressure on their employer in a dispute.

go slow tactics

also called " working to rule" it is an alternative to the strike, in which the labourers work more slowly than usual.

government expenditures

government purchases of goods and services, transfer

payments, and net government interest.

government securities

fixed interest securities issued by the government. They may be in the nature of bonds or other types of security and may or may not be redeemable. They may be issued to banks and other institutions in the money market or to the general public through banks or the post office. The treasury bill is a specific type of government security which is issued only within the money market, and particularly to discount houses which tender for these bills each week. The rate of discount at which they are allotted is a pointer to the general health of the economy and can influence the current minimum lending rate.

grade creep

tendency to re-grade or reclassify employees as surreptitious method of allowing increases in pay.

graded hourly rates

a form of payment system where employees are paid according to their Merit Ratings.

grading

the sorting of goods into quality classifications, e.g., meat men's suits, and cotton are all graded according to predetermined quality standards.

grant closeout procedures

the procedures specified by grant-making public agencies that define financial, reporting, and asset-retention or-protection steps that must be taken at the termination of a grant.

grant project

a grant that directs funding to specific project, in contrast to a general support grant.

grant receivable

an asset account in an organisation's chart of accounts and balance sheet. Grants receivable are posted when formal notification of a grant award has been received.

grapevine

the informal communication network of an organization. Often much more efficient than the formal one.

graph

a diagram that represents the way in which one quantity varies as another quantity does. A diagram consisting of points called 'vertices' or 'nodes' and I lines called 'edges' or 'links' in which each edge has a vertex at each end. (Also called a 'network').

gratuitous guest

an individual transported in a vehicle, such as a bus or ambulance, with permission of the operator but without payment.

gratuity

sometimes known as a lump-sum, it is an amount payable under some pension schemes at the time when the pension is due to commence. It is not liable to income tax.

gravy jobs

easy piece work jobs or those with loose rates. May also be known as fat work. Jobs on which it is difficult to earn bonus may be known as learn work or stinkers.

gray collar

describing workers whose jobs lie midway between blue-collar and white-collar employment for jobs containing elements of each.

gray market

a term for transactions that are conducted outside the usual business channels but are not illegal.

green paper

a publication of the government with a green cover—usually a proposal to which the government is not committed but would like public comment on.

green river ordiance

a law passed by a local government to restrict door-to-door selling. The name is derived from Green River. Wyoming, one of the first places to pass such an ordinance.

grievance procedure

the arrangements for settling disputes arising on the shop floor between trade union members and management.

In most other industrial countries these arrangements tend to be formal, written agreements, often enforceable at law. Under the continental and American systems of Collective Bargaining most substantive agreements, i.e. those dealing with terms and conditions of employment, tend to carry their own negotiating procedures for the settlement of disputes. In Britain, however, there has traditionally been a clear distinction between substantive and procedural agreements, and, in both cases, much less emphasis on formality and enforceability. Almost all industries have some kind of dispute procedure, including arbitration (Arbitration, Industrial), though there are considerable differences in terms of complexity, speed and general effectiveness. Historically most industry-wide procedures have developed piecemeal, often as a result of Strike action, and may therefore still reflect an anachronistic balance of bargaining power between management and trade unions.

In the engineering industry the provisions for avoiding disputes required any worker concerned to first raise any question in person with their foreman. If the worker was not satisfied they went with the Shop Steward to the departmental manager. Subsequent stages might take the form of a works committee (if one existed), or a works conference with official representatives of the appropriate Trade Union and Employers' Association, and then a local conference at which a panel of employers not directly involved in the question at issue met to hear the two sides of the case from the union and the firm concerned. If no agreement was reached the final stage was a central conference at which a panel of national representatives of the Engineering Employers' Federation formed 'courts' to hear the case of the firm and of the workers. Only when this procedure was exhausted and no agreement reached did strike action become constitutional.

gross annual value

the rent that could be obtained for a year for a piece of land if it were let in the open market, on the condition that the landlord would pay for all repairs and the tenant would pay all the rent.

gross business product

that part of gross national product produced by business activity.

gross fund

a term applied to carities and pension fund and any other funds which are exempt from tax, particularly income tax and capital gains tax:

gross income

revenues from services, investments, contributions, and all other sources, prior to any deductions such as expenses or the funding of reserves.

gross lease

a rental contract that requires the lesser to pay all (or most) expenses for the leased property, including such items as taxes, insurance, maintenance, and utility fees.

gross margin

the difference between the total cost of goods and their final selling price. Gross margin may be expressed as net sales less the cost of goods sold. Since markdowns, shortages, and discounts have been deducted in computing gross margin, the figure is not the same as maintained markup. Gross margin is often used synonymously with the term gross profit. The former term is more usually found in retailing and the latter in manufacturing usage.

gross national product (GNP)

the total value (at current market prices) of all goods and services produced by a nation over a specified period of time (commonly one year).

gross profit (or gross income)

it is the excess of revenue over cost of sales. Converse represents gross loss.

gross profit ratio

a ratio by which performance of a product or of its management may be measured; it is computed by the formula; gross profit divided by net sales.

gross reach

total number of opportunities

for people to see the advertisements contained in a schedule; the sum total of the readership of each publication multiplied by the total number of insertions.

gross returns on net assets

gross profits before payment of interest and depreciation earned from the employment of fixed assets expressed as a percentage of the cost of these assets.

gross sales

sales revenue before deductions have been made for returns and allowances, but after sales and excise taxes have been deducted. It represents the total amount charged to all customers during the accounting period. When returns and allowances are deducted, the resultant figure is the vendor's net sales.

group decision method

a method of solving a problem affecting a manager and some or all the group of people he manages, in which the manager states the problem at a meeting of the group and asks the group to decide on a solution. The manager's task is, then, not to present his own solution but to draw the best possible solution from the group.

group incentive payment

incentive payment that is related to the value of quantity of work done by a group of workers within a factory or other production unit.

group interview

a selection interview at which two or more applicants for a job are interviewed simultaneously–often conducted as an informal conversation.

group method of training

in the training process groups can be used to satisfy a variety of learning goals. When the objective is to enable specialists from different backgrounds to learn to work together or to combine forces to attack a problem, a group can be formed and put to work on appropriate tasks. The group thus becomes a source of knowledge and information available to its members. It may also serve as a vehicle through which its members learn about groups and about each other's behaviour from observation and discussion whilst engaged upon a common task. In this process the members of a group can obviously become important influences on each other, sometimes with lasting effect upon an individual's behaviour. Learning about inter-group behaviour may be similarly fostered by involving several groups in a common task that requires interaction between them. In all of these instances a member of the training staff is present, primarily to assist group members to learn from what is happening to them.

In pursuit of the first objective-helping experts to learn to work together-the British Army has used carefully structured groups in courses for senior officers at its Staff College for more than sixty years. The method was later adapted for the training of managers in industry and administrators in the public service by the Management College at Henley; variants of the method are now widely applied in Britain, the Commonwealth and Scandinavia.

The use of small groups as vehicles for learning about behaviour from personal experience has taken subtly different forms in the USA and Britain. In the USA Kurt Lewin and his followers developed basic skill-training groups, whose objectives were to help participants to diagnose group problems and to improve their skills in dealing with interpersonal relation and leadership. Later, the goals of these T-group changed more towards self awareness, so the process became known as 'sensitivity training'. In Britain, as a result of work by W.R. Bion at the Tavistock Institute, the emphasis was initially more upon group than individual behaviour. Consequently training in small groups along the Tavistock model became a method of gaining insight into the unconscious forces influencing group behaviour and attitudes towards authority.

A common ingredient in these small-group methods was a tension-creating phase resulting from a deliberate refusal by the staff to give structure to the proceedings. Lewin believed that individuals were stimulated by uncertainty to experiment with their behaviour, whilst bion, as a 'group consultant', took a role rather like that of a psychoanalyst with a patient. In a typical T-group the trainer may begin by stating the purpose of the group and then lapsing into silence, leaving an apparent power vacuum. This gives scope to the group members to create a social system that will satisfy their own goals and needs but that poses problems of power, influence and the degree of intimacy demanded. The trainer's contribution may then be to express personal feelings, thereby legitimating members to do so and to show that he or she cares about the members. The trainer also tries to help their understanding of what is going on by occasional comments, in addition to managing time and deciding the sequence of events.

During the 1960s there were pressures for a return to the original concern of sensitivity training with increasing the competence of individuals and their personal skills-Interpersonal Skill Development. Blake and Mouton introduced structured task training as a part of their Managerial Grid approach to organization development, during which individuals in phase one receive face-to-face feedback on their management styles from members of six-strong problem-solving groups Teams. The managerial-grid approach postulates an ideal management style that all managers should try to adopt, so feedback from the group becomes important as a means of shaping behaviour in a prescribed direction. In Britain a similar use of feedback associated with relatively simple group problem-solving tasks has characterized a management training approach used by Ralph Coverdale and a number of other trainers in industry.

group of ten

the richest and most influential members of the International Monetary Fund : Belgium, Canada, France, Federal Republic of Germany, Italy, Japan, Netherlands, Sweden, UK and USA. These countries signed the 'General Arrangements to Borrow' in 1962 by which they agreed to lend each other through the IMF up to US dollars 6000 million to forestall or cope with an impairment of the international monetary system.

group problem-solving

or group decision making. Process in which a manager presents a problem to a group of subordinates in order to elicit a solution by discussion with and between them.

group psychology

people do not just get together; they get together for a purpose.

group selection techniques

where, in personnel selection, a number of candidates for a vacancy are interviewed or assessed together, and judged partly on their relations with each other.

group technology

a production method involving the manufacture of parts in 'families' or groups of related parts, rather than in small numbers, hence achieving the improved resource utilization inherent in quantity production.

The basis of a group-technology production system is the definition and description of groups of families of parts. Similarity of shape (design classification) and/or similarity of manufacturing requirement (production classification) may exist. Although the two classifications are usually related, only a detailed investigation within a company will indicate whether this relationship exists and whether there are sufficient suitable parts to merit this type of production.

Several proprietary systems exist (e.g. the Opitz and Brisch systems), their main difference being the method of classification and coding. Two techniques-production-flow analysis and component-flow analysis-take account of the sequence of operations required in the manufacture of items, whilst the formation of production 'cells' is a common consequence of the adoption of group technology in batch production. → Cell Production; Flexible Manufacturing System.

group training

form of group dynamics training in which the trainees meet in small groups and each trainee studies the behaviour and group processes that take place in his own group.

group training scheme

an arrangement whereby two or more firms have common facilities for training.

group working

organizing of workers to increase the degree of autonomy and responsibility carried by the worker through the delegation of responsibilities to the work group.

growth

expansion of a business organization of the economy in general. The rate of growth in the latter is usually measured by the rate of change in the gross domestic product.

growth of the firm

the reasons for the growth of a firm can be divided into two categories: impersonal and personal.

It has been customary to play down the role of business leadership, or entrepreneurial ability, in contributing to the growth of firms. This accords with the approach to history that deals with political and economic forces rather than with great statesmen and monarch. However, students of the past growth of firms detect at least some qualities or skills that must be present for growth to take place, although their presence does not guarantee it. Sheer physical strength appears necessary and this must be coupled with an ability to work hard and concentrate entirely upon the business if needs be. Since uncertainty is part of the framework of life there must be present a willingness, almost a desire, to take risks. To this must be coupled a determination that can amount to ruthlessness, if necessary. Finally, in the past successful entrepreneurs have not always had technical or commercial training. However, the growth of knowledge in the field of management plus the general raising of educational standards means that this will be much less true in the future and we would expect successful entreprenenurs to have a training in science, engineering, accountancy or perhaps one of the newer areas such as marketing or corporate planning.

The impersonal forces that create the conditions for growth

can range from the possibility of government financial aid to the threat of competition in established markets. The existence of unexploited technical economies of scale will obviously favour growth, as will the possibility of marketing or managerial economies. Finally one should not neglect the internal pressure from research and product improvement departments.

To classify the growth patterns that emerge from a combination of these two sets of forces, economists have talked about three types of integration: horizontal, vertical and lateral (patterns of Growth). One should note, however, that although integration tends to imply takeover or amalgamation, expansion may also come purely from within the firm itself.

The parameters used to determine the growth of a company are varied. Turnover is often used, as are the value of assets, number of employees, profits or share of the market. More recently a further criterion has been used, namely net present value to shareholders and this may well be the most all-embracing criterion of growth for a company. (Present Value; Financial Management; patterns of Growth.

growth stage

that stage of the product life cycle during which demand for the product picks up momentum and competitive products are introduced into the marketplace. During the growth stage, production increases and profit rise until competition begins to drive down prices.

guaranteed wage plan

that part of a labour contract in which employes are guaranteed either employment or a stated amount of wages during a specific time period.

guarantee

a promise by one person (usually called the 'Guarantor') that he will make good any failure by a second person (called the 'principal debtor') to meet financial obligations owned to a third person. A promise, given by a manufacturer of goods which are sold by retailers, that the manufacturer will correct any defects in the goods found by a purchaser within a certain time. (In theory, it is the retailer's duty to correct defects and so the manufacturer is acting as guarantor of the retailer).

guaranteed bond

a bond issued by one company to another company (e.g., the parent company) guaranteeing that interest will be paid on the capital borrowed from the parent company.

guarantee pay

there is no general right to withhold wages merely because no work is available, although employers can reserve this right by inserting a suitable clause into their contracts of employment. Even where this has been done, however, legislation guarantees earnings up to a maximum of five workers day in any rolling three-month period. In 1985 the maximum per day was £10.50. The statutory guarantee does not operate where the temporary lack of work is due to industrial action involving any employee of the employer or of an associated employer. To qualify, an employee must have been emplcyed for at least one month, be available for work, and be prepared to accept any temporary alternative work that is suitable if the employer offers it.

Partly because the statutory maximum is fairly modest, it is not uncommon to find that trade unions have negotiated more generous 'guaranteed week' agreement with many employers in manufacturing industry.

guarantor

a person who promise that if a second person fails to fulfil some obligation then he will fulfil it instead or pay money up to a specified limit to compensate for any loss caused by the second person's failure.

guest worker

foreign national who is permitted to enter a country to work, but not settle there with his family.

guide chart profile method

type of job evaluation technique developed in the UK and using three factors; know-how, problem-solving and accountability in the context of a particular salary scale.

guild socialism

a moderate form of socialism that advocated social ownership of the means of production but management of industrial activity by the workers themselves, who were to be organized into guilds modeled after the medieval craft guilds.

haggle

process of discussional bargaining, prior to the negotiating of prices or terms of agreement.

hallmarks

the impressed stamps on gold, silver and platinum under the authority of the Goldsmiths Company and the various assay offices.

Hallmarking is of particular relevance to silver, partly because silver has traditionally been in more common use than gold, and also because of the facility for converting silver articles into coinage.

halo effect

a tendency toward distortion in an appraisal or performance rating on an individual caused by the reaction of the person doing the appraisal or conducting the interview. A high rating on one factor tends to result in a high rating on all other factors.

handbill

form of printed advertising delivered personally into the hands of likely prospects.

handicraft system

the practice of pursuing a craft or trade in a small shop largely by hand or with only simple machinery.

handout

inexpensive leaflet for free distribution at exhibitions or for promotional purposes, especially at point-of-sale.

harassment

words and/or actions that unlawfully or alarm another person. Harassment may include anonymous, repeated, offensively coarse or late-night phone calls; insulting, taunting, or physically challenging approaches, and other forms of anti-social behaviour.

hard copy

text or information in a form which can be read by the human eye, as opposed to micros copy or information stored on disc, tape or visual display unit.

hard core control

small group of directors or senior executives who effectively lead and direct a company usually in long term strategic issues.

hard-core unemployed

people who are unemployed because they lack the education or skills required by a complex economy.

hard core unemployment

another name for structural unemployment.

hard currency

a national currency used in international trade because it has a stable or rising exchange rate and is generally accepted as being easily convertible, e.g., American dollars or Swiss francs.

hard funding

money obtained from an organisation's regular sources of operating funds that is budgeted for activities. In contrast, soft funding implies that the money comes from a grant or other source that will not continue indefinitely.

hard news

news of value to general news columns of the press as distinct product news which may interest feature writers specializing in say, gardening, beauty, motoring, fashion, food and so on, or trade magazines which report new product news.

hard sell

punchy, persuasive, high-pressure advertising, employing five point formula of attraction, attention, desire, conviction and action. Opposite to soft sell.

hardware

formally, the mechanical, magnetic, electrical, and electronic components of a computer. Informally, any piece of computer or automatic dataprocessing equipment.

harmonization

achievement of common international conventions and regulations as with postal, civil aviation, customs and other operations.

harmony

essence of an advertisement or commercial reaching the desired theme or objective.

hawthorne investigation

a programme of research conducted at the Hawthorne plant (Chicago) of the Western Electric Co. into various aspects of individual and group behaviour. The main research took place during the period 1927-32 and must be the best known and most widely quoted investigation in the history of social research.

In November 1924 the Western Electric Co. commenced a series of short experiments to determine the relationship between different intensities of illumination and productive efficiency. The experiments were inconclusive and prompted the consideration that relevant variables of a psychological nature had been inadequately controlled. Accordingly advice was sought from academics, notably Professor Elton Mayo of the Industrial Research Department, Harvard Graduate School of Business Administration, and in April 1927 six female workers were isolated in a room where output could be measured whilst various conditions relating to rest pauses and hours of work could be varied, and the effects noted by an observer. This stage of the investigation, the Relay Assembly Test Room, lasted for approximately five years. The experimenters were surprised to discover that, although output increased fairly steadily throughout the first two years of the Test Room, the variables with which they were primarily concerned apparently had little effect on production. Instead, what seemed of particular importance was the change in social climate created by the experimental conditions, including the development of personal friendship amongst the girls and their freedom from supervisory pressures. This change in the social environment was associated with a marked change in the girls' attitudes towards their work.

Subsequent stages in the investigations overlapped with, and arose out of, the first. The apparent importance of employee attitudes to work and to supervision suggested the advisability of discovering more about the attitudes of employees generally. In September 1928, therefore, a programme of formal interviews was started, first in the Inspection Branch and later in other branches, so that by the end of 1930 well over 20,000 employees had been given the opportunity to talk confidentially with a member of the interviewing team. The data from the interviews revealed, inter alia, that there might be a connection between worker attitudes and productivity and that worker attitudes were considerably influenced by the other members of the work group to which the worker belonged; in other words, attitudes were less personal than social phenomena.

The final stage in the research was the systematic observation of such a work group. It consisted of fourteen men engaged in wiring, soldering and inspecting a 'bank' of telephone terminals. The Bank Wiring Observation Room was set up in November 1931 and continued until May 1932, when it was abandoned because of the economic depression. The investigators discovered that the operators adhered to a more or less fixed standard of output regardless of the existence of individual and group incentive payments and that they maintained output at that level consistently, this being achieved partly by exaggerating in the records the amount of work actually done and by claiming 'allowances' for work stoppages which, in fact, had not occurred. These breaches of company regulations were condoned by the men's immediate superior. The investigators noted the difficulty of the supervisor's position as he tried to satisfy the demands of his superiors without losing the essential goodwill of his workforce. This stage of the investigation, with its emphasis on work group and supervisory behaviour, was particularly important for its theoretical implications.

The value of the Hawthorne studies is inestimable. Industrial psychology was transformed as an academic discipline. Prior to the investigations the individual was viewed and treated as an isolated unit; after the investigations this view was no longer tenable. For the next thirty years research workers utilized the theoretical concepts generated by the investigations and directed their research along lines suggested by the Hawthorne findings. As a seminal work it is virtually without equal. Unfortunately the work contained too much that was new for it to be readily assimilated, even by its authors, and a grossly oversimplified interpretation of its contents helped to give rise to the Human Relations school; Organization Theory.

hay clerical battery

three part psychological test developed in the USA and covering, in four minutes each, number perception, name finding, and series of numbers.

hazard

a situation or event that introduces or increases the probability of occurrence of (or extent of loss arising from) an accident; such as slippery floors, unsanitary conditions, or congested traffic.

head-on position

outdoor advertising position directly facing traffic.

head on positioning

a market positioning strategy in which two products which are nearly identical compete with one another directly.

health and safety commission, the

this is responsible to appropriate ministers for the administration of the Health and Safety at Work etc. Act 1974. Member of the Commission are appointed by the Secretary of State for Employment after consultation with the TUC, CBI and local authorities. It reviews health and safety legislation and submits proposal for new or revised regulations. Its operational arm is the Health and Safety Executive. The commission also has responsibility for the health and safety of all persons (including divers) engaged in the offshore oil and gas industry.

health and safety legislation

every year about 1,000 employees are killed, and half a million injured at work through industrial injuries and diseases. The first Act to deal with health and safety at work was passed in 1802, and by 1974 no fewer than thirty-one Acts dealt with the subject. In 1972 a committee, under the chairmanship of Lord Robens, on Safety and Health at Work (Cmnd. 5034), made a number of criticisms of the old system: there was too much apathy at work about safety and health, too many haphazard and intricate rules and regulations, and the administration of the system was too fragmented. The far-reaching provision of the Health and Safety at Work, etc. Act 1974 are based on the recommendations of the Robens Report.

The 1974 Act seeks to provide a comprehensive and integrated system of law to: (i) secure workers' health, safety and welfare; (ii) protect other persons against health or safety risks arising out of or in connection with the activities of persons at work; (iii) control the keeping and use of explosives or highly flammable or dangerous substances, and generally prevent the unlawful acquisition, possession and use of such substances; and (iv) control the emission into the atmosphere of noxious or offensive substances from certain premises.

The Act establishes a Health and Safety Commission and Health and Safety Executive to be generally responsible for administering the Act and regulations made thereunder, together with the older legislation (such as the Factories Act 1961), which the 1974 Act and regulation will progressively replace. Section 2-9 of the Act impose a number of very extensive duties on various persons, contravention of which may lead to criminal proceedings. Thus section 2 requires every employer to ensure, so far as is reasonably practicable, employees' health, safety and welfare. Employers must also prepare and bring to employees' notice a written statement of their general safety policy and arrangements for implementing it. The Act also provides for the making of regulations requiring the appointment of safety representative by a recognized trade union. Section 3 of the Act makes it the duty of every employer and self-employed person so to conduct their undertakings as to ensure, so far as is reasonably practicable, that they and others not in their employment who may be affected are not thereby exposed to health or safety risks.

Section 6 requires persons who design, manufacture, import or supply articles for use at work to ensure, so far as is reasonably practicable, that the articles are so designed and constructed as to be safe and without health risks when properly used. Section 7 requires all employees while at work: (i) to take reasonable care for the health and safety of themselves and others who may be affected by their acts or omission at work; and (ii) as regards any statutory duty on their employer or other person, to co-operate with them to enable that duty to be complied with.

Section 8 forbids the intentional or reckless interference with, or misuse of, anything provided in the interests of health, safety or welfare. Section 9 forbids employees being charged for anything done or provided in pursuance of the legislation.

The Health and Safety Commission is empowered to issue codes of practice to provide guidance with respect to the sections 2-7 duties or regulations made by the Secretary of State for Employment under the Act. The Commission may also hold inquiries into accidents etc.

The 1974 Act is policed by inspectors with wide powers to enter premises, test materials and conduct investigations, etc. Where a person contravenes the legislation, an inspector may serve on them an 'improvement notice, requiring them to remedy the contravention. If an inspector believes that a particular activity occasions risk of serious personal injury, they may issue a 'prohibition notice' specifying remedial measures to be taken and fixing a time after which the activity will be prohibited until such measures are taken. The inspector can put the notice into immediate effect where they consider that the risk is imminent. Appeals against improvement and prohibition notices may be made to Employers Liability.

health care

provision by professional and paraprofessional personnel of services for the maintenance of health, prevention of illness, and treatment of illness or injury.

hearing

sound is produced by vibration and transmitted, usually through the air, by means of pressure waves. A 'pure' tone is produced by a sinusoidal pressure wave, the amplitude of which determines the loudness of the sound, and the frequency of which determines the pitch. Differences in timbre or quality of sounds are brought about by differences in complexity of waves, which can be regarded as consisting of a number of individual sinusoidal components.

The speed of sound in air is approximately 750 mph; in liquids and solids it is considerably increased.

In the human ear the tympanic membrane vibrates in response to pressure waves. The vibration is transmitted via the three bony occiscles of the middle ear into the cochlea, the spiral tube of the inner ear, wherein the mechanical vibrations are converted into hydraulic form and ultimately transduced into nerve impulses.

The frequency range of human audition extends from about 20 Hz to 20 kHz, there being considerable differences between individuals. Subjective loudness of sounds depends upon frequency as well as amplitude, the maximum sensitivity occurring between 4 and 5 kHz. In this frequency range perception of sound occurs at a sound pressure of about 0-0002 dynes/sq. cm. sound intensity levels are usually measured in decibels above this basal value (Threshold). The overall intensity level of normal speech, for example, is about 66 decibels (Speech).

Hearing is generally dichotic, that is, each ear gets a slightly different signal. Localization in the horizontal plane is brought about by the interpretation of differences in phase and intensity of signals arriving at each ear. It is necessary, however, for the listener to move his head in order to identify the elevation of the source.

Loss of hearing ability occurs as part of the normal ageing process and takes the form of a steady decline from the age of twenty onwards. High-frequency sounds are subject to greater loss with age than low frequency ones.

heat

various automatic physiological mechanisms, notably rate of blood flow and sweat rate, contribute to the maintenance of body temperature at a constant value near to 37° C. Only small increases (about 4° C) can be survived, although cooling to temperatures below 20° C is sometimes possible. Sensations of thermal comfort are affected by air temperature, humidity, rate of air movement and amount of radiant heat. Numerous attempts have been made to derive a single index to combine these atmospheric variables. The corrected effective temperature is probably the most useful of these indices and is derived from randiant temperature, wt-bulb temperature and rate of air flow. It is defined as the numerical value of the temperature of still saturated air that would induce an identical sensation. Comfort zones have been established empirically. Decrements in both physical and mental work output result from high temperature. Most work tasks become almost impossible to perform at corrected effective temperatures in excess of about 34° C. Temperature differences of only about 5° C at constant relative humidity separate 'impossible' from relatively easy performance. A similar difference in judgements results from changes in relative humidity of about 15 percent at constant temperature.

Several studies have demonstrated decrements in physical work performance at low temperatures. There is no evidence of corresponding mental work deterioration.

heavy half

that segment of the marketplace which represents numerically half of the consumers in the population, but which contains by a large majority most of a firm's actual customers.

heavy industry

the term applied to traditional industries like steel-making, coalmining and shipbuilding which were the basis of western industrialization in the nineteenth century and have always required heavy physical labour.

heavy users

consumers or customers whose purchases of a product are larger than average.

hedge

to protect oneself against financial loss; especially to make a transaction in a futures market for a commodity or for foreign currency which reduces the risk of loss from a commitment already made in connection with that commodity.

hedging

a method by which wholesale dealers in basic raw materials and food-stuffs or manufacturers of certain products can transfer risks of adverse price fluctuations to professional speculators in the commodity exchange.

hedonic goods

consumer goods whose attractiveness lies principally in that they give the purchaser pleasure.

heir

the heir or heir-at - law was the person entitled, by law, to the real property of a deceased person who left no will.

Henri Fayol (1841-1925)

Henri Fayol was a French industrialist. He joined a French mining company (Commentry-Fourchambault-decanzeville) in 1860 as an engineer and rose to the position of its managing director in 1888. Through his long practical experience, Fayol developed a general theory of management. He published a book, Administration Industrielle Generate, in French in 1916 which was translated into English in 1929 under the title. General and industrial management.

Fayol classified all business activities into six categories as given below:

(i) technical (production or manufacturing).

(ii) commercial (buying, selling and exchange).

(iii) financial (search for and optimum use of capital).

(iv) security (protection of property and persons).

(v) accounting (including statistics) and

(vi) managerial.

According to Fayol the first groups of activities are quite well known and, therefore, he concentrated his attention on the analysis of the sixth group, i.e. managerial activities.

According to Fayol, to manage is to forecast and plan, to organize, to command, to coordination and to control. Thus, Fayol classified managerial activities or functions into the following categories:

(i) planning.

(ii) organising.

(iii) commanding.

(iv) coordinating.

(v) controlling.

heroic theory

there are essentially two different theories of the process of invention: the heroic theory and the systematic theory.

According to the heroic theory, the credit for a particular invention belongs completely or mainly to one individual who has the unique inspiration. Thus the invention of the spinning mule is attributed to Crompton, of steam engine to Watt and so forth.

Heroic invention also called spontaneous invention can be

explained only in terms of chance happenings, the curiosity of an individual inventor or what Taussig called the " instinct of contrivance ".

heuristic

an adjective used to describe an exploratory method of tackling a problem, in which the solution is discovered by evaluations of the progress made towards the final result e.g. guided trial and error. Contrast with alogrithm.

heuristic method

training approach.

heuristic models

use of mathematical modelling technique that takes into account the fruits of practical experience of actually getting the work etc. in question done.

heuristic programming

operational research scientists sometimes use Simulation to tackle problems on which a rigorous mathematical analysis is not feasible. Simulation is a particularly useful approach to representing the behaviour in time of complex systems incorporating a large degree of uncertainty. Other problems may be complex because there are a large number of factors and constraints involved, which may be combined in an astronomical number of ways to produce feasible solutions. These problems are often not amenable to rigorous analysis or are particularly suited to simulation; heuristic programming provides an alternative non-rigorous approach, which has proved most useful. Such problems are typically managerial. Managers need to be able to distinguish the relatively few good approaches to a problem from the many feasible alternative available. They may do this by developing 'rules of thumb' by which they try to account either consciously or subconsciously (that is, by 'hunch') for all the factors or constraints involved. Owing to the limitations on the human brain's ability consciously to store and manipulate information and/or managers' lack of time, they may not be able to evaluate all promising alternative, so 'solutions' better than those adopted may escape their attention. Typically, the person responsible for production scheduling in a large jobbing shop faces this situation.

A computer, on the other hand, can store and manipulate large amounts of information quickly and, if it can be programmed to use similar rules of thumb to the manager, it is likely to produce better solution. The term 'heuristic' means a procedure or rule of thumb used to solve a particular problem and so heuristic programs have been written for computer to solve the problem by this method.

Heuristic programming is proving very useful and has

been used with success on problems of assembly-line balancing and job-shop scheduling, plant layout, warehouse location, stock control, resource allocation to large projects and portfolio selection.

hidden buyer

in purchasing a person other than the purchasing agent who, through his power to specify the characteristics of a product, is the real buyer. Technicians, managers, and others within an organization may have the capacity to exert such influence.

hidden cost

any of the costs of doing business that cannot be recorded by an accountant and so do not show up on a firm's balance sheet or income statement, for example, the losses resulting from a customer's failure to reorder and cancellations of orders are considered hidden costs.

hierarchy

any ordering or grouping of persons, things, or ideas by rank or level of organization or class. In organization and management, the term "hierarchy" refers to the structure of an organization, the job designations within it, and the persons occupying those jobs according to levels of increasing status and accountability.

hierarchy of effects

those stages (beginning with unawareness and ending with purchase of the product) through which consumers pass when responding to a firm's promotional efforts. In order they are: awareness, knowledge, liking, preference, conviction, and purchase.

hidden decision

any decision taken automatically and without question; for example, renewing a contact when due without reviewing its continued usefulness.

high pressure selling

aggressive selling activity to achieve sales revenue irrespective of a consumer's real need or resources.

Hind Mazdoor Sabha (Economics of Labour)

one of the major trade unions of India. Founded in 1948, it stands for the establishment of a democratic socialist society.

hinterland

area external to store or shopping centre from which custom is drawn.

hire purchase

the equivalent of instalment buying. The buyer pays an initial deposit, takes possession of the goods or receives the benefits of the services, and then makes regular payments to cover the reminder of the purchase price plus interest or carrying charges. The buyer does not take title to the goods until the last periodic payment or instalment is paid in full.

historical method

spending same amount on advertising as in the past but with adjustments to meet changing costs of different needs.

hoarding site

parcel of land or a building used for posters.

hobbesian model

organizational factors model showing balance between advantage to consumer and manufacturer.

holdback

an amount of money withheld from periodic payments to contractors to assure their compliance with contract terms. Usually the amount to be withheld is expressed as a percentage in the contract provisions. The amounts withheld are paid to the contractor after a designated official certifies that the contractor has completed work pursuant to the contract terms.

hold back pay

wages withheld by an employer for the purpose of calculating payroll periods.

holding company

a corporation operated for the purpose of owning and controlling the stock of other corporations.

holding gain

the difference in the worth of an asset from the time it was bought to a subsequent time (usually when it is sold, donated, or otherwise disposed of).

holding out

pretending that a partner who has in fact left a partnership is still a member of it and obtaining credit on the strength of his name.

hold order

in manufacturing, a written order directing that certain operations or work activities be interrupted or cancelled, pending a change in design or material.

home audit

market research for what is normally a combination of dustbin check and pantry check to obtain data on house-holds' choice and volume of consumption of consumer goods.

homeostasis

the significance of a number of physiological control mechanisms in maintaining constancy of the internal bodily variables was first recognized by W.B. Cannon, who coined the term homeostasis to designate these stages of equilibrium. In respect of many bodily variable it is necessary to control values within quite narrow tolerances in order to avoid severe damage or death. Examples of variables that are maintained by automatic physiological control systems include body temperature, blood-sugar level and blood pH. The concept of homeostasis may be enlarged beyond such autonomic activities and may include gross somatic activity including, for example, the hungry animal's search for food. Numerous symptoms of disease involve the breakdown of the usual homeostatic mechanisms, so that the individual is unable to make the usual effective adjustments to cope with environmental stresses. The ageing process is characterized by a slow decline in the efficiency of homeostatic mechanisms.

horizontal competition

competition between channel of distribution members at the some channel level, e.g., in retailing, department stores in head-to-head competition. Not to be confused with channel conflict.

horizontal cooperative promotion

promotional efforts sponsored by two or more members of a distribution channel who are operating at the same level. For example a number of manufactures may cooperatively sponsor events in support of American participation in the Olympic Games.

horizontal industrial market

a broad market for industrial goods—one which includes a number of industries. Products sold in horizontal markets have a relatively wide range of potential customers.

horizontal price fixing

resale price maintenance agreements between firms at the same level of the market, e.g., collusive agreement between two or more manufacturers of the same product to fix prices at an artificially high level. Generally horizontal price fixing has as its objective higher profits and or the restriction of competition.

horizontal vs. Vertical financial analysis

this method of classification is based on the modus operandi of analysis. Horizontal analysis refers to the comparison of the trend of each item in the financial statements over a number of years, or of companies. The figures for this type of analysis are presented horizontally over a number of columns. Such a column represents a year or a company. This type of analysis is also called Dynamic Analysis as it is based on data from year to year rather than data of any one year.

host country orientation

an overseas marketing orientation in which a firm's overseas subsidiaries are often managed by local people and are thus more responsive to the needs of the local consumer.

hosting

continental system of selling editorial space.

hot money

apart from its use in the world

of crime to describe stolen or counterfeit money, hot money is a term sometimes used in the sphere of international payments. It refers to funds that move quickly from one country to another in search of the highest rate of interest.

hot shop

creative studio which puts high value on novelty and topicality in the preparation of its advertising copy and designs.

hot shop agency

opposite to a modern service agency. Small executive team buying creative and other services and required and so keeping down overheads while not being inhibited by the limitations of regular staff.

hour-for-hour plan

payment by results system in which pay is directly related to the achievement of standard performance.

hours of work

the time during which an employee should be doing his job.

house account

significant customer, usually serviced at management level; because of the volume of business transacted, prices are keen and leave little or no opportunity for the payment of commission on sales.

house agency

an advertising agency wholly owned and operated by a large business organization to which it provides services which are, however, not necessarily exclusive to that organization.

household

a group of people who all live regularly at the same address and can be treated as a unit. There are two basic methods of identifying households: by defining 'housing units' and treating all the people living in one housing unit as household; by identifying groups of people who regularly live together as a family—usually defined as a group who are all catered for by one person for at least one meal a day.

household goods warehouse

a warehouse that specializes in storing household articles and furniture.

house journal

a regular publication, in the form of a newspaper or magazine, that is distributed to all employees of an organization and contains information of common interest.

house mark

a brand used by a firm or by group of firms on all products.

house organ

also, company magazine. A periodical issued by a business enterprise either for its own employees or for its customers, distributors, stock holders, or other outsiders with whom it has regular dealings.

house to house

calling direct on potential

consumers and users at their own homes for purposes of distributing or collecting information, leaving samples or direct selling.

housewife time

on radio, the time between the morning and afternoon drive times.

human capital

that part of an organization's capital represented by the ability, experience and skill of its work-force.

human communication

the process of communication between people; a relatively new field of study involving contributions from computer science, linguistics, logic, psychology and social science.

human engineering

an American term for Ergonomics.

human factor in efficiency

the necessity for constantly increasing efficiency is a basic fact of business life. Yet increasing generates forces which in the long run decrease efficiency and the problem is still unsolved; it may be worse than ever. So perhaps more can be gained by concentrating on weakening those forced which tend to decrease efficiency rather. than strengthening the forces which tend to increase efficiency. Basically the only out is to obtain the participation of the employees themselves in alleviating the factor that they have created to keep production down.

human relations

the discipline concerned with the application of the behavioural sciences (e.g., psychology, social psychology, sociology, and cultural anthropology) to the analysis and understanding of human behaviour in organizations.

human resource accounting

a concept that views the employees of an organisation as capital assets, like plant and equipment. While the concept is intuitively attractive, calculating the value, replacement cost, and depreciation of human assets poses significant problems.

human resources

a general term for all of the employees of an organisation or the workers in a society.

human resources management

the responsibility for making the best use of an organization employees. One of the major functions of personnel management.

humanism

an individualized philosophy and social doctrine of values that emphasizes personal dedication to and constant concern for human welfare in every real of human experience.

humanitarian

a person concerned with improving the health, welfare, and happiness of humankind;

a person engaged in activities to improve the health, welfare, and happiness of humankind; a true philanthropist.

humorous sell

an advertising message that jokes about the product being sold. This technique was very much in vogue in the late 1960s and early 1970s. Also called the soft sell.

hypodermic needle model

a largely discredited theory of masscommunication which held that the mass media have a direct immediate and powerful effect on the people receiving the media message. The people were seen as helpless victims whose attitudes and behaviour were influenced by the mass media messages much as if they had been injected with a hypodermic needle the Theory was superseded first by the two step flow model and later by the multistep flow model.

hypothecation

hypothecation is a charge against property for the amount of debt where neither ownership nor possession is passed to the creditor. In hypothecation, goods are in the possession of the borrower, but are charged equitable to the bank. Usually the hypothecation deed empowers the bank to require possession of goods to be handed over o him.

hypothesis

a testible assertion, statement, or preposition about two variables which are in some way related to each other.

hundi

an indigenous bill of exchange in India.

hurdle rate

a figure, set by the management of a firm, for the minimum internal rate of return that an investment project must have if it is to be accepted.

hyper employment

an alternative term for overall employment. It means that situation in which the demand for labour greatly exceeds supply. This situation generally arises during inflation.

hyper-inflation

the condition when all the equilibrating effect of inflation is lost and the value of the monetary unit sinks almost to zero.

hyping

promotional activity. Usually used with derogatory implication that claims are being made that will not be fulfilled. (Probably derived from hyperbole).

hypothecation

the pledging of property as collateral for a loan, the lender is not given title to the property but is given the right to sell it in case of default.

hypothesis testing

determining the correctness of assumed parameter, usually by sampling techniques.

IBM

international black market. Term used in West Africa, e.g., number of Ghanian credit to the pount sterling.

iceberg principle

in the evolution of marketing performance, the iceberg principle states that much valuable information is not represented adequately in summary data—that such summary data, in fact, is only the tip of the iceberg and that only detailed figures will reveal the submerged information.

iconic models

laboratory simulations of real life situations, particularly in engineering. These are models that look like the systems they represent.

idea marketing

the application of marketing principles in an effort to promote ideas, issues, causes, etc. Idea marketing may be carried on by profit and nonprofit organizations.

ideal market exposure

the degree to which a product receives exposure to potential customers so that it is sufficiently available to meet customer needs without exceeding them. Exceeding customer needs by providing additional exposure of the product is seen as adding unnecessarily to the total marketing cost of the product.

idem sonans

Latin for "the same sound". A doctrine holding that absolute accuracy in the spelling of names in legal documents is not required.

identifying consequences

we try to foresee impact on all the various company goals when consequences are likely to be both desirable and undesirable, both immediate and long-range, both tangible and intangible, both certain and only possible.

ideology

a system of beliefs that provides for the members of a group a moral justification for their individual and collective behaviour and that offers satisfying, although often grossly oversimplified, explanations of various social phenomena. All social groups develop ideologies, although it is seldom that any ideology is capable of precise definition or that all members of the group subscribe equally to all element of it. An ideology will reflect the values of the group members and serves to unite the group. The adherents of a given ideology have an emotional commitment to it and will tend to select supportive facts and to ignore or deny contradictory facts. The racist, for example, whose ideology stresses the inherent superiority of one racial group over another, will be strongly inclined to repudiate genetic evidence to the contrary. Where an ideology is patently demonstrated to be inadequate, its adherents may have recourse to the identification of scapegoats whose malevolent activities may then be claimed to have prevented the manifestation of phenomena consistent with the ideology: the ideology can thus be vindicated. For example, a manager whose ideology embraces the concept of the essential unity of interests of management and labour, may attribute recurrent industrial disputes to the activities of agitators.

idle

in cost accounting, equipment or labour that is not being used productively and hence represents a loss to the firm.

idle poor

habitually lazy people.

IFCI

in India the process of institutionalized industrial development financing dates back to 1948 when with its establishment the Industrial Finance Corporation of India (IFCI) was enjoined to assist industrial development particularly in the less developed areas in the country. In providing assistance the IFCI alongside the IDBI, the National Small Industries Corporation and organizations at State levels has not only emphasized the technical, financial and economic viability of projects but also the managerial capability of the promoters. It has been conscious of the need to ensure that its assistance while being of financial advantage to its beneficiary should fit in the economic strategy of the country and seek a social impact.

ignorance effect

a situation where commodities may be mistaken for other commodities for many reasons e.g. deceptive labels as well as price.

IIM

Indian Institute of Management.

IIPA

Indian Institute of Public Administration

illegal contracts

certain classes of contract which are not legally binding. Examples include those between firms in countries at war with each other.

image

metal perceptions or impressions held by an individual about himself, about others, or about products or services. How a customer sees himself and the way he fits into his environment influences his behavior in the marketplace.

image building

advertising and other promotional efforts intended to influence customers perceptions of a firm. For example, a business may engage in activities which enhance its reputation for being socially responsible.

image sell

a type of advertising message

which focuses on creating and conveying a particular image for the product or service being advertised.

imaginative approach

in advertising copy, an imaginative approach is one which concentrates on the possibilities for self-fulfilment and life-enrichment to be derived from the goods or product.

imitative entrepreneurship

it is characterized by readiness to adopt successful innovations inaugrated by innovating entrepreneurs.

It is one of the four types of entrepreneurship, the other three being:

1. innovating entrepreneurship.

2. fabian entrepreneurship, and,

3. drone entrepreneurship.

imitative segmenter

a segmenter which tries to offer an improved marketing mix to meet the needs of a target market already identified by an innovative segmenter. The products so developed tend to resemble or even duplicate the innovator's product.

imperfect competitor

anyone who buys or sells a good in large enough quantities to be able to affect the price of that good.

implicit costs

those expenses in a business which are less obvious and accountable than explicit costs, but which may affect the overall profitability of the business. They may include the owner's salary (even if the actual money is not paid out) or the rental value of the building (even if it is owned by the business, since it is not being rented out to others).

implied consent

the apparent acceptance of a proposed condition, course of action, or promise of outcome. Actions, and expressions can lead to the assumption of agreement to or acceptance of a proposed action or condition.

implied contract

a contract that is inferred from actions of the parties who fulfill promises without the existence of an expressed contract.

import

(1) to bring or transport goods into a country especially for the purpose of sales. (2) an import is any item brought into a country.

importance performance analysis

a marketing research tool employed to identify strengths and weaknesses in a company's performance as they are perceived by customers or potential customers.

import broker

in international trade, an import broker is an agent middleman who brings buyers and sellers together for the purpose of selling foreign goods in a domestic market. Import brokers provide the domestic buyer of imported goods with information about the availability of such goods. They also provide potential importers with information about the needs of the domestic buyers.

import duty

a tax imposed on the importation of goods into a country.

import licence

items for which restrictions are imposed against their importation could be had only when the government permitted the party to do so.

import prohibition

prohibiting by law or allowing only under defined conditions the imports of certain commodities.

imports

goods or services purchased from other countries, involving the use of foreign exchange. Imports, like exports, may be visible or invisible.

imports-restriction on trade

various restrictions apply to imports. Duty rates on some goods vary according to the type of product and the nature of any existing agreement with the supplying country. Tendencies to impose restrictions are countered both by fear of reprisals by the other country and by the general agreement on tariffs and trade. Other goods may be the subject of quotas, i.e., only a certain quantity may be imported in any one year. All nations have a list of goods, the importing of which is prohibited. Such lists vary widely from country-to-country.

import substitution

efforts by countries with poor trade balances, especially developing countries, to reduce imports by encouraging home production.

impoundment

the withholding by executives of budgeted or appropriated funds. There are several types of impoundment. Ones to confiscate funds after programme objective have been accomplished. A second made of impoundment is used to secure legal compliance.

impoverished style

a style of managerial leadership that exerts a minimum effort to get the required work done with the minimum of control considered to be appropriate to sustain organization membership.

impression cover

number of insertions it takes to cover the required percentage of population actually seeing the advertisement or commercial.

imprest

a cash advance whether for a float or to set off against anticipate expenses.

impulse buying

consumer purchases made without prior planning,

generally on the basis of the immediate appeal of the merchandise and its proximity to the point of sale.

impulse buying goods
phenomenon of self service, items being displayed to induce extra, unplanned purchases.

impulse goods
consumer goods that are normally bought by consumers without any previous planning (i.e., on impulse).

impulse merchandise
items which, because of their immediate appeal to the customer, are purchased with out prior planning or long consideration.

inc
abbreviation of incorporated when the word is part of the name of a corporation.

incentive
financial or other award provided to a subscriber, members enrolled, or beneficiary of a health service, prepaid, or insurance plan, usually in the form of cash or higher benefit levels.

incentive engineer
American term for a work study officer/engineer or rate fixer responsible for setting payment by results targets.

incentive payment system
a payment system of which inventive payment is a principle feature.

incentive plans
stimulating worker for higher outputs has led to the introduction of incentive plans in industry. Greater productive efforts are rewarded by suitable incentive payments. Norms or standards are carefully laid down either on the basis of past performance of the worker or through work measurements. Worker is paid incentive wages by reaching the standard or by exceeding the same.

incentive schemes
awards for ideas, increased productivity, record sales. Special organizations offer packages incentive schemes, particularly suitable for sales forces.

income approach
a method of appraisal used to determine the value of rental or lease property. Estimated net income from the property is spread over the life of a piece of equipment or property, and then discounted for the age of the equipment or property so as to determine its current value.

income averaging
the merging of lower income from prior years with present income, divided by the number of years, to achieve an averaged income as the basis for income tax payment. This reduces taxes in the current year.

income distribution plan
a financial programme for paying income to recipients, such as participants in a professional partnership. Allocation of income in a

distribution plan is accomplished by using one, or a combination of the following methods : (1) equal distribution to all participants. (2) production incentives paid proportionately to partners, according to the amount of income they produced. (3) payments proportional to the number of years of a partner's service to the partnership; (4) payments for performance of administrative functions. (5) payments for developmental activities which may contribute to future income. (6) consideration of outside income that contributes to the total income of the partnership; (7) allocation of outside income that contributes to the total income of the partnership; (8) subsidization of new members to compensate for lack of experience or client/patient base.

income fund

a mutual fund whose prime objective is to maximize current income (not, for example, to maximize future growth).

income of a person

the value of the goods and services which an individual can consume during a given period and still have the same amount of wealth (assets) at the end of the period as at the beginning.

income return

either the annual gain from an investment or the percentage figure found by dividing the annual gain by the initial price of the investment.

income segmentation

the subdivision of a population on the basis of the earnings of each segment.

income statement

usually designed as profit and loss account this statement is for the relevant financial year. The items appearing in it are in the nature of Revenue. It can be dissected under the following section : Gross Profit Section, Operating Profit Section, Net Profit Section : Appropriation Section.

income tax

from a business perspective, a tax on profits from business or work, but not on growth in the value of investments of property. For an individual, an income tax is a tax on personal income from work, less allowable deductions, credit, and other factors.

in company, in house

work handled inside the company's not put out to an agent or consultant. House magazines, exhibitions and print may be internal responsibilities.

incoterms

terms for use in international trade contacts drawn up by the International Chamber of Commerce. Incoterms include c and f, cif, ex-works, fas, fob and for.

increment

in personal management this

is a regular and usually automatic, increase in a scale of pay. In ergonomics it may refer to an increase in a stimulus from the environment of a standard amount, e.g., of illumination.

incremental payment system

giving pay increments arising from increased merit, age or service in accordance with a predetermined scale.

indemnify

to promise to someone that if he should suffer loss as a result of some specified event then he will be reimbursed (but he cannot claim more than he loses).

indemnity fund

used by an employers association, to compensate member firms for losses incurred by adhering to association policy during industrial action.

indent

a purchase order to an exporter or middleman to import certain goods within a specified time.

independent store

typically owned and operated by an individual, family, or partnership, the independent store is not a part of chain organization or ownership group, although it may be a member of a voluntary chain. These retail outlets are often general stores or limited-line store.

independent worker

one who works on his own account and not for an employer.

indexing

a strategy employed to mitigate the effects of inflation by tying increases in wages, taxes, interest rates, etc. to changes in a price index; i.e., as prices advance and retreat a variety of escalators are used to bring other aspects of the economy into line. For example, social security payments may betied to fluctuations in the consumer price index.

index linking

systematic adjustment of the value of transactions in line with changing prices, particularly in times of inflation.

Indian Institute of Management (IIM)

major qualifying body in the area of management science. In India, there are three IIM located one each at Ahmedabad, Bangalore and Calcutta.

Indian Labour Conference

tripartite body, comprising the representatives of the government, employers and labour, set up by the government of India for consultation and discussion relating to questions affecting labour.

indirect channel of distribution

the movement of products from manufacturer through

independent middlemen to the ultimate consumer or industrial user. The employment of middlemen in the channel of distribution leaves the producer with somewhat less control over distribution and with less contact with customers.

indirect cost

costs involved in doing business which cannot be directly related to a particular product or service or to a particular organizational unit. Included in this category are such expenses as the cost of heat and light, administrative expenses, building depreciation, etc. Also known as common cost.

indirect export

a method of exporting goods which involves the use of independent international marketing middlemen to enter the foreign market. These middlemen include the domestic-based export merchant, the domestic-based export agent, cooperative international marketing organizations, and the export management company. A firm interested in indirect marketing, may use any of these middlemen to reach the foreign market.

indirect labour costs

the costs associated with those members of the work-force not directly involved in the production of goods and services, but whose labour is essential to the running of the organization, e.g., maintenance and secretarial staff.

indirect materials cost

an indirect cost that relates to an expenditure by a firm on materials or supplies.

indirect question

oblique approach to gain information which might otherwise be withheld.

indirect review

where management reviews the progress of work, not by direct monitoring or inspection (direct review) but indirectly through feedback in the form of complaints returned work.

indirect taxation

a form of taxation which is not paid directly to the government is indirect taxation, but which is added to the cost of good and services, e.g., value added tax of the television licence in the United Kingdom.

indirect wages

synonym for indirect labour cost.

indirect worker

an employee of a firm whose work does not directly contribute to the manufacture of one of the firm's products. (Also known as an indirect).

individual brand

a particular product offered for sale by its producer under a unique brand name, i.e., none of the manufacturer's other products carry the same name.

individual consumer

the term usually refers to a

family.

individual face-to-face contacts

these contacts are in two classes: (i) the individual face-to-face contacts of superior and subordinate and (ii) the group face-to-face contacts in informal and formal meetings. Regarding the former it is obviously essential to have know channels of communication within the hierarchy. This is a common management precept. What appears to be one of the unrecognized barriers at this level is a failure to utilize the channels most productively, specifically the failure of the superior to listen to what the subordinate has to say before he offer information comment or advice on the subject under discussion.

individual training methods

individual as opposed to group training methods, including programmed instruction and personal job instruction.

induction

a process of introducing or orienting new employees to the environment of the organisation. It is very much a socialization or personalization problem. A new employee must be made to feel at home after he has been placed on a particular job. He must get himself familiarized with the new environments, new colleagues and new challenges. This will generate in him a sense of belonging and self-confidence.

induction method

films, videocassettes, slide presentations and literature to introduce new recruits to an organization.

induction procedure

(or induction programme) activities taking place when a new employee joins an organization of which the objectives are to acquaint the individual with the organization and his colleagues and to ensure that all the organization's records concerning the employee are complete.

induction training

devised for school leaver entrants or other new employees in a firm to familiarize them with company practices (practises) and procedures.

indulgency pattern

terant and lenient style of management.

industrial accident

accident suffered at work.

industrial advertising

advertising of products or services to industrial, commercial or business organizations.

industrial democracy

the concept of giving workers a voice in how they do their jobs, so that to some extent they help manage a firm or industry.

industrial disease

a range of disease and illnesses

which are caused by some aspect of work or its environment—for examples, asbestosis, silicosis, dermatitis etc.

industrial dispute

a conflict between management and workers or between their representatives, usually about pay or conditions of employment.

industrial distributor

mainly a wholesaler of goods to producers and manufacturers rather than to retailers, the industrial distributor may provide his customers with a wide range of services including calls by salespersons, the extension of credit, the stocking of large assortments, delivery etc.

industrial engineering

an American term for a kind of applied ergonomics which concentrates on the system of production and draw on various fields, including industrial psychology, operational research and time-and-motion study, as well as physics and mathematics.

industrial espionage

planned attempt by a company or its agents at obtaining secret or confidential information from within or about a rival company.

industrial injuries

employees who are injured in the course of their employment may claim damages from their employer if they can prove negligence or breach of statutory duty Employers' Liability.

In addition, and regardless of whether they can prove legal liability, injured employees who lose time off work will be entitled to statutory sick pay. This is payable by their employer at one of three flat rates, depending on earnings, for up to eight weeks' absence in any tax year. No payment is due for the first three days of incapacity. Where any incapacity for work lasts for more than eight weeks (so exhausting entitlement to statutory sick pay) the individual is then entitled to state sickness benefit, which is payable weekly for up to a further twenty weeks. After a total of twenty-eight weeks' incapacity, invalidity benefit takes over. Like sickness benefit, it is paid by the DHSS, though at a higher rate. It is payable for so long as the invalidity lasts, up to retirement if necessary.

Where an injury has some lasting effect, an employee becomes eligible after ninety day's disability (disregarding sundays) for disablement benefit. This is not a fixed sum but depends upon the extent of the loss of mental or physical faculty sustained. The degree of injury is expressed as a percentage as given in a table or scale of assessments. Where disablement is assessed at less than 20 percent a lump sum is paid and a weekly pension awarded for more serious disablement. The pension can be supplemented in certain circumstances by, for example, a special hardship allowance.

In order to maintain a claim for any of the state benefits individuals must be employed earners under the Social Security Act 1975, although they need have no minimum number of national insurance contributions provided their injuries were caused by an 'accident arising out of and in the course of employment. Disability caused by certain industrial disease is also covered by the national insurance scheme so long as detailed regulations have prescribed the disease as creating a special occupational hazard in one or more specific industrial operations. Sick Pay.

industrial law

in Britain the term industrial law is used for that branch of law which deals with Contract of Employment, the special provisions concerning particular aspects of employment (e.g. Health and Safety legislation) and the law dealing with collective labour relations, such as Trade Union Law and Collective Bargaining. In some other countries and increasingly in Britain this branch of the law is referred to as labour law.

British industrial law has come into existence by accident rather than by design. Part of it is represented by the common-law rules dealing with the master-servant relationship as modified over the centuries by statute as and when Parliament found it necessary to deal with particular abuses. Trade unions in Britain have by and large preferred to deal with their problems by direct negotiation with employers rather than by invoking legal sanctions, since they have had little confidence in the impartiality of the law when faced with industrial problems. Academically, the subject has been somewhat neglected in the past, although most law degrees offer it nowadays, at least as an optional subject. There is an industrial law society.

At one time British writers on industrial law could be divided into those who felt the scope of the subject should not be enlarged and those who saw the law as potentially a key regulator of the employment relationship and of industrial relationship generally. The volume of legislation over the last twenty years and the case law it has spawned make it increasingly difficult to continue to characterize the role of the law as largely abstentionist.

industrial market

the industrial market consists of all those organizations which are involved in production, manufacturing, providing services, wholesaling, and retailing, together with the many levels of government and a wide variety of institutions; i.e., all potential customers with the exception of individuals buying goods for themselves or their immediate families.

industrial purchasing

the buying of goods and services at the business, industrial, or institutional level. Most industrial purchasing is carried on by professionals skilled in negotiating prices and buying in large quantities. Also known as procurement.

industrial relations

this term is now used to describe the web of relationship that exists between employee or their trade union representatives, management and government. It usage is therefore much broader than its original industrial or manufacturing context and extends to issues and procedures concerning employment in any worker environment.

industrial relation act

the objective of the Industrial Relations Act 1971, abrogated 1974, was to provide a legal framework for the conduct of industrial relations in contrast to the pre-existing voluntarist system.

The Act contained four broad categories of provision: (i) the rights of employes; (ii) the registration and conduct of trade unions and employee associations; (iii) strikes and lockout; (iv) the reform of collective bargaining.

Unions affiliated to the TUC opposed this legislation before and after its enactment and adopted a policy of non-cooperation in the implementation of the Act. In particular, they refused to register and to co-operate with the institutions established under the Act, except in self-defence. Any affiliated unions not complying were expelled from the TUC. The TUC unions were particularly incensed by the making of their former legal immunities conditional on registration; by the constraint on the powers of trade-union officers; by the outlawing of the traditional pre-entry closed shop; by the new right of employees not to join a trade union or other workers' organization; by the provision for making collective agreements legally binding unless specifically provided otherwise by the parties; and by the arrangements for the use of the National Industrial Relations Court and the Commission of Industrial Relations to determine disputed bargaining rights.

In practice the Act was particularly effective in two areas: unfair dismissal and procedures. The unfair dismissal provisions continue as amended by the Employment Acts 1980 and 1982. With respect to procedures, many companies have been stimulated to improve their industrial relations system with the aid of the Industrial Relations Code of Practice, which remained in force when the Act was repealed and replaced by the Trade Union and Labour Relation Act 1974.

industrial relations management

in recent years interest in the role of managers in industrial relations has grown appreciably. Within the firm industrial-relations management may form only a part of the total responsibility of personnel management, irrespective of the size and influence of the personnel department; or it may be so significant for the enterprise that the industrial-relations manager has a seat on the board of directors whilst the personnel manager does not, although this is so far relatively rare in Britain. In practice there are dangers that differing industrial-relations policies are carried out by operational managers, personnel managers, and other service managers, e.g., industrial engineers. Increasingly, however, British management is moving towards more coherent, more rational and more positive industrial-relations policies.

The analysis of industrial-relations management has centred on the notions of strategy, style and frame of reference. Industrial-relations strategies are long-term policies that are developed by the management of an organization in order to preserve or change the procedures, practice or results of industrial-relations activities over time. They may be designed to curtail or, alternatively, to enhance trade unionism. They may be centralist or decentralist (i.e., they may involve pushing all industrial-relations decisions down to enterprise level). They may or may not involve employers associations. Also they can take a paternalist or human-relations approach or be coercive. Almost certainly they change over time according to economic circumstances and the power of unions.

A managerial industrial-relations style refers to the approach of managers to labour issues. The four pure types are directive (or authoritarian), paternalist (or welfare oriented), constitutional (i.e. accepting a 'web of rules' formed in negotiations with organized labour and governments) and participative (involving the workforce and their representatives in decision-making processes). In practice, however, actual industrial-relations styles are more complex. In Britain they include sophisticated paternalism, characterized by a deliberate attempt to avoid collective bargaining and often a refusal to recognize trade unions, constitutionalism, which is still typical where unions are strong and consultative management (very common, involving information-sharing and employee involvement but not full participation). The much publicized directive style of the so-called 'macho' managers is not typical of most British firms. In Britain in the 1970s, despite a preference for a unitary frame of reference, managers in many companies in practice adopted a pluralist position and encouraged the growth of Shop Stewards (including full-time convenors and other senior stewards), while providing a number of facilities for lay officers to carry out their unions duties. In the 1980s unitary perspectives have been reasserted far more and are evident in the growth of consultative practices and procedures and a number of direct appeals to the workforce. The different strategies of management have also been identifiable in the shift in preference for different collective bargaining levels in the 1970s and 1980s. In the earlier period managers helped to change the locus of bargaining by encouraging enterprise-level agreements with the workforce. Later, however, there was a preference to move to the head office at company level (i.e. above the establishment), where policies could be formulated that were applied consistently throughout the constituent work units and where managements were free to develop their ideas without recourse to either union or government. Nevertheless, practice still varies in Britain amongst different sectors and firms. Moreover, there are distinctive styles of management associated with Japanese concerns (paternalism and a pronounced unitary frame of reference) and with various national culture. Trade Union Types; Managerial Unionism.

industrial sociology

the study of the effects of societal processes on the environment of work and on the economy, e.g., the black economy or social change and its effects on economic life.

industrial trade union

where a single trade union represents all the workers in an industry instead of the more common situation, known as multiunionism, where union represent particular skills or types of worker whatever the industries in which they are working, many commentators have pointed to the multiplicity of trade unions in several industries as a root problem of industrial relations.

industrial training boards

originally established by the

Secretary of State for employment under the Industrial Training Act 1964 to ensure that the provision of training (Industrial Training) is adequate to meet the needs of the industries for which they are instituted. In 1978 there were twenty-six training boards, if one included the Foundry Industry Training Committee (technically a committee of the Engineering Industry Training Board), the Local Government Training Board (which was set up voluntarily) and the Agricultural Training Board (which had a different method of funding from the others).

Boards were initially appointed by the Minister of Labour and had to consist of a chairman with industrial or commercial experience; an equal number of persons appointed from the two sides of industry after consultation with the appropriate employers' association and trade unions; and people with educational or training experience appointed after consultation with the Minister of Education. A board has two main duties: to ensure that sufficient training is provided in its industry, and to publish information on such matters as the nature, content and length of training for different occupations. A board's authority extends to all forms of training and to any further education that should be associated with the training. It can approve training facilities and courses, lay down standards, impose tests, inspect and advise, and undertake research.

When first constituted under the Industrial Training Act, each board had the duty of imposing upon employers in its industry a financial levy and of making grants to employers in accordance with its assessment of the quantity and quality of the training provided. Following the introduction of the Employment and Training Act 1973, the Industrial Training Boards no longer had the duty to raise a levy, but had power to do so provided that the levy did not exceed 1 percent of the total wages and salary bill of an employer. The Employment and Training Act 1981 amended the Industrial Training Act 1964 and allowed the Secretary of State for Employment to abolish or change the scope of an industrial training board after consulting the → Manpower Services Commission. Under the 1981 Act, a board can still finance its operating expenses from a levy, but requires the support of the majority of employer members before a levy can be imposed.

In November 1981 the Secretary of State announced the abolition of sixteen training boards, the statutory system of training in the sectors of industry concerned being replaced by a voluntary system, to be based upon trade associations. This has left seven industrial training boards under the statutory system covering the construction, engineering, hotel and catering, clothing and allied products, offshore petroleum, plastics processing and road transport industries.

industry-wide agreement

or national agreement. Collective agreement or bargain between employers and trade unions on an industry wide basis. At the other extreme is workplace bargaining. In between are company agreements and factory agreement.

inelasticity

the relative insensitivity of a product's sales volume to changes in price. A product which has inelastic demand does not motivate its marketer to cut the price, since sales revenue per unit of product decreases more rapidly than unit sales increase.

inept set

in consumer behaviour, inept set refers to those specific brands which, for one reason or another, the buyer excludes from consideration when shopping a product category.

inertia

resistance to change in individuals and/or organizations; considered one of the major problems confronting marketing effort.

inertia selling

practice of delivering goods to people who have not ordered them and living them either to pay for the goods or to return them within a specified time.

infant industry

the newly established industrial units.

inference

judgment; reasoning based on facts, opinions, or observations that are indicative but not conclusive with regard to some circumstances.

inferential statistics

that portion of the field of statistic concerned with making inferences about some fact in a larger population on the basis of findings obtained in samples.

inflation

any increase in the general price level that is sustained and non-seasonal in character. The effect is to decrease the consumer's purchasing power.

influencer

in industrial purchasing, the influence, although he does not make the final buying decision, has input during the preliminary discussions regarding the transaction, generally on the strength of some technical expertise.

informal agreement

also called "gentlemen's agreement" the term refers to an agreement added by the members of a traded association to conform to certain trade practices.

informal communication

communication among people through informal contacts is known as informal communication or grapevine. It does not flow through the official authority relationships. It represents spontaneous expression of ideas and reactions. It is built around the interpersonal relations among the people working in an organisation. It is not established by management but it coexists with the formal communication system.

informal organization

unlike the outward face of the formal organization this reflects the inner life of the organization where communication proceeds via the grapevine, where life is lived in informal groups and productivity is determined by the group norm of a particular work group.

information gathering

this is the essential first step in setting up an information system, which requires a procedure for identifying and collecting information.

information management

this is concerned with applying information technology to the flow of information in an organization with the intention of ordering it in the best way to achieve organizational goals.

information retrieval

the process of recovering data from a data base. This process lies at the heart of a management information system. The most common example of information of retrieval is probably the checking by an airline booking clerk of the availability of seats on a particular flight.

information search

an activity by which consumers gather product information and weight alternatives. The search may be carried out internally, i.e., by the consumer consulting his memory for relevant information collected in the past, or it may be carried out externally, i.e., through the examination of advertising, discussions with friends or salespeople, etc.

information system for feedback

the more challenging and critical task before the manager is the setting up of an information system for feedback from the community. For, in the next decade the manager will have to be far more socially vigilant and aware than he is in present. By virtue of his status and position he will have the major responsibility of identifying the needs and problems of the masses.

information technology

information is essential to achieve concerted action by an individual or by an enterprise. Some working definitions are useful to clarify the technology of handling information:

Data. Numbers representing an observable object or event.

Information. Human significance associated with an observable object or event.

Knowledge. Theoretical or practical understanding of a subject.

Wisdom. Experience and knowledge judiciously applied.

These terms form a hierarchy; each item is built upon the previous one but adds to it in terms of human significance. Computers and information systems actually handle data, but present the result to the human user so that it looks like information, or even knowledge. So far, they make a poor job of appearing wise.

'Information technology' (IT) is a modern term. It was coined to mark the convergence of two technologies that had traditionally been separate: computing and communications. This convergence was made possible by microelectronics. A major advance came with the invention of the transistor in 1948, then in the early 1960s came integrated circuits (ICs) in which many transistors and other components could be fabricated on to a single 'chip' or crystal of semiconductor such as silicon. The capacity of these ICs developed at a remarkable pace, consistently doubling every year. By the early 1970s it was possible to fabricate more than 10,000 components on a single chip; this was termed very large scale integration (VLSI).

It turned out that the new technology was best suited to processing data that is in digital rather than analogue form. In an analogue representation, some continuously varying physical quantity (such as the variation in air pressure caused by the human voice) is represented by a continuously varying electrical signal. The signal is then an 'analogue' of the physical quantity, but it is not easy to process signals in this form accurately. In a digital representation, the physical quantity is described numerically. The numbers might, for example, represent a graph of sound-pressure as a function of time. The numbers are usually handled in 'binary' for, comprising only the digits 0 to 1; this is because it is technically easiest to handle numbers using devices that have only two physical states.

The emergence of IT has produced human problems as well as technical ones. People trained in one discipline find it difficult to understand the problems and reasonable of another discipline, where the traditions, in particular of co-operation and standardization, may be very different. Some of these problems have had effects of which the general manager needs to be aware, because it limits what the technology is able to offer in practice. The interface between operator machine is also receiving increased attention. Information System; Man-machine interface.

information theory

the study of information and the way it is communicated. It originated with mathematicians and engineers and draws heavily on concepts from these fields, but with advances in brain research it has also been used in linguistics and psychology.

informative advertising

a form of advertising which figures heavily in the pioneering stage of new product development and other situations in which the aim is to build primary demand. Informative advertising serves to tell customers about a new product, suggest new uses for a product, inform the market of a price change, explain how the product works, describe available services, correct false impressions, reduce consumers fears, and to build a company image.

infringement

a breach or violation of a right; also, the unauthorized making, use, selling, or distributing of something protected by a patent, copyright, or trademark.

in house training

as in–company training.

initial markup

when expressed in dollars, initial markup is the difference between the cost price of merchandise and its first retail price. When expressed as a percentage, it is computed as the difference between cost price and first retail price divided by retail price. In both cases markdown and stock shortages are not counted in the computation. Initial markup is sometimes referred to as original markup, initial mark-on, or markon.

inner directed

a person guided primarily by goals and ideals stemming from his/her own value system rather than by the opinions of others. Inner-directed people are often considered nonconformists by their peers.

inner pack

one of a number of packs which are then stored in multiple container, e.g., twenty individual cartons of cigarettes might be wrapped as a unit, a number of which are then packed in a fiberboard case.

innovating entrepreneurship

C. Larence Danhop classifies entrepreneurs into the following types:

1. innovating entrepreneur
2. imitative entrepreneur
3. fabian entrepreneur, and
4. drone entrepreneur.

Innovating entrepreneurship is characterized by aggressive assemblance of information and the analysis of results deriving from novel combination of factors. Men in this group are generally aggressive in experimentation and exhibit celerity.

innovation peripheral

another company's contribution to same product group, such as a different kind of nylon shirt with different properties and sales appeal.

innovative combiner

a marketing firm using the combined target market approach to identify a new combination of sub-markets. Innovative combiners are often followed into the marketplace by a number of imitators.

innovative segmenter

a segmenter that seeks out new submarkets, identifies unsatisfied needs, and attempts to develop a marketing mix to reach the new segment. Innovative segmenters are often followed into the market-place by a number of imitators seeking to utilize the newly identified market segment for their own products.

innovator

experimental buyer, first to try a new product or service.

in-pack premium

a free gift or other item placed within the package of the item being promoted by the manufacturer. For example, the "prize in every package" inside each box of cracker jacks.

input/output devices and media

for a computer to communicate with the outside world input/ output facilities are required. The data given to the computer are manipulated within it by electrical pulses. Initially they are hand-or typewritten on paper, so input facilities are required to convert them into electrical forms. Since computers operate very quickly, input facilities must be designed to operate as fast as possible. Similar considerations apply to output facilities.

There are several types of input facilities available and the type most suitable is dependent upon the particular application. Computer installations usually have two or more alternatives present to provide flexibility.

(i) Punch cards. These are basically the punched cards used in data processing since 1890. Information is coded by punching holes in alternative positions (usually twelve) in a vertical column. Cards are usually 'eighty column' or 'forty column' in size. The cards are 'read', that is the positions of the holes are 'sensed' by a card reader. Sensing is performed in a number of ways: (a) electrically-by passing the card between an electrically energized roller and a set of wire brushes. Where holes are present electric circuits are complete: (b) mechanically-a set of steel pins, each coincident with a punching position, is pushed down on the card face. Where a hole is present, the pin passes through, activating a mechanism: (c) photoelectrically-light is focused on the card, which is supported over a set of photoelectric cells, each coincident with a punching position. The presence of a hole activates the appropriate cell. Card readers performing this operation can 'read at 1,000 or more cards a minute.

(ii) punched paper tape. This consists of a continuous strip of paper or plastic tape $\frac{3}{4}-1$ in. wide. Data are recorded by punching holes laterally across the tape. There are between five and eight punching positioning, giving, 5-8 track tape. Data from the tape are read serially by a tape reader operating photoelectrically. Tape readers can read at 1,000 or more characters per second.

input output matching

the concept of decision control points leads to idea of input-output matching around each such point. Whether it is a chief executive or a departmental head or a plant foreman all such points in the organization structure should be amenable to input-output matching in a continuous manner. The period over which such matching could be done and the index to do it shall of course be different for various classes of decision control points.

inquiry test

method of testing advertisements or media by comparing the number of inquiries received.

insolvency

strictly, there are two forms of insolvency. Legal insolvency occurs when a business is unable to obtain the necessary cash to pay its debts; that is, the demands of all creditors of the business could not be satisfied despite realization for cash of all of its assets. Technical insolvency occurs when the business is unable to meet its debts at a particular time, despite the fact that it is not legally insolvent, and is therefore a particular result of mismanaging the timing of cash flows.

inspection buying

in industrial buying, the practice of purchasing a product only after every item has been carefully examined. This method is used primarily for products that are not standardized and require inspection. For example, one of a kind products such as cars and buildings must be inspected.

installment buying

also buying on time. Purchasing consumer goods, usually relatively expensive ones, and paying for them over a period of time, in periodic partial payments called installments.

installment credit

a consumer credit arrangement between retailer and customer, generally implemented for the purchase of expensive durable goods. Unlike revolving credit, the installment plan usually involves a formal contract which is secured by a down payment. The customer agrees to pay the balance at periodic intervals, each installment including interest and service charges which represent revenue for the retailer. Under this plan the store retains title to the merchandise until it is fully paid for, thus leaving the way open for repossession if it should necessary.

installment selling

involves taking in initial deposit against goods purchased and collecting the balance of the selling price over an agreed period of time in fixed installments.

institutional advertising

advertising intended to enhance the prestige, image, and reputation of a firm or institution rather than to promote a specific product or to induce an immediate response on the part of the target audience.

institutional expectancy chart

sometimes used following psychological testing in an attempt at predicting the levels of efficiency within a workforce, note being made of such factors as the number of workers expected to be of above-average performance.

institutional market

the institutional market consists of a wide variety of organizations, many of them non-profit, including schools, churches, hospitals, etc. The institutional market is a part of the larger industrial market.

in-store promotion

sampling, demonstration and sales promotion event organized by manufacturers in stores for foods, wines, washing machines, chewing gum, ironing boards, etc.

instr (test)

ability to follow instructions test.

instrument

1. a document intended to have a specific legal effect, e.g., written contract, a financial instrument or a statutory, instrument.

2. a device for measuring or testing either physical or mental attributes (e.g., a questionnaire or an achievement test).

instrumented store

a retail outlet in which information gathered and analyzed by computers has determined the optimum layout and shelf-space. Inventory control, ordering, and related functions are also determined by information gathered by computers, usually through point-of-sale scanning.

insurable risk

a risk that is one of a large, homogeneous group of similar risks that would incur a definable and quantifiable loss, for which the loss in individual cases is accidental or fortuitous; for which the potential loss is large enough to cause hardship.

insurance law

a contract of insurance is one whereby the insurer (generally an insurance company) undertakes in return for a premium to indemnify the insured against the financial consequences of the contingency insured against, up to the maximum amount stated in the insurance policy. The term assurance is sometimes used for those contracts where the contingency (e.g. death) is one that is bound to occur at some time.

Contracts of insurance have three general features;

(i) they are contracts of utmost good faith. This means that the insured must volunteer to the insurer all information about the risk that might influence the insurer's decision whether, and if so at what premium, to insurance. Failure to do so would entitle the insurer to disclaim his liability under the contract.

(ii) the insured must have an insurable interest in the subject matter of the policy. This means that the insured faces a financial loss in the event of the contingency materializing. If the insured lacks an insurable interest, the transaction would be treated as void, being in the nature of a gamble.

(iii) all contracts of insurance, except for life and accident insurance, are treated as contracts of indemnity and the insured may, irrespective of the amount of the policy, recover no more than the loss that they have actually suffered. If this loss exceeds the amount of the policy, no more than the sum insured for could be claimed.

insured loan

in the context of federal credit programmes, a loan for which a private lender is assured of repayment by the federal government for part or all of the principal or interest due. For example, a guaranteed student loan.

intangible assets

assets which have no physical existence (unlike, say, machinery or property) but which are still presumed to be of some financial value to the organization, e.g., copyright, goodwill, patent or trade mark.

intangible resources

with reference to a business organization, intangible resources include the firm's reputation in the marketplace, the relationship it maintains with customers, the quality level of its products or service, etc.

integrated learning system
combined and planned use of a variety of methods of instruction and teaching aids (e.g., audiovisual aids) to achieve specified goals.

integrated manager
a term describing the manager who likes to become part of the people, things, and processes he or she manages. Such managers are joiners and take pains to get involved with individual and groups about their work.

integrated marketing
a strategy in which all of a company's marketing efforts are handles by a single organization, generally a large advertising agency (sometimes called a superagency). These agencies are equipped to provide services such as direct mail, coupons and other promotions, publicity releases, and public relations activities as well as traditional advertising.

integrated pension plan
a plan that adjusts the employee's pension benefits downward to reflect the company's contribution to social security.

intelligence tests
tests designed to measure the mental alertness and capacity of a person to grasp and put together the elements of a novel or abstract situation. They measure the intelligence quotient (IQ) of the candidates regarding their reasoning, perception, numerical ability, etc.

intensity of distribution
intensity is said to be increased as the number of outlets (wholesale and retail) are increased.

intensive distribution
a marketing strategy in which goods are placed in the maximum number of retail outlets by the manufacturer or distributor, thus giving the product the widest possible exposure to the public. Also known as mass distribution and extensive distribution.

intensive selling
selling a greater volume to present customers through energetic promotional derive.

interacting skills
the skills used by marketing managers to influence others to implement the firm's marketing strategy. These skills include motivating employees of the firm as well as others on whom the firm relies (such as marketing research firms, advertising agencies, dealers, wholesalers, agents, etc.). For example, managing conflict within a channel of distribution is one area in which the marketing manager must utilize interacting skills.

interaction matrix
design tool used in arranging plant layouts, activity relationships, etc., particularly

where physical positioning is a vital consideration.

interactive medium

medium which permits the recipient to participate or to demand information, such as TV system whereby the viewer can communicate with an information base, terminals or other viewers.

interchangeability

removal of demarcations between types of labour and job, having the advantage for employers of more economical use of labour and for employees of greater job security.

interest tests

tests designed to determine the preferences but not the ability of an applicant for occupation of different kinds. Interest of the candidate in the job is ascertained to avoid maladjustment.

interim reporting

this includes the preparation of quarterly, half-yearly, and other interim reports and income statements, cash flow and funds flow statements, scrap reports, etc.

interlocking directorate

a situation in which an individual serves on the boards of directors of two or more competing corporations. This tends to create a monopoly by bringing the management of these corporations under a single control.

intermediate customer

a generic term for any buyer between the producer of the basic raw materials that are used to make the product and the ultimate consumer. Manufacturers, wholesalers, retailers, and other middlemen are all intermediate customers.

intermodal services

in transportation, such coordinated services as piggyback and fishyback which combine two or more modes of transportation, e.g., truck trailers on railroad flat-cars.

internal controls

accounting procedures for protecting a non-profit organisation's assets and ensuring the accuracy and validity of its financial reports; all of the coordinate methods and measures adopted within an organisation to safeguard its assets, check the accuracy and reliability of its accounting data, promote operational efficiency, and encourage adherence to prescribe managerial policies.

internal data

marketing information derived from a firm's own internal records. Included are such accounting records as profit and loss statements and financial ratios, sales revenues and costs, inventory data, etc. Also known as operating data.

internal marketing

management strategies for employee development, particularly for those employees involved in selling. The intent of internal marketing is to improve the organization's relations with its customers.

internal public relations

a programme of communications with an organisation's staff and members, typically utilizing newsletters and bulletins. Internal public relation programmes are intended to create and maintain morale and enthusiasm within an organization.

international department

that part of a firm charged with the conduct of foreign operations.

international forces

it refers to the role of the poor countries in the world economy.

international marketing institute (IMI)

an association of marketing executives which conducts summer programs both in the United States and abroad geared to improving the marketing skills of its membership. IMI maintains both a placement service and a library. It publishes a newsletter as well as export marketing for smaller firms. The association is based in Cambridge Massachusetts.

interpersonal skill development

interpersonal skills come to the fore when two persons interact socially. When Albert communicates his intentions to Barbara, verbally or non-verbally, he has to make assumption, for example, about her knowledge, feelings, attitudes, abilities and level of interest. And when Barbara responds, he in turn must listen with care or interpret accurately non-verbal signals or gestures, in order to assess whether or not she has understood his message.

Sending understandable message, listening, anticipating others' reactions to one's behaviour and interpreting their responses are all examples of interpersonal skills, which can be developed by training. Group Method of Training, for example, enable an individual to behave in front of others, to receive information about the effect of that behaviour on their feelings and attitudes, and to plan modifications if necessary. If people respond negatively to Albert because he continually interrupts them, the elimination of such interruptions can then become an appropriate learning objective for him.

The development of sophisticated interpersonal skills, like interviewing or negotiation techniques, may initially require instruction in the complexities of the process, illustrated by demonstrations of good practice, such as the skilful use of questions. Practice interviews or role played negotiations can then be organized, observed (preferably with the aid of videotape) and discussed with the participants to discover what went well and what behavioural modifications would lead to a more skilled performance next time. Similar feedback of a constructive nature from colleagues can be encouraged in the working environment when the skills are being used in earnest. Performance Appraisal.

In a training design suggested by Harrison and Berger for programmes concerned with interpersonal skill development, during the first one and a half hours participants consider the feedback they have already received within their organizations, complete a self-assessment questionnaire, and perform a variety of tasks with others. This phase enables participants to assess their own strengths and weaknesses and to diagnose their own training needs, which are then discussed with the training staff. Improvements are most commonly sought in the areas of communication, leadership and influence, decision-making and problem-solving. The next two and a half days are spent helping the participants to develop the skills they need. To this end, task situations are designed to meet individual requirements, taking into account the person's situation within their enterprise. A final day is then devoted to the practical problems likely to be encountered within the enterprise when the individual applies his or her newly learned skills.

interpolation

the process of estimating intermediate values between two known values.

intertype channel conflict

a form of distribution channel conflict which occurs when middlemen of different types (e.g., specially stores and department stores) attempt to impede the operations of one another in such a way as to create channel dissonance.

interview

in essence an interview is a form of conversion, between one interviewee and one or more interviewers, which is structured to a greater or lesser extent. It is probably the most widely-used method for the assessment of a person's ability. It is also the most subjective method.

interviewer

conducts research surveys, whether in the field or in discussion groups. For field work, matronly, self-effacing intelligent women and those with social science training preferred. Discussion groups usually led by people with psychological training. Men usually conduct industrial interviews.

interviewer bias
distortion in the results of an interview due to the intentional or unintentional intervention of the interviewer.

interviewing procedures
general types of interview include the connected conversation interview, the directive interview, and the non-directive interview. Types of interview used particularly in personnel section include the seven point plan, the five fold grading scheme, the panel interview, and group selection interviews.

interview technique
when writing feature articles interviewer should have written or unwritten questionnaires of information to be sought. First questions should not require act of memory, and should be simple, personal ones.

interview tension
condition suffered by respondent according to process adopted, e.g., anxiety during a tape-recorded interview. Interviews often more satisfactory if there are no obvious clumsy and inhibiting factors such as large note-books, clipboards or tape recorders and microphones.

in transitu
on the way.

intrinsic rewards
rewards which are internal to the employee such as job satisfaction or self-actualization, rather than external such as pay or fringe benefits.

introductory stage
the beginning (or pioneering) stage in the product life cycle during which the marketing effort is directed toward introducing the product (rather than the specific brand) to the consuming public. Many products fail at this stage because they never capture the interest of the consumer.

inventory
(1) the assets of a business other than those commonly referred to as "plant and equipment" i.e. inventory includes raw materials, semi-finished goods or work-in-progress, and finished goods to be either used internally or offered for sale. (2) a detailed, often descriptive list of goods held in stock for future sale.

inventory carrying costs
those costs of doing business directly related to goods held in inventory, including warehousing, deterioration and obsolescence, theft, and insurance charges.

inventory management
as stock control, but possibly taking into account plant, equipment, etc., as well as stocks and products.

inventory or stock-control problems
in this context inventory is defined as idle resources. The company usually needs to maintain some of its resources,

e.g. raw materials or finished good stocks, men or money, in reserve and therefore idle stock. The function of inventory control is to determine the best level for these reserves. Taking raw material stock as an example, we may say that some costs increase and some decrease as the level of stock is increased: (a) tied up capital, storage space, taxes and insurance costs, together with risk of obsolescence and spoilage all increase as stockholding increases. (b) shortage, ordering and purchasing costs generally all decrease as stockholding increases.

An inventory control system must be able to answer two question: how much to order and how frequently. The order quantity is determined so that it achieves an appropriate balance between the opposing costs above, and is sometimes known as the economic order quantity (EOC). Since demand for stock is not regular, allowance must be made for variability by maintaining a buffer or safety stock; this stock also has an associated cost and the objective is to keep it at a low level consistent with the service level requirements of management. This may be achieved by noting the frequency of demand in previous periods, by representing it on a statistical distribution (Normal Distribution) and by holding multiples of the standard deviation (Measures of Dispersion) to satisfy the service level: the higher the service, the greater the stock and the more the cost. Although the standard deviation is an important and useful measure of statistics, it is sometimes inconvenient to calculate. A more practical calculation is the mean absolute deviation (Measures of Dispersion) and is more commonly applied in stock-control problems.

The frequency of ordering depends upon accuracy of forecasting and length of lead time, i.e. the time between placing an order with a supplier and receiving the goods. The lead time may vary, again conforming to a statistical distribution with mean and standard deviation. This variation too will influence the level of safety in stock which will be required.

inventory profit

profits accrued on goods held in inventory during a period when the value of the goods increased.

inventory risk

the financial risk involved in carrying goods in inventory—because their value has decreased or because there is little demand for them.

investment

the use of money to make money by, for example, lending it for interest, buying property for gain in value, leasing property, and other ways.

investment adviser

a person who on a professional service basis gives advice to another person on investment situations.

investment deepening

investment which increases the total output of a given labour force by increasing the productivity of that force, within a given framework of technical knowledge.

investment opportunity chart

a grid or matrix representation of opportunities available to a firm in the marketplace. The chart is a tool used for strategic planning.

investory

this term has three related uses in a list of items in stock in a list of raw materials in the cost of materials currently being processed.

invisible hand

the terms invented in the eighteenth century by Adam Smith to support the policy of free trade as opposed to government intervention in the working of the market. The pursuit of self-interested economic behaviour by each individual was supposed to lead naturally when aggregated to the best interests of the whole society as if by the working of an 'invisible hand'. This idea is frequently claimed as the basis of the modern ideology of the free market.

invoice

a bill or statement, usually itemized, which is enclosed with a shipment of merchandise or mailed later by the seller. Information generally includes quantities shipped, prices of goods, terms of sale, discount, method of shipment, and other particulars including total amount due the seller.

isolated store

a free-standing building having no other retail outlets in the immediate vicinity and generally located on a highway or back street.

issues in organization

(i) What behaviour should defined by the organization structure? (ii) What behaviour is taking place outside of or in contradiction to the organization structure? (iii) Does the organization structure define how individual units are related to each other? (iv) Does the structure define how individual units are related to the overall mission of the corporation? (v) Is the definition of the organization structure sufficiently complete to reduce the need for direction from top management to a minium? (vi) Do managers make a disciplined effort to act according to the organization structure? (vii) Is it necessary for managers to act in contradiction to the organization structure in order to be effective?

issue management

PR activity to present an organization's position or views on a public issue.

item analysis

a technique to determine the effectiveness of different items on a test in its discrimination among the people who take it.

item number

manufacturing procedures, a number assigned to each line item, part, or assembly in a bill of material for purposes of identification. Item numbers are normally assigned sequentially for each bill of material.

jar

1. a wide mouthed container, usually of glass, stoneware, or plastic.

2. glass container usually for high viscosity materials such as pastes and greases.

jet propelled inflation

a name employed by F. Benham to refer to hyper inflation.

JIC

1. abbreviation of joint industrial council.

2. abbreviation of job instruction and communication.

jig and tool design

design of new jigs, tools and equipment to meet the requirement of a new production run, or the design improvement of existing jigs and tools for use in existing or modified production runs.

jingles

catchy tunes to which slogans or doggerel are set to gain memorable effect, as in TV and radio commercial May often be extended as slogans in press and poster advertising.

jm

abbreviation of job methods.

job

piece of work; to do a job of work = to be given a job of work to do; to be paid by the job = to be paid for each piece of work done.

job analysis

examination of a job, its component parts and the circumstances in which it is performed. Purpose and slant of job analysis very between job evaluation, vocational guidance, personnel selection, training, equipment, design, etc. Can be known as job study.

jobber

in the distribution of goods, an individual or a firm that intervenes between a wholesaler-distributor and the retailer. Jobbers may act exclusively as brokers or sales agents, carrying no inventory of the goods purveyed, or they may so organized and finance their activities as to provide warehousing facilities for the goods.

jobbing

doing small pieces of work.

job centre

government office which lists jobs which are vacant.

job classification method

non-analytical job evaluation

technique involving the allocation of jobs into pre-determined job grades/and or levels the characteristics of each grade will normally be defined in terms of level of responsibility or skill involved. Job classification schemes are often developed by means of job ranking.

job clinic

technique used particularly in sales training where specific problems encountered by an individual are discussed with two or three colleagues and solution suggested.

job club

organization which helps its members to find jobs.

job costing

practice or activity of allocating costs to specific jobs or items of production.

job cycle

the complete sequence of operations that a worker has to perform in order to complete a unit of his output.

job demands

the requirements a job has, and therefore what will be expected of the person who performs it.

job description

a document that outlines in broad terms the purpose, scope, duties, and responsibilities of a job for which a person is hired. Also known as position guide.

job design

process, or activity, of deciding on the tasks and responsibilities to be included in a particular job and of deciding on the methods to be used for carrying out those tasks.

job enlargement

expanding the content of a job to include new responsibilities that will usually require training and the acquisition of new skills.

job enrichment

job enrichment is based on the theory that job satisfaction and interest is the function of job content. It is applied as motivational tool whose basis is 'motivators' which satisfy higher order needs of the worker. It improves both efficiency and satisfaction by making the job meaningful. The job becomes meaningful to the worker when it provides a sense of achievement, recognition and an opportunity to use his skill, knowledge and ability and help personal growth and advancement. It makes the job challenging and full of responsibility.

job evaluation

a complete analysis of all the positions in a company, with a view to establishing their comparative value to the firm. Each job is ranked according to such factors as physical and/ or mental effort required, responsibility, skill and working conditions.

job evaluation for wages fixation

wages fixation on the value of jobs determined through the technique of job evaluation is gradually gaining ground in Indian industries although the technique has a much wider acceptance in U.S.A. and U.K. and other countries. The basis of any sound wages structure depends on correct determination of the worth of jobs.

job fragmentation

splitting an existing job up and dividing it amongst other jobs, or creating a new series of smaller jobs.

job induction

the informal orientation of a new employee which emphasizes the responsibilities of the job and the role the new employee will play in the department. Usually performed by the department manager or other direct supervisor of the new employee. Includes expectations, hours, schedule, hourly rate, pay schedule, etc.,

jobless

people with no jobs or the unemployed.

job lot

a broken lot, unbalanced assortment, or discontinued merchandise reduced in price for quick sale.

job mobility

the extent to which workers are prepared to change job, especially if a change requires geographical relocation.

job posting

a system that allows and encourages employees to apply for other job in their organization.

job production

manufacture of an article according to the specifications of a customer, or against specific order.

job restructing

job restructuring is concerned with job and work changes, i.e. the modification of the tasks and involvement of individuals. Restructuring that leads to the addition of further similar tasks is often referred to as job enlargement and can be seen as a horizontal change. Vertical changes involve increased individual involvement, perhaps through the addition of different tasks and duties. Such changes are generally referred to as job enrichment. Job restructuring, i.e. individual work and job changes, should be distinguished from organizational changes that generally concentrate on groups of workers → (Group Working) or aim to provide increased job variety for individuals without the modification of jobs, e.g. job rotation. Such organizational changes will often give rise to some form of job restructuring-indeed, in many cases job restructuring is possible only as a consequence of organizational changes.

job rotation

a technique of training employees by moving them from one job a another in a systematic way.

job satisfaction

the extent to which a worker is content with the rewards the gets out of her job, particularly in terms of intrinsic motivation.

job sharing

the procedure whereby two (or more) part-time workers make up one full-time job between them and share the accompanying pay on a pro-rata basis.

job shop

a functional organization whose departments or work centres are organized around particular types of equipment or operations, such as drilling, forging, wave soldering, and assembly.

job simplification

the process of using people like machines by reducing their job to consist of the smallest task possible with the least amount of discretion in it. It is particularly with the work on an assembly line.

job time

in work measurement the time for completing all the elements in a job.

job title

the official name an organization gives to the occupant of a particular job, e.g., sales manager.

job transition

the process of moving from one job to another, either within the same organization or between organizations. A time of heightened psychological activity and stress.

jobber

a middle man; a person or organization who purchases and sells goods or service to others.

join

to start work with a company.

joinder

situation where a union or person is brought in as a party to unfair dismissal proceedings if such a party has been instrumental in the dismissal through some sort of pressure.

joint

combined or with two or more organizations linked together.

joint consultation

structure or procedure developed in the circumstances of a particular organization for promoting understanding and common purpose between management and employees.

joint consultative committee

a committee established for the purposes of joint consultation.

joint demand

the simultaneous demand for two or more goods or services than generally are used together.

joint industrial council

a collective bargaining and/or consultative committee for an industry or public service with a constitution based on the model laid down by the Whitley Committee, which was set up by the government in 1916. Hence some Joint Industrial Councils are known as Whitley Councils (Collective Bargaining, Joint Consultation).

During the First World war the government became concerned about industrial unrest, much of which seemed to stem from the unofficial shot stewards movement (Industrial Democracy; Trade Union Types-Industrial Union; Shop Steward). It therefore set up the Whitley Committee to make suggestions for improving relations between employers and employees. The committee proposed the formation of Joint Industrial Council at industry level and Works Committees at the workplace, both representative of managements and employees; the extension of statutory wage regulation in industries badly organized in terms of trade unions and employers' associations (Wages Councils); the setting up of a permanent court of arbitration; and the authorization of governmental inquiry into disputes (Industrial Dispute). The policy suggested was adopted, although Joint Industrial Councils were not set up in industries where adequate collective bargaining arrangements existed. There are today some 200 Joint Industrial Councils or bodies of a similar character.

Although largely based on a model constitution, Joint Industrial Councils present considerable variety in structure, in their degree of authority in the industry, and in the nature and extent of their activities. While a few councils deal only with the negotiation of wages and conditions, most have at some time dealt with other matters. Conversely, there are examples of councils that do not negotiate wages. Among the matters dealt with are research, welfare, health and safety, and training, including apprenticeship. In some Joint Industrial Council industries there are District Councils, which may have a limited amount of local autonomy.

Joint Industrial Councils with District Councils have been established for local authorities in England and Wales, one each for white-collar and manual workers. There is a National Whitley Council together with Departmental Councils for the administrative and legal department of the Civil Service and, for government industrial employees, a council for each of the main employing departments. Food manufacture provides a private sector example. Sometimes there is a failure to agree on Joint Industrial Councils. The Food Manufacturing JIC, the Bacon Curing JIC, the slaughtering Industry JIC, and the Cocoa, Chocolate and Confectionery JIC all failed to agree, for example, in 1980. In those cases, there may be intervention by ACAS.

joint ownership venture

a form of joint venture in which foreign and domestic investors join to create a local business. Each firm shares in the ownership and control of the new firm. Some foreign governments require joint ownership as a condition for entry into their markets.

joint product

two or more products that inevitably result from processing a single raw material and that are of equal importance, so that none can be designated as the major or primary product.

joint promotions

a marketing effort, generally widely advertised, aimed at increasing sales. The cost of the promotion is shared by the two participating companies. Joint promotions are used to introduce new products or services or to revitalize those already established. They are commonly employed to push undifferentiated products or services, e.g., airline tickets, soap, hosiery, hotels, etc.

joint venture

a business contract or management effort between two persons, companies, or organizations involving risk and benefit sharing.

journal

house journal-magazine produced for the worker in a company to give them news about the company.

journalizing

the initial recording of an accounting transactions in a journal.

journeyman

the traditional term for skilled worker who has completed a craft or trade apprenticeship but is not yet a master craftsman in self-employment. In previous times such a worker would need to travel around offering his skills to a master until such time as he could set up in business for himself.

judge

person who decides in a legal case. To make a decision about someone or something.

judgement

legal decision or official decision of a court.

judgement sample

a form of nonprobability sample in which researchers select subjects who they judge to be good prospects for accurate information. This form of sample selection relies on the predisposition, and hence the bias, of the researcher. In some cases, such as in award nominations, the judgment sample is desirable, since it uses experts who are thought to be especially qualified in the area of interest.

judicial
referring to the law.

junior
younger or lower in rank.

junior department store
not as large as the traditional department store, the junior department store carries a relatively wide variety of merchandise in a departmentalized form of organization. Prices are often moderate and major appliances and furniture are usually not included in the merchandise offering. In many respects the junior department store is a large specialty store.

junior level management
the term applied to managers who are relatively low in the hierarchy of an organization because they are junior in age and/or level of responsibility and authority.

just
fair and reasonable.

justice
fair treatment in law. Fairness and reasonableness.

justify
to give an excuse for or to give a reason for.

just in time production
a Japanese approach to the process of production which emphasizes tight scheduling of materials into and out of the process, with a very low inventory of stock carried on - site. The aim of the process is to prevent bottlenecks in production and ensure a smooth flow of throughout. It is also claimed that this approach reduces costs, increases job satisfaction and improves quality.

just noticeable difference
a formula developed by German scientist Ernst Weber to measure how large a change must occur to be noticed in human perception. The change, or just noticeable difference is not an absolute quantity but rather an amount relative to the intensity of the original stimulus. According to Weber's formula, the stronger the initial stimulus, the greater the secondary stimulus must be if it is to be recognized as different. The formula is used by marketers trying to determine how much of a difference must be built into a product to differentiate it from its competitors as well as in setting prices. In the latter application, the theory maintains that the more expensive an item is originally, the larger the price drop required before it is seen as a bargain by consumers.

juvenile
young (person).

kanban
the basis for the Japanese system of just-in-time production. It involves requesting items only as they become necessary in the production process.

key
important.

key repertory grid

a technique used in market research to obtain opinions from respondents about production and their brand images. The materials are presented in threes and the respondents are asked to say why one is different from the other two and why these two are similar.

key resource

a vendor whose past dealings with a retailer have been excellent and from whom the retailer has consistently bought a substantial portion of its merchandise.

key result area

a major area of grouping of activities and their results that are 'Keys' to an organization's survival and success. Key result areas are integral to organizational planning, management, and evaluation, and are absolutely essential for managing by objectives.

kickback

illegal commission paid to someone (especially a government official) who helps in a business deal.

kinked demand curve

a form of demand curve commonly found in oligopolistic markets. With few members operating in an industry, any price rise by one member results in a reduction in sales revenues as customers buy from competitors. Any price cut invites the competition to retaliate in kind. The kink in the demand curve is at the point where demand above the point is elastic and below it's inelastic.

kiting

an unauthorized borrowing or theft of money through the continuing action of drawing and cashing a cheque on one bank, following that shortly by a covering deposit in the form of an unrecorded cheque on another bank, that cheque, in its turn, bring covered by a cheque drawn on a third bank, the process possibly continuing undetected through several banks.

knock off

(informal) to stop work.

knocked down

descriptive of articles that have been taken apart to reduce the cubic foot displacement or to improve the unit as a shipping format.

know

to learn or to have information about something.

know how

skill or ability in a particular field; knowledge about how something works or how something is made.

knowledge of results

the process of giving people feedback on their performance of a task. In the study of learning this has been found to increase someone's motivation to perform better.

knowledge worker

a term sometimes used for a person working in the communication of information particularly in information management.

laboratory

place where scientific research is carried out.

labourer

person who does heavy work.

labour intensive

(industry) which needs large numbers of worker or where labour costs are high in relation to turnover.

labour intensive industry

an industry which makes greater, relative use of human labor than it does of machinery and automation. Labor costs in such industries are therefore relatively high. The construction and garment industries are examples of labor intensive industries.

labour management relations

a general term referring to the formal and informal dealings and agreements between employees or employee organizations and managers.

labour relations

the totality of the interactions between and organization's management and organized labour.

labour-saving

which saves work or which needs little labour.

labour-turnover

the percentage of the total labour force of an organization leaving its employment and being replaced over a given period of time, usually a year.

lack

not having enough. Not to have enough of something.

ladder

series of steps made of wood or metal which can be moved about, and which you can climb.

laggard

in the diffusion process, laggards are the last group of consumers to buy a product or service. They are frequently older, tradition bound individuals of low economic and social status.

language

efficient communication depends largely upon the existence and use of an appropriate language, whether the communication is between human beings or between operators and machines. Languages for human communication exhibit an enormous complexity: their vocabularies are large and the rules by which words can be assembled into meaningful utterances are many. Over and above the questions of literal meaning are the further complications associated with the emotive overtones of statements, and the aesthetic value of certain word juxtapositions.

Apart from the natural languages, extensive use is made of other information sources during person-person communication, such as the interpretation of posture and gesture. Other indirect means of communication between people involve special-purpose symbol systems such as those used in mathematics, musical notation, maps and engineering drawings. Very little research has yet been done in an attempt to study the efficiency of such language systems or to produce superior ones.

The study of language in the context of operator-machine communication is still in its infancy, but will certainly occupy an ever-increasing role in human-factors studies as technological innovation proceeds. Obvious examples of areas where some progress has already been made include telephone dialling codes, aircraft instrumentation and computer auto codes.

The existence of an appropriate language facilitates not only efficient person-person or operator-machine communication but also contributes a good deal to the way in which an individual can handle problems. Mathematics provides a ready example. It is a simple matter to evaluate the 134+69 using the familiar Arabic notation, but extremely difficult to solve the same problem translated into Roman notation, CXXXIV+LXIX.

large

very big or important.

largely

mainly or mostly.

large scale

involving large numbers of people or large amounts of money.

last

coming at the end of a series. Most recent or most recently.

last in first out

redundancy policy, where the people most recently appointed are the first to be made redundant.

late majority

in the diffusion process, the late majority includes those consumers in the mass market who are slow to purchase new products and services. Members of this group are likely to have below average incomes, relatively little social prestige, and to be relatively unresponsive to innovation.

lateral

referring to the side.

law

rules made by central government or local government or a court, by which a country is governed and the activities of people and organizations controlled. All the laws of a country taken together.

law of demand

a law stating that as the price of a product is raised the demand for this product will diminish, i.e., consumers purchase more goods at a low price than at a high price. Also known as the law of diminishing demand.

law suit

case brought to a court.

lawyer

person who has studies law and practises law as a profession.

lay

to put.

lay off

to lay of workers = to dismiss workers for a time (until more work is available). Action of dismissing a worker for a time.

lazy

(person) who does not want to work.

leader

person who manages or directs others.

leader pricing

a strategy in which the prices of certain items (called leaders, or loss leaders) are established at levels so low that they yield little or no profit. The objective of this practice is to increase customer traffic flow and to create the general impression of store-wide low prices.

leadership

a widely-applied term that usually refers to the personality characteristics and the behaviour of people with authority and influence and responsibility for leading groups. The term is also used to refer to the group of people officially responsible for running an organization.

leadership performance

executives, because of their status, duties and authority, are said to be in the position of leadership. If leadership is considered as something that influences persons, executive performance would be leadership performance. More specifically, it would be acts which influence the acts of others.

leadership style

an imprecise term that refers to the blending of a person's knowledge of leadership theory and skills with his or her own personality and values under different organizational circumstances to yield a "style" of leadership behaviour. Some people are relatively rigid and can use only one or two leadership styles; others are more flexible and may have many style options available to them.

leading

most important.

lead time

time between the start of a task and its completion.

leak

to pass secret information.

learner training

the learners are those who join industry for semi-skilled jobs without any prior knowledge about the elements of industrial engineering. They have, therefore, to undergo a program of education training. For this purpose, it may become necessary to send them to vocational school for sometimes for the study of workshop mathematics and learning operation of machines. After this, they may be assigned to regular production job.

learning

process of receiving and assimilating information or skills.

learning and training

in view of the variety of different occupational skills that personnel are called upon to acquire, it is impossible to lay down a set of simple and comprehensive rules by which training programs should be devised. None-the-less there are some general principles of human learning that must be observed in the development of any training program.

Little or no improvement will result from unmotivated trainees. Appropriate incentives, such as cash rewards, promotion prospects or the attainment of status and reputation, may serve as methods for producing an adequate motivational level.

Generally speaking, learning will be facilitated by short periods of instruction followed by rest or at least a relief from novely. As skill is acquired, the length of the training session may be increased.

It is essential that trainees should be provided with information about their achievement. This should be accurate and comprehensive and should be given as soon as possible after each trial. One of the advantages of using automatic machines as trainers is the speed and precision with which they may display result of trials.

In many cases it is advisable to present the trainee with an overall view of the total task before detailed instruction about the individual task element is provided. In this way, the trainee is able to build up a correct view of the whole skill and bring about an appropriate synthesis of the elements when these have been learned. In certain types of skilled activity this synthesis (perhaps involving elements of timing) is the essence successful performance.

Habit interference occurs when practice at one activity brings about a decrement in another. This may be minimized by making as different as possible both inputs and outputs which might be confused. Consistency in training procedures similarly minimizes interference. Thus meticulous standardization is required when, for example, several different instructors contribute to a training program.

There is a good deal of evidence to contradict the widely held misconception that older people cannot benefit from training. It is, however, usually the case that more time is required by an older person to acquire new knowledge and skills.

(Industrial Training).

learning curve

a graphic representation of the fact that as production increases, unit costs decreases; i.e., when a great many items are manufactured, each individual item will be cheaper because the manufacturer has learned to reduce expenses and to increase efficiency.

leap frogging

communication which by-passes the official chain of command.

lease

a contract renting land, a building, space in a building, or equipment, typically for at least one year but often longer. Under a lease, title (or ownership) does not change. Leasing is an alternative to purchasing capital items (that is, an alternative to incurring capital costs).

leased department

a department or area within a store operated by an outside organization, although often not so identified to the customer. Generally the store supplies the space and those essential services such as lighting, security, etc. in return for a flat fee or for a percentage of the leased department's sales. Shoes, jewellery repair, photo services, etc. are leased departments frequently found in department or discount stores.

least preferred co-worker

a technique developed by the American psychologist Freed Fiedler to assess the extent to which someone in an position of leadership is predisposed to deal more with the task confronting the group of the interpersonal relations of its members. The technique involves asking people about their least preferred co-workers.

leave

permission to be away from work. To go away from. To resign.

leaver

book who has left.

legal

according to the law or allowed by the law.

legal aid

legal advice offered by the state.

legal guardian

an individual or agency who is legally designated to act on behalf of, or have responsibility for, a patient who is considered legally incapable of acting on his or her own behalf.

legally

according to the law.

legal reserves

the percentage of total funds that an insurance company or bank must set aside to meet possible claims.

legal tender

a lawful medium of exchange, such as money.

legislation

law.

legitimate power
legitimate power stems from three sources: shared value acceptance of a social structure or the sanction of a legitimizing agent. In a manufacturing company a foreman assigns work to line workers. They do not work because they accept the management structure of the company which makes it legitimate for the foreman to assign work.

leg time
the number of days between the date a service is rendered and the receipt of a claim by an insurer, service plan, prepaid plan, or other third party for processing and payment.

leisure
time free from work or other obligations.

leniency
not being strict in dealing with subordinates.

letter
piece of writing sent from one person or company to another to give information.

letter of credit
a written instrument issued by a bank to a buyer of goods which is evidence of the buyer's good credit standing. The letter of credit is presented to the seller of the goods by the buyer, the seller delivers the goods to the buyer and collects his money from the bank which issued the letter of credit which, in turn, collects from the buyer. The letter of credit is useful in international trade where the buyer has been unable to establish a line of credit with the seller of goods.

level expenditure method
a method of developing media advertising schedules in which each segment of the campaign is treated equally.

level premium
an insurance premium that remains unchanged throughout the life of the policy for which it is paid.

leverage
influence which you can use to achieve an aim. Borrowing money at fixed interest which is then used to produce more money than the interest paid.

leverage ratio
an organisation's total debt divided by its total assets; one of many accounting ratios used for assessing an organization's financial health.

levy
money which is demanded and collected by the government.

liability
legal responsibility for damage or loss, etc.

liability insurance
insurance that compensates the insured for any or specific liabilities or losses.

liaise
to inform someone of what is being done, so that actions are coordinated.

liaison
keeping someone informed of

what is happening.

licence

official document which allows someone to do something.

license

to give someone official permission to do something.

licensing

(1) an agreement between the creator of a product or line of products and a manufacturer in which the creator (licensor) give the manufacturer (licensee) permission to use his name in the marketing of a product in return for a royalty, usually computed as a percentage of sales. (2) a form of joint venture in which a domestic manufacturer seeks entry into a foreign market by granting a licence in the foreign market permission to use a manufacturing process, trademark, trade secret, etc. in exchange for a royalty or fee. The partnership thus formed allows the domestic manufacturer entry to the host country market with minimal risk, since the licensee is providing the means of production. The licensee, on the other hand, gains access to a well-known product or product line.

licensure

a formal process by which a government agency grants an individual the legal right to practice an occupation, grants an organisation the legal right to engage in an activity.

lien

a claim, charge, or liability against property that is allowed by law, rather than one that is part of a contract or agreement.

lieu

in lieu of = instead of.

life

time when a person is alive.

lifestyle

the behaviours, activities, values, and beliefs that influences the physiologic, psychosocial, environmental, economic, and religious aspect of a person's daily life.

lifestyle segmentation

the decision of a market into subgroups based on the way the members of each group live. Particular attention is given to the activities and interests of the members of each group.

light industry

the term applied to industries like electronics or clothing which tend to be smaller in scale and require less physical labour than heavy industry.

lighting strike

sudden strike.

limit

point at which something ends or point which must not be passed.

limited line store

a retail outlet in some respects similar to the specialty store in that it carries a limited number of product lines but has considerable depth in the lines it carries. Limited lines stores are often known by the name of the product they sell, e.g., shoe store, furrier, bakery, flower shop, etc. Also known as limited assortment stores.

limited service wholesaler

a wholesaling middleman who, like his full-service counterpart, takes title to the goods he resells, but who provides fewer services in an effort to reduce costs. Known also as a limited function wholesaler. Included under this term are the following enterprises: drop shipper, wagon distributor, cash and carry wholesaler, rack jobber, mail-order wholesaler, and producer's cooperative.

limitations on management's freedom

the objectives are the boundaries that management sets on its freedom of decision. They establish the kind of things that management can do and those that are outside its objectives. There are also other limitations on the freedom to make decisions, but these are not self-imposed, although, in an indirect way, they may be the result of previous decisions. The first of these limitations is shortage of money, men, and materials; therefore, many business decisions will mirror the economist's definition of 'the application of scarce means to alternative ends'. One of the advantages of large scale organisation is that it is less limited by shortages of money or men. The second, and often stringent, limitation on manager's freedom of decision is that imposed by outside agencies such as the government or trade unions. A third limitation comes from people's attitudes.

limited

restricted or not open.

line

line of business or line or work = type of business of work. Bottom line = last line on a balance sheet indicating profit or loss.

line and staff (1)

line functions are those that are specifically charged with the responsibility for directly achieving the objectives of the organization. Staff functions are those responsible for assisting the lines. This classification by function seems gradually to be losing favour as the closely interdependent nature of the various functions in the organization is increasingly recognized. Given such interdependence, it seems neither logical nor useful to attempt to classify departments according to their implied contribution to the attainment of organizational objectives. Accordingly many writers now regard the description of some functions as primary, with the relegation of others to secondary status, as more likely to lead to confusion than to clarity in the analysis of organizational relationship.

line and staff (2)

a line relationship is the authority relationship between superior and subordinate in the chain of command. A staff relationship is a service or advisory relationship. These usages derive from a (mistaken) analogy with military organization. The concept of a line relationship is reasonably unambiguous, but in military as well as in industrial organization non-line relationships are too complex to permit the use of a single classificatory term. A production department, for example, is likely to interact with the maintenance department, production scheduling, progress department, budget control, personnel department and so on. It would seem very probable that each relationship so established would differ significantly from each of the others. Organization theory, however, has not yet developed a terminology that gives recognition to these differences. The existence of staff relationships violates the principle of unity of command although this violation has been obscured by the insistence that, in theory, such relationships are advisory. Recently, however, there has been a greater willingness to recognize that may 'advisory' relationships involve functional authority and the organizational difficulties frequently result from the failure to make this explicit.

line and staff conflict

the line and staff departments of an organisation are generally found to be at loggerheads with each other. The line department complains that:

(i) the staff people encroach upon their authority and prerogatives.

(ii) the advice given by staff people is mostly academic and unhelpful in achieving production goals.

(iii) when a project is unsuccessful it is the line people who are blamed and held responsible for its failure but when it is successful staff people receive credit.

Staff departments complain that;

(i) line people are generally ignorant and bull-headed. They resist new ideas.

(ii) line people distrust, non-co-operate and even sabotage staff plans.

(iii) staff has not enough authority to translate its advice into action.

(iv) line departments receive preferential treatment in matters of staff allowances and other facilities on the basis that they are earning departments.

line and staff concept

a term used in organisational theory to denote the different functions performed in an organisation by managers who are directly responsible for achieving the organisation goals ('line') and those who perform supportive functions like marketing or personnel ('staff').

line and staff organisation

according to Louis Allen, line functions are those which have direct responsibility for accomplishing the primary objectives of the organisation. Staff refers to those elements of the organisational that help the line in the attainment of organisation objectives by providing advice and service. Line executives exist to take and execute decisions while staff executives exist to provide specialized knowledge for taking decisions. Line and staff organisation is designed to maintain a proper balance between centralization and division of work. It seek to combine the advantages of specialization and unity of command. Under this type of organisation there is a direct line of authority as in the line organisation. In addition, specialists are attached to line managers to advise them on important matters. These staff officers do not have any power of command. Staff relationship is purely advisory and staff experts cannot issue instructions to subordinates outside their own departments. They simply provide information and suggestions which are not binding on line managers who have the ultimate authority to take decisions. Line and staff organisation came into existence due to the inability of departmental managers to investigate, think and plan and at the same time execute the plans. It is an improvement over the other types of organisation because it provides the benefits of specialization absent in line organisation. At the same time, it avoids the confusion and conflicts which exist in functional organisation due to the absence of unity of command.

linearity

the assumption of linearity is close enough to reality also. The influence of each element must be directly proportional to the quantity of each element involved in any problem. LP is relevant when the problem to be solved is a production process involving a straight-line relationship with a number of alternative methods for reaching the objective. A hierarchy of management problems ranging from those most suited to quantitative treatment (on the technical side) to those in which quantification is most difficult (on the human and value side) can be solved mathematically.

linear programming

a mathematical technique employed to pick the best choice from among several alternatives. The economic theorists approach to the analysis of business behaviour and business problems is based on the concept of optimization. This, however, does not mean that in applied operations research work the analyst pretends to be able to find the best of all possible decisions.

line assistant

the line assistant in an organisation assists his chief in the whole range of his duties, except where a more limited delegation is made. He helps the principal to manage the function; that is, he assists with overall planning, organizing, direction, coordination and control. Although the line assistant is in the direct chain of command, he is staff to his superior because he exists only to advise, counsel and act for his principal. The line assistant has no responsibility apart from that of his principal; therefore, he has none to redelegate.

line manager

an executive in a firm having a line organization, i.e., a direct line of responsibility and control from top to bottom. The line manager has direct responsibility for certain operations which represent the primary mission of the organisation.

line of credit

the maximum amount of credit a customer has with a bank or other lending institution.

line printer

a high-speed computer printer that prints a line at a time rather than a character at a time.

line staff relationship

study of company organisation brings to light frequent instances of friction and conflict between line and staff. What is at the root of the difficulty? Both line and staff have their viewpoints. Line managers most often have these complaints about the staff organisation: staff tends to assume line authority, staff does not give sound advice, staff steals credit, staff fails to see the whole picture.

line structure

the extension of a line of products by its manufacturer beyond the range currently produced. For example, the extension may involve products at higher and/or lower prices or products at different levels of quality.

liquid assets

cash and other current assets that can be rapidly converted into cash.

liquidated claim

a claim which has been settled (by full or partial payment or consent to no payment) or made part of an agreement (payment in whole or in part or no payment, as expressed in the terms of the agreement) by the parties to the claim or by court order.

liquidated damages

the money amount established

by the parties to a contract that must be paid in the event one or more of the parties fails to fulfil the terms of the contract.

liquidation

winding up or closing of a company and selling of its assets.

liquidity ratios

liquidity implies a firm's ability to meet its short-term obligations when they become due for payment. It is a prerequisite for the very survival of the firm. Liquidity ratios measure the short term financial strength of an enterprise.

liquid ratio

liquid ratio is ratio of liquid assets to liquid liabilities or current liabilities. It is concerned with the relationship between liquid assets and liquid or current liabilities. For the purpose of computation, the current assets and current liabilities could be classified as follows:

current assets—(i) liquid assets and (ii) deferred assets;

current liabilities—(i) liquid liabilities and (ii) deferred liabilities.

list

several items written one after the other.

list price

the list price may be at the point of production; i.e., it may be the manufacturer's price to the distributor or retailer as represented on a list or in a catalog, but more often list price is meant to indicate the retail price suggested (and sometimes advertised) by the manufacturer before any discounts or other price reductions are made.

litigate

to go to law or to bring a lawsuit against someone to have a dispute settled.

litigant

person who is involved in a civil action in court.

litigation

going to law or bringing of a lawsuit against someone to have a dispute settled.

litigious

(person) who likes to bring lawsuits against other people.

loading

assigning work to workers or machines.

loan

to lend or advance money or other property or persons for temporary use; a sum of borrowed money. For accounting purposes, a loan is an account receivable by the lender and an account payable by the recipient.

loan package

a financial proposal that provides data that a lender and borrower need in order to decide whether or not a loan will be granted and accepted.

loan value

the maximum amount that can be borrowed against the cash value of a life insurance policy.

local
referring to a particular area, especially one near where a factory or an office is based.

local advertising
advertising sponsored by local businessmen who provide products or services in the local market. When conducted by stores it is frequently called retail advertising despite the fact that some retailers are national advertisers.

local brand
goods marketed in a particular geographical region such as bread, beer, etc.

locally
in the area near where an office or factory is based.

location of industry and regional problems
the depressed economic conditions of the 1930s in the UK drew attention to the plight of several areas dependent upon old-established industries such as coal, iron and steel, textiles and shipbuilding. The problem of these areas was that their basic industries were depressed and alternative employment opportunities rare.

The location of an industrial enterprise depends upon two sets of costs: transport costs and processing costs. Transport costs cover the cost of transporting materials and fuel to the point of manufacture and transporting the finished product to the market. Processing costs depend upon the cost of raw materials, labour, capital equipment and managerial expertise. On the whole there is little evidence of regional variation in processing costs and thus location has been determined in the past by the incidence of transport costs. The majority of our old-established industries are materials-dominated and hence were located close to coal, iron ore and adequate water supplies. On the other hand the new and growing industries have been freed from the coalfields by the development of new fuels and since, on the whole, transport costs to the market have dominated, they have settled close to the large centres of population in the Midlands and the South-east. Thus, we have the present situation of areas of high unemployment with too little diversification, too much labour and too few jobs. This has meant that when the rest of the economy is booming, Development Areas, as they are sometimes called, are just beginning to grow and hence they suffer when brakes to the economy are imposed.

Since the 1930s government policy has varied both in the amount and type of aid and the areas to which it has been applied. Following the White Paper Regional Industrial Development (Cmnd. 9111) and the submissions received in response to it, a 'new' approach to regional problems was launched in November 1984 under the 1982 Industrial Development Act. This takes account of the criticisms of previous policy, which included the extravagance of the existing system, the lack of emphasis on job creation and a dislike of the primacy given to automatic grants. The new policy, according to the Industry Minister, aims to be more cost-effective, putting more emphasis on job creation and reducing the current bias towards capital-intensive investment.

The new policy creates two categories of assisted area, replacing the previous three-tier system, and extends the coverage to 35 percent of the working population. Intermediate Areas will be eligible for selective regional assistance, whilst Development Areas will be eligible for the new regional development grants as well. Thus automatic grants are being concentrated on the areas of greatest need (15 percent of the working population). The new rate of capital grant is set at 15 percent but there is to be a ceiling of £10,000 for each new job created. Alternatively, labour-intensive projects will receive a grant as a fixed sum for each job created, currently set at £3,000. In addition certain service activities will now be eligible for regional development grants. The effect of the new policy is that in 1687/88 it is expected that expenditure on regional industrial incentives will total nearly £400m, some £300m less than if present policies had continued.

lock

device for closing a door or box so that it can be opened only with a key.

lock-in

a loan that does not permit prepayment. The borrower is "locked-in" for the period of the loan.

lock out

to shut the factory door so hat workers cannot get in and so force them not to work until the conditions imposed by the management are met.

lockout

industrial dispute where the management will not let the workers into the factory until they have agreed to the management's conditions.

lockup agreement

an agreement between an acquiring company and a company targeted for takeover that makes the targeted company unattractive to any other company.

locus of control

a dimension of personality in which people who have an internal locus feel they have control over what happens to them, and people with an external locus tend to attribute their experiences to outside forces or other people.

logistical marketing function

any marketing function which involves the transportation and physical distribution of goods and services. Logistical marketing functions include storage, assorting, assembling and related tasks.

logistics

a term that was originally used in the military sphere to describe the organizing and moving of troops and equipment. It is now often applied to any detailed planning process in an organisation which entails the distribution or redistribution of resources.

logo

generally one or more letters worked into some distinctive typographic or calligraphic design. Logos are often in the form of initials (representing the name of a brand or company) but the logo of the coca-cola-company, which is entirely written out, is probably the most famous in the world. Also known as a logotype, a signature cut, or a sign cut.

long

for a large period of time.

long distance

long distance call = telephone call to a number which is not near.

longhand

handwriting where the words are written out in full and not typed or in shorthand.

long-range

for a long period of time in the future.

long-term

for a long time ahead.

long term financing

any loan that has a term of more than ten years.

long term original issues

all long-term debt other than that issued to refinance existing long-term debt. It includes long-term debt issued to pay back existing short-term obligations.

longwall method

a method of production in the United Kingdom coalmining industry which led to a change in shift work and other practices as the result of the introduction of new mining technology. These changes meant that there was one long coal-face of two hundred yards being worked by three shifts of miners with different tasks as opposed to one team on a ten-yard face who did the whole job.

loose

not packed together.

lose

not to have something any more.

loss leader

refers to a product or service sold at a loss for the seller in order to attract customers to buy other products or services.

low

not high or not much.

low ball price

the promotion of a product, usually by telephone, at a very low price calculated to lead customer into a store. Upon arrival at the store the customer is informed by the salesperson that management will not allow him to sell the product at the promised price and attempts to pressure the customer into buying a more expensive item.

loyal

(worker) who supports the company he works for.

loyalty

company loyalty = dedication of staff to the company and its objectives.

luddite

the term used to describe workers who are obstinately opposed to the introduction of new technology into their workplace. It derives from the followers of Ned Ludd, an early nineteenth century British worker, who saw new machinery as threat to their traditional craft skills and working practices and opposed its introduction violently.

machine

device which works with power from a motor.

machine direction

the direction in which the fibres lie, while running in a paper-making machine is called machine direction. This is also known as 'grain' of the paper. Paper folds easily in the machine direction, as the pull of the machine has already stretched the length of the fibres almost to the maximum.

machine finished (m.f.)

this refers to the finish of the paper. Paper is fully treated to dry completely by running on a series of cylinders.

macrosegmentation

a strategy employed in industrial marketing in which market potential for products or services is established by examining broad segmentation variables such as the data provided by the Bureau of the Census.

magazine

paper, usually with picture, which comes out regularly, every month or every week.

mail order retailing

a form of selling in which personal contact and store operations have been eliminated. The retailer contacts potential customers through the use of direct mail, catalogues, television, radio, magazines, newspapers, etc. Merchandise is described in words and pictures, customers order by mail or telephone, and orders are filled by the seller through the mail or via parcel services.

mail order wholesaling

a form of wholesaling in which personal selling has been eliminated. Mail order wholesalers send catalogs to retail firms and/or other wholesalers along with instructions on how to order goods. Mail order wholesalers often handle the merchandise of several small manufacturers who cannot afford to produce their own catalogues but who desire market exposure for their products. Many mail order wholesalers are found in the stationary and printing field.

mail survey

also Postal Survey. A survey in which contact with respondents is made through the medium of the postal service.

main

most important.

main heading

brief statement of chief topic or subject in a chapter or other composition.

maintain

to keep in effective condition. Maintenance refers to the work necessary to keep something in a satisfactory condition. An organisation is maintained by being kept in a sound operating condition.

maintained markup

the difference between net sales and the cost of goods sold. The maintained markup figure (expressed as a percentage of net sales) does not reflect deductions for cash discounts and workroom costs, and represents the actual markup which was achieved for the selling period.

maintenance marketing

that form of marketing appropriate to a marketplace in a full-demand condition. Monitoring the market for changes in customer demand is of primary importance in maintenance marketing.

majority

larger group than all others. Number of votes by which a person wins an election.

major premise

in a syllogism, the proposition which contains the general truth from which the particular inference is deduced.

make

type of product manufactured.

makegood

repeating an advertisement without change, or refunding space or time charges, as compensation for an advertisement omitted or containing a significant error.

make or buy decision

choice between manufacturing a component of a product in the company's own plants or purchasing it from an outside supply or suppliers.

make-ready

process of making adjustments to increase or decrease the printing impression in specific areas. If over the plate called 'overlay' if under, called 'underlay.'

make up

to compensate for something.

maladjustment

state in which a person falls short of being able to do what is expected of him by others or by himself.

mall
in shopping center design, the mall is composed of pedestrian walk–ways which may be enclosed (and thus heãted and air conditioned) or open to the sky. In larger centers, the mall provides access to the anchor stores as well as the inward-facing smaller shops.

man
person or ordinary worker.

manage
to direct or to be in charge of an organization or part of one.

management
those persons charged with the responsibilities of determining company or organisation policy and planning and directing operations.

management accounting
accounting, which is primarily concerned with providing information relating to the conduct of the various aspects of the business, the cost or profit associated with same portions of business operations, is called management accounting. Management accounting provides assistance to the management in all of its functions. By providing the accounting information in the required form, and at the required time, it enables management to perform its functions effectively. It makes available the relevant information after modifying the same suitably for effective planning and decision-making. It helps to replace intuitive decision-making system with scientific decision-making ones. Control refers to observing whether the actual results correspond to plans, and taking suitable action if there are deviations. Management accounting helps to prepare accounting information for the use by managers of an organization in budgeting, decision-making, planning and formulating policy. Management accounting includes such tools as budgetary control, standard costing, etc. which greatly help the management to exercise its control function effectively.

Tools of management accounting. The following tools and techniques are used in management accounting to assist management:

(i) analysis of financial statements.

(ii) ratio analysis.

(iii) funds flow analysis.

(iv) cash flow analysis.

(v) cost volume profit analysis, differential cost analysis, etc.

(vi) budgetary control and standard costing.

(vii) management reporting.

management audit
a review designed to evaluate management efficiency and to identify areas in need of management improvement within an organisation. Management audits are used

to ensure effectiveness in meeting organisational goals. It is an inspection and evaluation of organisational performance, including one or more of the following: organisational structure and compensation, operational effectiveness, quality of services and products, market effectiveness, fiscal performance and integrity, customer (client or patient) relations, professional relations.

management buyont

a situation in which the management of an enterprise make a bid to own it, whole or in part, by buying out the original shareholders, then operating as a separate concern on their own behalf.

management by crisis

a management style that tends to set up crash programmes to deal with problems as they arise in an organization rather than focusing on long-term planning or the overall objectives of the organization. It is a style that suits a manager inclined to authoritarian management and is a way of making short-term crisis management into a permanent arrangement.

management by exception

the management concept based upon the assumption that if there are adequate control signals to warn of deviations from acceptable operating standards, the only action required by management is the establishment of standards and the correction of such deviations.

management by objectives

a term proposed by the American management specialist Perter Drucker in the 1950s to emphasize the importance of setting objective for and by each individual member of an organization as well as the various branches of the organization. Drucker also emphasized the element of self-control and taking responsibility for one's own work. As an objective and a quantifiable measure of performance this technique has since become very popular with senior management, though its application in practice has often been more top down and formalized than Drucker had intended.

management calender

a working calender that displays significant events, periods of heavy workload, and other data, and which is used for planning by an organisation's staff or committee members and directors.

management contracting

a form of joint venture in which a domestic firm provides management expertise to a foreign company. The foreign company provides the capital investment.

management control

control is one of the five managerial function. It involves the setting up of processes and machinery to find out whether the organization is carrying out its four functions of organizing planning, deciding and implementing the objective of the company in the best manner and whether it is moving satisfactorily towards the goals set.

management cycle

a conception of the program management processes or function in which the "center thrusts of power" are innovation/motivation and staff development.

management development

training of managers currently employed to improve their performance in their present jobs and/or to fit them for promotion.

management education

management education is that part of education which gives far more knowledge and skills in the design and improvement of organisation and systems than what is being done in conventional management program. This is equally so in the case of public sector where there is a great deal of data, but enough has not been done to convert the data into meaningful information for decision-making and planning.

management first line

managers directly over the rank and file.

management general

overall management as opposed to management of a speciality.

management information system (MIS)

any formal process that provides the managers in an organisation with facts they need for interpretation and decision-making. Most management information systems use computers to collect, store, manipulate, and retrieve information for planning, organizing, directing and controlling administrative activities (and sometimes clinical activities) concerned with the provision and utilization of services, programmes, projects, and products.

Increasingly, management information systems include decision-analysis tools and incorporate relational approaches for examining data, in order to create options for administrative and clinical decision-making and evaluate probabilities and risks of decision alternative.

Many management information systems also automate routine decision processes and the rules and procedures by which decisions are made and action taken.

management middle

managers above the first-line supervisors who do not participate in decisions on overall policy.

management prerogatives

the prerogatives management believes it cannot share with if it is to have freedom to manage effectively.

management prerogative—limitation on

the management might agree to some kind of employee participation where it does not touch the question of management prerogative. But imminent fear stems from growth of participation through collective representation and the proposal for extending it through redistribution of share-ownership of public ownership.

management process school

George R. Terry gives the following advantages of using the management process methods:

(i) an inclusive, easy-to-understand, conceptual framework of management is offered. This school fosters the idea that management is a distinct activity that can be identified, taught and practised

(ii) a foundation for the study of management is provided: It supplies helpful guidance for management education, development and progress. It promotes understanding of what management really is.

(iii) contributions by other schools of management are feasible: A simple and convenient framework is provided to which the best contribution of other schools can be added so that the best contemporary thought concerning the particular managerial activity can be employed.

(iv) flexibility is provided, innovation and progress are encouraged. While constant and rigorous, it is neither too broad nor too precise. Applicable to a variety of situations, its user is given the needed leeway to suit a particular set of circumstances.

(v) the knowledge and the art of management are recognized. How best to utilize them in a practical situation is encouraged.

(vi) genuine assistance to practitioners of management is supplied: the process pattern enables a manager to correct out and to understand thee problem. Is it primarily one of planning, organising, actuating or controlling or is it a combination of several or all of these? The straight forward and practical approach helps the manger to put his or her knowledge and skill to use and determine objectives and the means to their attainment.

(vii) management principles are derived, refined and used. These principles serve as needed bench marks, for useful management research, give increased meaning to management, and assist in management application.

(viii) the development of a purposeful philosophy of management is encouraged and expedited. The process school is not mechanistic. Each phase of its application requires drawing from the manager's values, beliefs, and understanding of the goals, resources, and environments with which she or he is working.

management science

the application of scientific methods, and particularly quantitative methodology to the practice of management. The application of a behavioural science or social science perspective to the study of management.

management service

any service intended to help management function more effectively, such as data processing or market research.

management style

the general approach a manager has to dealing with other people at work, and in particular the exercising of his or her authority with subordinates. This style is often characterized as tending toward authoritan management or democratic management, depending on the personality of the individual manager, but people can also have somewhat different approaches when faced with different situations.

management team

a vague term generally referring to a group of mangers who, in addition to their distinct responsibilities are held jointly accountable (by a senior manager or governing body) for an organisation's performance in meeting established goals or providing services that fulfil the mission of a program within budgetary and revenue constraints.

management top

the company policy makers (sometimes just president).

management type flow chart

this is a fully illustrated chart, depicting a horizontal and departmentalized flow of work. In this chart, each operation or step involved in a procedure is described in a short and descriptive sentence. This chart is read from left to right and is used by the management for reference purposes. The preparation and use of flow chart offers the following advantages:

(i) these charts give information about office work in a logical and systematic manner.

(ii) these reveal defects in office systems and procedures.

(iii) these can be prepared and used easily.

(iv) the charts provide a graphic picture of the flow of office work.

management work plan

a record used in program or organisational management, usually as part of a management-by-objectives process. A management work plan supports and provides greater detail than a management-by-objectives form.

It emphasizes task and resources management.

manager
one who plans, organizes, motivates, coordinates, and controls the work of other people.

manageress
woman who runs a shop, or a department.

managerial
referring to managers.

managerial economics
the application of economics to the kind of practical business decision that a manager has to take. As well as economics the field draws on operational research, management accounting and marketing.

managerial functions
managerial functions refer to the kind of activities managers perform as managers perse, regardless of the specific types of managers they are. Managerial functions are performed in the course of coordinating and carrying out key enterprise functions. A useful and often used division of managerial function is: planning and innovation, control, organization, staffing, direction, leadership and motivation.

managerial grid
type of management training in which trainees attempt to solve a number of problems in groups, and thus discover their individual strengths and weakness.

managerial psychology
the systematic study of the role of the manager in an organization and in particular the relationship between supervisors and supervises. This area of study is a part of industrial psychology.

mandatory
mandatory issues = bargaining issues that directly affect employees' jobs; mandatory meeting = meeting which all members have to attend.

man Friday
male employee who does a variety of tasks.

man hour
work done by one person in one hour.

manifest
obvious or apparent. List of goods in a shipment.

manned
with someone working on it.

manning
people who are needed to do a work process.

manpower
number of workers in a country or industry or organization.

manpower analysis
an analysis of the employees in an organization that attempts to identify patterns and trends in their employments. It will examine, for instance, the distribution of employees by age, sex, skill, job title and length of service. It is the first stage of systematic manpower planning.

manpower plan
there are plenty of tools available to improve the quality and effectiveness of employment forecasting and the alert personnel manager will take steps to see that the

broadest possible application of these techniques is being utilized. Like most other challenges in managing a business the solution appears to lie in establishing effective communication or perhaps more accurately an effective integration. No one person or group in most organizations is likely to have at hand all the information necessary or desirable in making a detailed and useful manpower plan.

manpower planning

the process of forecasting both the numbers and the kinds of employees that an organization will be required over a given period of time and taking steps to ensure their supply. Ideally this should be an integral part of an organization's personnel policy from recruitment to retirement, including selection, promotion and training.

manpower services commission

under the Employment and Training Act 1973 the manpower service commission (MSC) was set up to run the public employment and training services. The MSC is separate from the Government but accountable to the Secretary of State for Employment. The Secretary of State for Education and Science is also fully involved in the consideration and approval of the MSC's plans and proposals affecting non-advanced further education in England. In respect of its operations in Scotland and Wales the MSC reports to the Secretaries of State for those countries and a Committee for each country advise the Commission on manpower, training and the implementation of its plans and programmes nationally.

The first objective of the MSC is to safeguard the provision of skilled manpower for the present and future needs of industry. This involves the Commission in the promotion of occupational training in a form that enables entrants of different ages and educational backgrounds to acquire agreed standards of skill appropriate to the jobs available, and that opens upon opportunities for adults steadily to increase their skills and knowledge during their working lives. The second major objective-one of those contained in the New Training Initiative (Cmnd.8455) of 1981-is to move to position where all those under age of 18 can continue in full-time education, or have planned work experience. Other objectives of the MSC include the provision of an efficient, accessible and cost-effective employment service, and the provision of a range of services to help job-seekers who have particular difficulty in obtaining suitable work or training.

The MSC has ten members who serve for a term of three years. They comprise a chairman, three members appointed after consultation with the

Confederation of British Industry, three appointed after consultation with the Trades Union Congress, two after consultation with local education authorities and one with professional education interests. In pursuit of its objectives, the MSC is organized into three operating divisions (employment, Training and a Skill centre Training Agency) and two support division (Resources and Planning, and Personnel and Central Service).

MSC. programmes are paid for mainly by grants-in-aid which cover about 70 percent of the total outlay. The rest, including activities such as the Community programme, Community Industry and Sheltered Employment, is paid for directly by the Department of Employment or from receipts for services provided. In 1983/4 the Youth Training Schemes provided training and work experience for 354,000 young people, of whom 80 percent were school-leavers, whilst the training opportunities scheme for unemployed adults enabled 66,200 people to complete training course. Another 113,000 long-term unemployed were provided with temporary full-time or part-time work or projects under the Community Programme, provision for which is to be doubled in 1986/7. Plans were also announced in 1985 to expand the Youth Training Schemes, so that in 1986, 16 year-old could receive two years of job-related training, and 17-year old one year, leading to a recognized vocational qualification.

In 1983 the MSC promoted a Technical and Vocational Education Initiative to establish projects run by local education authorities for 14-18 year-old, which incorporated work experience as an integral part of the programme. In 1984 the Government gave the MSC new responsibilities by enabling it to purchase a more significant proportion of work-related, non-advanced further education provided by local education authorities, thereby discharging the function of a national training authority.

man-to-man ranking

arranging employees in order according to their skills or other criteria.

manual

a compilation of directions and instructions in book or booklet form.

manual worker

someone employed on the shop floor of an organization doing physical rather than mental work, whether the work is skilled or unskilled.

manufature

to make a product for sale, using machine. Making a product for sale, using machines.

manufacturers' agents

independent agents who sell manufacturers products on a commission basis; they often sell the products of several different manufacturers.

manufacturer's branch office
a wholesaling establishment from which a producer or manufacturer conducts sales activities and which includes warehousing or other storage facilities from which merchandise may be shipped to customers. These establishments are sometimes known as captive jobbers, distribution centers, captive wholesalers, or district offices.

manufacturer's brand
nationally advertised goods offered for sale by their producer or marker. Manufacturer's brands often carry a distinctive and widely recognized brand name or trademark. Also known as a national brand

manufacturer's sales office
an establishment owned and operated by a producer or manufacturer from which sales are solicited by a permanent staff of salespeople employed by the company. Sales offices carry no inventory and thus operate like drop shippers in that they have no warehouse from which goods could be shipped to the customer.

manufacturer's store
retail outlets operated by the manufacturer of a product, e.g., automobile tires, for the purpose of selling the product and providing services to the customer. Also known as producer outlets.

manufacturer wholesaling
a practice in which a manufacturer assumes the duties commonly performed by a wholesaler or other middleman within the channel of distribution.

margin
difference between the money received when selling a product and the money paid for it. Extra space or time allowed.

marginal
marginal cost = cost of making a single extra unit above the number already planned.

marginal analysis
analysis to determine the point at which the cost of extra input of one factor (e.g., another employee or another machine) will pay for itself.

marginal cost
the amount of money expended to produce ones additional unit of a product or service.

marginal income analysis
an approach to financial planning that seeks to break down costs according to how they behave in order to quickly determine break-even points, gain a measure of the profitability or loss level of a product or service, and obtain a basis for sound pricing.

marginally punched card
cards used in hand tabulation where the holes are punched on the border of the card.

marginal men
groups not fully accepted by the society in which they live.

marginal revenue
the amount of money accruing from the sale of one additional

unit of a product or service.

marginal size
the size, greater and less than which will give rise to diseconomise.

marginal tax rate
the tax rate (or percentage) that is applied on the last increment of income for the purpose of computing income taxes.

marginal untility
the amount of satisfaction a consumer receives from the acquisition and use of one more unit of product.

margin of error
deviation from the true figure originating in a complete census; the smaller the sample the larger will be the margin of error. Can be calculated beforehand in certain condition.

marital status
condition of being married or not.

market
(1) An aggregate composed of a prospective buyer (or buyers) and a seller (or sellers), that brings to focus the conditions and forces which determine prices. (2) The aggregate demand of the potential buyers of a commodity or service. (3) The place or area in which buyers and sellers function. (4) (as a verb): To perform business activities connected with the flow of goods and services from producer to consumer or user.

market analysis
measurement of the extent of a market and the determination of its characteristics.

market anticipation
efforts made, generally on the basis of market research, to guess how customers will behave in the marketplace at some time in the future.

market build-up method
a forecasting technique in which information from a number of market segments is gathered, separately analyzed, and then added together to form a more or less complete picture of the marketing environment for the purpose of forecasting sales.

market composition
the buyers of a product according to their identifying characteristics e.g., age, sex, occupation, etc.

market data
data which may be primary (direct from the phenomenon studied) or secondary (existing records or published material) which relate to the characteristics, composition and behaviour of markets.

market division of authority
in marketing management, a form of organization in which line authority is organized so that it corresponds to the structure of the marketplace or to the way a firm's customers are segmented. This practice is prevalent in firms which market their products to two or more industries or who distribute their product through two or more channels.

market factor
a variable in the marketing environment which may affect demand for a product or service.

For example, the number of teenagers will affect the sale of phonograph records, or high interest rates will affect the sale of new homes.

market factor index

when a number of market factors are taken together, analyzed, and expressed in relation to a base number, a market factor index has been created, such an index is used in the projection of future sales trends.

market financing

the general business function of providing and managing funds and credit which is directly related to the transactions involved in the flow of goods and services from producer to consumer or industrial user.

market forces

the factors determining supply and demand in a given market.

market grid

a device employed in market segmentation studies in which a total market is subdivided in an effort to more precisely target potential customers. The information is frequently presented in the form of a grid.

marketing

the performance of business activities connected with the flow of goods and services from producer to consumer or user.

market information function

one of the facilitating marketing functions. The market information function includes the collection, analysis and distribution of the information needed by marketers in the performance of universal marketing functions.

marketing against the competition

a strategy in which a firm focuses its marketing efforts on the strengths and weaknesses of its competitors rather than on the wants and needs of its customers. For example when Pepsi-Cola determined that Coca-Cola was weakest in marketing to younger consumers they focused their advertising attack on this vulnerable area.

marketing and labelling

it implies putting marks or labels on the packets. A mark or a label may provide information regarding weight, size, price, date of manufacture and expiry, etc., about the product. A mark may be printed, attached or affixed on the packet. It may carry instruction as to the handling or opening of the packet.

marketing as usual approach to shortage

an approach to actual or anticipated shortages of ages of the raw materials required for production. When companies feel they cannot produce enough goods to meet customer demand they may assume that such shortages are temporary and continue to produce the same quantities of their products and sell to the same customers.

marketing audit

a systematic comprehensive evaluation as a firm's marketing philosophy, objectives and strategy with a view toward implementing corrective action if deemed appropriate. The audit may be applied to on-going marketing programs (a control audit) in an effort to determine their effectiveness or to completed programs (a review audit) in an effort to evaluate their results.

marketing communication
all those messages transmitted from sender to receiver which involve the buyer–seller relationship. In addition to formal promotional messages informal non-systematic communication such as word of mouth is also included.

marketing company era
a stage in the evolution of marketing (from roughly the mid 1960s to the present) during which marketing departments took on dominant roles in many manufacturing organizations.

marketing concept
a philosophy of marketing that emphasizes the supreme importance of the customer. Fundamental to this philosophy is an understanding of what the customer wants in any given market and this is usually ascertained by extensive market research.

marketing department era
a stage in the evolution of marketing during which the marketing department in a firm, although still subordinate to production and sales, is beginning to influence the development of the company marketing program.

marketing environment
the set of external factors that affect the market in which an organization operates, i.e., cultural, economic, legal, political geographical etc.

marketing ethics
those standards, values, moral principles, etc., which govern the marketer's behaviour in the marketplace.

marketing function
a major specialized activity or related group of operations performed in marketing.

marketing information system (MIS)
a marketing information system is a complex of persons, procedures, and equipment which, in concert, collect information relevant to marketing decision-making. It is more broadly based than marketing research in that the system gathers data from within the firm as well as externally in the marketing environment. The system provides for the evaluation of the collected data to determine its usefulness to the executives responsible for planning the firm's marketing strategy.

marketing management
marketing management is primarily concerned with the stimulation of sales and promotion of consumers satisfaction. It includes

analysis of markets, determination of marketing goals, sales forecasting and formulation of marketing plans, policies and procedures. An important function of marketing management is to evolve an appropriate marketing mix, i.e., planning and development of a satisfactory product for a particular market demand and fixation of its prices.

marketing manager
that executive responsible for the firm's product planning and marketing strategy development. The marketing manager directs marketing research activities, formulates goals for the sales force, develops a sales promotion and advertising strategy, sets pricing policy, establishes budgets for particular lines, and engage in other marketing activities aimed at maximizing the firm's position in the marketplace. The marketing manager may also be known as the vice president marketing or the director of marketing.

marketing mix
the blending of product, price, distribution channels, personal selling, and advertising into a suitable marketing programme for the firm.

marketing myopia
a term coined by Theodore Levitt in a Harvard Business Review article (September-October, 1975) referring to a short-sighted, narrow view of marketing.

marketing objectives of
(i) securing consumer satisfaction. (ii) coordinating production with consumption. (iii) maximization of profits without unfair trade practices. (iv) service to the society, improving quality of life.

marketing opportunity analysis
an analysis of the marketing environment in an effort to ascertain where changes might occur and to determine when problems might develop. Marketing opportunity analysis is commonly employed in marketing planning and strategy development, particularly with respect to the activities of competitors.

marketing plan
a program covering all methods and procedures for marketing the product or products of a business.

marketing planning manager
that executive who, in organization serving a number of markets, supervises the marketing research efforts as well as a number of market managers. The marketing planning manager is essentially a strategic planner. Sometimes known as a market development manager.

marketing policy
a course of action established by a business to secure consistency of its marketing procedure under recurring and essentially similar circumstances.

marketing program

the overall plan maintained by a firm which blends all its strategic plans. The marketing program is the responsibility of the entire firm, not just one division. When the various plans are quite different, there is little concern for how they all fit together. When they are similar, however, the some sales force may have to carry out several plans. Consideration is always given to the way each plan competes for the firm's limited financial resources.

marketing research
the gathering, recording, and analyzing for a business of all facts about problems relating to the market for and promotion and selling of its goods or services.

marketing research firm
an outside firm contracted to provide marketing research to a company.

marketing strategy
the logical, comprehensive plan of action through which a firm intends to reach its objectives in the marketplace. Marketing strategy is primarily concerned with the implementation of company policy and with those marketing activities through which the company's goals are to be achieved.

market intelligence
general information relating to the market or markets, of an unsystematic kind, i.e., which is not the result of systematic study by scientific methods.

market minimum
the rate of sales for a product or service which would be achieved without any demand stimulating expenditures such as advertising or promotion.

market mix
the combination of different aspects of an organization strategy for marketing a product, e.g., advertising market research, production and public relations. The guidelines for the most appropriate mix are sometimes expressed as the 'four Ps'—project, price (market), position and place.

market news
specific information about conditions in the marketplace having an immediate bearing on the conduct of business, e.g., news of crop failure quickly commodity traders.

market niche
a unique place of gap in the market for a given product.

market penetration pricing
a market strategy in which goods are priced low enough to have immediate wide appeal in the marketplace. The object of market penetration pricing is to quickly capture a significant share to the market.

market period
in the marketing process, that period from the time a product is manufactured (or a commodity is produced) until the time it is sold. During this period costs are fixed and the amount of product does not vary. Price will be determined by current demand.

market place
in its broadest context marketplace refers to the marketing environment.

market positioning
those efforts aimed at establishing a product or service in a particular niche or segment of the marketplace. Market positioning strategy usually includes those promotional activities which differentiate the product from competitors and which vividly establish the product's image in the minds of potential customers. Also known as positioning, product positioning, or target positioning.

market potential
the expected sales of a commodity, a group of commodities, or a service for an entire industry in a market during a stated period.

market price
a price determined by supply and demand in the marketplace. Prices for farm products are almost always set in this way.

market research
systematic gathering and analysis of information about prospective purchasers or users of different products or services, in order to help development and marketing people make better decisions about introducing new products or services, increasing market penetration with existing ones, conducting public relations and advertising programmes, using follow-up methods and improving future sales.

market segment
a subdivision of a population (commonly ultimate consumers), the members of which share similar identifiable characteristics, e.g., wealth, style, education level, marital status, sexual orientation etc. A firm may develop different marketing programs for each segment of its target market.

market segmentation
the process of identifying the market for a product from the markets for other similar products, by relating consumer habits, preferences and characteristics, to those associated with the product.

market share
the amount of total demand in a market which a particular organization supplies over a given period of time.

market share analysis
an analysis of a firm's sales which takes into account the activities of a firm's competitors and views the company as a participant in the general marketplace. Market share analysis is a more precise measure of performance than sales volume analysis.

market size
the number of buyers and prospective buyers of a product or brand.

market strategy
a plan for the marketing of a product. There may be one or more strategies employed including: product differentiation (the product is

carefully distinguished from its competitors) price competition (the product is marketed at a competitive price relative to competing products) market segmentation (the product is targeted for a particular customer segment) and other strategies calculated to promote and sell the product.

market survey

an overall appraisal for a product or service that an organization offers or proposes to offer to a market. It will normally indicate not only the market situation for the commissioning organization but also the position of competitive forces and future trends. The investigation will frequently be made by the collection of previously unknown data, but may be made by the collation of existing information (Desk Research). The former pattern is most common in consumer markets where few official or trade statistics are available; the latter is more common in industrial and agricultural markets. The original investigation may occasionally be conducted via a census of a total relevant population, but will generally involve the selection of representative respondents (Sampling) by either quota or random sampling procedures. A uniform, structured questionnaire may be used to gather the relevant information and the findings published as a report. Where the survey examines a market of considerable complexity, or involves interviewing a well-informed population concerning the product or service-e.g., Architects, computer technologists-a less structured approach may be used in the questioning. A wide variety of other research methods are available and are sometimes used, either in conjunction with or in place of the questionnaire survey or desk-research investigation (Marketing Research).

Some controversy centres around the method of report presentation that allow the findings of such a survey to be most effectively communicated. The Market Research Society lays down a code for its members, insisting that they provide sample, time and methodological details, etc.

market target decision analysis

a system used to identify target markets for goods and services through an analysis of the various segments which make up the total market. Frequently the information is presented in the form of a grid to facilitate decision making.

market testing

a marketing research technique in which a new product or service is introduced, usually in a limited, carefully selected geographic area (a test market), in an effort to predict its performance in the marketplace. Market testing also provides management with the opportunity to correct production problems before a total market commitment has been made. Also called test marketing and product testing.

market value
the current price that a particular item would fetch in the market.

markup
the difference between cost price of merchandise and its retail price. Markup may be expressed in dollars or as a percentage. If stated as a percentage it may be based on either cost price or retail price.

mass
large group of people.

mass market
the mass market does not include "everyone". Each organization selling to the mass market targets a large and widely dispersed (but clearly defined) group of consumers who are its potential customers.

mass merchandising
the retailing on very large scale of goods (largely staples) at prices lower than those commonly found in department and specialty stores. Mass merchandising is characterized by: 1) an emphasis on products whose market is not highly segmented 2) customers who are willing to sacrifice sales assistance and store services in return for lower price, 3) high volume and a rapid stock turnover rate and 4) a very highly competitive marketplace.

mass produce
to manufacture identical products in large quantities.

mass production—new style
the specific technique for applying this principle is systematic analysis of products to find the pattern that underlies their mutiplicity. Then this pattern can be organized so that the minimum number of manufactured parts will make possible the assembly of the maximum number of products. The burden of diversity in other words is taken out of manufacturing and shifted to assembly.

mass production—old style
mass production is the assembly of varied products—in large number or small out of uniform and standardized parts. In the manufacturing mass production is today the prevailing system. It is and with good reason considered to be the typical system of an industrial society though process production may soon become a wrong contender. This old-style mass production is based on a misunderstanding. It is the essence of genuine, mass production that it can create a greater diversity of products than method ever designed by man. It does not rest on uniform products. It rests on uniform parts which can then be mass-assembled into a large variety of different products.

mass promotion

sales promotion activities concentrated at a particular time e.g., the Christmas season.

mass publication
periodicals having a wide variety of appeal and a large general circulation.

master
skilled worker, qualified to train apprentices.

master agreement
a collective bargaining contract that serves as a model for an entire industry or segment of that industry. While the master agreement serves to standardize the economic benefits of all of the employees covered by it, it is often supplemented by a local contract that deals with the particular circumstances of contractual agreement with the various local unions.

master lease
the primary lease controlling an entire property and any leases or subleases that are written subsequently.

master of business administration
the academic qualification in management education which is generally accepted as a prerequisite for a professional career as a manager. The qualification is also becoming increasingly sought after in India but not in other industrialized countries like Germany and Japan which have alternative routes into management.

masthead
name of publication and staff, usually boxed and appearing in each issue.

matching concept
in accounting the matching of costs and revenue in an effort to relate expenses to the income they helped to produce i.e., to determine a firm's net income for a given period usually one year.

matching grant
a grant made under the condition that additional funds be raised from other sources.

material management
logistic activities concerned with the movement of production materials from their place of origin to the site of manufacture and with the movement of semifinished products within the manufacturing facility.

maternity
becoming a mother.

maternity leave
a period of time off work granted to a female employee to have a baby, after which she is entitled to return to her job.

mathematical programming
this is generic term used to describe a set of related mathematical techniques used in operational research to solve resource scheduling (Allocation Problems; Optimization).

The most commonly used member of the family is known as linear programming (LP), so-called because there is a straight-line relationship between the variables in the problem. An example would be if the total cost of producing a batch of an item is directly proportional to the batch size. That is, if it costs £10 to produce 100 items, it costs £20 to produce 200, £30 to produce 300, etc. If all the variables present in an allocation problem are related in this simple way, it may well be appropriate to use LP. Surprisingly, many problems have been found to fulfil these requirements, and the technique is used extensively. There are a number of sub-techniques of LP that are appropriate for particular problems. The most generally applicable is the simplex method, whilst others are the transportation method (so called because, among other applications, it can be used to find the cheapest way of transporting goods from factories to warehouses) and the assignment method (useful for finding the best way of assigning workers to jobs).

In some problems all the variables do not have linear relationships and non-linear programming techniques have been developed. Among these are quadratic programming (where there is a squared relationship between some of the variables), and stochastic programming (where the exact relationships between some variables are uncertain).

mathematical school of management

under this school theorists see management as a system of mathematical models and processes. Perhaps the most widely known groups are the operations researchers or operations analysis. The abiding belief of this group is that, if management or organisation, or planning, or decision-making is a logical process, it can be expressed in terms of mathematical symbols and relationships.

mat or matrix

a paper-match impression of printing plate, from which a lead casting can be made to reproduce the material on the original plate.

matrix organization

flexible organization structure where authority depends on the expertise needed for a particular task and overall responsibility is shared between several persons.

matte

dull finish on illustrations. Needed to prevent glare from stills on television.

maturation

development consistent with mental or chronological age.

maturity

maturity curves = rate of pay increases based on age and length of service.

maturity stage

that stage of the product life cycle in which demand level off and profits begin to decline. Levels of competition have increased to the point where a shake-out is taking place in the market.

maximization
making as large as possible.

maximize
to make as large as possible.

maximum
the greatest number, value or score. The value of a variable when it cases to increase and starts to decrease (mathematical).

maximum benefit amount
a cap or limit on the benefits that an insurance plan will pay in a specified calender period, usually one year.

MBA
Master of Business Administration degree awarded to graduates who have completed a further course in business studies.

MD
Managing Director.

measure
way of calculating size or quantity or value.

mechanic
person who works with engines or machines.

mechanical
worked by a machine.

mechanics of reading
habits developed in connection with reading but apart from the reading process itself, such as following lines or print from left to right across the page, from top to bottom of a page, and from one to another.

mechanism
action of machine or system.

mechanistic
very formal and structured.

mechanistic and organic management
terms used by T. Burns and G.M. Stalker to differentiate two contrasting systems of management. The mechanistic system is characterized by a precise subdivision of the total organization into sections, each with its own semi-discrete objectives. Co-ordination is achieved by superiors in the hierarchy and by formal procedures. Individual tasks and responsibilities are precisely specified and the majority of interactions are between superior and subordinate. There is, in other words, a heavy emphasis on formal organization. In contrast an organic system place considerable reliance on the members of management forsaking their specialist preoccupations and adapting their behaviour in voluntary and spontaneous co-operation with colleagues in pursuit of common objectives as the situation may require. Rights and responsibilities are assumed or conceded with changing circumstances. Very little use is made of formal authority; most interactions, even those between supervisor and subordinate, are, or resemble, consultation between colleagues.
Burns and Stalker do not suggest that either system of management exists in its pure form to the total exclusion of any elements of the other, but their research indicated a clear division between those

managements that emphasized the mechanistic system and those that emphasized the organic. The mechanistic seemed to work when the organization was operating in comparatively stable conditions, so that events could be foreseen and anticipated by the devising of appropriate procedures. The organic was most suited to situations of rapid change and uncertainty, when fluid organization practices were necessary to achieve the swift responses required. (Bureaucracy; Formal Organization.

mechanistic organization

a term introduced by two British sociologists and management theorists, Lom Burns and George Stalker. It denotes a relatively closed and formal type of organization with a high degree of bureaucracy, in contract to an organic organization.

media

avenues through which public relations messages are transmitted. Common media (singular is "medium") include newspapers, magazines, radio, books, music, paintings, cartoons, posters, leaflets, brochures, speeches, window displays, car cards, trade or business papers, envelop stuffers, calenders, motion pictures, slide films, television, radio, newspapers, magazines.

median

a measure of central tendency which divides a group of scores in half with half the scores falling above the median score and half below.

media of advertising

magazines, newspapers, trade papers, television and radio bill boards and direct mail. Advertising is thus the modern means of informing the consumers about the products made available by the manufacturer or seller. Advertising has become a specialized branch of management. It is through advertisement that firms increase the sale of their products. The purpose of advertising is to inform, to persuade and inspire the consumers to buy the goods.

media research

research into the relative efficiency of different advertising media, and of different forms of particular advertising media, in reaching audiences.

mediate

to try to make the two sides in an argument come to an agreement.

mediation

attempt by a third party to make the two sides in an argument agree.

mediator

official mediator = government official who tries to make the two sides is an industrial dispute agree.

medical

referring to the study or treatment of illness.

medical check up

medical or physical examination of the candidate is an important step in the selection procedure. A qualified medical expert appointed by the organisation should certify whether the candidate is physically fit for the job.

medical test
physical examination determines the physical fitness of the selected candidate for the job. It is also necessary for the protection of the employer against the risk of claims for compensation from individuals who are already affected by disabilities. The medial examination should be both general and thorough. The finding should be carefully recorded as to give a complete medical history, the scope of current physical capacities and the nature of disabilities, if any.

medium
any vehicle used to convey an advertising message, such as television, magazines, or direct mail.

meet
to come together with someone.

meeting
coming together of a group of people.

megabyte (MB)
a unit of measure of the storage or memory in computer hardware, meaning one million bytes.

member
person who belongs to a group or a society or an organization.

membership group
a reference group to which an individual actually belongs and with which he interacts. The group may be primary, e.g., family, neighbours, friends, co-workers, etc., or it may be secondary, e.g., voluntary associations, clubs, athletic teams, trade unions, religious organizations, etc.

memo pad
pad of paper for writing short notes.

memorandum or memo
short message sent from one person to another in the same organization.

memory
a function of cognition which refers to the storage of information with reference to a computer, an electronic form of storing information.

mental ability
an untechnical term meaning intelligence or mental maturity.

mental age
level of development in intelligence expressed in terms of the age at which the average child attains that level.

mental deficiency
term for all degree of lack in intelligence.

mental measurement
quantitative determination of a person's abilities and tendencies.

mental set
an attitude.

mental test
measurement in which interest centres on the

differences between different individuals responses.

mentor
person who is respected and looked up to by less experienced members of staff.

menu
a list of computer programmes, operations, options, instructions, files, questions, and other functions displayed on a computer monitor in order to assist an operator.

mercantile credit
credit at the trade level, i.e., credit extended by manufacturers or wholesalers to other channel members such as retailers. Such credit avoids the need for COD shipments or for limiting business to a cash-and-carry basis.

mercantilism
rules which appear to increase the wealth of a country, largely through governmental action, e.g., imposition of tariffs.

merchandise mart
a facility in which exhibition space is rented on a permanent basis to manufacturers and wholesalers so that they may display their products to potential customers, usually distributors and retailers, not the general public. Marts are often devoted to a particular line of products, for example, apparel or furniture.

merchandising
(1). (broad definition, which overlaps that given later for product planning): the planning involved in marketing the right merchandise or service at the right place, at the right time, in the right quantities, and at the right price. (2) (narrow definition): the buying functions as performed by wholesalers and retailers.

merchant
a middleman who takes title to the good he buys and who, in turn, resells them. Most merchants are wholesalers or retailers and are variously known as traders, distributors, dealers, storekeepers, etc.

merger
combination of two companies, generally through an exchange of stock.

merger conglomerate
merger of companies in entirely different fields.

merger horizontal
mergers of companies producing the same type of products or services.

merger vertical
mergers of companies with their suppliers or their marketing outlets.

merit
quality which deserves reward.

meritocracy
society or organization where advancement is based on a person's natural ability rather than on his or her background.

merit rating
formal periodic reporting in writing on how well individual employees are doing their jobs. Similar to Appraisal except that appraisal is generally used for rating of managers.

merrick differential piece rate system

it is a system which has three steps. Upto 83% of the standard output straight piece rate is paid. Above 83% and upto standard output a bonus of 10% of the time rate is paid. An additional bonus is paid for output above the standard.

metaphor

a figure of speech in which a word or phase literally denoting one kind of object or idea is used in place of another in order to suggest a likeness or analogy between them.

method

way of doing something.

micro

shortened, colloquial form of microcomputer.

microcomputer

a relatively small and cheap computer that has been designed for specific applications.

microeconomics

the part of economics that deals with small-scale issues like the prices of individual products, the performance of individual companies, or even a family budget.

micro-macro dilemma

in economics, the realization that what is beneficial for some producers and consumers may not necessarily benefit society as a whole.

microship

a tiny piece of silicon, containing a complete electrical circuit used extensively in the manufacture of the microcomputer.

microwave relay

sending broadcasts from one point to another by ultra high frequency signals.

mid–

prefix middle.

middle

in the centre or between two points.

middle level management

it consists of the heads of divisions or departments and branch managers. These are persons of intermediate rank who plan and control department activities. The department or functional managers are responsible to the top management for the proper functioning of their departments.

middleman

an individual or an organisation acting as a link between others, especially between producers and consumers or retailers, e.g., a furniture wholesaler to a literary agent.

middle management

a management whose position in the hierarchy of an organization is higher than junior management and lower than senior management is part of middle management, and this accounts for most managers in most organizations. Middle managers are typically in charge of the constituted units that make up an organization, responsible for the work of other people but with little or no say in the making of policy or the taking of organization wide decisions.

migrant
person who moves from one place or country to another, usually to work.

militant
(person) who very actively supports and works for a cause.

military leave
US unpaid leave or absence from work by workers who are in the armed forces or who have to do their military service.

milking
a strategy in which a company prices an established product above the level which would ordinarily be justified by production costs and competitive conditions in the marketplace.

milk round
visiting of universities and colleges by employers, in order to find promising new employees.

mimeographing
a trade-mark process for reproducing typewritten or handwritten matter.

minimal
the smallest possible.

minimize
to make something as small as possible. To make something seem not very important.

minor
less important.

minority
number or quantity which is less than half of the total. Small number of people in a larger group, who may suffer discrimination.

minor premise
in a syllogism, the proposition which introduces the minor term. It is the second proposition.

mirror writing
writing words or numbers backward. The term was derived from the fact that such writing can be read when held before a mirror, which reverses the order of the letters or numbers.

misappropriate
to use illegally money which is not yours, but with which you have been trusted.

misappropriation
illegal use of money by someone who is not the owner but who has been trusted to look after it.

miscarriage of justice
decision wrongly or unjustly reached by a court or decision which goes against the rights of a party in a case, in such a way that the decision may be reversed on appeal.

misconduct
illegal action or action which can harm someone.

misdirected marketing effort
marketing efforts which are based upon incomplete; inconclusive, incorrect, or misleading data. Misdirected efforts are often the result of management's inability to accurately calculate marketing costs.

mismanage
to manage badly.

missionary salesman
a salesman employed by a manufacturer to make contact with and work with his customers or those of his

distributors, usually for the purpose of developing good will and stimulating demand.

mission identity
the company perceived by its customers in terms of its goals. Sometimes referred to as company image, mission identity is more accurately the sense of purpose which keeps a firm on track.

mission statement
a detailed statement of the goals and objectives of an organization calculated to provide the members of the organization with a sense of direction.

mistake
wrong action or wrong decision.

misunderstanding
lack of agreement or mistake.

mixed brand strategy
a marketing strategy in which a manufacturer produces a number of similar products under different brand names, or in which a middleman or retailer sells products under different brand names, or in which a middleman or retailer sells products under dealer or generic names as well under manufacturer names.

mixed economy
in economics, this refers to the kind of economy in which the ownership of the means of production is partly in the private sector and partly in the public sector.

mixed dextral
right-handed and left-eyed.

mixed sinistral
left-handed and right-eyed.

mobile
which can move about.

mobility
being able to move from place to another.

mock interview
a training device for interviewers, in which they conduct interviews, according to given instructions, with a respondent who has been instructed to behave in certain ways.

mock up
a scale model used for study, testing, or instruction.

model
(1). a person employed to pose in photographs, style shows, or other activities.
(2). a representation of large entity, to provide a smaller, inexpensive means of visualizing it. A model of a new skyscraper, for instance, may be shown in a company's lobby or used in photography to approximate the appearance of the building.

modelling
a form of learning from observing a model which goes much further than copying or imitation. Children especially may generalize from the model behaviour to a wide range of similar behaviour of their own invention.

model, mathematical
a description of a system (a machine or a situation) in which the factors are expressed in mathematical terms in such a way that effects of various changes in the real system can

be simulated by changing the values given to the mathematical terms.

model release
a document signed by a model allowing use of pictures of the model.

modem
from the term 'modulator-demodulator. It is an electronic device that converts information from a computer into a form suitable for transmission by telephone thus enabling communication with other computers.

moderate
not too large. Not holding very extreme views.

modification
change.

modify
to change or to make something fit a different use.

momentum
movement forward.

monitor
(1). TV receiver used to watch broadcasts or closed circuit signals.
(2). to review a broadcast station's content.

monitoring skills
the skills used by marketing managers to develop and manage a system of controls and provide feedback on the results of marketing activities. These controls may be annual plan controls, profitability controls, and/or strategic controls.

monopoly
control of the sale of a product by one supplier.

monospony
a situation is which one buyer can control or greatly influence the price of a product through being the only buyer, or the most powerful buyer, in particular market.

montage format
a form of advertising found in the print media and on television in which a number of pictures or image are juxtaposed in such a way that an overall impression is created in the mind of the viewer.

monotype
typesetting machine that produces single characters and casts them into lines.

montage
composite picture of two or more scenes; also, a series of dissolves or scenes in rapid sequence to show of events, personnel changes, etc.

Monte Carlo technique
techniques used in operations research that make use of the laws of probability.

month
one of twelve periods which make a year.

month end
the end of a calender month, when accounts have to be drawn up.

monthly
happening every month or which is received every month.

moonlight
informal to do a second job for cash (often in the evening) as well as a regular job.

moonlighter
person who moonlights.

moonlighting
doing a second job.

morale
feeling of confidence or satisfaction.

more
written at the bottom of a page of copy indicating more to come.

morgue
the department of a publication that contains clippings, reference materials, illustrations, and other source materials. It sometimes incorporates the traditional library of reference works.

motile
motor minded.

motion
moving about. Proposal which will be put to a meeting to be voted on.

motion study
study of the discrete motions performed in doing a task in order to determine whether it can be performed more efficiently.

motivate
to inspire, impel and encourage action. Motivation encompasses all the actions undertaken by a leader to encourage higher productivity. They includes selection, placement, compensation, communication, participation and development.

motivation
the act of arousing or stimulating an inward urge to action in order to achieve a goal.

motivational
referring to motivation.

motivation research
a type of marketing research that seeks to determine subconscious reasons why consumers buy given products, or at least the reasons that they are unwilling or unable to express clearly.

motivation to participation
the most effective of all organizational devices is to achieve business participation in community rehabilitation, ending pollution and maintaining the ecological balance even though no single device is likely to be adequate alone. New and distinctive business abilities will be needed. Means must be found for new initiatives as well as ways to make funds available such as through anti-pollution bonds or other comparable devices.

motivation, psychology of
when we mange a business we are not managing just a department or an organisation but primarily the people who compose the department, the people who are part and parcel of the organisation, the people who were managed by our predecessors and they will be managed by the posterity as well. How do these react to varying situations, phenomenal changes in systems conventions, tastes, habits, aptitudes and in essence the totality of the enormous changes that envelop them? The changes brought about by social, political

economic and other factors may have a salient effect on the people, may even change the order of priority which they fix for themselves but it is quite doubtful whether the people will change basically.

motive
a conscious or unconscious factor which will determine an individual's behaviour towards a goal or in any situation.

motivation skill
it is only through proper understanding of the hopes, fears, aspirations, disappointments and failures of a person that a manager can decide as to how to motivate his subordinates. He must find out why people behave as they do. The needs of every person can be classified broadly under bio-genic group, socio-genic group and ego group.

mount
a base (wood or metal) used to raise the height of the plate to that of a type for printing by the letter press process. A plate is mounted on a base to raise it to type height.

moving average
in time series analysis, the moving average is the basis upon which predictions are made contingent upon the average outcomes of experiences over two or more recent time periods. Moving average for sales, for example, assumes that the sales figures for the next period will be the average of the sales figures for a given number of previous time periods.

MSC
Manpower Services Commission.

multinational company
a company whose interest cut across national boundaries, one which allocates its resources and its marketing efforts on a world-wide basis. (Also called "transnational company" and "international company".

multinational marketing
marketing efforts in more than one foreign country which may include the operation of production and distribution facilities and the employment of local labour and management personnel.

multiple
many.

multiple branding
a marketing strategy in which a firm gives each item in a line of products separate brand name as, for example, a large cereal manufacturer may market several dry breakfast foods under different brand names as part of an effort to reach various segments of the market and to dominate supermarket shelf space.

multiple channel approach
impressing an idea or subject on an audience by utilising many types of media and communications, to "surround" them with it.

multiple choice question
question framed in such a way as to give the respondent

several possible answers from which to select that which is appropriate.

multiple correlation

in statistical analysis, the comparison of the effect of several independent variables on a single dependent variable. Each independent variable is carefully weighted to determine its effect.

multiple effect

using a communication device that stimulates many others to disseminate the same information. For example, a folder of press stories that members of an organisation in many areas use with local media.

multiple packaging

the packaging together of two or more items (men's underwear, cans of beer, packages of chewing gum, etc.) as a means of encouraging multiple purchases on the part of the consumer.

multistage pricing

a planning strategy in which a broad price policy is developed by integrating a series of individual pricing decisions into a coherent price framework for the firm.

multistage sample

a sample selected by stages, the sampling units at each stage being sampled from the larger units chosen at the previous stage.

multivariable segmentation

a form of market segmentation in which more than one factor (age, race, etc.) is employed to segment the population.

muscular work

movement is achieved by muscular contraction. The energy required for contraction is stored in the muscles within the large glycogen molecules. These disintegrate to produce glucose, the breakdown of which liberates energy and produces lactic acid as a waste product. No immediate supply of oxygen is required for this series of reactions, but an 'oxygen debt' is created, in that oxygen is required for the further breakdown and removal of the lactic acid. Thus, in the long term, the amount of oxygen consumed is proportional to the amount of physiological work performed. It must be noted that a certain expenditure of energy takes place without obvious movement, since work is done by such muscles as the heart, in addition to those involved in the maintenance of posture. Numerous equipments and techniques are available to measure the rate of oxygen consumption and hence the physiological energy-cost of any activity of human performance. This energy-cost provides one index for evaluating different methods of performing a particular task.

narrative

description of something as a story.

narrative material

reading matter which tells a story.

nation
country and the people living in it.

national
referring to a particular country.

national advertising
advertising sponsored on a national or regional basis, generally by manufacturers or producers. Also known as general advertising.

national efficiency
at the country or total economy level use can be made of the following measures as:
(i) level and rate of growth of real GNP (Gross National Product).
(ii) level and rate of growth of real per capita income.
(iii) rate of utilization of key factor inputs (plant, material, power, etc.).
(iv) useful output in relation to total output.
(v) level and rate of growth of total real industrial output.
(vi) physical output and growth rates for specific major commodities.
(vii) total industrial employment and rate of growth of same.
(viii) level and rate of increase in industrial labour productivity (in terms of output per man hour or year).
(ix) level and rate of increase in industrial output per capita and per gainfully employed citizen.
(x) value-added contribution of overall industrial sector to GNP and trends over time (in percent).
(xi) value-added per industrial employee and trends over time.
(xii) incremental capital-output ratios and trends.
(xiii) ratios of inventories to output produced and sold.

national environmental constraints
(i) the percentage of the total population and those presently employed in industry who can read, write and do simple arithmetic calculations, and the average years of schooling of adults.
(ii) specialised vocational and technical training. Extent, types and quality of education and training of this type not directly under the control or direction of industrial enterprises.
(iii) higher education. The percentage of the total population and those employed in industry with post-high school education, plus the types of quality of such education. The types of persons obtaining higher education.
(iv) special management development programmes. The extent and quality of management development programmes which are not run internally by productive enterprises, and which are aimed at improving the skills and abilities of managers and for potential managers.
(v) industry and manpower utilisation. The extent and degree to which the types of formal education and training in a given country fits the needs of productive enterprises and

all levels of skill and achievement, and the degree to which manpower utilisation is effective.

national growth and management

the objectives for national growth as set forth by our planners, are:

(i) a sizable increase in national income so as to raise the level of living of the people in the country.

(ii) rapid industrialization and utilization of nation's economic and natural resources.

(iii) a large expansion of employment opportunities; and

(iv) reduction of inequalities in income and wealth and a more even distribution of economic power.

nationalization

the process by which a state takes over the ownership of a private company or industry and brings it within the control of the public sector. This may be due to practising the ideology of socialism or to the attempt to save a strategic part of the economy from collapse or foreign ownership.

nationwide

all over a country.

natural

normal.

natural classification of expenses

an accounting practice in which expenses are grouped into classes based on the kinds of expenses involved, e.g., rent, salaries, supplies, raw materials, taxes, interest, etc. rather than on the function of the expenditure, e.g., the costs of operating a particular department. Also known as ledger expenses or object of expenditure cost.

natural monopoly

a condition in the marketplace in which, because it best serves the public, there is only one seller. Public utilities are examples of natural monopolies in which prices are regulated by a public agency.

natural products

raw materials which occur in nature, such as fish, game, lumber, metals, minerals, oil, and coal.

need awareness

the degree to which consumers may be cognizant of their needs and willing to discuss them with others. Three degrees or levels of need awareness are generally described; conscious, preconscious, and unconscious.

needs

what is necessary.

negative

meaning "No".

negative option plans

a form of direct marketing in which the customer (who may or may not be a member of a "club") is shipped a preannounced product at regular intervals unless he advises the seller not to ship before a predetermined data. The Book-Of-The-Month Club is a typical negative option plan. All such arrangements are regulated by the Federal Trade

Commission.

negativism
marked resistance, the tendency to do the opposite of what one is requested to do.

neglect
not doing a duty.

neglected
not well looked after.

negligence
lack of proper care or not doing a duty (with the result that a person or property is harmed).

negligent
showing negligence or not taking proper care.

negligently
in a way which shows negligence.

negligible
very small or not worth bothering about.

negotiable
which can be discussed so that an agreement is reached.

negotiable instruments
a negotiable instrument is a document embodying a debt of a sum of money, where the document enjoys the quality of negotiability. Normally a debt of money may be transferred (assigned) by the creditor to a third party, but this assignment may be made in writing, written notice of it must be given to the debtor and the third-party assignee acquires no better title to the debt than was possessed by the assignor. With a negotiable instrument, however, the transfer may be effected by mere delivery of the instrument without the necessity of either a written assignment or written notice to the debtor, and the third party who receives such an instrument in good faith acquires a good title to it, irrespective of the title of the transferor. The only exception to the rules about transfer apply to bills of exchange and promissory notes, which require a written endorsement for purposes of transfer. Whether or not an instrument enjoys the quality of negotiability depends largely upon commercial custom. Negotiable instruments include bank notes, bills of exchange, cheques, promissory notes, treasury bills and dividend warranties. It is unlikely that further instruments will be added to this list by commercial custom, but statute law could be used to create further negotiable instruments.

negotiate
to discuss a problem formally with someone, so as to reach an agreement.

negotiated contract
a contract to buy goods or services in which the buyer and seller negotiate its specific terms. Negotiated contracts are frequently employed instead of competitive bidding when there is a sole supplier and thus no competition in the marketplace.

negotiation
the essence of the collective bargaining process. It refers to the discussion of terms and

conditions of employment by employers and employees, or their representatives, with a view to reaching a mutually acceptable outcome.

negotiator

person who discuses with the aim of reaching an agreement.

neighbourhood shopping center

a small shopping center, often arranged on the strip plan, which serves its surrounding community—typically persons living within five minutes of drive time. Neighbourhood centers are frequently anchored by a supermarket of variety store and may include service retailers (beauty shops, card shops, etc.) and stores selling convenience goods (drug stores, etc.).

nepotism

giving preferential treatment to someone who is a relative or friend (especially giving a job to a member of the family who is less well qualified than other candidates).

net

pay or price, etc. after all deductions have been made.

net benefit

a decision criterion based on the same information and used for the same basic purpose as a cost/benefit analysis. A net benefit is calculated by subtracting costs from benefits (a cost/benefit analysis divides benefits by costs).

net current assets

the aggregate of all current assets (including cash) less current liabilities. It is also known as working capital.

net income

revenue and gains minus expenses and losses.

net profit

is the excess of 'revenue and gains' over 'expenses and deprives'. It results in an increase in the proprietor's equity. Net loss is the deficiency of revenue and gains' as compared to 'expenses and deprivals' and leads to decrease in the owner's equity.

net sales

sales revenue after returns, allowances, discounts, cancellations, and taxes (sales and excise) have been deducted for the accounting period. Net sales represent the actual sales dollars the company will receive.

net total assets

total assets less current liabilities.

network

link-up of two or more broadcast stations to carry the same material.

network chart

it involves:

(i) determination of work breakdown structure.

(ii) development of network logic indicating the sequence inter-relationship and interdependence of activities and events.

(iii) estimation of activity timings based upon some assumption of resources.

(iv) calculating of earliest and latest completion times, floats

(slack) etc.
(v) identification of critical paths.
(vi) time-cast trade off, where possible for redetermining activity timings.

networking
linking people scattered geographically into a single work group by electronic means, e.g., teleworking.

net worth
in business, a synonym for owner's equity, i.e., the excess of assets over liabilities in an enterprise.

neutral
a term referring to any third party who is actively engaged in negotiations in order to facilitate an agreement.

neutrality laws
US laws relating to discrimination which must be observed by organization.

new
recent or not old.

new product planning process
those stages through which a product passes in the development process. Included are idea generation and screening, analysis and evaluation, product development and production, branding, test marketing and positioning, and finally, full scale marketing and product.

new push theory
budgets play an important part in the "push". Finance people are usually asked to scrutinize all budgets carefully. They are directed to cut out all "the lace and niceties" and "get down to essentials". In short a new pressure upwards is expressed somewhere in the budgets in terms of a "tighter" figure. The results may be as expected. Human efficiency rise say 10% and production is increased. A new level of efficiency is stabilized at 80%.

news
information about things which has happened.

newsletter
a publication in letter-size format, usually issued periodically.

newsprint
coarse-quality paper used for printing newspapers.

newssheet
leaflet distributed by an organization, giving the latest news about itself.

new technology
the term often used to describe the applied micro electronic devices to be found in the electronic office.

new unsought goods
products offering new ideas and applications of which the consumer is not at all aware. The marketing of such goods requires informative promotion so that potential customers will accept and seek out the product.

nick
a small grove across the belly of a type. It helps the compositor to place the type in the correct way while composing by hand.

night
period of time from evening to

morning.

no-attention job
job that can be done with minimal concentration.

no-claims bonus
reduction of premiums on an insurance policy because no claims have been made.

no demand
a condition in the marketplace in which there is no need or desire on the part of consumers for a product or service being offered for sale.

nominal
very small (payment).

nominate
to suggest someone or to name someone for a job.

nomination
act of nominating someone for a job.

nominee
person who is nominated for a job.

noncommercial advertising
advertising by nonprofit organizations to promote public interests (such as automobile safety or equal rights), encourage contributions to charities or other philanthropic causes (such as the American Red Cross), and promote political causes.

non-comparable bases
unlike numbers or magnitudes used as standards or reference in two or more sets of data, which invalidate comparisons between the sets of data.

non-conformance
act of not conforming.

non-contributory
non-contributory pension plan or scheme = pension scheme where company, not the employee, pays, all contributions.

non-directed interview or nondirective interview
interview which is not conducted round certain fixed questions, and which therefore encourages open discussion.

non-executive
non executive director = director who attends board meetings and gives advice, but does not work full-time for the company.

nonlinear programming
an operations research technique that may be used when some of the variables in the mathematical models are raised to a higher power (e.g., X^2)

nonoccupational policy
an insurance policy providing protection against off-the-job injury and illness. Injury or sickness covered by workers compensation insurance is excluded. Group accident and sickness policies are often nonoccupational.

non personal communication channels
media that carry messages without personal contact or feedback. Nonpersonal communication channels include mass media (such as direct mail), atmospherics (environmental factors designed to stimulate sales and or establish a particular image), and events (such as grand openings).

non price competition
competition in the marketplace based on factors other than price. A firm may emphasize service, terms of sale, delivery, attractive packaging, extensive promotion, or the product's reputation in an effort to gain a competitive advantage.

nonprocess input/output
the requirements for inputs and outputs that are associated with the process but that are not directly connected to it, should be detailed. These may include data on raw material characteristics the results of optimization calculations that are performed on other computers, changes in production requirements, special reports and data that are transmitted to remote special locations. The type of reports and their frequency are important since they can result in the necessity for additional output devices that in some cases must be remote from the PCCs site.

non-profit organization
any organization whose ownership resides entirely with its members and whose financial operations are not intended to yield a profit for shareholders, e.g., clubs or neighbourhood associations or charities.

non-resident
person who is not considered a resident of a country for tax purposes.

non-sampling error
error due to imperfect select, bias in response, observation, recording, etc. An error in sample estimates which cannot be attributed to sampling fluctuations.

non store retailing
a form of retailing in which a traditional store building is not involved, i.e., in which the retailer and customer transact their business through such means as: 1) direct mail 2) door-to-door sales 3) in-home or party-plan selling 4) telephone sales, 5) catalog sales, 6) interactive television, or 7) vending machines.

non-taxable
which is not subject to tax.

non traceable common costs
those expenses in a business which cannot be assigned to a particular function, e.g., executive salaries, interest payments, etc.

non-union
company using non-union labour = company employing workers who do not belong to trade unions.

non-verbal communication
communicating a message, using facial expressions or body language, but without speaking.

norm
the usual quantity or the usual rate.

normal
usual or which happens regularly.

normal distribution
the distribution of data from a random sample of the population. When these data

are plotted on a graph they show up as a symmetrical bell-shaped curve with scores clustered around the average and declining towards either extreme.

normally
in the usual way.

norms
values of an organization or of society.

no-strike agreement or no-strike clause
agreement or clause where the workers promise never to strike.

notice
piece of written information. Official warning that a contract is going to end or that terms are going to be changed.

notice board
board fixed to a wall where notices can be put up.

notification
informing someone of something.

notify
to tell someone something formally.

numeracy
literally, the ability to count—the numerical equivalent of literacy. The term is used more widely to include people with no fear of dealing with statistics or mathematics and the ability to handle quantitative methodology.

numerical control
direction of machines by magnetic tape or punched cards.

nutrient
a food substance that is digested and absorbed by the body and utilized as food and energy to sustain life.

nutrition
the science of food, nutrients, and other substances found in food. Nutrition is concerned with the actions, interactions, and balances of food and its component substances in relation to health and disease. The processes by which an organism ingests, digests, absorbs, transports, utilizes, and excretes food substances is also part of this science. In addition, nutrition examines the social, economic, cultural, and psychological implications of food and eating.

obit
obituary. A biography of a dead person.

object
to refuse to do something or to say that you do not accept something.

objection
to object to something.

objective
goal or purpose towards which work is directed.

objective test
a test which can be scored with a minimum of dependence upon individual interpretation of the answers.

obligation
duty to do something.

obligatory
necessary according to the law or rules.

observance
doing what is required by a law.

observation

the research technique in which the researcher observes certain predetermined phenomena, such as the reaction of shoppers to displays or the numbers passing a poster site, rather than questioning subjects directly, as in interviewing.

observational methods
research techniques in which the interviewer (observer) gathers information by observation rather than by questioning respondents.

observe
to obey (a rule or a law).

observer
person who observes.

obsolescence
situation where a worker no longer has the knowledge or skill to perform efficiently or where a machine is out-of-date.

obsolescent
becoming out of date.

obsolete
no longer used.

obstruct
to get in the way or to stop something progressing.

occupation
job or work.

occupational
referring to a job.

occupation clue
clue suggesting nature of employment.

occupy
to live or work in a property (such as an office). To take up a certain amount of time.

odd
odd numbers = numbers which cannot be divided by two. Odd jobs = small pieces of work, not connected to each other, and paid for individually.

odd-job-man
person who does various pieces of work.

odd line pricing
a method of ascribing prices ending in odd numbers, especially five, seven, or nine, to convey the impression of a lower price.

off
not working or not in operation.

offence
crime or act which is against the law.

offender
person who breaks a law or regulation.

offer
statement that a company is willing to do something. To offer someone a job = to tell someone that he can have a job in your company.

office
building or set of rooms where a company works or where business is done.

office as a memory centre
records relating to different activities of an organisation are prepared and maintained in the office. From such records relevant data can be obtained as and when desired. An office serves as a storehouse of information. In the absence of well preserved records, an organisation has no guide and has to rely on memory, hearby, conjecture, or chance. Therefore, an office is known as the brain of an organisation.

office as a control centre
an office collects feedback information on results and enables the management to keep a check on various activities of the business. As a control centre, it monitors the progress of work and prevents unwarranted deviations. It also helps them to take remedial actions.

office bearer
person who holds an office, especially person who is a member of a union council and holds the office of secretary or treasure, etc.

office charts
an office chart is a graphic representation of the organisation structure of an office. It is a diagrammatically form which shows the major office functions and inter-relationship among them. It is a diagram of the formal authority—responsibility relationships existing between various departments or units of the office. It depicts graphically the working relationships in the office showing who is to do what. An office chart is a blue print of an office. An office chart contains the following information:

(a) departments and positions in the office.

(b) names and status of office personnel.

(c) flow of authority and responsibility.

(d) channels of formal communication.

(e) line and staff relationship.

office employment
working conditions in offices are governed by the Offices, shops and Railway Premises Act 1963. The act defines an office as a building, or part of a building, used solely or mainly for office purposes, i.e. one of the following: administration, handling money, telephone or telegraph operating and clerical work in general, including writing, bookkeeping, sorting papers, filing, typing, duplicating machine calculating, drawing and the editorial preparation of matter for publication.
The provisions of the Act dealing with health, safety and welfare largely repeat the corresponding provisions of the Factories Act, adapted to meet the special needs of office employment. The provisions of the Act are enforced by the inspectors of the Health and Safety Executive as far as offices situated in factory buildings are concerned, while other offices are supervised by district and borough councils. Like the Factories Act, the 1963 Act will be replaced eventually by the new machinery set up under the Health and Safety at Work Act 1974.

office layout
office layout refers to the systematic arrangement of furnitures, machines and other facilities within the office space available. It implies the placing of people and equipment within each department or section of

the office so as to make the best possible utilization of accommodation or floor-space available.

office manager

an office manager is the officer who is entrusted with the task of managing an office. His job is to guide the office staff in the performance of clerical work. An office manager is known by different names, e.g. Administrative Manager, Manager—Office Service, Administrative Officer, etc. Office work is basically a service function and, therefore, the office manager is basically a staff executive. But he is given substantial functional authority.

officer

person who has an official position.

office, roles of

every organisation has at its very centre the office which gives life to the whole organisation. An office breathes life into modern organizations in the form of prompt, up-to-date and accurate information. Without an office, the organisation may be like a house built on sand. It is in the office that plans are conceived, records are kept and progress is evaluated.

office services

this includes maintenance of proper data processing and other office management services, communication on best use of latest mechanical devices.

official

from a government department or organization.

officialese

language used in government documents which can be difficult to understand.

officially

according to what is said in public.

official publications

also government publications and official statistics. Statistical and other factual material in published form, from government department sources; a high degree of accuracy can be assumed as public sanction is high.

off price retailing

the selling at retail of merchandise, often carrying status or premium labels, at less than "regular" prices. In contrast to discount retailing (where the discounter pays the same price for his merchandise as everyone else and sells it for less than traditional retailers) off-price retailers buy merchandise at cut-rate price and pass the savings along to their customers.

offset lithography

printing process in which image is transferred to a rubber roller and printed onto the paper.

off-the-job

off-the-job-training = training given to workers away from their place of work (such as at a college or school).

ohio-state psychological examination

a test used to predict ability to

do academic work at the secondary, college and university levels. The test measures vocabulary, language usage, and achievement in reading.

old

having existed for a long time.

old age

period when a person is old.

old boy network

using long-standing key contacts to appoint people to jobs or to get a job or to do business.

old fashioned

out of date.

oligopoly

a situation in which a few sellers can control or dominate a market. Such a situation is widely regarded as an incentive for the seller to form a cartel.

ombudsman

official who investigates complaints by the public against government departments.

omnibus questionnaire

a questionnaire which contains questions on several different topics, it can contain MR as well as opinion questions.

omnibus survey

in market research this is a wide-ranging form of survey that seeks to obtain data on many topics for a number of clients.

on call

ready to be called to work at any time.

on demand

a term indicating the requirement for immediate action in the form of payment of the delivery or representation of some item or sum of money, usually as a result of a legally binding obligation.

one level channel

a marketing channel in which there is only one intermediary, commonly a retailer, between the producer and the consumer.

one man

one-man business or firm or company or operation= business run by one person alone with no staff or partners.

onerous

heavy or needing a lot of effort or money.

one sided

which favours one side and not the other in a negotiation.

on-line

term used when computer input or input is directly connected to the computer.

on-the-job

on-the-job training = training given to workers at their place of work.

on-the-job test

it is on the basis of the result of various tests that a candidate is finally selected, but before he is given a job on permanent basis, it would be better to try him out for a few weeks in the factory itself. It is only by observing workers actually at work that one can find out whether he can work harmoniously with his fellow-workers and his behaviour towards the higher management. It is then that he can be finally selected or rejected.

on-the-job training

a form of training that is given to people at their place of work, and usually during working hours. In the United Kingdom it often involves sitting next to nellie.

op ed

opposite editorial. The page facing the editorial page in newspapers. Some are now devoted in part to statements from non-staff sources.

open

at work or not closed.

open account

(1) a policy under which a vendor extends interest free credit to his customers on a short term basis. Commonly, bills are payable in full at the end of 30 days. The practice of recording such transactions in a ledger gave rise to the popular term "on the books." (2) any credit account in which there remains a balance to be paid.

open door

a term used to describe unscheduled and unlimited access or admission to, or availability of a person, service, or facility, a policy adopted by a manager to assure open feedback and the participation of all employees in issues relating to management actions, policies, organizational performance, and employees beliefs and attitudes.

open end

broadcast material in which time is left at beginning or end for addition of material by the station.

open-end agreement

a bargaining agreement providing for a contract that will remain in effect until one of the parties wants to reopen negotiations.

open ended

with no fixed limit or with some items not specified.

open ended question

question for which no fixed alternative responses are given. As compared with Closed Question which has fixed alternative answers, e.g., Multiple Choice Question.

open-end lease

a lease that may involve a balloon payment, based on the value of the item leased, when it is returned to the lessor.

open house

an event in which a company invites its employees, dealers, suppliers, and/or its community to visit it and see how it operates. A device of employee, dealers, stockholder, supplier, dealer, and/or community relations.

opening

act of starting a new business.

open mortgage

a mortgage that can be paid off at any time before its maturity (the time it ends) without a penalty.

open office

an open office implies a big room or hall in which the staff and equipment of several departments are accommodated. Each department or section of the office is allotted a separate space in the hall without being partitioned by walls. The space may be demarcated by counter high filing cabinets or shelves.

open plan

open plan office = large room divided into smaller working spaces with no fixed divisions between them.

operate

to work; to make something work or function.

operating cycle

the time gap between the purchase of raw materials and sale of finished products in a manufacturing firm.

operating ratio (OR)

this is the ratio of cost of goods sold plus operating expenses to net sales. This is closely related to the ratio of operating profit to net sales. For example, if the operating ratio is 80% then the operating profit ratio would be 20%.

operation

business organization and work.

operational

referring to how something works.

operational definition

a definition of something which is based on the operation of the factors which produced it, e.g., inflation is defined by the movement of prices and the real value of money. The term is also used more loosely to mean a 'working definition' or a 'rule of thumb'.

operational planning

the operational planning, monitoring and control system is primarily meant to take care of five areas of management:

(i) planning and optimization of physical resources.

(ii) planning for financial requirements.

(iii) up-dating the time estimates and controlling project time duration.

(iv) anticipating delays and taking corrective action well in time.

(v) controlling costs.

operation research

application of quantitative methods to the solution of management problems. It includes a "systems approach" in which a large number, rather than a few factors, are considered positively by a group of scientists from different fields.

operations research for management

there is a new concept in management. It helps companies to solve such diverse business problems as directing salesmen to the right accounts at the right time, dividing the advertising budget in the most effective way, establishing equitable bonus systems, improving inventory and reordering policies, planning minimum cost. Production schedules, and estimating the amount of clerical help needed for a new operation. Operations research makes possible accomplishments: (a) it helps to single out the critical issues which requires executive appraisal and analysis, and (b) it provides factual bases to support and guide executive judgment. Thus, it eases the burden of effort and time on executive but intensifies the potential of their decision-making role. In this sense operations research contributes toward better management.

operation research for problem solving
current research on the machine simulation of higher mental processes suggests that we will be able to programme much of the top job before too many decades have passed. There is good authority for the prediction that decade or two a digital computer will be the world chess champion and that another will discover and prove an important new mathematical theorem, and that in the somewhat more distant future "the way is open to deal scientifically with ill-structured problems to make the computer coextensive with the human mind.

operative
referring to the working of a system.

operator
person who works a machine.

opinion
they ρver expression of an attitude.

opinion leader
a person whose opinions are widely respected (especially within a reference group), who is often a trend-setter, and who influence the purchase decisions of others.

opinion polling
a form of survey research in which respondents are asked their opinions regarding goods, services or political candidates.

opinion research
research into the nature of individual and group opinion on certain topics, e.g., political opinion.

opportunity
situation where you can do something successfully.

opportunity cost
the value of the benefit sacrificed by choosing a particular alternative or course of action.

opportunity forecast
a form of business forecast in which an effort is made to predict future conditions in the marketplace which might present opportunities for new products, the reduction in production costs, or the avoidance of changes in the marketing environment which might prove detrimental to the organization.

oppose
to try to stop something happening; to vote against something.

opposite
opposite number = person who has a similar job in another company.

optical reader
electronic reader of printed material.

optimisation
any attempt to maximize or

minimize a specific quantity, usually called an "objective"; also, a determination of the best mix of inputs to achieve an objective.

optimum

the course of action that minimizes overall losses or maximizes overall gains.

optimum price

the price at which the highest profit potential occurs, determined by relating the movements of sales volumes to the increases and decreases in selling prices.

optimum utilization of manpower and natural resources

as a means of balanced regional development industry must utilize local manpower and natural resources to the full. The objective should not be to mass-produce the goods on modern, expensive machines but to get these goods produced by the masses. Action should be taken to implement projects that utilize such resources effectively and efficiently.

optional

not necessary according to rules.

oral

referring to speech, as opposed to writing.

oral communication

oral communication implies communication through spoken words whereas written communication is through written words. Oral communication can be of two types:

(a) face to face, conversation.
(b) through mechanical devices, viz., telephone, loudspeaker system, paging system, dictating machines etc.

order

arrangement of records (filing cards, invoices, etc.).

ordering costs

all those costs of doing business which directly relate to the ordering of goods and services including operating expenses associated with the order and receiving departments.

ordinary

normal or not special.

organ

journal or magazine.

organic organization

type of organization with little formality in its structure and procedures.

organisation

the division of work into managerial positions in the corporate structure and the adaptation of the structure to the people in the organisation.

organisational

referring to the way in which something is organized.

organisational behaviour

the behaviour of an organisation acting as an entity, rather than that any individual member.

organisational climate

the ethos of, or commonly perceived feeling about, an organization. It is based on tangible factors like the prevailing management style, the clarity of goals and values, the time horizons etc.

organisational consumer

organisational consumers include manufacturers, wholesalers and distributors, retailers, and government agencies, and non-profit organisations. The use the products they buy to make other products, to maintain the organisation's operations, or to be offered for resale.

organisational culture
this term denotes 'culture' as the term is not only the shared belief, value, attitudes and expectations of its members to make up the culture of an organisation, but also the unquestioned assumptions about its traditions and ways of doing things.

organisational goals
the normally stated objectives which are the basis for the existence and the maintenance of an organisation.

organisational loyalty
the basis of the contract between an organisation and its members. It is usually assumed to be something the individual owes the organization-rarely the other way round.

organisational pathology
writers on organisational theory from a human relations viewpoint have proposed that an organisation can be healthy or unhealthy, just like any of its individual members.

organisational shape
the profile of the levels of hierarchy in an organisation, the extent to which it is a flat organisation or a tall organisation.

organisational symbols
symbols uniquely associated with a particular organisation. These may be internal (annual dinner, founder's picture or slogan) or external (logo or trade mark).

organisational types
any attempt to classify organisations along one or more dimensions, e.g., formality, as in mechanistic organisation and organic organisation.

organisation and methods
the application of work study techniques to the structure and procedures of an organization in order to improve the efficiency of the organization's systems.

organisation audit
an audit of all aspects of an organisation operations. In practice this is usually the same as a management audit.

organisation charts
management should decide whether it wants an organization chart and, if so, what kind. The chart helps to show what has been decided. It will also be useful for showing to newly appointed managers and inquiring visitors.

organisation convenience
a course of action that meets the (usually financial) interests of the organisation as a whole rather than the interests of members or customers, e.g., moving to a cheaper, but less accessible location.

organisation development
planned and integrated effort to improve the effectiveness of

an organization through the restructuring of its processes on the basis of behavioural science.

The application of an organization-development programme involves a careful diagnosis of the organization's shortcomings, the preparation of a strategy for change and the marshalling of the physical and intellectual resources that the programme is seen to require. Typically organization development, as the term implies, seeks improvement in the total organization, or in a quasi-autonomous sub-organization, recognizing that to be effective change in any one part of the system requires supportive change in other parts.

Organisation development conceives the ideal organisation as being characterized by comparative clarity in the objectives established at all levels, a high degree of commitment to those objectives, open and honest communications throughout the system, open expression of disagreements, a constructive approach to conflice resolution and aculture that supports personal integrity and growth.

organisation formal

the official relationships of the positions in a corporation, generally shown on an organisation chart and embodies in job descriptions.

organisation, informal

the unofficial (interpersonal) relationships in an organisation not shown on the organisation chart and even not consistent with it.

organisation theory

the study of the structure and functioning of organizations and the behaviour or groups and individuals within them' (D. S. Pugh).

Despite the importance of formal organizations to modern societies, they have been objects of systematic study for little more than one generation. During the nineteenth century various industrialists published their own personal philosophies of management, either describing the organization of their own factories or explainning the enlightened nature of their treatment of their labour force. However, it was not until the early days of the present century that attempts were made to formulate general propositions concerning organizational structure and processes. Early contributions to an understanding of organizations came from three main sources: the scientific management movement, industrial psychologists and the classical theorists. The primary concern of all three was to increase managerial efficiency.

The scientific management approach, pioneered by F. W. Taylor, concentrated on shop-floor organisation and developed techniques for studying, analyzing and measuring the work of the operative, and for scheduling and recording work-in-progress. It may be argued that the 'scientific managers' were more concerned with the problems of analysing and improving performance at shop-floor level that with the creation of general theories of administration, although Taylor's determination to maximize managerial expertise led him to advocate the use of functional authority and to suggest an appropriate structure. Their work also did much to stimulate interest in management as a rewarding subject for intellectual application.

The First World War further focused attention on industrial problems and academic behavioural scientists became increasingly involved. Psychologists, both in Britain and In the USA, studies the problems of personal adjustment experienced by the newcomer to factory work and sought to systematize the hitherto haphazard process of selection, placement and training. Research was conducted to ascertain the effect on the operative of various elements in the organizational environment such as heat, light, ventilation, hours of work and the number and distribution of rest pauses.

Between the two world wars, classical organization theorists sought to develop principles of management that would guide general managers in their task of structuring and administering business organizations. The contributions came almost entirely from practising managers and reflected their concern with practical problems such as departmentalization, co-ordination, control and the distribution of authority.

organising

organising comprises if:

(i) breaking down work into operative duties.

(ii) grouping operative duties into operative positions.

(iii) clarifying position requirements.

(iv) selecting and placing individuals on proper jobs.

(v) providing personnel facilities and other resources.

organize

to arrange things or people in a certain way so that they work more efficiently.

orientation

introduction of new employees into an organization.

ostracism

rejection of a member or members of a group by others.

ostracize

to reject and refuse to have anything to do with a member or member of a group.

out

on strike.

outfit

small, sometimes badly run,

company.

outhouse

working outside a company's buildings.

outlet

used in connection with the distribution of goods. That point or place where goods and services are available to buyers; usually used to mean retail outlet.

outline

the skeleton or gist of an article or a programme.

out of court

a dispute settled between two parties privately without continuing a court case.

out of date

old fashioned or no longer modern.

out of pocket

having paid out money personally.

out of work

with no job.

out-placement

help in finding another job, given by an employer to an employee, who has been made redundant.

output

the volume produced or put out. The relationship of output to input (the resources expended in producing), gives the measure of productivity. The concept or productivity is relevant to marketing and to MR, in so far as efficiency is a desirable goal. Thus the relationship of the resources expended (input) to the results (output) is most pertinent.

output media

in data processing, paper printouts and forms, tapes, diskettes, embossed plastic cards, and other matter and devices on which processed information appears.

outtake

filmed or taped material not used in the final programme.

outvote

to defeat in a vote.

outwork

work which a company pays someone to do at home.

outworker

person who works at home for a company.

over

more than.

overachiever

person who tries too hard and achieves more than he is really capable of.

overall

covering or including everything.

over bought

an inventory position in which too much stock of a certain kind has been purchased for resale.

over-capitalization

a company which is not earning sufficient profits to sell its securities at par, is called to be 'over-capitalized'. Over-capitalization means that the company is not in a position to employ all its capital profitably.

overcompensation

an extreme form of compensation.

overconforming

this term is sometimes used to describe a person who is excessively slavish to the demands of authority or the convention of social norm.

overhead
costs that do not vary with output over a period of time.

overleading
learning in which practice or repetition continues beyond the point required for adequate mastery of the task. Overlearning is not usually considered harmful, e.g., it is not thought possible to learn something too well.

overlearning
continuing the learning process beyond the level of skill needed.

overmanned
having more workers than necessary.

overmanning
having more workers than are needed to do a company's work.

overpaid
paid too much.

overproduce
to produce too much.

overqualified
having too many skills for a job.

overrepresent
to give one group more representatives than another.

overrun
to go beyond a certain limit.

overseas
across the sea or to foreign countries.

overseas sales branch
in direct export, the overseas sales branch is a branch or subsidiary of the exporting firm, located in the host country. This allows the exporter greater exposure and control in the foreign market and also avoids total reliance upon a domestic-based export department employing an independent, international, marketing middleman.

overseer
person who supervises other worker.

overshoot method
a technique for forecasting economic activity based on the theory that whenever business activity rises beyond the normal trend level, a reaction is bound to set in.

overstaffed
with more workers than are needed to do the work of the company.

over stored
a condition in the marketplace in which there are more stores in an area than can operate profitably.

over the counter
stocks not sold on a registered exchange.

overtime
hours worked beyond the normal working time.

overworked
having too much work to do.

own
to have or to possess.

owned funds
these funds are those that have been contributed by the owners of the business, i.e., proprietors, partners or shareholders as the case may be. Ownership funds are the real risk capital. Generally, it remains invested in the business as long as the business continues to exists.

Owners of business can withdraw these funds from the business only at the risk of the closure of the business.

owned goods service
a service which involves existing products already owned by the customer, e.g., automobile repair service, alteration of clothing by a tailor, tree trimming etc.

owner
person who owns something.

owner's equity
the owner's contribution towards the assets of a business entity. It could be expressed as the total assets of an entity less such claims of outsiders or liabilities and includes both contributed capital and retained earnings.

ownership
act of owning something.

pa
personal assistant.

p.a.
per annum.

pabx
private automatic branch exchange.

pacemaker
organization which helps another to change by giving advice or offering support.

package
group of different items joined together in one deal.

packaged environment
a physical entity such as a theme park, stadium, shopping mall, or cultural center which has a highly developed identity calculated to enhance the presentation of goods and services.

package testing
research into the form, size, colour, usage, etc., of packaging to ascertain what will be most acceptable to consumers.

packaging (in marketing)
the wrapper or container in which a product is enclosed to facilitate distribution and use. The marketing approach towards the design of packaging has undergone substantial change in recent decades. Protection of the contents, the original purpose, is now deemed only one of many functions performed by the packaging; it is seen as a vitally important part of communications in consumer markets (Marketing Communications Mix). In industrial markets particular attention is paid to the problems of handling, storage and shipment, especially through the use of bulk packaging which breaks out into smaller packs (Design). This latter pattern is familiar also in consumer markets. Eight general principles have been evinced for good packaging: (i) it should be integrated in design, particularly in terms of colour and typography, with the other communications media of the organization; (ii) it should be designed to be eye-catching; (iii) it should establish its own identity; (iv) it should be appropriate to the product in terms of users' subjective expectations; (v) it should be aesthetically pleasing; (vi) it

should invite handling; (vii) it should be well constructed, as durable as necessary for its purpose and convenient in use, paying particular attention to pack size for, e.g. storing table use; (viii) it should be designed specifically to communicate with its market segment (Market Segmentation).

packing order
the hierarchy of status relationships formed among farmyard hens by their practice of pecking each other. The most pecked hen has the lowest status. The term is now routinely (and therefore dangerously) applied to status relationships in human groups. Similarly, the term he-pecked has long been part of everyday speech though it is applied to males rather than females.

page proof
the proof of an entire page.

paid
with money given.

paid up poiicy
a policy of endowment or whole life insurance on which no more premiums have to be paid. Sometimes where a policyholder wishes to cease paying the premium but not to cancel the policy this may converted to a paid-up policy at an agreed valuation.

paired comparisons
method of assessment where items to be assessed are each compared with all others and a final score for each obtained.

palletization
in physical distribution, palletization is the arrangement of products on low platforms, or pallets, for efficiency of movement. Goods so arranged are moved as a unit by motorized lift trucks.

pallets
flat trays of varying sizes and design for holding materials or parts during movement to or in production and also for handling finished products: they are often moved by form lift trucks. Also known as skids.

pamphlet
a printed piece of a few pages, with a paper cover. Often interchangeable with "leaflet", except that a pamphlet may contain more pages that the word "leaflet" will permit.

panacea
a universal remedy for all problems in an organization; ideally it should be cheap, painless and change nothing important, which is why reorganization is such a great favourite.

panel
a selected sample of persons who are interviewed about, or who maintain records or, their purchases, viewing or listening habits, etc., used either for continuous research on one topic, or maintained by a research organisation for use in ad-hoc surveys.

panel method
research methods for which a more or less permanent group of respondents (the panel) is used. Consumer Product Testing Panel: a panel is

consumers who are given new products to test in use, before they are marketed. Consumer Purchasing Panel: a panel of consumers who are asked to record their purchases in a dairy. Radio Audience Panel Or Television Audience Panel: a panel of listeners or viewers who are asked for their opinions of programmes and who may also be tested on their awareness of associated advertising material. Retail Audit panel, also Stock Audit: a panel of retailers who agree to permit their stocks to be checked at regular intervals by an observer (auditor).

panel on takeovers and mergers
a body working under the auspices of the stock exchange to supervise takeovers and mergers. The rules under which the panel operates are many and complicated but their intention is to ensure that takeovers and mergers are conducted so that all parties to them are treated fairly.

pantry check
an observational method in which the observer records the brands of goods in a housewife's kitchen and/or pantry.

paper profit
a profit arising from the change in market value of an asset which has yet to be realised. A person who buys shares for Rs. 1,000 and later finds that they are worth Rs. 1,500 but does not sell them is said to have made a paper profit of Rs. 500

paper tape
strip of special paper into which encoded data are punched to provide input to a computer or other data-processing machine. The width of the tape varies according to the number of holes which may be punched across it: 5,6,7, or 8 hole tape plus feed hole are the most common. Also known as punched tape and perforated tape.

paperwork
office work, especially writing memos and filling in forms.

par (par, value)
the price which a security bears on its face, sometimes called 'face value', thus a loan which is priced at Rs. 1000 and repayable at the same amount is said to be repayable at par.

parachute
large, usually tax-free, sum of money given to an executive who retires from a company before the end of his service contract.

paradigm
a detailed example or model of a particular process.

paragraph analysis
the process of finding the main idea of a paragraph together with its details perceived in their right relation to the idea.

parallel running
running of a computer and former systems side by side during interim period before placing all work on the computer.

parameter
mathematically this is a

constant in an equation that defines the form of the curve. In psychology it is constant that defines the curve of a psychological function like learning. In statistics it takes the form of a measure of a total population of scores. The term is sometimes used loosely, and wrongly, as wrongly as if it were 'perimeter'.

parametric programming
a type of mathematical technique concerned with the allocation of resource. It is used in situations where the various parameters of a problem are allowed to take on different values.

parametric statistics
statistics that deal with a normal distribution or other population of scores.

parity
being equal.

Parkinson's law
law, based on wide experience, that in business the amount of work increases to fill the time available for it.

parpetual inventory
an inventory the accounting for which is kept current by immediately recording each addition to or subtraction from it.

part exchange
a transaction involving the purchase of goods by one person from another where part of the purchase consideration is satisfied by the handling over of different goods and part by means of a cash payment. Part exchange is usually found where second-hand goods are exchanged between individuals with a cash adjustment to allow for their difference in value.

partial proprietor
a stockholder (an individual, company, or institution) who holds a considerable proportion of a company's stock but not a controlling (51 percent or more) amount.

participant observer techniques
an observational method in which the observer participates with the subject in some activity and records the subject's observed behaviour.

participate
to take part in an activity or enterprise.

participating preference share
a preference share which carries a right over and above its preferential right to share further in profits once the dividend payable to the holders of ordinary shares exceeds a stated level.

participation
the term used to describe the involvement of people in the performance of the organisation they work for, e.g., by employee ownership of profit sharing.

participative
where both sides take part.

participative management
as organisations have proliferated in size and specialisation, the problem of control and integration of supervisory and staff levels has become increasingly

worrisome. The best answer until now has been participative management. But information technology promises better answers. It promises to eliminate the risk of less than adequate decisions arising from garbed communications, from misconceptions of goals, and from unsatisfactory measurement of partial contributions on the part of dozens of line and staff specialists.

partly paid shares
shares in a company on which an amount less than the full nominal value have been paid by their holders. The unpaid part of the capital may be called up by the company at any time and remains a liability of the shareholders in the event that the company is wound up.

part method
a technique of learning in which the material is broken down into smaller parts to be learned separately and then recombined.

partner
person who works in a business and has an equal share in it with other partners.

partnership
a legal relationship of an association of individuals for participation in activities or the accomplishment of purpose who have contracted to place money, effects, and labour in commerce or business with a proportional sharing of profits and losses; an unincorporated business organisation consisting of two or more partners.

partnership act
legislation which defines partnership and governs its conduct.

part-time
not working for the whole working day.

part-timer
person who works part-time.

party
organization or person involved in a legal dispute or legal agreement.

pass
permit to allow someone to go into a building.

pass a dividend
the action by a company of failing to pay a dividend at a time in the financial year when a dividend is usually paid. When the directors decide to pass a dividend it is usually taken to mean that the company is in difficulty. Either its profit is very low or it is making an actual loss.

passalong rate
a term used with reference to the print media indicating the number of readers who may see a newspaper or magazine in addition to the initial subscriber or purchaser. Also referred to as readers per copy.

pass book
a book issued by a bank or building society in which are entered details of an account with a customer. It has to be presented on the occasion of each transaction in order to be made up to date. The traditional

pass book is being phased out by most institutions in favour of computer produced statements.

passenger count
an observational method in which the observer or some mechanical device, records the total number of people, cars, etc., passing a certain point during a specified period.

passers-by
persons who pass a certain point during a specified period.

passive fund management
an inactive custody of a fund of investments.

paste-up
a layout in which illustration and type material are combined on one sheet for reproduction as a single engraving.

patent
a monopoly right, awarded by law to an individual or group, granting sole right to make, use or sell an article or process they have invented. In the United Kingdom a patent normally lasts for twenty years during which time the patent holder is protected from any attempts by others to copy their invention.

paternalism
used to describe a "fatherly" style of management where the employer is overprotective towards his employees.

paternalistic
(employer) who is overprotective towards his employees.

paternity leave
short period of leave given to a father to be await from work when his wife has a baby.

path goal theory
a type of contingency theory of leadership which is based on the expectancy theory of motivation. It concentrates on maximizing the performance of subordinates in a given situation with the leader of manager having an enabling function of clearing a path for his or her subordinates towards their personal goals at work.

pathological
pertaining to disease.

pattern bargaining
bargaining between unions and an employer, in which the unions refer to past collective agreement made with employers.

pattern of growth
firms may grow either by internal expansion or by merger and takeovers; the patterns of growth are frequently referred to as horizontal and vertical integration. In recent years many firms have diversified their activities and are frequently described as conglomerates.

Horizontal integration refers to a situation in which a firm grows by extending the production of its existing products or services. This may be because the firm has unexploited technical and marketing economies of scale and thus grows from within. An example of this would be the expansion of Asia into the South of England and

Sanisbury's into the North of England. However, a firm may recognize deficiencies in its own organization and see in a rival a way of remedying them: such motives appeared in the inquiry into the proposed merger of Montague Burton and United Drapery Stores in 1966. Alternatively a firm may try to buy market share and expertise, and became apparent in the inquiry into the proposal merger of GKN and AE in 1984. Vertical integration refers to a firm growing either into retailing and additional production processor or into the ownership and manufacture of raw materials and components. Clearly a frequent way of accomplishing this end is to acquire other firms, but it need not necessarily be so. The motives for vertical integration, are usually fear of supplies or outlets being curtailed and the desire, with modern manufacturing methods, to maintain even flows of production. A desire to safeguard their supply of good quality true steel was one reason why tube investments purchased the round oak steel works in 1953. Similar fears prompted the purchases in the 1950s of Briggs Motor Bodies and Fisher & Ludlow by Ford and BMC respectively. The development of courtaulds, in the textile industry, is an example of vertical integration by internal growth and by mergers and takeovers, as is the development of Bass in the brewing industry.

Diversification, leading to possible designation as a conglomerate, refers to growth in the direction of different products, which may have a common technical base, use existing marketing facilities or have no relationship at all. The uncertainties of economic life are one reason for this pattern for it ensures that all one's resources are not tied to one product or market segment. Another reason may be that although technical economies in the existing product range have been exhausted there are still marketing and managerial economies unexploited. Yet another reason may be the existence of surplus funds available for investment. A good example of this type of development is ICI, with its diverse interests in agricultural chemicals, drugs, petrochemicals and fibres. The term conglomerate generally refers to the particular nature of the business organization, generally consisting of a holding company and a group of subsidiary companies engaged in dissimilar activities. In recent years the two most successful conglomerates have been the Hanson Trus and BTR. The Hanson Trust has taken over such dissimilar companies as London Brick and Everready Batteries. In 1983 BTR took over Thomas Tilling, itself a conglomerate, in the largest UK conglomerate merger so far. At the time the Director General of Fair Trading argued that the bid had no industrial logic behind it and since there was little or no industrial overlap between the two companies it was allowed to go ahead without reference to the Monopolies Commission.

pawn
to pledge an asset with a pawnbroker as security for a cash loan.

pawnbroker
one who lends cash on the security of some personal possession of value, usually jewellery. The borrower may redeem the item within a stated period of time by repaying the amount of the loan with interest. In the event of the default of the borrower the pawnbroker is entitled to sell the subject of the pledge.

pay
salary or wage or money given to someone for regular work.

payable
which is due to be paid.

pay and file
a system of dealing with taxation, used in the USA, whereby the taxpayer submits payment of the amount of tax due at the same time as submitting the statement of income on which the calculation is based.

pay as you earn
the method of charging income tax to wage and salary earners. An employer is required by law to deduct the appropriate amount of tax from payments of wages and salaries before they are made. The amount deducted is then accounted for by the employer to the income tax authorities.

pay-as-you-go-plan
a pension plan in which the employer pays pension benefits to retired employees out of its current income.

payback
the amount of money a new product must earn (calculated as net income before depreciation but after taxes) to recover the initial investment made in its development.

payback method
a method of evaluating capital expenditure projects. By this method the additional income or expected savings per annum are compared with the net outlay, by dividing the latter by the former. For example, if the savings of Rs. 200 are obtained from an investment of Rs. 1000 the payback period is five years.

paycheck
salary cheque given to an employee.

pay-day
the day on which workers are paid. It is normally the same day in each week or in each month.

paye
pay as you earn.

payee
a person to whom a negotiable instrument (such as a check) is made out. For example, "pay to the order to John Smith".

pay freeze
a situation in which wages and salaries are held at existing levels. It might be imposed by a government as a policy to reduce inflation or by a company wishing to contain its costs. A pay freeze is very difficult to maintain for more than a short period of time.

payer
one who makes a payment.

paying in book
a bound book of paying in slips issued by a bank to customers who frequently pay in cheque or cash. Each slip has a counterfoil which provides a record of the deposits made with the bank.

payin in slip
a blank from which must be completed by a customer wishing to make payments of cheques or cash into his or her bank account. On it must be written details of the deposit.

pay master
one who controls the payment of cash. Although the term can be used as the title of an office it is often used colloquially to indicate the ultimate source of funding and, therefore, the one with financial power. The government, for example, is the paymaster for public sector salaries.

payment
giving money.

payment in advance
payment made before the end of an accounting period in respect of benefits to be received in a subsequent period. Insurance premiums and payments of rates are common examples of payments in advance. They are treated in the balance sheet as current assets. Where they are relatively small in total amount they are frequently amalgamated with debtors.

payment in kind
payment for work done in goods and services rather than money.

payment of bonus act, 1965
the act applies to every factory and other establishment in which 20 or more persons are employed during an accounting year. The act also applies to an employee drawing Rs. 1,600 per month as salary or wages. According to this Act every employer is bound to pay to every employee who is qualified for the minimum period of service of 30 working days during an accounting year a minimum bonus of 4 percent of the salary of the wages earned by the employee during the accounting year of Rs. 40 whichever is higher irrespective of whether the employer has had any profit or not. The bonus is to be paid within a period of 8 months from the close of the accounting year. This Act also lays down a limit of maximum of 20 percent of the total salary which may be paid to the employees as bonus.

payment on account
a payment made by a debtor of part only of an amount owed. Where a debtor makes frequent

payments on account this is often regarded as a sign that he or she is in financial difficulty and it may signal an imminent bad debt.

pay off

to pay all the money owed to someone and terminate his employment.

payout (or payoff) period

the time it takes for an investment (e.g., in a new machine) to pay for itself.

payroll

list of people employed and paid by a company. Money paid by a company in salaries.

payroll deduction

a specified amount of money withheld from the earnings of an employee to finance a benefit. A payroll deduction may be a set payroll tax, such as the Social Security tax, a required payment for a benefit, such as a health insurance premium, or a voluntary deduction, such as a fixed amount for a savings account.

payroll giving

a system whereby a person in receipt of wages or a salary can agree to regular deduction which are then given to charity.

payroll tax

a tax charged on employers and depending on the number of people they employ. Although the idea has been discussed there is currently no explicit payroll tax imposed in many countries. It could be argued that the employer's contribution to national insurance payments in a form of payroll tax.

payslip

a document given to an employee to explain how his or her net payment of wages or salary is calculated. It will show the gross amount and the amounts of any deductions such as income tax and national insurance.

pbdit

profits before depreciation, interest and taxes, which amounts to gross cash flow.

pbr

payment by results.

peace dividend

the amount by which the population at large is expected to benefit from a reduction in governmental defence expenditure consequent on a more peaceful world. It is likely to be felt in the form of reduced taxation.

peak

highest point.

pecuniary

involving money. If a person is said to have gained a pecuniary advantage from some situation, this means that they have acquired some money out of it.

peer

person who is of the same age or at the same level as someone else.

peer review

a review of some person's activity by some other person involved in the same activity. A peer review of the work of an Auditor would require an examination of that work by another auditor.

peg
to hold something at a certain point.

pegged exchange rate
a rate of exchange between two currencies which is never permitted to fluctuate. It may, in practice, be very difficult to achieve.

penalize
to punish or to fine.

penalty
punishment (such as a fine) which is imposed if something is not done.

penalty clause
a clause contained in a contract whereby one part agrees to pay a stated penalty to the other in the event of a delay in the completion of the contract.

penetration pricing
a strategy in which a new product is introduced into the marketplace at a lower than usual price in an effort to rapidly penetrate the market and build sales volume. Sometimes called impact pricing, as the strategy is also calculated to increase consumer awareness of the product.

penny pinching
acting so as to cut costs to the minimum at every opportunity. The use of the term often implies that the amounts served are small relative to the inconveniences suffered.

penny share
a share in a company which is quoted in the stock exchange at a very low amount. It usually arises where the company, whilst maintaining its existence, has no commercial success and pays no dividend.

pension
money received regularly after retirement as part of either a private or government scheme.

pensionable
able to receive a pension.

pension cost
the cost to a company of providing a pension for its employees. The amount borne by the company is likely to be part only of the total cost, the rest being borne by the employees themselves.

pensioner
person who receives a pension.

pension fund
a fund built up over a period of time by contributors in order to provide subscriber with a pension on retirement. The purpose of the fund is to keep money belonging to the prospective pensioners separate from that of the employing company. The actuarial value of the fund's liabilities can be determined from time to time so as to ensure that its size is adequate to meet them

people blindness
a fundamental truth about today's class of rising young executives is that many of them will fail to reach their goals. They will fail, not for lack of competence, but because they have a "people-blindness" that, time after time, traps them into making a technically good decision that just won't work

in practice. They haven't learned that an executive succeeds or fails not so much because of what he does, but because of what he is able to get somehow else to accomplish.

pep
abbr. programme evaluation procedure. A name sometimes used to describe pert.

peppercorn rent
a rent which consists of a trivial payment, for example 1 penny per annum. A peppercorn rent enables the legal status of a tenant to be created whilst in effect allowing him or her to occupy the property rent free.

per
at a rate of; per hour or per day or per week or per year.

per annum
in a year.

per capita
for each person.

perceived value pricing
a strategy in which the price of a product or service is based upon the buyer's perception of its value rather than on the seller's cost of production.

percentage
the occurrence rate per hundred of any phenomenon.

percentile
a point in a distribution of scores so selected that a certain percentage of cases are above it and a certain percentage of cases are below it.

perception
mental awareness and integration of sensation.

perceptual mapping
a marketing research tool in which a number of factors such as product attributes, customer preferences, and particular brands are plotted on a chart on the basis of computer analysis. Since various factors tend to form clusters, it is possible for marketers to distinguish between various competing brands and to spot open niches in the market place.

perfecting
the operations of printing the second side of paper, after having printed the first side is known as 'perfecting'.

perfect market
the situation (condition) where all the potential sellers and buyers are promptly aware of the prices at which transactions take place and of all the offers made by other sellers and buyers and where any buyer can purchase from any seller and vice versa.

perform
to carry out work. Performance refers to the process of accomplishing work to the point at which it is ready for measurement or evaluation. Performance implies continuing activity or observation until a designated end point is reached. A manager performs a function by working it constantly. Performance can be accomplished in part by delegation.

performance
way in which someone or something acts.

performance analysis
a method used to compare the actual performance of a marketing plan with the expectations for the plan.

performance appraisal
conventional programmes of performance appraisal within the ranks of management tend to treat the individual as though he where a product under inspection on the assembly line. In a model method launched by a few companies in the U.S. (among them General Mills Ansul Chemical and General Electric) have been experimenting with approaches which involve the individual in setting 'targets' or objectives for himself and in a self-evaluation of performance semi-annually. Of course the superior plays an important leadership role in this process, one in fact which demands substantially more competence than the conventional approval.

performance appraisal interview
an interview between an employee and his or her line manager, usually conducted once a year, at which an assessment is made of the individual's job performance and how it relates to training needs, promotion opportunities, etc.

performance bonds
an amount deposited by a contractor against the possibility that the contract will not be completed. In that event the sum deposit will be used in meeting compensation.

performance monitoring research
research, generally in the form of interviews or questionnaires, employed to monitor a particular marketing program and to provide the marketing manager with the feedback required to evaluate the firm's marketing activities.

performance rating
production is achieved in any organisation with the association of men, machine and raw materials and it is the responsibility of the management to provide for best possible interaction of the same so that productivity is maximised. Variables affecting ultimate output are numerous and all of them are not equally important.

performance sampling
a work measurement technique of random sampling by observation the effort or performance level of employees to determine the rate of speed at which an operator is working compared to a normal worker.

period
length of time.

periodical
a newspaper appearing at an interval of a week or more.

peripheral equipment
auxiliary machines used in conjunction with computer, e.g., highspeed printer card reader and magnetic tape unit.

perks
informal extra items given by a company to workers in addition

to their salaries (such as company cars, private health insurance).

permanency

being permanent.

permanent

which will last for a long time or for ever.

permanent difference

a difference between accounting profit and taxable profit which persists in the long run. It is to be contrasted with a timing deference. Both terms arise in connection with deferred taxation. Examples of permanent differences are those caused by expenses not allowable for tax, i.e. those not incurred wholly for the purposes of the business.

permanent file

a file kept by the auditor of a company to record information of permanent significance about the client. The permanent file might contain copies of the company's memorandum and Articles of Association and of the names and addresses of its directors.

permanent health insurance

an insurance enabling the insured person to make claims in the event of ill health. It is a term of such a policy that the acceptability of the risk and the amount of the premium are fixed at its inception. These cannot be changed if there is a subsequent deterioration in the health of the insured.

permanent interest bearing shares

securities issued by a building society which are traded on the stock exchange. The holders are not, as are ordinary depositors with the building society, able to withdraw the funds from an account.

permanently

for ever.

permission

being allowed to do something.

permission to deal

the permission granted by the Council of the Stock Exchange to a company allowing its shares to be bought and sold through the stock exchange. Many conditions regarding the number of shares available, the past history of the company and the information which it undertakes in future to supply have to be met before the permission is granted.

permit

official document which allows someone to do something.

eerpetual inventory

system of continuous stock recording so that the stock of each item is known at all times. This facilities regular checking with quantities actually in store and obviates closing down for stocktaking: also known as continuous inventory, or continuous stocktaking.

perpetuity

a matter which continues for ever. The law does not favour perpetuities and there is a rule against them in trust law.

per pro

per procurationem with the authority of; the secretary signed per pro the manager.

perquisites
(formal) perks.

persistent unemployment
unemployment which is constant, owing to lack of skills or lack of jobs.

person
someone or man or woman.

personal
referring to one person.

personal account
an account with a real person and distinguished from a nominal account. Accounts with debtors and creditors are examples of personal accounts.

personal allowance
an amount allowed to be deducted from a person's income in determining the amount subject to income tax. A married couple is given a higher total personal allowance than two single persons.

personal bias
bias which derives from the personal disposition, preconceptions, etc., of an interviewer, editor, observer, etc.

personal development plan
establish a personnel development plan and integrating it into overall personal planning efforts are sometimes more difficult than obtaining a good manpower plan.

personal equity plan
an investment plan undertaken by an individual with an approved plan manager such as a bank. This type of plan was created by statute and has the characteristic that, provided the rules are observed, all income and capital gains accruing to the plan are free from taxation.

personal finance
that area of financial matters which concerns individual people. It will include the provision of mortgages, loans, insurance and savings opportunities. Personal finance has become a large industry.

personal identification number
a secret number issued to the holder of a credit card or debit card which is used when cash withdrawals are made from automatic dispensing machines. It is envisaged that eventually the personal identification number may take the place of a signature in authorising transactions entered into with these cards.

personal interview
face-to-face interview between the interviewer and the respondent, as compared with a telephone interview, or a mailed questionnaire contact.

personality
person's character or general nature.

personality tests
tests designed to judge the emotional balance, maturity, and temperamental qualities of a person. These are designed to test the characteristics that make up his personality. Tests may follow any of the three methods: (a) experimental methods, (b) rating method or (c) the question answer method.

personal ledger

a section of the whole ledger containing accounts with real persons. Thus the sales ledger and the purchase ledger are examples of personal ledgers.

personally

in person.

personal pension plans

a scheme whereby an individual can save money to purchase a pension on retirement. It is normally operated by an insurance company and would be used by a person whose occupation does not automatically provide a pension.

personal representative

the person who deals with the affairs of a deceased person. It is a general term which applies equally to an executor or an administrator.

person job fit

the extent to which the personality of an individual fits harmoniously with the job he/she does. On the goodness of fit between the two will depend the crucial factors of work like job satisfaction, productivity and stress.

personnel

people who work in a certain place or for a certain organization.

personnel department

a department of an organisation that provides for the planning and management of the organisation's human resources, including recruiting, interviewing, and screening of job applications, planning and classification of new positions, compensation and benefits planning, implementation and maintenance of compensation schedules and job classifications, providing new employee orientation, development and maintenance of a position control system, developing and maintaining an equal employment opportunity and affirmative action programme, conducting labour relations and negotiations, and performing risk appraisals.

personnel function

a service performed for the management of an organisation that typically includes assistance in staffing and manpower planning, recruiting, selecting, training, evaluating, and in compensating, disciplining, and terminating employees. The personal function also usually includes assistance to management in such areas as labour (or union) relations, affirmative action programmes, and the prevention of discrimination on the basis of sex, race or age.

personnel management

a specialized function concerned with all aspects of the management of human resources in an organisation from recruitment to retirement and including conditions of employment, selection, training, placement, promotion and the welfare function.

personnel manager

a personnel manager is expected to be a leader with high intellectual powers and a philosopher who gives to the organisation a vision of future for leading human relations in an organisation towards more prosperous and progressive policies.

personnel policy

formulation and development of personnel policies becomes important to a company when:

(i) the organization has reached a size that requires many decision-making centers that will act consistently.

(ii) situations requiring decision occur frequently.

(iii) a record of decision-making criteria is needed to evaluate the effectiveness of the criteria as the result of decision become known.

The process of developing a personnel policy involves assessing its appropriateness to the organization. It must be acceptable in all the situations in which it might be used as basis for decision testing against each of the organization's major functions to make certain that all operating, legal, financial, marketing, and public relations considerations had been taken into account.

The policy should also be tested against community practice to assure that the reputation of the firm is being maintained at as high level as its business and financial situation will permit. The maintenance of a competitive position in the community in these matters can assist the organization with its employees, its public, its bankers, its stockholders, and its customers, and thereby facilitate the survival and growth of the organisation.

personnel records—types of

personnel records contain detailed information regarding the employees in an organisation. These records are maintained pertaining to individual employees or group of employees taken together. Important types of records are: (i) job records; (ii) employment records (iii) wage, salary and administration records (iv) accidents, health and safety of employees records (v) discipline and termination records (vi) industrial disputes records (vii) confidential reports.

personnel specification

a statement of the personal features deemed to be required for the effective performance of a given job or position, as derived from job analysis, and covering: knowledge, required, educational standard and qualifications, previous experience, personal qualities and mental calibre, together with any special characteristics deemed relevant.

person to person

telephone call where you ask the operator to connect you with a particular person.

pert

program evaluation review technique. A more elaborate version of the critical path technique which takes more factors into account.

peter principle
an idea introduced in 1969 by Laurence J. Peter and Raymond Hull in a light-hearted study of occupational incompetence, which subsequently became the subject of more serious debate and controversy. Its continuing appeal suggests that the Peter Principle concurs disturbingly with the beliefs and perhaps the experience of many people who work in organization.
The premises of the principle can be stated quite briefly. Incompetence in organizations is universal. In every kind of organization people are to be found who are incapable of performing their jobs, and the causes of this phenomenon are not random. They derive from certain characteristics of the rules governing the placement and promotion of employees. One of these is that employees are frequently promoted from positions of competence to positions in which they act incompetently. This type of promotion is so common that it has come to be embodied in a dictum that states that 'In a hierarchy every employee tends to rise to his level of incompetence', or, The cream rises until it sours'. Thus the final promotion is typically from a level of competency to a level of incompetence, and upward mobility will end in an unsuccessful promotion as regards performance.
From this principle is derived Perter's Corollary, which states that 'In time, every post tends to be occupied by an employee who is incompetent to carry out its duties.' Organizational collapse is only avoided because the work that has to be done is performed by those who have yet to reach their personal level of incompetence.
The validity of the principle and its corollary are stoutly defended by Laurence Peter. He claims that their existence can be seen in many case studies, some of which he quotes to very good effect. There is the case, for example, of R. Driver, the autocratic teacher, ascending the educational hierarchy to become Assistant Superintendent. At this level he is expected to participate in school-board policy discussions, using democratic procedures that are completely alien to his previous experience. He seeks to dominate the board by an autocratic style that leads its members to regard him as incompetent. He receives no further promotion. Citing these case histories is as near as Peter wishes to come to objectivity.
There is, however, a further defence. This is an hilarious treatment of apparent exception to the principle, exotically categorized as the percussive sublimation, the lateral arabesque. Peter's inversion, hierarchical exfoliation, and the paternal in-step. These are

organizational manoeuvres or devices to maintain the consistency of the hierarchy and to deceive people outside it by pseudo-promotions, obscurantism and the rejection of super-competence. The purpose of these subterfuges is to preserve the principle that nothing fails as well as success.

petition in bankruptcy
a formal application to the court asking that a named person be judged bankrupt. It is usually presented by a creditor who has not been paid but may be presented by the insolvent person him or herself.

petroleum revenue tax
a tax levied in respect of profits from the exploitation of oil deposits.

petty cash
a small revolving cash fund (usually containing from twenty to fifty dollars) commonly kept in a cash box and maintained by a secretary or receptionist. The petty cash fund is used to pay for small, unexpected, incidental items as the need arises, without prior authorisation and without the necessity for writing a check. It is called a "revolving fund" because each time the fund is drawn down to a predetermined minimum level, the vouchers or notes are reconciled with the remaining cash and the fund is replenished.

petty cashier
a person who is responsible for the custody and accounting for petty cash.

phase
period or part of something which takes place.

phase in
to bring something in gradually.

phase out
to remove something gradually.

philanthropic voluntarism
the issue facing managements today is not one of philanthropic voluntarnism and not one of superficial public relations. As Professor Baumol of Princeton University, U.S.A. observes, business organisations will not serve the national interests (must less their own) by undertaking to behave like philanthropic institution. Such a transformation is neither feasible nor desirable.

phonetic alphabet
the analysis of a word into its phonetic elements for pronunciation purposes; commonly used as a synonym for phonics.

phonetic approach
a procedure for studying words by associating appropriate sounds with printed forms.

phonetics
the science of the sounds of letters as used in speech.

phonics
the science of the sounds of letters as applied to the pronunciation of words in reading.

phonogram
a letter or group of letters forming a sound that can be articulated.

physical (examination)
medical examination.

physical distribution management (PDM)
the planning monitoring and control of distribution and delivery of manufactured goods, including the use of transportation, warehousing, agents and retail outlets.

pica
twelve points make a pica body. This is the basic unit of measurement in printing.

picket
striking worker who stands at the gate of a factory to try to persuade other workers not to go to work.

picketing
act of standing at the gates of a factory to prevent workers going to work.

picking up
this is a difficulty mainly associated with ink. It may also be due to unmatured paper. It commonly occurs when a large solid area is printed. When a coated paper is used the trouble could occur if the ink is very stiff.

pictograph
a record or story consisting of pictorial symbols.

picture clue
an element in a picture which provides meaning.

picture frustration test
a type of test used to indicate the subject's attitudes and motives towards a certain topic through the subject's interpretation of pictures shown to him; a projective technique.

piece
small part of something.

piece rate
rate of pay for a product produced or for a piece of work done and not paid for at an hourly rate.

piecework
work for which workers are paid for the products produced or the piece of work done and not at any hourly rate.

pie chart
a circular chart dividend into segments to represent categories of data often in percentage form. Also known as sector chart.

piferage or pilfering
stealing small amounts of money or small items from an office or shop.

pigmatic primaries
the basic colours used in trio colour printing to produce a visible spectrum of colours. They are Yellow, Red and Blue.

pilot study
a term used in market research or survey research, e.g., when a proposed questionnaire may be tested on a few respondents before being used on a large scale study, to see whether the questionnaire needs revising and whether the study itself is worth doing.

pilot survey
a test run of a study on a small sub-sample to evaluate the planned methodology, etc.

pin
letters standing for personal identification number.

pink form
an application form for shares

in a company, printed on pink paper and giving the person using it a right to preferential treatment when allotments are made. A company issuing shares may give pink forms to employees or to others having an existing connection with the company.

pin money
small amounts of money earned casually by a person to supplement his or her main income.

piracy
strictly the term means the seizing of goods from ships on the high sea, i.e., outside any jurisdiction. The term is now, however, applied to certain infringements of rights, e.g., the use of computer software which has been illegally copied rather than purchased.

"pitch"
the idea that the source wants to get across to his audience. To "make your pitch" is to present your argument.

place
where something is or where something happens.

placement
putting someone in a job.

placement test
in such a test, products or packs are delivered to selected usage points for trial to be followed up by interviews collecting information on performance and attitudes towards them.

placing
a method of obtaining a subscription for shares in a company. The shares are not offered publicly but are issued to persons or institutions who have previously agreed to take them.

plaintiff
person who starts a legal action against someone.

plan
a proposal designed to guide and direct work to be performed. Plans consist of five major elements: objectives, policies, programmes, schedules, and budgets.

planned economy
an economy under the central direction and control of the state, e.g., under the ideology of socialism, which would decide on matters like pay and production in the absence of market forces.

planning
setting the objectives to be accomplished by a corporation (or a segment of it) over different periods of time and deciding on the major methods of reaching them.

planning and preparing advertisements
usually restricted to advertisements that are carried by media of mass communication (such as newspapers, radio, television and posters) and sometimes, direct-mail advertising, other forms of advertising (e.g., by giving away calenders or pencils with an advertisement of them) are included in sales promotion.

planning function

comprise offsetting uncertainty and change; focusing attention on objectives; gaining economical operation and facilitating control.

planning long range

generally, the preparation of plans for five years or more ahead.

planning permission

the right which attaches to a piece of land to use it in a specified way, usually by creating a building on it, and which is given by a local authority following an application to it. The grating of planning permission may increase the value of a piece of land many times over.

planning strategic

a complete review of basic company objectives and methods of achieving them, which may results in major changes in either or both.

planning technical

the process of planning short-run changes within the budget.

plant

industrial machinery and equipment. Large factory.

plant and machinery

equipment used in a productive industrial process. Plant and machinery is shown in a balance sheet as a fixed asset. It is subjected to depreciation so that its cost is spread over the period of its useful life. For tax purposes capital allowances may be claimed in respect of expenditure on plant and machinery.

planting

placing publicity material with the media.

plant layout

layout problems occur at four levels in an industrial context: (i) factory location – Location of Industry; (ii) labour of departments within the plant; (iii) layout of facilities within departments; (iv) workplace layout— Work Study; Ergonomics.

Items (ii) and (iii) can be considered the macro and micro versions of the same problem, which is to obtain a relative location of departments and facilities to achieve most efficient operative.

The arrangement of production facilities is determined in the main by the type of production. There are three types of facilities layout.

(1) layout by process (layout by function). All facilities for performing the same or similar functions are grouped together, i.e. lathes, milling machines, etc., are found in separate areas. Layout by process is associated with jobbing in small-batch production and has the following characteristics: (a) it allows specialized supervision; (b) facilitates the provision of service; (c) failure of machines or absence of workers does not disrupt production excessively; (d) good machine utilization; (e) operations may be missed and 'bad' jobs delayed because of the necessary flexibility of control; (f) high work-in-

progress.
It is appropriate where there is a variety of products; small batch sizes; intermittent demand for products.

(2) layout by product (flow or line production). One product or component is produced in one area with the necessary facilities. Layout by product is associated with mass and large batch production and has the following characteristics: (a) little material handling is necessary; (b) good machine utilization; (c) low work-in-progress; (d) production control is facilitated; (e) minimum floor space is required; (f) machine breakdown disrupts production; (g) production is created to fastest machine; (h) effective use of labour, i.e. minimum training, job specialization, etc. Job Analysis.
It is appropriate where there are large batch sizes or continuous production; standardized design; stable demand; a continuous supply of material.

(3) layout by fixed position. Used where the material or principal component is fixed or must remain in one position, e.g., the building of aircraft, shipbuilding, civil engineering. Unlike in the previous layouts the facilities move to and from the product. It is characterized by; (a) poor facility utilization (particularly on remote work, e.g. civil engineering); (b) the ability to accommodate variety in product, changes in design, etc.; (c) satisfaction for intermittent demand.
The product, and hence parts to be manufactured, and the method of manufacture will determine machinery requirement. Storage, inspection, etc. will be required, and total space requirements for each area or department can be calculated, making allowance for movement, development, etc.
The criterion used for layout planning is normally materials handling or transport cost, so an investigation of the pattern of interdepartment or interfacility movement is required before a layout may be developed using one of the many techniques. Plant Layout Techniques.

plant layout study
an analysis of all the factors involved in the siting of machinery, workplace, ancillary equipment, storage facilities, process flow and services, and of the design of the functional aspects of the building that house them, in order to produce a layout which will minimise the cost of production.

plant register
a classified record of plant normally giving details of origin, cost, date of purchase, depreciation, repair costs and location.

plant replacement reserve
a reserve created by retentions of profits for the purpose of meeting the costs of replacing plant. As the depreciation

charge causes retentions equalling the original cost of the plant, the additional plant replacement reserve is required only when replacement costs are rising. It is, therefore, in essence a form of inflation accounting. The plant replacement reserve is legally a revenue reserve but will probably be treated as a capital reserve.

plastic money
term applied to any form of credit card, charge card or debit card.

plate
piece of metal bearing relief of incision for printing impression; also, sensitised glass used in camera or printing plate used in offset.

plateau
a temporary halt in the progress of learning, during which added units of practice bring no improvement.

plough back
to allow profits to accumulate in a business rather than to be withdrawn by the proprietors so that the extra resources thus made available can be used in financing the expansion of the business.

plug
a free and favourable reference.

pluralism
sharing of authority by several levels for departments in an organization.

plus
added to. More than.

pluvius policy
a type of insurance taken out by the organisers of an event to protect themselves from the risk that its financial success will be affected by adverse weather conditions.

poaching
enticing employees to work for another organization or enticing members of a union to join another union.

pocket calculator or pocket diary
calculator or diary which can be carried in pocket.

pocket money
a small amount of money given to a person regularly for small amounts of personal expenditure. The term is often applied to an allowance given by a parent to a child.

point
the fixed unit of measurement in printing. All materials used in the composing room are cast to the multiples of the point. It standardises all composing room materials.

point hour ratio
shows the relationship between the total number of hour points earned and the number of semester or term hours for which the student is enrolled. An indication of scholarship.

point industrial society
a concept associated with the American sociologist Damel Bell in which the reserve sector could become an alternative basis to manufacturing industry for the creation of wealth in society following the adoption of new technology.

point line system
the system of aligning the various sizes of type bodies in a line is called the point line system. This is one of the advantages of the point system.

point of sale (POS)
the place where the final act of purchasing occurs, e.g. the counter of a retail store.

point-of-sale advertising
a form of advertising material that is below the line and placed in retail outlets, i.e., the point at which the sale is actually made.

points rating method
the method of job evaluation by the detailed analysis of component job factors. Each factor is defined precisely and given a range of points values, so that every job can be assessed numerically within the established range.

poison pill
an onerous contract with a collaborator entered into by a company to deter an unwelcome takeover. The contract will not be enforced if the takeover were successful.

policy
a general principle laid down for the guidance of executives in handling their jobs.

policy formulation for planning
the use of policies assists managers in answering what to plan. At all organisational levels better understanding of what is to be accomplished as well as the means of accomplishment is fostered by the use of sound policies. Confidence of the manager is enhanced since a manager operating within a policy gains assurance that one's actions are in keeping with the wishes of, and will be backed up by, one's superiors.

polite
behaving in a pleasant way.

political contribution
amounts paid by a company to a political party. The accounting significance of such amounts is that they must be disclosed in the annual accounts. They are also a disallowable expense in computing the liability to corporation tax.

poll
a survey of the attitudes, opinion, and/or desires of a specific group of people.

poll tax
a tax the main characteristic of which is that every member of the population pays the same absolute amount regardless of circumstances.

pool
typing pool=group of typists, working together in a company, offering a secretarial service to several department. Unused supply.

poor
without much money.

population
also universe. A group of persons which is being investigated and from which some are selected in a systematic fashion to form a sample.

portable

which can be carried.

portfolio

a collection of investment. The term usually refers to a collection of investments of a similar type. Thus an investor may hold a portfolio of stock market securities. A company may invest in a portfolio of real capital projects. A property company may hold a portfolio of properties for rent. The term is sometimes extended by analogy. Thus an accountant may have a portfolio of clients and an insurance company a portfolio of risks.

portfolio planning

assumes that managing the diversified firm resembles managing a portfolio of investments. Each firm is unique in such things as growth, cash flow, profits, and tax benefits.

portfolio selection

the objective of portfolio selection is to base the choice of an investment opportunity upon the aggregate characteristics of a collection, or portfolio, of investments. The term can be applied to the selection procedures of either an investor on the Stock Exchange or a company engaged in (Capital Budgeting).

Traditional approaches to investment selection were concerned simply to maximize the overall rate of return from a portfolio. However, influential work by Markowitz recognized that the investor will typically require either the maximum return consistent with a prescribed measure of portfolio risk, or its corollary, namely the minimum exposure to risk consistent with a specified rate of return. Portfolio risk was shown to comprise both the possible variation in expected returns of individual securities and the degree of association (or lack of it) between the return of one investment and that of another.

Although the Markowitz model and later variations have been applied to selecting portfolios of securities quoted on the Stock Exchange, little progress has been achieved in improving, in general, the methodology of capital budgeting.

portfolio theory

a theory of diversification carried out in order to reduce risk originally applied to stock market investments, the theory may now be applied to any risky portfolio. The essence of portfolio theory is that diversification will succeed in reducing overall risk only if the risks of the individual components of the portfolio are not positively correlated.

position

work grouped for performance by one individual.

position audit

the study of a company's position in relation to its environment. Before determining a long-term strategy for a company a corporate planner needs to know where the company stands today and what factors have shaped its past. The planner needs to be able to identify the reason why the company's profits have moved as they have, whether it has gained or lost a share of the market, how effective its research department has been and so on, thus gaining an insight into the company's current strength and weakness. It is also necessary to know what lies ahead in the environment so as to identify any obstacles and opportunities. The position audit is the summary of these four main factors that the corporate planner needs before a strategy can be devised for the company. —Corporate Planner; Obstacles and Opportunities; Strategy; Strengths and Weaknesses.

positioning of various departments

according to Newman and Summer it involves four basic considerations.

(i) the balance and emphasis we wish to give to various departments. (ii) the way we overcome limits to the effective span of supervision of each executive. (iii) the provision we make for dynamic change, and (iv) how we manage to integrate organising with the other phase of management (planning, leading and controlling).

position paper

a document that presents an organised exposition of an organisation's position on a given issue. It may be used with the media, with government bodies, or in other ways.

post

job or paid work in a company.

postal order

a document purchased at a post office which enables the purchaser to send small amount of money through the post with little risk. The recipient's name is entered on the postal order before despatch and, as an additional protection, it may be crossed so that it is payable only through a bank. A charge is made for the service in the form of a poundage added to the purchase price.

post balance sheet event

an event occurring after the date of the balance sheet put before it has been finalised by its being approved by the Board of Directors. There is a standard dealing with accounting for post balance sheet events. This standard classifies such events as either adjusting events or non-adjusting events. The former require an amendment to the balance sheet while the latter do not.

post-cessation receipts

amounts received by a business after it has permanently finished trading. Their significance is that they will be subject to income tax either as received or as an addition to the profit of the business is its last year of trading.

post-dated cheque

a cheque on which is given a date later than that on which it is actually issued. The effect of post-dating a cheque is that the payee cannot present it for payment until the lapse of a period of time. This may be to allow for an agreed period of credit or to enable to drawer to assemble the funds for payment of the cheque.

postential

possible. A person's ability to become something in the future.

poster research

research undertaken to discover the content, form and number of posters required to achieve the desired impact of the advertising message, or the most effective location of posters.

posting

the action of recording a financial transaction by means of an entry in the ledger. Posting is usually done from a book of prime entry.

posting and bidding

advertising a job internally so that employees can apply for it.

post office

the Post Office has a primary responsibility for providing postal services. Because, however, it has a public office in a very widespread network of locations it is also the point at which people deal with the government for many purposes, e.g., savings and collection of social security benefits.

posture

correct posture is essential in order that maximum working efficiency may be attained and if discomfort and the risk of injury are to be minimized. Two complementary programmes are necessary to achieve these goals: equipment of all types must be properly designed for the people using it and training schemes are necessary in order to teach safe and efficient ways of deploying the body. The latter programme is usually confined to the lifting and handling of heavy articles, but might well be extended to include such simple postures as those of standing and sitting.

Occupational studies of the design of equipment in relation to posture have included examinations of motor-vehicle cabs, aircraft and space-vehicle cockpits, computer consoles and crane cabs.

Fairly extensive studies have been carried out into the nature of seated posture and the design of chairs. The main weight of the body, when seated, should be upon the bony ischial tuberosities and very little pressure should be exerted on the underside of the thighs. Nothing should press behind the knees, and it should be possible for both feet to be placed upon the floor or upon a foot-rest. Backrests should provide proper support in the small of the back and should be shaped to accommodate the natural curvature of the spine.→ Ergonomics.

posture of receptivity
readiness of a person to receive and respond to communications from a given source.

potential acquisition valuation method (PAV)
systematic approach, involving ten stages, to evaluate investment proposals. Analyses costs involved and expected return on investment i.e., annual net income.

poundage
the fee charged by the post office when it issues a postal order. It is paid in the form of an addition to the price of the postal order.

pound cost averaging
an advantage claimed for the system of investing in shares (usually through a Unit Trust or shares in an investment trust) by means of regular equal amounts. The effect is that when prices are low more units and when they are high fewer units are purchased. The average price paid is then lower than the strict arithmetical mean of the prices experienced.

poverty
the condition of having an inadequate supply of money, resources, goods, or means of subsistence. Poverty is a difficult concept to define in practice, and there is no single national definition of poverty.

poverty trap
the situation where an unemployed person in receipt of social security benefits cannot take up employment without finding his or her net income reduced because of the consequent loss in benefits.

power
strength or ability.

power of attorney
a legal authority given by one person to another to allow the latter to deal with the former's money and other assets as though they were his or her own. The power may be given when the person giving it has become, through age or infirmity, unable to conduct his or her own affairs, or where a long absence abroad is contemplated.

p.p.
per procurationem. To p.p. a letter = to sign a letter on behalf of someone.

practical experience in management
(i) a thorough understanding of how a particular organisation works, what it principles are, how and why they were developed. (ii) a thorough knowledge of and respect for the people who were smart enough to invent these principles and make them successful. (iii) a realization that an individual can succeed in a particular organisation only when he discovers how to contribute within a previously established framework and only when he is writing a song that someone else must sing.

practice
way of doing things.

preacquisition profit
a revenue reserve of subsidiary company which came into being

before the holding company acquired control. Under the acquisition method of constructing a consolidated balance sheet a preacquisition reserve is unavailable for distribution to the members of the holding company.

precinct principle
organisation of a campaign through delegation of local responsibilities to chosen leaders in each community, as in the precincts of a city in a political campaign.

precoded questionnaire
a questionnaire that has been coded before it is sent to a respondent or administered in the field.

preconceived idea
a predetermined point of view unmodified by the introduction of new and relevant concepts; a prejudice.

predator
a company seeking to take over another company whose existing management does not support the takeover.

predecease
to die before another person. The provisions of a will, may be affected if one of the persons named in it as a beneficiary predeceases the testator.

predecessor
person who had a job or position before someone else.

predetermined motion time system (PMTS)
name given to any work measurement system which lists motions to accomplish manual or clerical tasks and a standard performance for making each motion.

predictive validity
assessing the validity of selection tests, by comparing the employee's performance in tests with his subsequent job performance.

preface
an introduction to a book, in which the writer declares his intentions.

preference inventory
an American personality and selection testing system.

preference shares
preference shares are those which carry with them certain preferential rights in priority to the equity shares. They enjoy: (i) preferential right to receive dividends before they are paid to ordinary shares and (ii) preferential right as to return of capital in the event of the winding up of the company. Preference shares may be cumulative or non-cumulative. They may be redeemable or irredeemable.

preferential
showing that something is preferred more than another.

preferential creditor
a creditor in a bankruptcy or a winding up who is entitled by law to priority of payment over other creditors. Preferential creditors include creditors for wages, salaries, rates and tax.

prefix
one of more syllables added at the beginning of a stem word to change or modify is meaning.

prejudice

bias or unjust feeling against someone.

prejudiced
biased or with unjust feelings against someone.

preliminary announcement
an announcement by the directors of a company concerning the results achieved during a year after the end of the year but before full audited accounts are published.

preliminary expenses
the expenses involved in setting up a company. At one time these might be regarded as capital expenditure and recorded as an asset on the balance sheet. Never regarded as good practice, this has now been made illegal in many countries and preliminary expenses must be off. This may be don against profit or; if there is one, against the share premium account.

premise
a proposition stated or assumed as leading to a conclusion; either of the first two propositions of a syllogism.

premium
insurance premium=annual payment made by the insured person or a company to an insurance company.

premium bonus system
incentive system in which the gain resulting from increased output is shared between employees and employer in agree proportions.

premium savings bond
a form of investment offered by the government to private savers and available for purchase at post office. No regular interest is paid on the bond but an equivalent amount is made available for a range of cash prizes. These are awarded to those holders who are successful in the regular draw. The prizes awarded on premium savings bonds are completely free of tax.

prepaid expenses
amounts already paid which will fall to be treated as expenses in a forthcoming period. An example of a prepaid expense is an insurance premium where the benefit of the cover provided, for some part of it, relates to a subsequent accounting period. A prepaid expense should appear on the balance sheet and be classified as a current asset.

prepare
to make ready for use. The process of getting something ready for presentation or final use. For example, a policy is developed, then prepared in written form for presentation to management.

prescribe
to direct specified action. This implies that action must be carried out in a specified fashion. A manager may prescribe on his own authority or through derived authority from a superior. When authority is derived, the source should be stated.

present

happening now. Being there when something happens.

presentation
the reporting of a survey, its results and the conclusions based thereon, by the researchers to the sponsor.

present value
the value at the present time of the prospect of receiving a sum of money at some future time after allowing for the time value of money. Present value is a concept vital to the appraisal to capital projects. It is calculated by applying a discount factor to the amount actually to be received.

present value method
a method of evaluating capital expenditure projects based on a modification of the discount cash flow method. An appropriate rate of interest is stipulated at the outset.

preside
to be chairman.

president
chief executive of a company or a club.

press agentry
seeking publicity by creating news of a flightly or dubious sort.

press conference
a meeting called to inform members of the press about an event or news subject, and to provide them an opportunity to ask questions and explore their areas of interest in the subject.

press release
a formal statement made by an organisation to representatives of the media in the hope that it will be publicly disseminated (published or broadcast). Press releases are written descriptions of past or uncoming events or activities of significance, or statements about the organisation's position.

press research
research relating to the medium of the press.

prestel
a network of computers accessed by telephone and operated by British Telecom. Subscribers obtain access to a large amount of regularly updated information on financial and other matters. Transactions, such as the payment of bills, the ordering of goods and dealings in investments, may also be undertaken through prestel. It was established in the mid-1970s and is the first such service in the world.

prestige
the reputation and standing of a person, institution, or group.

pre-tax
before allowing for taxation. Thus the pre-tax profit of a company is the amount it has earned before allowing for corporation tax.

pretesting
sampling techniques in a survey to be confident they are right before setting up the complete survey pattern.

preventive maintenance
the periodic inspection of plant and equipment at predetermined times to

foreshadow the state of wear or to disclose and rectify faulty parts or conditions. The purpose is to undertake running maintenance regularly instead of at ad-hoc times to meet actual breakdowns.

preventive mediation

an action undertaken to avoid last-minute crisis bargaining. Negotiating parties sometimes seek preventive mediation before they reach an impasse.

preview

the act of asking a preliminary survey of chapter, book, or other written composition.

previous

which happens earlier.

price

the amount, usually expressed in monetary terms, for which a product is offered or sold.

price and incomes policy

a policy that government follow whether their ideology is in favour of state intervention in the market or having a laissez-faire economy. The object of the policy is to reduce inflation and unemployment and the means of achieving it is to have a reduction in pay and in prices.

price earnings level or ratio

multiple of stock market price of a security on the basis of its current earnings per share. For example, a stock selling at Rs. 100, and having current after-tax earnings of Rs. 10 a year would be at a 10-to-1 price-earnings level.

price-earning ratio

the relationship between the market price of a company's shares and the earnings per share.

price index

a mathematical quantity derived for the purpose of measuring movements in the general level of prices. A price index is essentially a form of average, weighted according to the relative importance of its components, and expressed as a percentage of its value at some defined base date. The best-known price index is the retail price index published monthly under government auspices.

price leader

a product pricing behaviour is followed by other products manufactured or marketed by other companies in the same industry.

prices, theory

a firm's pricing policy is an important element of its competitive strategy but it must be considered in relation to product and promotional policies. As far as traditional micro-economics is concerned, interest in prices stems from their role in allocating scarce resources rather than their determination within the firm. This partly explains the many disagreements over methods of pricing among economists and businessmen.

If the firm is selling in a perfectly competitive market (Market Models), then it has no pricing because price is determined by the market. The forces of demand and supply interact to determine the price that will clear the market and the individual firm strives to sell as much as it can at this price. In practice the system does not work perfectly, shortages and excess supplies occurring because of imperfect foresight or poor weather conditions. This means that either the Government enters the market, or producers attempt to organize themselves, in order to stabilize prices and incomes. Such a pattern applies to many agricultural commodities and industrial raw materials.

For the firm selling in other than a perfect market (Market Models), the appropriate price to set is that which satisfies its objectives. If profit maximization is the objective, the profit-maximizing output occurs where marginal receipts and marginal costs are equal (this is the first-order condition). The price of this output can then be read off the demand curve.

Output op is the profit-maximizing output, because at this output marginal receipts and marginal costs are equal. The price at which this output can be sold is PR. From the basic model several variants have been developed to explain the observed behaviour of firms in different structures. Thus the existence of price discrimination leads to a price discrimination model, whilst the suggested stability of prices in oligopolies has given rise to the kinked demand curve, which enables stability and profit maximization to be preserved in the model.

pricing

pricing refers to the process of fixing the money value of a product or service. It is the value of the product to be obtained from the customer. Price is determined by the top executive in such a way that it brings the largest volume of sales with sufficiency margin of profit. A number of considerations are involved in the pricing of products, such as cost of product, extent of competition, nature of product, etc. A sound price policy will help in increasing both the customers satisfaction and business profits.

pricing (accounting information for)

there has been considerable controversy concerning the appropriate accounting data for the making of pricing decisions. In particular some accountants contend that fully allocated unit costs are appropriate, whilst others have suggested marginal or variable unit costs. The argument between the two schools suggests that some contenders do not always appreciate that a realistic pricing policy requires attention to both demand and competitive factors. The marginalists suggest that if price is above the marginal or variable cost of the product, the firm will be better off, whereas the fully allocated costs school contends that all costs must be covered if the firm is to make a profit in the long run. A proper perspective is perhaps that marginal cost sets a lower limit on price, although demand and competitive factors should be paramount in arriving at a price that is likely to be in accord with the achievement of a long-run profit objective. Moreover an unimaginative application of fully allocated unit cost to pricing could result in economic disaster for a firm. If, for instance, the sales volume is falling, then the addition of a share of fixed overhead costs to each unit for pricing purposes will increase price further, causing the sales volume to fall even more.

priestman system
a premium bonus system of wage payment, first used by Priestman's of Hull in 1917, applicable to the employees who work in groups, a group bonus being paid in addition to the ordinary time rate.

primacy effect
the finding that, under certain conditions in the process of learning, the first one of a series to be learned is remembered best.

primary
basic.

primary group
a small group (such as the family) characterized by direct, intimate, personal relationships between people who depend on each other for support and for satisfaction of emotional needs.

primary market
(1) a market for a good in which the sellers are the producers of the good. (2) a market for securities in which the sellers are the issuer of the securities.

primary ratio
an overall measure of business efficiency, based on the widely employed criterion of the return on capital employed.

primary standard data
a form of predetermined motion time system which is a simplified version of methods time measurement. Data are expressed in milli-minutes (0,001 of a minute) at a 100 on the 0/100 British Standard Scale.

prime cost
the aggregate of direct material cost, direct wages and direct expense.

prime entry
the original record of a financial transaction made in journal, day book or cash book. A book of prime entry is not part of the double entry system but provides a source from which posting to the ledger can be done.

prime time
broadcast hours when the potential audience is largest-usually weekday evenings.

principal
person or company which is represented by an agent. Money invested or borrowed on which interest is paid.

principle
basic point or general rule.

print
standard vertical size measurement unit 1/12th of a pica or 1/72th of an inch.

printed sources
also published sources. Data which are printed and published and which are usually generally available.

prior charges
all types of debentures, preference shares and other stock ranking for payment of interest or dividend in precedence to the ordinary shares.

prior year adjustment
an adjustment contained in a set of accounts which relates wholly to a matter which occurred in a previous period. It will normally arise because some error in an earlier year's accounts has been discovered, or bacause there has been a change in accounting policy to which it is desired to give retrospective effect.

private
belonging to a single person, not a company or the state.

private company
a company which, by its articles of association, restricts the transfer of its shares to those approved by the directors. A private company is designated by the term limited (often abbreviated to Ltd.) in its name. Its shares may not be quoted on the stock exchange as the shares of such companies must be transferable without restriction.

private investor
an individual person who holds investments for his or her own private benefits. Recent government policy in many countries has been to encourage an increase in the number of private investors.

private ledger
a section of the nominal ledger containing accounts confidential to the proprietor and therefore kept separately. Typically, the private ledger will contain accounts relating to capital, profits and drawings. It is most likely to be encountered in very small business where such matters are the concern only a sole proprietor who may wish to keep information about his or her personal income and wealth from employees.

privately
away from other people.

private sector
industries or activities that are considered the domain of free enterprise.

privatisation
the process of returning to the private sector property (such as public lands) or functions owned or performed by government.

privatised industry
an industry that has undergone privatisation.

privilege
advantage associated with a certain position or situation.

prize
a sum of money or a valuable

object awarded to a person in recognition of some achievement or following success in a draw. Prizes are not normally subject to taxation.

probability

the degree of likelihood of an event occurring measured statistically according to the mathematical theory of probability in which the occurrence of an event is regard regarded as being governed by the laws of chance.

probate

the process of proving that a will is genuine, and distributing the property of an estate as provided in a will; also, in some states, the name for a court that handles the distribution of decedents' estates (dead persons' property) and other matters.

probation

trial period for a new employee.

probationary period

period during which a new employee is on probation.

probe

use to obtain further information when the initial inquiry does not produce a satisfactory response, or to make sure at interview that the respondent has answered the question fully.

problem

thing to which it is difficult to find an answer.

problem identification

problem identification is a major task case studies. Frequently, it requires deep and concentrated thought. A common criticism by the non-professional is that the case does not include all the facts. This is true; few case studies can include all the facts. But managers seldom have all the facts, a concept itself subject to wide interpretation by the researcher. So while not prefect case studies do have a definite sense of reality. Attempting to determine a solution without full knowledge may be frustrating but actually it is part of the essence of managerial problem solving.

problem of adjustment

the problem of getting smooth operations becomes acute because the superior has to uphold, at the work level the standard policies and rules which have been originated by other groups and see to it that workers conform to them. This is not an easy task, because people do not like to conform to matters when they have say in them and when they feel their point of view is not taken into account. This is not a popular way of evoking spontaneity of cooperation. But supervisors as well as workers are repeatedly exhorted to conform to conditions over which they very little say. Often these conditions fail to take into account what is of vital importance to men in their work situation.

procedural

referring to procedure.

procedural agreement

an agreement that sets up a procedure to regulate conflict between the parties concerned. The procedural agreement has always existed in the British system of industrial relations but the → Industrial Relations Act 1971, repealed 1974, defined the term as including that collective agreement, or part of it, that relates to consultation, negotiation or arbitration machinery for dealing with terms and conditions of employment or other questions arising between employer(s) and worker(s) or their organizations; negotiating rights; facilities for officials of trade unions or other workers' organizations; and grievance, discipline and dismissal procedures.

The → Industrial Relation Code of Practice stresses the need for clarity in procedural agreements and lists their desirable contents. Procedural agreements can theoretically be distinguished from 'substantive agreements', which concern the substance of agreements on remuneration, conditions or work, fringe benefits, etc. In practice, however, the two often overlap→ Collective Bargaining; Shop Stewards.

procedure

a predetermined series of steps to be taken in doing a task.

procedure charts

a chart or diagram showing the general sequence of operations in a clerical procedure: a type of process chart, although process chart symbols are not usually used.

proceeds

the amount of money arising from a transaction or series of transactions. Thus, the proceeds of a sale of fixed assets will be the total amount received from them. The proceeds of the share will be the amount of money raised by it. The terms usually imply that all costs associated with the transaction have been deducted.

process

series of steps or stages that make up an activity.

process blocks

blocks made from a colourful design or picture of reproduction by the letter press process.

process chart

a graphical representation of the sequence of events depicting a process. The chart enables the process to be more readily visualised and provides a basis for examining and improving it using work study techniques. Normally process charts use symbols to record the nature of events making up the process.

process control mechanism

acts which help to adjust operations to predetermined standards on the basis of information reaching a manager which gives him the opportunity for corrective action and is his basis for basic control. He cannot exercise control, without such information. And he cannot do a complete job of managing without controlling.

product differentiation

the packaging and advertising of different brands of virtually identical products in order to create differences between them in the mind of the consumer; the process of designing and producing a range of the same basic products in order to appeal to different segments of the market.

product

goods and services produced, usually for sale.

product costing

a method of costing in which costs incurred in the manufacture, processing or handling of several products are assigned to the operations directly relative to each particular product and/or service.

product diversification

the introduction of alternative or additional products which are in a different field from the products at present being produced by the company.

production

showing something. Making or manufacturing of goods for sale.

production control

(1) procedures and means by which the manufacturing plans or programmes are determined or put into operation. Includes the issuing of operating instructions concerning timing, quantities, and completion dates, and the collection, recording and analysis of data of control manufacture in accordance with plans. (2) the function of directing, regulating and coordinating the movement of materials and the utilisation of machines and labour in regard to quantity, quality, time and place, and comparing planned output with the output achieved. (3) sometimes used to cover production planning, although production control is usually regarded as a complementary function.

production innovation

a product whose production breaks new ground for an organisation, either because of the process involved in producing it or the market it is aimed at.

production management

(1) the planning and control of production processes and quality, as well as production quantity, and all production-serving activities, including the purchase of production materials, and the maintenance of plant and equipment, i.e., the planning and control of all phases of manufacturing. (2) may also include responsibility for the industrial engineering, or work study function.

production planning

the function of setting the limits or levels of manufacturing operations in the future, consideration being given to sales forecasts and the requirements and availability of men, machines, materials and money.

production system
in unique product management first job is to get an order. In mass production the job is to build an effective distributive organisation and to educate the customer to adopt his wants to the range of product variety. In process production the first task is to create, maintain and expand a market and to find new market.

production unit method
a method of calculating depreciation in which the amount charged to the profit and loss account in the year is proportionate to the amount of product turned out by the asset. The method is based on the idea that the productive life of an asset will expire according to the extent to which it is used.

productivity
output per man-hour.

productivity bargaining
collective bargaining that seeks increases in productivity in exchange for increase in wages and benefits. These are two basic approaches to productivity bargaining; integrative bargaining and pressure bargaining.

productivity criteria quotient (PCQ)
a method of comparing the relative change in productivity of machines at different times. Certain critical elements of design and construction which have a direct bearing on how well a machine does its job are established for each type of machine. Each element is given a weight of 1,2, or 3: actual changes in machine design and construction are then studied and improvements affecting effectiveness are tabulated while changes that do not effect performance are ignored. PCQ numbers provide a yardstick or estimate of the extent of change in a given type of machine by comparing the PCQ for two years.

productivity measurement
measurement of the productivity of any organisation, programme, or individual. This is particularly problematic in the nonprofit and public sector because of the problem of defining outputs and of quantifying measures of efficiency, effectiveness, and impact.

product life cycle
a term used in marketing to describe the different stages that every product goes through from its development and introduction to the market, via its initial sales and its established sales, to its eventual decline and withdrawal from the market.

product management
a method of apportioning managerial responsibility on the basis of products or product groups. The product manager has overall responsibility for all aspects of the product, from design and development, through production of sales and marketing.

product mix
the composite variety of goods produced or marketed by a producer or sold by a wholesale or retail organisation.

product planning
long range planning which provides good discussional material because products are familiar objects, they have wide interest and they illustrate many excellent examples of planning techniques.

product planning and development
supply of products according to the needs of the customer is the foundation of business and trade. Customers purchase only those products which provide their maximum utility. Goods are produced in anticipation of demand. They must be of good quality and should be capable of satisfying all the demands whenever it comes.

product testing
research into the acceptability of new products, and modified products, to potential consumers.

profession
work which needs special skills learnt over a period of time, and tested by examinations, group of specialized workers; the legal profession.

professional
referring to one of the professions.

professional indemnity insurance
a form of insurance which can be taken out by persons offering a professional service, such as accountants. The policy idemnifies the insured against the direct financial consequences of an error in their work.

professional manager
the professional manager is an individual who manages an organization by applying modern management technique to develop and expand the business, to achieve and attain the ambitions, aspirations and expectations of the owners and society. Such a manager need not necessarily be an owner though divergent views are expressed as to the desirability or otherwise of his sharing the ownership of a business which he manages. The professional manager tackles all operating problems by applying scientific methods. Such methods include a well-planned, organised and systematic human approach to all organisational responsibilities.

professionalism
showing a professional attitude.

proficiency
skill or being capable of doing something.

proficiency testing
the assessment of technical knowledge and skills related to the performance requirements for a specific job, whether such knowledge and skills are acquired through formal or informal means.

proficient

capable of doing something well.

profile

brief description.

profit

money gained from a sale which is more than the money spent.

profitability

(1) the ratio of profit to capital; in its simplest form profit after taxes but before dividends divided by total assets and expressed as a percentage. (2) also used figuratively for any activity when the output from it is greater than the total of the resource used.

profit after tax

the profit of a company after allowing for the corporation tax due on the profit. The figure must be shown in the company's published profit and loss account. It is the find out of which dividends may be paid.

profit and loss account

a summary of revenues earned and expenses incurred for a determine period resulting in the calculation of profit (excess of revenues) or loss (excess of expenses). The summary is frequently extended to include taxation on profit and dividends declared, but these are strictly appropriations or profit and belong to a separate summary called appropriation account.

profit before tax

the profit of a company before any deduction has been made in respect of corporation tax. The amount must be shown in the published profit and loss account.

profit centre

person or department which is considered separately for the purposes of calculating a profit.

profiteering

the making of an unfair or disproportionately large profit by exploiting a situation. Profiteering might occur, for example, if traders put up prices excessively for a product which is in short supply but has not, in fact, cost them any more to buy than usual.

profit forecast

a forecast by the management of a business of a profit expected to be made in a forthcoming period. Managements are not obliged to make profit forecasts but they may do so if, for example, they are seeking to raise extra finance or wish to fight off a takeover bid.

profit (in accounting)

an accounting profit (or loss) is conventionally defined in terms of the increase (or decrease) in a firm's net assets resulting from its ordinary business activities. Thus item such as profits from the sale of assets other than output of products and capital contributions from investors are excluded from the calculation of the change in the value of net assets. An alternative but equivalent definition of accounting profit, for any given time period, is in terms of the difference between the total amount of revenue from sales of products (or

services) for that time period and the amount of assets and resources consumed in earning those revenues. (Profits).
The principal defects of the traditional method of business-profit measurement may be said to be the accounting conventions relating to the Valuation of Assets used in arriving at the change in the value of net assets. In particular the use of historic cost as the valuation base may result in estimates of profit that do not accurately reflect 'reality', particularly in periods of inflation (Changing Price Levels, Accounting for). The measurement of profit (income) is interconnected with the problem of the measurement and valuation of capital. The adoption of alternative concepts of capital valuation would in turn result in different profit measurements. The accounting concept of profit merely represents one of a number of alternative concepts (Valuation of Assets).

profit making
a business is the only human organisation whose existence depends on profit. As EIIs and Walton point out governments can tax churches, can call on members for support, and the family can survive without profits, but a business requires profits to justify its existence. Profit making is a basic goal of business and the profit concept underlies marketing. Profit goals are achieved in the market place and the basic task of the marketing manager is to serve consumer needs profitably in a way which will be consistent with long range survival goals.

profit maximisation
the policy of striving to achieve the greatest possible return from the resources employed in a venture.

profit percentage
the percentage of the final price of a product which represents profit to the business organisation.

profit planning
the formulation of plans leading to a realistic level of profit and the implementation of those plans.

profit-relate pay
an element of the pay an employee which depends on the profit of the business. In advanced countries such pay has been more lightly taxed than other income.

profit sharing
the distribution of part of firm's profits to some or all of its employees, based on the profitability of the firm. A qualified profit sharing plan must provide specific criteria and formulas for which persons get what share of the profits.

profit sharing scheme
scheme where workers get a share of the profits of the organization they work for.

programme
in relation to computers, the schedule of instructions in machine terms, which directs the sequence of operations

carried out by the machine.

programmed instruction
course of instruction carried out by each trainee at his or her own speed.

programmed learning
a form of learning involving a system of self instruction, based on conditioning, where a task to be mastered is broken down into small steps. The subject is given feedback about his mastery of each step as he goes along.

programming support
the type of programming support that is required to install and operate the PCCS should be determined. This affects the amount of primary storage that is required as well as the I/O and the secondary storage device that must be included in the system configuration. This area is particularly difficult for the inexperienced, and competent assistance must be acquired.

progression
moving forward in stages.

progressive
which moves forward in stages.

progressive proofs
a set of engraver's proofs used in colour process printing, showing each colour plate separately and in combination.

project grant
a grant of funds to a public or private organisation for a specified purpose, such as development of an emergency medical service system or conduct of a containing education programme. Project grants are usually discretionary. Applicants are typically chosen on the basis of merit, often competitively. The amount of a project grant is usually based on the estimated cost of achieving the goal of the project.

projective alternative
some kind of forecast is crucial to the analysis of alternatives. We must predict what is likely to happen if we take action A or alternative B or likewise for each alternative on our list. For some decisions the tie between a proposed alternative and a result is almost mechanistic and we can predict outcomes with precision.

projective listening
imaging the effects of one's own words on other people in order to improve direct communication skills.

projective techniques
tests designed to determine the personality traits of subjects, in which the subject's free responses to certain stimuli are noted, analysed and interpreted by qualified testers.

promote
to give someone a more important job or to move someone to a higher grade.

promotion
special activities designed and intended to create and stimulate interest in a person, product, organisation, or cause.

promotional mix
personal selling, advertising, sales promotion and packaging are the activities undertaken

to accomplish selling objectives. These objectives are mutually interdependent and management has to blend them in proper proportion so as to produce a coordinated sales programme to be known as a 'Promotional Mix.'

promulgate
to publish; to announce officially; to put out formally.

proof
a specimen or trial impression taken from the matter set for printing.

proofreader's marks
a set of standard symbols and abbreviations used to indicate corrections in a proof.

propaganda
an effort to influence the opinion of others.

proportional tax
a tax that takes a constant proportion of income as income changes.

proposal
materials organised to offer plans for a programme or services. A proposal may be used as a presentation or submitted by mail or hand delivery.

proprietary
owned, as in the case of property; private; profit-making; owned and operated for the purpose of making a profit, whether or not one is made.

proprietor
owner of a business.

proprietress
woman owner.

prosecute
to bring (someone) to court to answer a criminal charge.

prosecution
party who brings a criminal charge against someone. Lawyers representing the party bringing a criminal charge against someone.

prospect
future possibilities for a person or organization.

prospective
person who could be appointed to a job.

prospectus
a document inviting an application for shares or other securities. A prospectus relating to shares in a company must contain information prescribed by law. This includes financial particulars for the previous 5 years, if applicable, and a statement of future prospects.

protect
to defend something against harm.

protection
act of protecting.

protectionism
a policy of government which has the effect to giving competitive advantage to home industry by imposing duties on goods imported into the country.

protection money
money illegally demanded from an individual or business under the threat that some violence will otherwise be committed. The payment protects the payer from that violence.

protest
statement or action to show

that you do not approve of something.

protestant ethic

max weber's term for the view that making money is a worthy occupation and that hard work and individual competitive effort are qualities to be admired for their own sake.

prototype

a trial version of a product. The original version of a product as compared to later versions.

privident society

a mutual organisation which uses the savings of some members to finance loans to other members at reasonable rates of interests and with reasonable terms of repayment.

provision

an amount set aside, by charging it in the profit and loss account to provide for depreciation or for any known liability the amount of which cannot be determined with complete accuracy. A provision is thus to be distinguished from an accrual which is to provide for a known liability to known amount. Any amount set aside for an unspecified purpose is properly known as a reserve.

provisional

temporary or not final or permanent.

provisional allotment

an allotment of shares to be confirmed if and when the shares are paid for. Such an allotment is made to existing shareholders in the case of a rights issue. Letters of provisional allotment are negotiable and can thus be sold in the market by shareholders unwilling to make further investment in the company.

provisionally

not finally.

proxy

a person designated by a stockholder to represent him at the company's annual meeting and vote his shares. Also used for the card that the stockholder uses to appoint his proxy.

proxy fight

combative effort by a stockholder or group to win the voting support of stockholders holding the controlling number of shares.

proxy statement

document required by government regulation and stock exchanges, detailing for stockholders all information pertinent to a request for their vote or proxy on any question or group of questions to be acted on at a meeting of stockholders.

prudence

a principle of accounting to the effect that accounting statements should be prepared on a cautions basis, avoiding undue optimism. It has been said that the purpose of a balance sheet is to show that the financial condition of the company is at least as good as that stated and not to show that it is not or may not be better.

psychic income

satisfaction, other than

monetary, from a job.

psycho-galvanometer
instrument used to study psychogalvanic response (reflex), which is the production of an electromotive force in the skin resulting from mental activity.

psychogenetic
originating in the mind, with no known physical basis.

psychologist
one who studies human behaviour.

psychology
science of human behaviour.

psychometrics
way of measuring intelligence and personality where the result is shown as a number on a scale.

psychosis
a relatively severe mental disease, i.e., one in which there is loss of, or disorder in, mental processes.

public (plural, publics)
any group of individuals that a public relations programme seeks to influence. A committee of three may be a public; so may a firms' stockholders, its employees, its customers, its community; so may a legislature, the entire nation, the world.

public accounts committee
this committee is appointed to play the role of improving the system of financial management and discipline and observing standards of financial propriety.

public administration
an old-fashioned term, dating from the time when the systematic study of administration was considered a public sector activity. It has been largely superseded by the terms Business Administration (when followed as part of a Master of Business Administration course) and Administrative Science.

publication of accounts
the accounts of company are published when they are made publicly available. This is done by filling a copy with the register of companies.

publication standard
financial statements prepared and audited with the same attention and care as statements intended for publication as part of the annual accounts. It follows this that publication standard statements should show a true and fair view of their subject

public cells in public enterprises
if every enterprise were to have public cells with sufficient competence, it should be possible to prepare corporate plans for each unit as well as for its sectors. The aggregate of these corporate plans would be the right source of information for the central planning body to prepare national plans for the sectors, based on resources, inter-industry analysis etc.

public company
a company having no restriction on ownership or transfer of its shares. It is distinguish by the use of the letter PLC as part of

its name. They stand for public limited company. A company must be a public company before it can be quoted on the stock exchange. Not all public companies are quoted, however.

public enterprises selection board

for the selection and recruitment of top managerial posts in public sector undertakings, the Public Enterprises Selection Board was set up by the Government of India under the Ministry of Finance in August, 1974.

public goods

commodities typically provided by a government that cannot, or would not, be separately parceled out to individual since no one can be excluded from their benefits. Public goods such as national defense, clean air, and public safety are neither divisible nor exclusive.

public image

the amalgam of ideas and belief of the general public or a social group about a person, organisation, etc.

public interest group

an organised pressure group seeking to develop positions and support causes relating to a broader definition of the public goods as opposed to any specific social or economic interest.

publicity

a technique of public relations. A message purposefully planned, executed, and distributed through selected media to further the particular interest of the client without specific payment to media.

public opinion

the most prevalent expressed belief of a public.

public opinion poll

an enumeration of those holding certain opinions regarding an event, etc.

public ownership

ownership by the government on behalf of the people.

public relations

(1) the function of management concerned with evaluating public attitudes, identification of the organisation's policies and procedures with the public interest, initiating action to gain public acceptance, understanding and goodwill. (2) activities concerned with developing in the public a high regard for an organisation by establishing. (a) internally to employees the conviction that the organisation is a good one; (b) externally to the public at large that the organisation is important and beneficial. (3) the deliberate, planned and sustained effort to establish and maintain mutual understanding between an organisation and its public.

public relation function in communication

one obvious objective for the public relations function is to make sure that business institutions perform as servants of people. The tradition of individuality must be preserved within the context of a society that is technological and progressive, in short the kind of society in which the individual increasingly functions as part of social and economic groups without sacrificing his personal identity.

public relations
directing and influencing relations with the public.

public sector
industries or activities run by the government.

public sector objectives
public sector come into being for a variety of reasons, such as:
(i) inability of private sector to muster enough venture capital.
(ii) to develop backward regions, and thus correct regional imbalances.
(iii) to create employment in areas of chronic unemployment.
(iv) for strategic reasons.
(v) to prevent concentration of economic power in private hands.
(vi) for revenue motives; and
(vii) to produce consumption items at cheap prices, and so on.

public undertaking
the sole criterion is whether such state activity directly or indirectly would be conducive to the benefit of the society. Leon Duguit says in his Law in the Modern State: "whatever is essential to the smooth running of society is a public service". Governments have been forced by the logic of events to assume more and more functions so that the sphere of state activity has constantly widened and diversified. The First World War made a strong breach in the laissez faire doctrine. The world- wide and unprecedented economic depression of the thirties called upon the governments everywhere to come out with bold economic policies.

public utility
an organisation that provides an essential public service, like the supply of water or electricity, whether it is part of the private sector or the public sector.

published surveys
surveys which are generally available in published form.

puffery
exaggeration or unsubstantiated material appearing in publicity.

puff-sheet
a publication that survives by consciously giving favourable mentions to advertisers and others who aid it financially.

pulp
term used to describe magazines printed on rough wood-pulp paper, as contrasted with "slicks" which are magazines printed on coated or calendered stock.

pulse rate
the measurement of pulse rate, usually expressed in beats per minute, has long been used in clinical diagnosis. It has value too in the assessment of work loads, since both physical work and mental stress produce increases in pulse rate. A

similar effect is also brought about by increases in ambient temperature.
Considerable variation exists between the resting pulse rates of different individuals, and it is consequently necessary to use an index of work based upon proportional increase in pulse rate above the basal value for any particular individual. Heavy muscular work (such as running or cycling) will produce maximal values in the region of 200 beats per minute.
Studies on motor-vehicle drivers and aircraft pilots have suggested a close relation between variations in pulse rate and the stress brought about the performance of certain critical manoeuvres.

punch
emphasis of vigour in story or broadcast material.

punched card
card into which code symbols are punched to represent the responses given to questions.

punctual
tending to arrive at a place at the right time.

punctuality
tendency to arrive at a place at the right time.

punitive damages
damages awarded on an amount exceeding any actual damage suffered by the plaintiff with the intention that the defendant should suffer some element of punishment for the conduct which is complained of.

purchase day book
a book of prime entry in which is recorded the purchases made by a business on a day-to-day basis. The entries are subsequently posted to the creditors accounts in the purchase ledger and the purchases account.

purchase journal
the journal used to record items ordered and purchased by an organisation. It contains information about the date of each item ordered and purchased, the nature of the item, the purchase-order number, the amount of the purchase, and which subsidiary or general ledger account is affected by the purchase.

purchasing
the acquisition of raw materials, components, goods and services for conversion, consumption or resale. The term is more specifically used within business to describe the work of the industrial buyer, who purchases primarily for conversion and consumption in the manufacturing process, or that of the retail buyer, who resells to the consumer. The objective of the function can be usefully defined as to purchase the right quality of material, at the right, time in the right quantity, from the right source, at the right price. This definition illustrates the complexity of the role, particularly when long-and short-term considerations are noted. Just as in Marketing,

it is a matter of judgement as to how the purchasing mix is brought into balance.

The role of the purchasing careful involvement with production, marketing and engineering colleagues for example, product design, and with production and finance on inventory levels. The purchasing manager should be closely involved in make or busy decisions and with Value Analysis, value engineering cost-reduction schemes. In retailing the purchasing manager will need to be closely involved in marketing and distribution. The average manufacturing company spends more than half the mcney it receives on goods and services, so the impact on the concern of the efficiency and effectiveness of its purchasing management can be substantial. For example it can be shown that a 5 percent saving in purchasing costs can be equated with an increase in sales revenue of 25 percent. The converse is also true, where a loss of 5 percent can erode profit to a similar extent. In retailing the proportion will be even greater, 80 percent is not uncommon.

A major part of the operational aspect of the role involves the appraisal and selection of suppliers. With the increasing internationalization of business this implies a wide knowledge of potential sources and, among other things, alternative transportation methods, and the ability to appraise potential comparative currency movements. In making source decisions managers should aim to obtain the materials/ services they require at the lowest cost to their companies rather than at the lowest price. In many manufacturing concerns the purchasing manager will be responsible for receiving and storing purchased items, scheduling their receipt with suppliers, keeping company production schedules and disposing of scrap and surplus materials and equipment. A further responsibility will often be the management of the raw material and component inventory.

From the strategic point of view the purchasing manager should exercise perception in understanding the company's supply market environment and be able to project its trends. Among the aspects that need to be considered in this respect are potential competition for available resources; vulnerability in respect of supplies (e.g. single sources, political risks); anticipated supply-cost trends; the impact of technological, legal, political or social factors on the company's supply market in the future; changes in the structure of specific supply markets (e.g.

concentration) and their effect on the company.

put in

to have an ad printed in a newspaper.

put out

to send out.

pyramid

shape like a triangle with a wide bottom rising to a point at the top.

pyramid hierarchy

an organisational structure having different levels of authority with fewer people at each succeeding level, so that a chart of the hierarchy would look like a pyramid in shape.

quadruplicate

in quadruplicate=with the original and three copies.

quads

these are large metal spaces wider than thick spaces. They are cast to various sizes as 1 cm, 2 cm, 3 cm, and 4 cm. They are used for filling up short lines.

qualification

formal document or proof which recognizes that a person has completed a specialized course of study or has a special skill.

qualification shares

a number of shares which a director of a company is required, by its Articles of Association, to hold before he or she is entitled to take office. Not all companies require directors to hold shares before he or she is entitled to take office.

qualified

having formal recognition of skill in a particular activity or having passed special examinations in a subject.

qualified audit report

an auditors' report which expresses reservations on certain matters of concern to the auditor. This may be in terms that indicate that the accounts to which the report refers are inaccurate or misleading and fail to give a true and fair view.

qualify

to qualify for = to be considered, to be entitled to.

quality

what something is like or how good or bad something is.

quality assurance

that function within a business that review the product or service after completion for determination of the degree of excellence that was accomplished.

quality circle

a technique developed in the 1960s by American and Japanese engineers. Each circle consists of a small local group or employees trying to solve practical problems about the standard of quality of the product they are working on. Membership of the circle is completely voluntary and is seen by management as a way of improving the participation and motivation of the work-force, as well as providing the bonus of increased quality, and perhaps as a result decreased costs.

quality control

the procedure of establishing acceptable standards with defined limits of variation in quality of material, size, weight, finish or other characteristics for goods or services, and maintaining these standards.

quality control, statistical
control of product quality by sampling techniques.

quality market
a market in which the quality of a product is more important to the customer than the price.

quantitative methodology
the use of research methods in behavioural science or social science which are concerned more with the precision and generalizability of the data being collected than their richness of content or complexity, e.g., having a narrower but sharper focus than qualitative methodology. The experiment and the structured questionnaire are the most common methods used.

quantitative research
research in which answers to questions are processed to produce number or percentage of people in different categories, accordingly to the make up of the simple and structure of the questionnaire, giving particular answers.

quarter
a period of time equal to 3 calender months, i.e., one—quarter of a year. It is conventional billing and accounting period.

quarterly
occurring once each quarter or three months period four times each year.

quartile
one of the three point on a frequency distribution which divide it into equal quarters.

quassi subsidiary company
a company which does not fulfil the legal definition of a subsidiary company set out in the companies Act but which nevertheless is effectively controlled indirectly by another company.

question
words which need an answer.

questioning aptitude
term used to describe the critical examination of an activity or procedure by asking a series of systematic questions.

questionnaire
a series of questions dealing with matters relevant to the topic being studied, administered to a group of individuals (the sample) with the object of obtaining data.

queue
line of people waiting one behind the other. Series of documents (such as orders, application forms) which are dealt with in order.

queueing
in erogonomics this term is used to describe a way of dealing with sensory overload in which all the stimuli but one are put on hold by the brain unit that one has been processed.

queuing problem

the problem of determining the facilities to be provided when the need for them varies at random, for example, the optimum number of thicket windows in cases where there may be long queues some times and no customers at all at other times.

quick assets

assets which are highly liquid. Cash and bank balances are good examples.

quick ratio

the relationship between average debtors (receivables) and average turnover.

quick succession relief

a relief given against inheritance tax where a person inheriting money then dies within 5 years so that the sum becomes liable to tax for a second time.

quid pro quo

something done in exchange for another thing done or given.

quit

to resign or to leave (a job).

quoins

wedge-shaped small wooden pieces of a mechanical device used to tighten the matter in a chase.

quoram

the minimum legal number of people required to be in attendance before a meeting can officially take place.

quorum

minimum number of people who have to be present at a meeting to make it valid.

quota

quantity restrictions placed on business transactions usually by a regulatory body.

quotations

this is hallowed metal furniture used to fill up the open space in a page.

racial

of or referring to a person's race.

racism or racialism

belief in racist ideas or actions based on racist ideas.

racist

(person) believing that people of certain racial or ethnic groups are inferior.

radio research

all research relating to the medium of ratio.

raiding

enticing workers to work for another organization or enticing members of a union to join another union.

raise

increase in salary.

random

done without making any special choice.

random error

a sample selected at random, i.e., in which each item or member has an equal probability of being selected.

random sample

a sample selected at random, each member of the universe having an equal chance of being selected.

random sampling

the process of sampling data at random from a population so that inferences can be made about the population from findings about the sample. The crucial condition is that each individual in the total population has an equal of being chosen.

random selection
a method of selecting sample units so that each possible sample has a fixed and determinate probability of selection.

random walk theory
the theory that stock market prices follow a random path and that therefore their future course is not predictable. The random walk theory arises from the efficient market theory of stock market behaviour.

range
series of items within certain limits.

rank
position in a company or an organization. To classify in order of importance.

rank and file
ordinary members of a trade union.

ranking
in a certain position.

ranking method
a simple method of job evaluation in which jobs are placed into a predetermined number of grades or levels progressing from the simplest to the most difficult.

rank order
the ordering of responses, e.g., opinions, preferences, according to the relative frequency of the responses given by members of a sample.

ransom
an amount demanded illegally for the return of a kidnaped person or a stole object of value. The threat is usually made that the person will be killed or the object destroyed if the ransom is not paid.

rapport
unconstrained, intimate, and friendly relationship between two persons.

rate
degree or level. Money charged for time worked or work completed.

rateable value
a notional annual rental value attributed to property in many countries which formed the basis of charging the form of local property tax known as rates.

rate of interest
the percentage which annual interest bears to the capital sum on which it is paid. Thus a rate of interest of 10 percent means that Rs. 1000 invested for 1 year would earn Rs. 100.

rate of pay variance
a variance caused by a difference between the rate of pay of labour envisaged in establishing a budget and that actually experienced.

rate of return
a simple method of evaluating capital expenditure project in which the rate of return anticipated from the proposed investment is compared with a predetermined target.

rates
a form of local taxation paid by property owners. At one time it was paid by domestic as well as

business property occupiers.

rate setting
an old fashioned term for the process of setting piecework rates of pay for a job. The process is more often included now under the term work measurement.

ratify
to approve officially.

rating
assessing something by assigning a certain grade.

ratio
mathematical expression to show the relationship between two amounts.

ratio analysis
a method of judging company performance by examining the relationships between various figures, e.g. the ratio of profits to investment.

rationalisation
term applied to improvement of industrial efficiency in Germany in the 1920s.

rational management
the opposite of participative management. The term is usually used to denote a management style that emphasizes objective measures of input rather than human relations.

ratio norm
norm for different kinds of ratios either as an average over-time of the same firm, or an industry average or an average of a cross-section of firms, to evaluate and control performance.

rat race
competition for success in business or in a career.

raw
in the original state or not processed.

raw materials
materials acquired for incorporation into a manufactured product. Raw materials are normally valued at cost for accounting purposes.

reaction time
the interval between the arrival of a stimulus and the initiation of the appropriate response is one of the fundamental lags in human control mechanisms and has formed the subject of many psychological experiments over the last hundred years.

With practice, subjects are able to reduce this lag to less than 0-2 second. Accurate measurement reveals that the reaction time is a function of numerous variables. The sensory modality, for example, is one such variable; reactions to sounds are swifter than those to lights. Again, faster reaction will follow from intense signals than from weak ones. There is considerable variation between different individuals in their speed of reaction, and in any one individual such factors as the level of motivation play an important part. Reaction times increase when a subject is faced with choice; this increase is logarithmic. The practical significance of this result is that operators' decision time must be allowed for, and that the amount of variety of both input and response should be kept as low as possible in order to achieve fast reactions.

reader's guide to periodical literature
an index to magazine articles and periodical literature.

readership
the numbers reading a publication. The term is difficult to define, for it must be stated whether purchase, subscription, exposure to, etc., of the publication are understood.

readiness
a physical, mental, and emotional preparedness for a given learning activity.

reading
a process of securing meaning from symbols; a physical, mental, and emotional activity of identifying, interpreting, and evaluating messages conveyed through the medium of printed symbols.

reading deficiency
lack of adequate skills in reading.

reading laboratory
a reading clinic or workroom in which corrective and remedial work in reading is carried on.

reading level
the stage of development which a person has reached in reading skill.

reading maladjustment
inability to adjust to the use of the reading process.

reading vocabulary
words that can be identified and understood in context or in isolation from the printed page.

readmost
terms used in assessing the effectiveness of an advertising in the press. Respondents are asked to indicate whether, if they noted an advertisement they then 'read most' of its copy. This data can then be expressed as a percentage of total readership.

readvertise
to advertise again.

readvertisement
second advertisement for a vacant post.

real
true or not an imitation.

realisable income
the profit of business calculated on the basis of valuing all its assets at realisable values. It is one of the concepts employed by Edwards and Bell on their book 'Theory and Measurement of Business income'.

realisable value
the amount which would be received if an asset were sold. It is argued that this basis of valuation, not commonly used in practice, would show more clearly the alternative uses forgone of the resources employed in the present business.

realisation concept
a fundamental accounting concept which states that profits should be recognised only when they have been realised or when realisation is assured.

realised profit
a profit which has become available in the form of cash, usually following the sale of the asset in which it is embodied.

real time
a period of time during which an on line computer is processing the data about particular situation while that situation is actually in progress thus allowing for instant updating as in an airline or hotel reservation system.

real-time operation
term used of a computer that is processing data fast enough for it to be used to control an operation.

real wages
disposable income left after paying taxation, etc., the buying power of a certain income as opposed to the actual money received.

reapply
to apply again.

reappoint
to appoint someone again.

reason
thing which explains why something has happened.

reasonable
sensible or not annoyed.

reassess
to assess again.

reassign
to assign again; to assign someone to a new position.

reassure
to make someone calm or less worried.

recall
in surveys using a random sample, it is necessary for the individual specified in the sample to be interviewed. Thus, if contact is not established on the first call, it is necessary that the interviewer makes one or more recalls.

recall method
used in telephone interviewing. Method in which the respondent is telephoned and asked questions, for instance, on radio or television programmes seen during a specified period, usually the day prior to the interview.

recap
recapitulation of subject matter, series, or programme.

receipt
paper showing that money has been paid or that something has been received. Act of receiving something.

receipt and payment accounts
an account of the activities of an organisation for a period of time in terms of the amount of cash received and paid under a number of headings. It takes no account of accruals or prepayments.

receiver
one who manages a company with a view to orderly liquidation. When a receiver is appointed, normal trading is suspended except to the extent that it assists in the process of liquidation, e.g., by allowing the sale of a going concern.

recency effect

the finding that under certain conditions in the process of learning the last one of a series to be learned is remembered best.

reception

place (in a hotel or office) where visitors register or say who they have come to see.

recession

fall in trade or in the economy.

recipient

person who receives.

recognize

to know someone or something because you have seen or heard them before.

recognition

act of recognizing.

recognition of revenue

the inclusion of revenue in the profit and loss account. Revenue may be recognised when a contract of sale is made or, alternatively, when the cash has actually been received. It is regarded as bad practice to recognise revenue before either it has been received in cash or its ultimate receipt has become certain (i.e., there is a legally enforceable debt).

recommend

to offer or suggest for use. Recommendation describes the presentation of plans, ideas or things to others for adoption.

recommendation

the advice or information regarding operations based upon research results.

reconciliation

an explanation of the difference between two figures which purport to express the same quantity. A reconciliation may be needed, for example, between the amount of cash shown in a business's balance sheet and that shown on its bank statements due to such items as unpresented cheques.

reconsider

to think again about a decision which has already been made.

reconstruction

a process of amending the financing arrangements of a limited company. It may include the writing off of accumulated losses by the reduction of capital or the amendment of the rights of particular classes of shareholders. Reconstructions are normally undertaken to place a company on a sound financial footing for a fresh start after a period of difficulty.

record

document which give information. History of past performance.

recordative work

routine recording and classified posting of financial transactions and events.

recorded delivery

a service operated by the post office whereby a signature is obtained on a delivery of a letter. It is thus possible to verify its arrival. It is a useful service for the transmission of documents which are important but of little intrinsic monetary value.

recourse

the right to require payment

from a person other than the one having a primary liability. If for example, the drawee of a bill of exchange fails to honour it on maturity the holder may have recourse to other persons who have endorsed the bill since it was first drawn.

recoverable

capable of being realised. The recoverable value of an asset is that amount which can be converted into cash, either by immediate sale or by a process of realisation in normal use.

recovery of expense

the absorption of indirect costs into the costs of departments, specific products, production units or cost centres by the application of an appropriate formula.

recovery stock

the shares of a company which are currently at a depressed price because of temporary factors having an adverse effect on the company but from which it is believed that it will recover.

recreation

leisure time.

recruit

new member of staff.

recruitment

obtaining applicants for a job.

recruitment function

the purposes of a recruitment function include seeking out evaluating, obtaining commitment from place and orienting new employees to fill positions required for the successful conduct of the work of an organization. Business enterprises enter into this activity recurrently to add to maintain or readjust their total manpower complement in accordance with business requirements.

red

the colour in which negative figures are traditionally recorded. Thus to be in the red at the bank is to have a bank overdraft. For a business to 'go into the red' is for it to make a loss.

red circle rate

US pay rate that is above the minimum rate for an employee's evaluated level.

redeemable shares

shares issued on the terms that the holders will at some future date be repaid the amount which they invested in the company.

redeploy

to move workers from one place to another or to give workers totally different jobs to do.

redeployment

moving workers from one place to another.

red tape

rules and regulations which creates a lot of paperwork.

reduce

to make smaller or lower.

reducing balance

one of the methods available for calculating the amount to be charged as depreciation. The amount is calculated by applying a fixed percentage each year to net book value of the asset. Since this steadily declines, application of the reducing balance method means that a greater part of the asset's value is charged in the early part of its life than is charged in the later part.

reduction

lowering (of quantities, prices, etc.).

reduction of capital

a process whereby the share capital of a limited company is diminished either by repayment or by writing down its value. In either case there are safeguards to ensure that the interests of creditors are not prejudiced. There are two circumstances in which a reduction of capital might be sought. The first is where a company finds itself with excessive funds for which no profitable use can be found. This might occur if there has been a permanent diminution in the level of business available. In this case the company might repay part of the capital rateably of its shareholders. The second is where a company has large accumulated losses where there are no prospects of recovery. The debit balance on the profit and loss account may then be extinguished by writing an appropriate amount from the nominal value of the shares so that for examples, Rs. 1 shares are reduced to 50p shares.

redundancy

loss of job by a person whose skills are no longer needed.

redundancy consultation

in an attempt to promote greater workplace consultation and to prevent redundancies from being declared without warning. Part IV of the Employment Protection Act 1975 requires employers who propose to dismiss employees as redundant to first consult any recognized trade union in advance. Recognition can be formal or informal and may be implied, for example from an employer's practice of negotiating terms and conditions of employment with the shop stewards of a particular union. The duty to consult arises whether or not the particular employees likely to be dismissed are themselves members of the union or qualified to receive a redundancy payment. It is sufficient that the individuals affected belong to a class or grade of workers that the recognized union ordinarily represents in the bargaining process when negotiating with the employer.

Essentially the duty to consult means that employers must provide recognized unions with advance information about proposed job losses. The reasons for the redundancies must be given in writing, together with details of the numbers and descriptions of employees likely to be affected, as well as the proposed method of selecting those to be dismissed. Where a recognized union puts forwards counter-proposals, an employer must consider them. He need not agree to them however, although he must give his reasons if he rejects any such representations. The 1975 Act lays down a timetable for consultations. It must begin at the earliest opportunity and in any event not later than ninety days before the first dismissal takes effect where one hundred or more employees are to be dismissed at any one establishment within a period of ninety days. If between ten and ninety-nine employees are likely to be affected within a period of thirty days, then consultation must begin at least thirty days in advance. Where fewer than ten employees are concerned there is no specified minimum period and consultation must begin at the earliest opportunity.

A recognized union may complain to an industrial tribunal that the employer's duty has not been discharged. If the complaint is upheld the tribunal may make a 'protective award' in favour of the affected employees. Depending on the seriousness of the employer's default the award may be up to ninety days pay for each employee where one hundred or more are redundant, thirty days pay where there are fewer than one hundred, and up to twenty-eight days pay where no more than nine workers are affected. There is a defence where special circumstances (such as a sudden and unexpected loss of business) make full compliance not reasonably practicable.

Regardless of any obligation to consult a recognized union, an employer has the further, and quite separate, duty to warn the Department of Employment of impending redundancies. The DE must be given at least ninety days advance notice in writing where one hundred or more redundancies within ninety days are contemplated, and thirty days warning where between ten and ninety-nine such dismissals are expected within thirty days. Failure here is penalized either by a prosecution and fine or, more commonly, the DE withholding up to 10 percent of any redundancy rabate due to the employer.

redundancy payment

a payment made to an employee who has been dismissed by reason of redundancy. There is a statutory entitlement of redundancy pay for all employees, the amount depending on length of services and level of pay. Many employers pay more than the statutory minimum.

redundant

(ability or skill) which is no longer needed or is useless. Person who loses his job because his skills are no longer needed.

re-employ

to employ someone again.

re-employment

employing someone again.

re-engage
to re-employ a person, but not necessarily in the same job.

re-engagement
employing someone again, but not necessarily in the same job.

referee
person (such as a former employer) who can give a report on someone's character or ability or job performance.

reference
written report on someone's character or ability or job performance, etc. Person who reports on someone's character or ability, etc.

reference marks
these are marks used in the text page to draw the attention to footnotes. They are six in number:

1. Asterik or Star
2. Single dagger
3. Double dagger
4. Sections
5. parallel
6. Paragraph.

refer to drawer
a form of words written by a bank on a cheque drawn on it. Although it literally invites the payee to consult the drawer of the cheque it amounts to a refusal to pay the cheque, usually because funds are not available in the account on which it is drawn.

refined data
with all this information at hand with a continuous feedback loop established for comparison and verification of the resulting refined data a truly valid and useful manpower plan can be developed. The prediction of a 95 percent probability of securing an order that could not be filled without the addition of 10 or 20 experienced computer programmers within a short time would have a compelling impact on any recruiting plan.

refresher course
course of study designed to revive skills or knowledge in people who have forgotten them or are out of practice.

refund
to pay back an amount previously paid. Thus the purchaser of goods which prove to be unsatisfactory may be refunded the purchase price by the seller.

refusal rate
the percentage rate of non-response to a questionnaire over the total number of responses sought. Converse of Response Rate, which represents the percentage rate of responses to the total sample number.

region
large area of a country.

regional development grant
a grant given by the government to encourage companies to establish business in regions of the country which are economically depressed.

register
official list. To write something in an official list.

registered office
an address to which official

notifications to a limited company can be sent and thus its address for legal purpose. Every company must have a registered office. This is very often not its business address but that of a bank, an accountant or a solicitor.

registered post

a service offered by the post office whereby the material is handled in a secure way and a signature obtained on delivery. It is thus possible to verity safe delivery. Where the material is lost or damaged in transit compensation may be claimed.

registered security

a security, ownership of which is recorded in a register maintained by the organisation issuing the security. It is to be contrasted with a bearer security. Most company shares and government stocks are registered securities. Transfer of ownership is achieved by means of the execution of a transfer document which acts as an authority for the appropriate amendment to the register to be made.

registry

an organisation that conducts a registration programme for health personnel and the list of individuals it has registered.

regressive eye movement

turning the eyes to the left to retrace a part of a line while reading from left to right across a line of print.

regular

which happens or comes at the same time each day or each week or each month or each year.

regular fold

when a sheet is folded on its longer side at right angles, it is called regular fold.

regulation

laws or rules.

reimburse

to pay someone back for money which he has spent.

reinforcement

the process of strengthening the likelihood that a given behaviour will occur by providing it with some form of reward. This is the basis of all conditioning.

reinstate

to re-employ someone in the same job (from which he was dismissed).

reject

to refuse to accept or to say that something is not satisfactory.

rejection

refusal to accept.

related intelligence mechanisms

three intelligence structures whereby an organisation can regularly search its environment for information. Each intelligence structure must also provide an appropriate coding procedure since most information channels are not multipurpose.

relations

dealing (with other people or other organizations).

release

end to an employee's contract

with an organization.

release date
used of research reports. The date on which the results of a study are published or are presented to the sponsor.

reliability
the extent to which a result is due to systematic effects, i.e., will persist from sample to sample.

reliability tests
statistical tests designed to give estimates of the reliability of data.

relief
person who takes the place of another, who is sick or on holiday.

relieve
to come to work to take the place of another worker at the end of a shift.

relocate
to establish an organization in a new place, to the established in a new place.

relocation
establishing an organization or a worker in a new place.

reluctant manager
a term introduced to management science in the 1980s by two British writers, Richard Scase and Robert Goffee. The term describes a manager suffering from a certain alienation form his job because he sees the reward for his efforts as being insufficient to compensate him for the stress he feels. This reluctance seems to be found more as the amount of bureaucracy in an organisation increases.

remedial reading
clinical procedures in which particular effort is made to discover the exact cause or causes of deficiency and means of removing or mitigating these casual factors, coupled with instructions designed to remove special reading deficiencies.

remedial transfer
transferring an employee to another more suitable job after he or she has not performed well in the present position.

remunerate
to pay someone for doing something.

remuneration
payment for services.

remunerative
(job) which pays well.

renew
to continue something for a further period of time.

renewal
act of renewing.

reopen
to open again.

reopening
opening again.

reorganize
to organize in a new way.

reorganization
new way of organizing.

reorganization of a firm
(i) the principle of the objective every organisation and every part of the organisation must be an expression of the purpose of the undertaking concerned or it is meaningless and therefore redundant.
(ii) the principle of specialization

the activities of every member of any organized group should be confined, as far as possible, to the performance of a single function.
(iii) the principle of co-ordination
the purpose of organizing per se, as distinguished from the purpose of the undertaking, is to facilitate co-ordination; unity of effort.
(iv) the principle of correspondence
in every position the responsibility and the authority should correspond.
(v) the span of control
no person should supervise more than five, or at the most, six, direct subordinates whose work interlocks.

repetitive question
a question which is very similar in form and purpose to other questions asked on the same questionnaire.

repetitive work
work which involves repeating the same task over and over again.

replace
to put someone in the place of someone else.

replacement
act of putting someone in the place of another.

report
the document prepared to contain all that information which is relevant to the planning, execution and results of a study.

represent
to act on behalf of someone.

representation
the managerial function of representing the company to outside groups, agencies, or individuals.

representative
used of samples. That which reflects the characteristics, in similar proportions, of the universe.

representative action
a class action; also, a lawsuit brought by one stockholder in a corporation to claim rights or to fix wrongs done to many or all stockholders in the company.

repression
the rejection and shutting out of the awareness of a reaction pattern (thought, feeling, impulse, memory) in order to avoid distress.

reprimand
official criticism given to an employee. To criticize someone officially.

repudiate
to refuse to accept.

repudiation
refusal to accept; refusal to perform one's obligations under an agreement or contract

requisition
official order for something. To put in an official order for something.

resale price maintenance
the practice in which the manufacturer fixes the minimum price at which the goods are to be sold to ultimate user or consumer and imposes sanctions on price cutting.

research and development
the first stage of a product life cycle in which science and technology is applied to the development of new products. The term is also used more generally to describe any systematic activity within an organisation aimed at giving it a competitive edge in the future.

researcher
the executive who undertakes and directs a market research study.

research on decision-making
the traditional economist's picture of the businessman is of a rational being who, under the pressure of competition, carefully weighs the costs of one action against another and is preoccupied with marginal costs and marginal utility. Managers, even though they may consider this description of business behaviour to be too academic, will probably still stress the rationai element in their decisions although they may allow that the decisions made by others are often not as objective as they should be.

research techniques
the procedures and methods employed to gather information on the subject of a study. The procedures selected for use in any particular study constitute its methodology.

resent
to feel annoyed about something.

resentful
feeling annoyed about something.

resentment
feeling of annoyance at something.

reservation of title
a condition attached to the supply of goods that title in them will not pass from the seller to the buyer until payment has been made in full. Normally a creditor for goods supplied would rank below may prior interests in the event of the bankruptcy of the customer.

reserve
an amount of money or other negotiable instrument set aside by an insurance company to assure the fulfillment of its commitments to pay future claims.

reserve capital
that part of the nominal capital of a business which has not yet been called up. It is thus a reserve which can be drawn on in case of need.

reserved responsibility
that portion of a manager's work that he performs himself and does not delegate.

reserve fund
reserve represented by investments outside the business specifically earmarket for use in case of need.

reserve price
a price set in advance of a sale by auction below which a sale will not be concluded. The function of a reserve price is that a seller can be assured thereby that the object of the sale will not be sold at too low a price because of lack of

interest at the sale.

residence
act of living or operating officially in a country.

resident
person or company considered to be living or operating in a country for official or tax purposes.

residual
remaining after everything else has gone.

residual income
that part of the income of a segment of a business which remains after all costs, including the cost of the capital employed in the segment, are taken into account. The concept of residual income is one which has an application in the measurement of divisional performance.

residual value
the value left in a fixed asset after it has reached the end of its useful life. It would be taken into account in determining the recurrent charge of depreciation.

residue
that which is left from the estate of a deceased person after all specific bequests have been fulfilled. It may often be the major part of the estate and be left to a named individual.

resign
to give up a job.

resignation
act of giving up a job.

resolution
decision to be discussed at a meeting.

resources
strength or advantage of a person or organization.

resources development
activities for creating, procuring, constructing, training, and committing resources for the achievement of an objective or goal, the conducting of a programme or activity, or the rendering of service for a given period or on a sustained basis.

responsibilities
job duties.

responsibilities of management
management carry all the responsibilities and duties that are incumbent upon it as a leader of the growth and planning process. It is management's job to see that conditions conducive to rapid growth are created, for therein lies the destiny of the country. This imperatively imposes upon management the responsibility to develop people. As a very vital part of this responsibility, management must multiply itself for taking on the responsibility, for more and more growth.
Another important responsibility of management is innovation which only means more and better people, goods and services. The innovation always results in creating new conveniences, new wants, lower prices, new techniques, better and new product, new designs, efficient and effective methods, better uses of capital materials, machines and people

and a development of better human beings.

responsibility
the work assigned to a person.

responsibility accounting
making the executive a cost centre responsible for the financial results of the field for which he is accountable.

responsibility centre
an area of business activity under the responsibility of a defined person or group of persons. If a budget is prepared for a responsibility centre its manager can be made fully accountable for any variance which occurs.

responsibly
in a responsible way.

responsive
(person) who listens and does what someone asks.

restrain of trade
any activity which interferes with the operation of a free market process fixing or preventing a new competitor from entering the market.

restrict
to limit or to impose controls on.

restrictive
which limits.

restrictive labour practices
arrangements imposed by employees by which labour is not used efficiently, there being no social or economic justification as far as society as a whole is concerned.

Many restrictions on the use of labour are now generally regarded as desirable. On economic grounds it may, for example, be more efficient to prevent excessive hours of work, since people when tired tend to produce poorer performances. A normal working week of sixty hours might not in some cases be excessive in terms of efficiency but would now be unacceptable on social grounds. Many such restrictions are incorporated in the safety, health and welfare provisions of the Factories Acts.

Some restrictive labour practice that are the product management decisions may or may not be justified, according to circumstances. Overmanning seems indefensible at time of high employment, but the retention of labour during a temporary recession may make both economic and social sense if it prevents the dispersal of a trained and experienced workforce.

Restrictive practices may be formal and agreed, as between trade unions and management, and even subject to a written agreement after collective bargaining, as in various types of apprenticeship regulations. They may be informal and by no means 'agreed', for example where work groups set their own standards of performance. Trade unions may or may not be involved. In any event, management acquiesces to them and shares the responsibility for their existence.

Restrictive labour practices may occur through Demarcation, low effective performance resulting from employment of craftsmen's mates, overmanning, restriction on output, unnecessary overtime, excessive tea breaks and bad timekeeping practices.

Restrictive labour practices are most marked in industries where there is little security of employment, e.g. shipbuilding, docks. They are also marked where trade unions have considerable bargaining strength, e.g. in the printing industry, where unions have extensive control over entry to employment as well as over job. Management weakness is another facilitating factor, e.g. in the newspaper industry, where the product is perishable, where there is considerable competition between employers, and where there is no external pressure such as foreign competition. Tradition and convention, e.g. among crafts, can be significant, although many restrictive labour practices are new, having sprung up with new work situation.

It is primarily management's job to eliminate or reduce restrictive labour practice by improving its handling of industrial relations generally. Unions can help by improving their structure and education programmes. Governments can assist in the last resort, e.g., the Devlin Inquiry into the docks.

In recent years the issue has become less contentious as unemployment and productivity have both risen sharply. Indeed, the focus of attention has shifted to the acceptance or otherwise of new technologies by the workforce and trade unions.

restrictive practices

(1) a limitation upon production, products, services, sales, purchases, suppliers, customers, markets, research, etc., agreed unilaterally or by agreement between two or more organisations. (2) labour practices which limit the full utilisation of manpower resources.

restructuring cost

the costs involved in making substantial organisational changes to a business. They would normally not be expected to recur and might, therefore, be discounted in predicting future profits from an analysis of current accounts.

restructuring of industry

a term often used to describe the decline of heavy industry, with its attendant unemployment, and the increasing importance of the service sector and of information technology.

result

something which happens because of something else.

resume

to start again.

resume or resume
US summary of a person's life story with details of education and work experience sent to a prospective employer by someone looking for a job.

resumption
starting again.

retail audit
also shop audit. Continuous research with a panel of retail distributors to study inventory levels and the performance of specific products at the retail level.

retail banking services
banking services provided to individual members of the public as opposed to those provided to businesses and institutions.

retailer
type of economic unit specialising in buying goods for resale to, or creating services for sale to, final consumers.

retailer survey
survey of the attitudes, opinions and behaviour of retail distributors in connection with overall performance of particular products.

retail price index
a figure, calculated monthly which reflects the cost, of set of basic goods and services used by most of the United Kingdom population. It is generally used as an indicator or changes in inflation and the cost of living and is often the basis for collective bargaining and for government policy - making.

retained profit
that part of the profit of company which has not been distributed to the members in the form of dividends. It is a cumulative amount and each year's retained profit, if any, increases the total. Retained profit is a revenue reserve and will appear as such on the balance sheet.

retainer
an advance fee paid to a professional to assure the availability of his or her services in the future.

retention
keeping employees on the staff, and not losing them to rival firms.

retention preference
the relative standing of employees in an organisational reduction-fee-force (RIF) process. Their standing is determined by such factors as veterans preference, tenure group membership, length of service, performance appraisal, and critical skills.

retire
to stop work and take a pension. To make a worker stop work and take a pension.

retirement
act of retiring from work.

retirement fund
a fund established and maintained to pay employees following their retirement, under terms specified in the employing organisation's retirement plan. Retirement funds, established in conformity with qualified retirement plans, may be tax-exempt or tax deferred.

retirement on the job
a term sometime used on an employee who experiences such alienation from this job that he does the minimum possible in order to retain it while he waits for retirement.

retrain
to train someone for a new job, or to do the same job in a more modern way.

retraining
act of training again.

retroactive
which takes effect from a time in the past.

retroactively
going back to a time in the past.

retrospective
taking effect as though it has occurred at an earlier date. Normally legislation is not made retrospective as this would imply uncertainty as to the legality of any action which might be taken.

return on capital
(1) trading profits as a percentage of total capital employed, i.e. total assets less current liabilities. Return on shareholders' capital. Trading profits less debits as percentage of total capital employed less debits (not often used). Return on equity capital. Total profits less debits, interest and preferred dividends as a percentage of shareholders capital less debits and preferred capital.

return on capital employed
profit related to the investment of capital required to produce it. It is used as measure of performance but is subject to distortion due to difficulties in determining both profit and capital employed.

returns
the completed schedules or questionnaires which are sent back to the researcher by the respondents or by the interviewers.

revaluation
the process of placing a different valuation on an asset from its current recorded value. Revaluation is a comparatively rare event in account on the basis of historical cost and is used only where balance sheet values have become conspicuously misleading.

revaluation accounting
revaluation or replacement value accounting is mainly concerned with ensuring that capital is maintained in real terms and profit is calculated on this basis.

revenue
money received from all source. Unless otherwise stated, gross receipts represent receipts prior to the deduction of expenses.

revenue bond
a bond that is redeemed only with revenues generated from the completed, operations project for which the bond was sold. This is the typical bond issued for the financing of projects.

revenue expenditure
expenditures of cash which are undertaken to maintain asset values (e.g., repairs) or to obtain current revenue (e.g. raw

material purchases, factory payroll).

reverie

a lower form of thinking. Dwelling upon a series of recollections without attempt to control their direction. Day-dreaming.

reversal tendency

the tendency of an individual to reverse letters or words while reading.

reversed block

a block the background of which is printed but not the letter or designs which appear as white.

reverse takeover

a situation where a company which was threatened by takeover responds by taking over the prospective bidder.

review

to examine critically. Review implies close scrutiny of something to determine its suitability or accuracy. For instance, a programme is reviewed preparatory to approval or authorisation.

revised operational procedures

these outline what specific activities are to take place in the performance of specific work. In writing and using ROP the management must concentrate on the changes that are required. This is the information the employee really needs to know to carry out the change.

revolving credit

the facility to borrow money up to a certain specified amount and to replace one borrowing with another as the former is paid off so long as the overall limit is not exceeded.

revolving fund

a fund established to finance a cycle of operations through sums of money received by the fund.

reward

money or other gains from effort.

reward power

reward power is based on one person's perception of another ability to reward him. It increases in direct proportion to the amount of rewards a person sees another as controlling. Within an organizational setting giving someone a raise or bonus, promoting him to a job with more responsibility, expanding his budget—these are highly used as reward power to influence a person to do a better job for the organization.

rewrite man

journalist who writes stories from material provided by others.

rhochrematics

the flow process from raw material source to final consumer. The concept embraces the basic function of producing and marketing as an integrated system and involves the selection of the most effective combination of transporting, processing, handling distributing goods.

rid

to throw something away because it is useless.

rigid

not flexible or which cannot be changed.

rigging a market

acting in a market in such a way that the prices established bear no relation to those which would have been produced by a free interplay of supply and demand.

right to work

the term may be used in a number of senses. The written constitutions of some countries include this 'right' among the constitutional rights of their citizens. In this context it merely implies that the government of the country should follow an economic policy that will achieve a state of full employment. In the USA and in some other countries the term 'right to work legislation' has been used to describe measures intended to prevent trade unions from insisting on a Closed Shop, thus debarring non-unionists from securing employment. Similarly in Britain some judges have used the phrase to justify controlling the way in which trade unions admit and expel members, particularly where the union operates a closed shop policy. A third meaning that has been given to this term is the implication that employees have a kind of property right to their jobs so that in the event of their dismissal for some reason other than misconduct, their employer should have to compensate them for the loss of their property. The Redundancy Payments Act 1965 introduced this principle, though in a somewhat limited form, into British law. In some continental countries dismissed employees have a right to appeal to an independent tribunal, which may order their reinstatement. In Britain this principle operated only in respect of employees who had to leave their jobs because of call-up for the armed forces. Under the provisions of the Trade Union and Labour Relations Act 1974, in connection with the Unfair Dismissal of Employees an — Industrial Tribunal may order the reinstatement or re-engagement of an unfairly dismissed employee.

A final meaning of the right to work is the right of all citizens to follow their chosen calling or profession without being denied entry by unreasonably restrictions, such as those based on considerations of colour, creed or sex.

rights issue

an issue to the existing shareholders of a company of the right to subscribe for additional shares pro rata to their existing holding. Where a relatively small amount of extra finance in required a rights issue represents an economical way of raising it. Shareholders not wishing to invest more in the company may sell their rights on the market.

rise

increase. Increase in salary.

risk

the likelihood, or the statistical probability, of failure in an enterprise; the essence of being an entrepreneur, and therefore of capitalism. The term is also used for the probability of damage or loss; the essence of insurance.

risk and uncertainty (in financial management)

several distinction have to be made in discussing financial risk and uncertainty. Modern decision theory generally follows the distinction made by F. H. Knight between risk and uncertainty. Risk is said to refer to matters against which one can be protected by applying ordinary insurance principles. That is to say, it applies to situations where the outcome is not certain but the probabilities of the alternative possible outcomes are known or can be accurately estimated by practical experimentation or the use of statistical data. Uncertainty is said to be present where the outcome cannot be predicted even in some probabilistic sense. Risk management is important in each of the three major areas of responsibility for the financial manager, namely Capital Structure, Capital Budgeting and Working Capital.

(i) Capital structure. Risk here derives from the relationship between equity capital and debt finance and is usually called financial risk. It can be viewed in terms of (a) the respective volumes and (b) the income-distribution effect of the two types of funds. Borrowing (which for some purposes includes preference-share issues also) increases the shareholder's risk and uncertainty. It does so by imposing a charge on profits and cash flow that must be met before shareholders become entitled to the residue either in the form of payment of dividends or re-imbursement of capital in the event of liquidation. To the extent that borrowing is used to finance investment, so the variability of profits accruing to ordinary (equity) shareholders is increased by the incursion of interest commitments. Since the average return to all investors in the company is generally expected to exceed the rate of interest payable on the debentures and loans, the expected return to ordinary shareholders must increase to the extent that the firm is debt financed. However, when the rate of profit falls below that of the rate of debt capital, the return to equity holders fall further because of the existence of debt. Thus equity holders gain the possibility of higher incomes but at the cost of greater expected variability of income. Since investors are generally assumed to be averse to risk, the question for financial management is what is the rate of compensation, in terms of increased expected rate of income (or dividends), for given additional amounts of financial risk; much of the discussion of 'gearing' revolves around this question. For both the valuation of investment and the cost of capital issues this is a central question.

(ii) capital budgeting. Risk that is inherent in the cost and revenue structure, and therefore in the profit structure, of a firm is generally referred to as business risk. The task facing the investment analyst is to assess the likelihood of variation in the expected return from a proposed investment and the effect that this may have for the enterprise as a whole. This process can be undertaken by employing→Risk Analysis and the principles of → Portfolio Selection. Whilst the measurement of risk is reasonably straightforward, it is a much greater problem to specify an attitude to risk, i.e. to develop standards by which the acceptability or otherwise of different combinations of expected value and variability of return may be judged.

risk capital

capital such that its remuneration and ultimate repayment depend entirely upon the outcome of a business activity as opposed to being dependent on a contract.

risk free rate of return

the rate of return which may be obtained from an investment in which there is no risk whatsoever, i.e., the return is known with complete certainty.

risk management

the function of planning, organising, directing, and evaluating a comprehensive programme of activities to identify, evaluate and take corrective action against risks that may lead to patient injury, employee injury, and property loss or damage with resulting financial loss or legal liability; all of an organisation's efforts to protect its assets, reputation, and human and physical resources against loss.

risk taking in business

In earlier days, status and prestige in society accrued for the most part to the civil service, to the military and to government officials. The operator in the market place was definitely second class. Also, stability of the society was the desideratum, certainly not change in any disturbing degree. Development, however, does involve, and more than that depends upon economic promotion and management and the changes in society which such activity entails. A development responsibility of the government therefore includes support, recognition, and encouragement of business managers. The significance of this point becomes even more clear when it is remembered that the government's intervention in the economic matters frequently involves the use of public officers in business activity. These specialized officers in economic affairs, like the specialists in science and technology, should receive the status and recognition and compensation due to the importance of their functions in comparison with the administrative class in the civil service.

ritual

automatic activity or behaviour that has a cultural origin in an organisation, society, or sect.

roam

abbr. Return on Assets Managed. An alternative term for return on investment or capital, specifically designed to focus attention on the investment in stock and debtors when evaluating new marketing proposals.

robot

part played by someone in a workplace or organization.

robotics

the study of robots, their design, manufacture and applications.

role

the part or character, taken or played, by a person in a situation or group.

role ambiguity

a situation in which an individual is unclear about the role expected.

role and responsibilities of personnel manager

(a) formulation of personnel policies, plans, programmes, and procedures.

(b) undertaking personnel research for better advice to management.

(c) developing an effective system of recruitment, selection, training, placement, appraisal etc.

(d) establishing effective communication system.

(e) advising management in negotiating with employees.

(f) facilitating the growth of cordial work relationships.

(g) designing schemes of motivation and welfare.

role conflict

situations in which individuals are subjected to stress due to the fact that the performance of their role or roles seems to require incompatible or impossible behaviour.

Role conflict can arise from several source. It may be due to a lack of compatibility between role and personality: individuals are uable or unwilling to perform the role, although wishing to do so, or, at least, to avoid the consequence of not doing so. It may be caused by lack of clarity in the role so that individuals are unable to perform because they do not know what behaviour is expected of them Or the expectations may themselves be conflicting, as in the case of industrial foremen, whose subordinates expect behaviour from them which is incompatible with that expect by their superiors. Again, the demands of different roles may conflict. For example, a young executive seeking to establish himself in his career may be required to work long

hours and to travel frequently on company business, activities which conflict with the behavioural requirements of his roles of husband and father.
Reactions to role conflict will vary with the individual and the situation but may include the rejection of one of the conflicting roles, deception of one of the groups or persons to lead them to believe that their expectations are being fulfilled when in fact they are not, escape from the situation by resignation, transfer or illness, or increasing anxiety and emotional tension.

role learning
learning attempted solely through repetition without any attempt to find order or meaning in the material.

role model
a person after whom an individual will model his/her own performance of a given role.

role of experimentation in operation research
operations research is the application of experimental science to the study of operations. The theory, or model, is generally built up from observed data or experience, although in some cases the model development may depend heavily on external or a prior information. In either event, the theory describing the operation must always be verifiable experimentally.

role overload
an extreme form of role conflict where the number of different roles expected of an individual are simply too great for her to contain.

role playing
acting out a situation, often used as a technique in human relations training.

role relationship
any relationship between two people which is defined by the role play, e.g., boss and subordinate.

role transition
the process of switching from one role to another a process in which socialization is of great importance.

role underload
the opposite of role overload. A situation in which an individual feels that his/her role is not big enough for him/her.

rorschach ink blot test
projective test in which subjects are asked to describe what forms and objects they see in a series of ink blots on paper.

roster or rota
list showing when different members of staff will due certain duties.

rotary printing
printing by plates mounted on a cylinder that rotates against paper. In letter press, separate plates may be mounted on a cylinder. Gravure and offset use a single cylinder plate.

rotate
to do tasks in turns.

rotation
taking turns.

rotogravure
printing by means of a

sensitised copper cylinder on which the image to be reproduced is etched. "Roto" is the familiar abbreviation.

rough
preliminary draft of manuscript or visualisation of graphic.

roundup
story prepared from material derived from various sources.

routine
normal or regular way of doing something.

routing
cutting out a part of a plate or engraving so that it will not print.

rowan system
in this plan if the worker completes his job in less than the standard time the wage payment time saved is calculated as a percentage of the time allowed and the worker is credited with a bonus for the time saved in the same percentage.

royalty
a fee paid to an author or composer on each sale of published work for which he holds the copyright, or to an inventor for the use of an invention for which he holds the patent.

ruckler plan
a group incentive scheme in which all hourly employees are eligible. Precise productivity increase are measured monthly and these gains are shared between employer and employees.

rule
general way of conduct.

rule of thumb
unwritten but accepted operating practice that are considered to be average; practical and generally accepted business practices and principles.

rumour clinic
US information service for employees which corrects false rumours which might be circulating in an organization.

run
to manage or to organize.

running cost
the recurrent cost of operating a particular activity. It is to be contrasted with capital cost. The running costs of a factory include raw materials, wages, fuel, light and heat, etc.

running number
consecutive numbers entered on each of a series of questionnaires, for identification and control purposes.

rural market potential
marketing in India has been essentially urban–based since it has been assumed that the buying power exists only in the urban areas. The rural sector has largely been neglected. But companies, both private and public have now realised the potential that exists in the rural markets and have started a move towards tapping this vast market.

rural market potential
marketing in India has been essentially urban-based since it has been assumed that the buying power exists only in the

urban. The rural sector has largely been neglected. But companies both private and public have now realised the potential that exists in the rural market and have started a move towards tapping this vast market.

rush
copy to be handled quickly is so marked.

sabbatical
paid or unpaid time off, for the purposes of research or study or travel.

sack
to get the sack=to be dismissed from a job. To dismiss someone from a job.

sacking
dismissal from a job.

saddle stitching
the binding of a publication or booklet by means of wire staples through the centre fold. This method of binding permits the pages to lie flat when opened.

s.a.e.
stamped addressed envelope.

safety
freedom from danger or risk.

salaried staff
employees who receive regular fixed payments, as opposed to those who are paid for the time worked, or the tasks completed.

salary
regular payment for work done, made to an employee usually as a cheque at the end of each month; amount paid to an employee, shown as a monthly, quarterly or yearly total.

salary structure
the arrangement of pay within an organization such that different grades of employees doing different jobs will receive different rates. These rates would be based (originally) on the process of job analysis and job evaluation increment of pay.

sale and leaseback
a single business transaction in which a piece of equipment or machinery is sold to an individual or business, which then lease it back to the original owner.

sale of good
a contract for the sale of good is contract whereby the property in goods is transferred by the seller to the buyer for a money consideration, called the price. These contracts are governed in the UK by the Sale of Goods Act 1979.

It is important to ascertain when the property in goods passes from the seller to the buyer, since the risk of loss or damage passes with the property. The Act states that the property passes at such time as the parties want it to pass and certain rules are laid down to indicate the position where the parties have not clearly expressed their intention (Romalpa Clauses). The parties may attach certain terms to the contract; if these terms are vital to the very existence of the contract they are known as conditions, while if they are merely subordinate terms they are called warranties. Both conditions and warranties may be either expressly stated in the contract or may be implied into the contract by law. A breach of a condition entitles the buyer to treat the contract as discharged and to claim damages, while a breach of warranty entitles the buyer to damages only.

Where goods are sold by description there exists an implied condition that the goods supplied will correspond to the description and that they will be of merchantable quality. Where the buyer has indicated to a seller, who is selling goods in the course of a business, the particular purpose for which the goods are being bought, there is an implied condition that the goods supplied will be reasonably fir for this purpose, except where it can be show that the buyer did not rely on the seller's skill and judgement in advising him. Two further implied terms in the Act state that the seller shall transfer a good title to the goods, and that the bulk of goods sold by sample will match that sample. Breach of these terms entitles the buyer to the return of any money paid and a release from their own obligations under the contract, plus a claim for damage if appropriate.

The protection granted to the buyer has been substantially increased by the Unfair Contract Terms Act 1977. This Act restricts the ability of a seller to exclude or limit their liability under a contract for the sale of goods for breach of implied conditions and warranties. In the case of a consumer sale any clause in a contract for the sale of goods exempting the seller from liability for breach of the above conditions and warranties is to be treated as void and any attempt at exemption is a criminal offence. Where the sale is between two business the exclusion of the implied terms is possible if the exclusion clause in the contract is deemed to be reasonable one in the circumstances.

sale on return

goods supplied on the basis that if they are not sold or used they may be returned to the supplier. If a business acquires goods on sale or return, it does not undertake the risk that it will not be able to find customers for the goods. In accounting for such an item the company supplying the goods should treat them as stock at cost until the sale is confirmed. The profit on them does not, therefore, figure in its profit and loss account until that time.

sales

money received for selling something or number of items sold.

sales account

that account in a double entry system in which is recorded the amount of the sales of business. Its function is to collect together all such items for an accounting period at the end of which the total is transferred to the trading account.

sales analysis
study of company sales records to determine what customers are buying—what models, what sizes and so on.

salesclerk
person who sells goods to customers in a store.

sales cost
the cost of making sales, i.e., including the cost of physical distribution, transport, storage, advertising, sales personnel, administration, etc.

sales coverage
the relationship between the number of prospective customers in a territory and the number that can be effectively called upon by the salesman at an optimum call frequently.

sales girl
girl who sells goods to customers in a store.

sales journal
a book of prime entry in which is recorded the sales made by a business on the day-to-day basis.

saleslady
woman who sells good to customers in a store.

sales ledger
a portion of the ledger containing all the accounts of persons to whom sales on credit have been made.

salesman
man who sells an organization's product or services to customers.

sales management
supervision and organisation of selling, and coordinating selling with other functions of the business.

salesmanship
it is a virtue that brings potential buyer into contact with a seller in such a way as to affect the transfer of goods. It is an art of creating demand for goods, which one has to sell. Salesmanship performs the function of feedback from consumer to manufacturer. It minimises the gap between the products and the consumer. Salesmanship is the science and art of selling your point of view, starting with the other man's viewpoint and leading his mind to the point where he will accept the goods. Salesmanship involves winning the buyer's confidence and make him permanent customer. It is a face to face persuasive communication between a seller and prospective buyer. Salesmanship is advantageous to both the seller and the consumer. The sellers gain as their sales increase and the buyers benefit through expert advice in regard to choice of goods. The salesman helps the consumers by explaining to them the various attributes and uses of the product. He also helps the dealers by giving them timely information regarding market conditions.

sales mix

the proportion of total sales which each of the range of products bears to the whole. The significance of the sales mix is that some products are likely to produce a larger gross profit than others.

sales planning
devising the strategy and means of accomplishing the overall sales objective, to include the establishment of standards of sales performance, control of aggregate and individual achievement and expense.

sales policy
the defined sales objective of any organisation and its means of accomplishment, supplying the basic framework within long-range forecasts are made and the day-to-day sales operation is conducted.

sales potential
estimated total market for any class of production or service.

sales promotion
certain promotional activities of manufacturers and wholesalers that complete personal selling and advertising. Consumer sales promotion includes consumer contests, premiums, sampling and types of consumer public relations. Dealer and distributor sales promotion includes stimulating dealers and distributors, and providing them with management aids, advertising assistance, display materials, traffic stimulation, and sales training.

sales quota
a sales goal assigned to a salesman, or the sales branches or department of a company, for use in the management of sales efforts.

sales returns
goods sold to a customer and then accepted back. This may be because they are damaged or because the customer has been permitted to cancel the sale as a gesture of goodwill. Sales returns are accounted for as a reduction to sales.

sales returns journal
the book of prime entry in which are recorded the sales returns as they occur.

sales tax
a fee that is payable to a state government and is collected by retailers as a percentage of sales made.

sales turnover
the rate at which stocks of the goods are sold and replaced in the organisation's inventory per annum. Since investment in inventory represents the working capital tied up, the smaller the total inventory and the faster the turnover, the greater will be utilisation of working capital.

saleswoman
woman in a ship who sells goods to customers.

salvage
a person who rescues abandoned property, for example, by taking in tow a vessel which has been left unattended in a storm, is entitled to some fraction of the value saved as a payment for

the service even though not explicitly contracted to give it.

sample
a selected and representative part of a group of units (the population or universe).

sample design composition
the plan made for the sample composition together with the procedures followed for selecting the sample.

sample size
the number of members of a sample.

sample survey
survey carried out on a sample of the universe, the results of which are regarded as applying to the universe.

sampling
the process of selecting, usually at random, a finite number from a large group or population, on the assumption that the selected group may be regarded as representing, for a particular purpose, the whole group.

sampling error
inaccuracy due to the fact that a sample may not be perfectly representative of a population, i.e., due to the fact that only a sample of values is observed.

sampling frame
a specification of the information available relating to the population to be studied, in sufficient detail so as to make possible the location of particular units, should they be selected for the sample drawn.

sanction
permission.

sandwich course
course of study where students at a college or institute spend a period of time working in a factory or office as part of their course.

sandwitch lease
a transaction in which a person or organisation leases property and then sublets it for more money; this is often done in leasing an office building and renting out office space in it to others.

satisfaction
feeling of being happy or good feeling of happiness and contentment.

satisficing
adopting a policy of achieving satisfactory results without necessarily achieving the best which might be possible.

satisfy
to give satisfaction or to please. To fill (the requirements for a job, etc.).

satisfying
adopting a course that is merely "good enough" from all viewprints, rather than seeking the best possible course (term used by Herbert A. Simon).

saturation
the point at which further penetration of a market is impossible or excessively costly.

saturation point
level at which any further expansion of distribution in a market is unlikely to be achieved and where further sales are restricted to the potential arising from replacement needs or

population growth.

savings-account loan
a loan secured by funds on deposit in the same financial institution.

scab
informal & pejorative worker who goes on working when there is a strike.

scalar chain
the chain of command.

scalar
working according to a scale.

scale
system which is graded into various levels.

scam
a fraudulent activity usually such that a relatively small amount of money is obtained from a large number of people.

scanlon plan
a group incentive scheme whereby employees and employers agree to a standard labour cost on a per unit basis.

scanning
the act of examining point by point. Generally the term is used to describe paid reading for a specific purpose.

schedule
a time sequence or the accomplishment of specified work.

schedule planning
planning concerns scheduling which is affixing time value to each needed activity and to the total project. Scheduling gives vitality and a practical meaning to a plan.

scheduling
the determination of times in the future when specified tasks should be completed.

scheme
plan or arrangement or way of working.

scheme of arrangement
an agreement between a company and its creditors which will allow an insolvent business to continue.

schever system
a German production planning and control system involving the use of specialised wall chart and direct telephone communication between factory operators and production control staff.

school leaver
person who has left school and has not yet found a job.

scholl of management theory
Frank P. Carracciolo has specified 6 main classes of management theory:
(i) the process school According to this school, management means (a) analysing processes, (b) establishing conceptual framework of process and (c) identifying principles underlying the process.
(ii) the empirical school. This school believes that by analysing the experience of successful managers or the mistakes of unsuccessful managers, management can learn about applying the most effective techniques. The school recommends case study approach for drawing general conclusions and enumerating principles.
(iii) the human behaviour school. The exponents of this

school of thought suggest the application of existing and newly developed theories, methods and techniques of the relevant social science to the study of human relations from personal dynamics or cultural heritage. This school puts more emphasis on motivation of the individual and on human psychology and sociology.

(iv) the social system school. The theory was founded by Chester Barnard who went into the cooperative, biological, physical and social aspects of the individual's environments. His theory emphasis formal organisation concept which consists of a cooperative system in which individuals not only communicate with each other but are also willing to contribute action towards a conscious common purpose. It is under this theory that managements are said to perform highly effective functions in socialist societies, where workers are motivated by a determination to show result and are fired with the zeal to achieve common purpose.

(v) the decisional school. This school emphases on rational approach to decision-making through the selection of a course of action from various possible alternatives. The theory can be expanded to examine the nature of organisation, structure, psychological and social reactions of individuals, and groups in order to provide the bases for decisions and value judgements.

(vi) the mathematical school. According to the exponents of this school, mathematicians provide the people in management the means of seeing many problems more clearly, the need for establishing goals and measures of effectiveness. They are helpful in getting people to view the management area as a logical system of relationships and enable the management to review and recognise information systems, so that mathematics can be given sensible quantitative meaning.

scientific management
school of management which believes in the rational use of resources in order to maximize profits.

scoop
a story which is the exclusive property of one newspaper, possession of which means victory over competitors.

score
credit or value given to a specific response to a test item. Sum of the credits obtained on all the items of a single test.

score-keeping
the process of data accumulation or record-keeping which enables interested parties (internal and external) to ascertain how the organisation is performing.

scrap
unwanted material emanating from an industrial process. Scrap may sometimes be sold

for use by someone else but may sometimes involve a cost in its disposal.

screen
two plate glass pieces cemented together with specific fine lines drawn at specific distances in a square. The screen breaks the original into tiny dots according to its tonal values.

screening
examining candidates to see if they are suitable for a job.

screen pattern
the final result in printing tri-colour blocks where the screen is kept at one angle for all the colours. This is also known as the 'Moire' effect.

scrip dividend
a dividend given in the form of extra shares instead of cash. It thus represents a capitalisation of part of the profit and loss account. A scrip dividend is often offered as an alternative to cash at the option of individual shareholders.

scripophily
the activity of collecting share and stock certificates for their inherent interest or attractiveness rather than out of any concern for their underlying investment value.

script
a face of type that resembles handwriting. Also in broadcasting, the written material used to produce programme or commercial.

search
looking for new managers for organizations usually by approaching managers in their existing jobs and asking them if they want to work for another company.

search problems
these problems were first identified during the war when tactics for searching the oceans for hostile submarines were developed. An oil company faces similar problems in searching an area of desert for oil deposits. In both cases with the resources available (aircraft or money) a decision must be made on what search tactics to use. A large area can be searched quickly, thereby increasing the chances of passing over a submarine, say, but reducing the chances of spotting it should the searcher pass over it. Alternatively a smaller area can be searched slowly, thereby reducing the chanced of passing over a submarine, but increasing the chances of spotting it should the searcher pass over it. Probability theory and statistical analysis have been applied to this problem to determine the optimum search policy.
Account auditing is a similar type of search problem and these techniques have been applied to a very limited extent to auditing in large organizations.

season
one of four parts in which a year is divided into (spring, summer, autumn, winter). A period of time when something usually takes place.

seasonal
which lasts for a season or which only happens during a particular season.

seasonality
seasonally adjusted figures=statistics which are adjusted to take account of seasonal variations.

seasonal unemployment
a form of unemployment that peaks at certain times of the year due to the nature of the industry in question, e.g., construction or tourism.

season ticket
a pass giving unlimited access to some service for a specified period of time. A person undertaking a daily rail journey, for example, may acquire a season ticket which entitles him or her to travel the journey as many times as wished during the period of currency of the ticket as opposed to purchasing a fresh ticket for every journey.

second
to lend a member of staff to another organization for a fixed period of time.

secondary
second in importance.

secondary data
data maintained by an organisation for use in its normal course of operations, and which can be used for evaluative purposes; evaluation data which already exist prior to the initiation of an evaluation study.

secondary stock
shares in a company which is smaller or less actively than the giants of the stock market.

second class
an inferior and, therefore, cheaper service. Letter sent by second-class mail, for example, cost less to send but are likely to take longer in transit.

second day story
a follow-up story based on one that has already appeared. This type of story also carries a second-day head, conveying the hint that it records not a fresh event but developments.

second generation
computers which use transistors and magnetic cores. Generally faster than first generation machines.

secondment
being seconded to another job for a period.

second mortgage
a mortgage on a property which is already the subject of a mortgage. Provided that the value of the property is sufficient it may provide security in this way for more than one loan.

secretary
person who helps to organize work or types letters or files documents or arranges meeting, etc. for someone.

secretarial
referring to the work of a secretary.

secret reserve
a reserve which does not appear on the face of the balance sheet. It is made by writing down assets to below their true value.

secure
safe or which cannot change.

securities and exchange board of India (SEBI)
an official body having the responsibility of overseeing the operation of the stock exchange in the country.

security
job security = being able to rely on a steady job and the income which comes from it.

seed money
the initial financing needed to start a project which is to be supplemented with larger, more permanent funding at a later date.

segment
a distinguishable portion of a whole. Thus a segment of a business's activity will be one which can be clearly identified and for which figures can be prepared.

segue (pronounced say-gway)
an uninterrupted transition, as when one scene moves directly into another in a motion picture.

select
to choose.

selection
choosing among the candidates for a job opening.

selection of personnel
selection means making a choice by preference. This choice by preferences is based on comparison between two factors: (i) what the job requires for successful execution, and (ii) what the applicant has to offer. For the most part, the better the balance between these two factors, the better the selection work and the more likely the attainment of a satisfactory working force—George Terry.

selective attention
singling out particular objects from among many for concentration of the mind.

selective dissemination of information system (SDI)
dissemination of information to meet the specific individual needs of research and development staff.

selective distribution policy
the policy of selling only to dealers and distributors who meet the seller's requirements such as size of orders, volume of purchases, profitability, or area or type of distribution.

selective reinforcement
tendency to pick out many ideas or messages that concern an opinion or attitude already held.

self-administering test
test in which instructions are so complete that a person can give the test to himself.

self-appraisal or self-assessment
a person's own assessment of his or her capabilities and character.

self-confidence
feeling confident in your own ability.

self-confident
(person) who is confident in his or her own ability.

self-cover
printed matter in booklet form without a protective cover.

self-employed
working for yourself or not on

the payroll of a company.

self enrichment

it is a virtue which can be achieved through self-disclosure and group feedback, sensitivity analysis tests, management effectiveness seminars, self-analysis etc. If a manager adopts the following five steps to maturity, he could successfully operate in an organization; self-examination; self-expectation; self-realisation power; self-education; and broadened perception.

self-evaluation

in management self-enrichment can be achieved through self-disclosure and group feedback, sensitivity analysis tests, management effectiveness seminars, self-analysis etc. If a manager adopts the following five steps to maturity, he could successfully operate in an organisation:

(1) self-examination.
(2) self-expectation.
(3) self-realisation power.
(4) self-deduction.
(5) broadened perception.

The answer to the various questions we ask ourselves in the above areas will disclose the extent to which we differ from others.

self-image

idea that a person has about his or her own character and abilities.

self-instruction

teaching oneself.

self-insurance

the consequence of a decision that it is more economic to stand the risk of a loss than it is to pay a premium to an insurer to take it.

self-made man or woman

person who is rich and successful because of his own work, not because he inherited money or position.

self-mailer

printed folder prepared for mailing without an envelope.

self-regulation

the process whereby in industry imposes upon itself codes of practice and other rules of conduct and polices them. It is an alternative to regulation by statute.

self-selected group

a group which is selected by virtue of their common response to some stimulus or their possession of some common identifying characteristic, e.g., those who respond to a mail questionnaire.

self-service store

retail outlet in which the customer is free to select goods from open displays, without the assistance of sales personnel.

self-starter

person who can be relied on to take the initiative in a new situation without asking for instructions.

seller's market

a market situation in which sellers have more power to influence prices and conditions of sale than buyers, usually because demand exceeds supply. Always contrasted with buyer's market.

selling

the personal or impersonal process of assisting and or persuading prospective customers to buy a commodity or a service, or to act favourably upon an idea that has commercial significance to the seller. (This definition includes the combined activities of personal selling and (promotion).

semantics jungle

when intelligent men argue about basic problems, some of the trouble lies in the meaning of key words. The semantics problem is particularly severe in the field of management. There is even difference in the meaning of the word "management". Most people would agree that it means getting things done through and with people, but is it people in formal organisations, or in all group activities? Is it governing, leading, or teaching? The greatest single semantics confusion lies in the word "organisation". Most members of the management process school use it to define the activity-authority structure of an enterprise and that they are "organising" when they establish a framework of activity groupings and authority relationships.

semi-

half.

semi-skilled

worker who have had some training.

seminar

teaching of a small class of advanced students.

senior

older; in a higher rank; (worker) who has been employed longer than another.

seniority

being of higher rank; being an employee of the company longer.

senior management

the term applied to managers who are relatively high in the hierarchy of an organization because they are senior in level of responsibility and authority and often in age as well.

sensation

impression received by the sense organs.

sensitivity analysis

an analysis of the components of a budget with a view to discovering which of forecasts on which it is based are most critical.

sensitivity training

a form of training for managers which is designed to make them more sensitive to their effect on others. Conducted by the conference method.

sensory deprivation

a situation in which people are deprived of the usual stimulation their senses encounter in daily life. Apparently when people are isolated from sensory stimulation as far as possible in a laboratory they quickly become bored and start to hallucinate. It may be that when we have nothing in our environment for our brains to work on and make sense of, we feel a need to provide our sensations and make sense out of nothing. Something similar seems to happen in particularly monotonous and boring jobs.

sentence completion test
projective test in which subjects are asked to fill in the blanks in sentences or phrases.

sentiment
instinct and feeling. The sentiments of those involved in a market will often have a big influence on prices particularly in the absence of any objective information.

separation
leaving a job (resigning, retiring or being fired or made redundant).

sequential sampling
a variant of activity sampling requiring continuous assessment of the observations instead of assessment after all observations are completed; observations continue to be taken and assessed until a predetermined accuracy level: has been reached.

sequestrate
to take and keep (property), because a court has ordered it.

sequestration
taking and keeping of property on the order of a court, especially seizing property from someone, who is in contempt of court.

sequestrator
person who takes and keeps property on the order of a court.

serial bonds
bonds of the same issue, put out at the same time, that have varying dates of maturity, so that the entire debt does not fall due at once. Usually, the groups of bonds carrying the longest term (in years) pays a higher rate of interest than bonds with shorter terms.

series bonds
group of bonds put out at different times with different cash-in dates, but all belonging to the same financial package; often, a complex mortgage.

serifs
small decorative lines on letters at the ends of elements. The most distinguished feature of some faces. The lines, or "flares", at the ends of the elements in the individual letters of the text and display type used in books are properly called serifs.

service activities
staff may perform service activities by carrying out specified work for the line. For example the personnel department may recruit, select and employ people for the line and other staff departments. The purchasing department may buy materials and supplies for the line. Finance may install accounting, budgetary and reporting system for the line organization.

service charge
a charge added by such establishments as hotels and restaurants to the total bill as an amount to be distributed to

staff. It takes the place of a gratuity and removes the voluntary element from the process of recognition by a customer of good service.

service of finance

the payment of interest on loans and dividends on shares. Such payments are required to be identified on a cash flow statement.

service sector

that sector of a mixed economy which is concerned not with the conversion of raw materials or the production of goods but with providing a service, such as advertising, education, health or transport.

services

activities or intangible accommodations, sold as such to consumers or businesses, or provided in connection with the sale of goods. (Examples of consumer services are hotel operations, laundry operations, charge account credit, free store purchase delivery. Examples of business service enterprises are mercantile agencies, advertising agencies, marketing research agencies, freight forwarders.)

servomechanism

a system that has control over another system. Feedback from the system under control enables the servomechanism to regulate its input so that a constant output is maintained. Athermostat is the usual example given of servomechanism but homeostasis in the body can also be seen in this way.

session

meeting or period when a group of people meets.

settle

to solve a problem or dispute.

settlement

solution to a problem or dispute.

settlor

one who creates a trust, other than by means of a will, for the benefit of named persons.

set up dominant system

in this system if the original set-up is correct, output will be standard.

seven' point plan

list of items used in assessing the potential of job candidates.

severance pay

money paid as compensation to an employee who loses his job through no fault of his own.

severe disability allowance

a social security benefit paid to persons who suffer from a severely disabling condition.

sex

one of two groups (male and female) into which people can be divided.

shake out

complete change, where weak or inefficient people or companies are removed.

share

one of many parts into which a company's capital is divided.

share account

a type of account offered by a credit union that is similar to the time-and-savings accounts offered by commercial banks and thrift institution.

share capital
the part of a company's financing which is represented by the total nominal value of the shares which it has issued.

shareholders' equity
that which remains of company's value after all prior claims against its assets have been met. The balance sheet value of shareholder' equity is the total value of share capital and reserves.

share premium account
a statutory capital reserve required where a company issues shares at a price in excess of their nominal value.

share shop
an establishment to which members of the public may go for the trouble free buying and selling of shares.

sheet
time sheet = paper showing when a worker starts work and when he leaves work in the evening.

shelf life
one unit of stock in a profit-making corporation.

shelter books
magazines that feature home furnishings.

shift
group of workers who work for a period, and then are replaced by another group.

shift work
the process of dividing the whole 24-hour day into work periods often of eight hours each, e.g., midnight 8.00 a.m. to 4.00 p.m. Shift work is used to obtain maximum use of plant in manufacturing or of the workforce in the service sector especially that part of it which includes the emergency services where continuous cover is required.

shipping charges
the cost of transportation expense for delivery of products from seller to buyers.

shop
place where goods are stored and sold.

shop, closed
an arrangement, embodied in a union agreement, under which the employer can hire only people who are already members of the union for jobs within the bargaining unit.

shop floor
place where goods are manufactured.

shoping list test
projective test in which subjects are asked to describe the character and possible behaviour of the individual who would purchase the assortment of items shown on a list.

shop, open
a shop in which it is not necessary for anyone to be a union member in order to get or keep employment.

shop steward
elected trade union official who represents workers in day-to-day negotiations with the management.

shop union
a union contract arrangement under which the employer may hire people who are not members of the union for jobs

in the bargaining unit, but they must all join the union after a certain length of time, for example, after a sixty-day probationary period.

short
for a small period of time.

shortage
lack or not having enough.

short-term planning
the projection of a plan for the next one to three years; usually a moving plan which is reviewed and revised quarterly for the first future year and half-yearly for the second and third future years.

shorthanded
without enough staff.

shortlist
list of some of the better people who have applied for a job, who can be asked to come for a test or an interview.

short-range
short-range forecast = forecast which covers a period of a few months.

short staffed
with not enough staff.

short term
for a short period in the future.

short time
reduced working hours.

short time working
a situation in which a workplace is forced to work a reduced working week because of shortage of orders. This is seen as a temporary measure to cut labour costs while retaining the workforce intact.

shoulder of type
the part of the type unit that projects horizontally above or below the ends of the character cast upon it. The shoulder does not print.

show of hands
vote where people show by raising their hands which way they have voted.

shut
closed or not open.

shut down
to shut down a factory. Shut down .

shut out
locking of the door of a factory or office to stop the staff getting in.

sibilant sound
a hissing speech sound. The sibilants in English are S, Z, SH, ZH and CH.

sick
ill or not well.

sickness
being ill.

sickness benefit
a social security benefit payable to those who are prevented by illness from working.

sick pay
pay given to workers who are off work for reasons of illness or injury. As well as statutory provisions there are many occupational schemes and these are sometimes regarded as a fringe benefit of a job.

side
on the side = separate from your normal work, and hidden from your employer.

sidebar
a secondary story that accompanies a main news story or feature article, sometimes in a box set into the larger

story.

sideline

business which is extra to your normal work.

side stitching

in binding a magazine or booklet, a method of stitching through the edges of the folded pages from front to back. The pages will lie flat when opened.

sight approach

the method of teaching children to read by recognising word wholes by sight, as contrasted to the phonetic method by which words are analysed into sound parts.

sight word

a word that is memorised as a whole.

sign

to write your name in a special way on a document to show that you have written it or approved it.

signature

1. The formalised construction of a company's name as it appears on stationery, advertisements, and other printed material. Often used interchangeably with logotype.
2. A printed sheet containing 4, 8, 12, 16, 32 pages, folded into one unit and forming a portion of a book or pamphlet.

significant influence

the influence by a company over the activities of another company which thereby fails to be treated as an associated company. It is defined as being participation in the financial and operating policies of the company without necessarily having full control of them.

sign on

to start work, by signing your name on a contract of employment. To give someone a job by offering a signed contract of employment.

silk screen

a method of printing based on the stencil principle. Ink is squeezed through a cloth screen that has the design to be printed imposed upon it in reverse.

silver circle rate

system whereby pay increases are based on length of service.

simo chart (simultaneous motion cycle chart)

a simo chart is used to record the co-ordinated movements of the limbs of one or more workers, the movement being described in terms of fundamental motions on a common time-scale.

The simo chart is used under similar conditions as the two-handed process chart (process charts), but normally results from the analysis of a motion film, and utilizes→ Therbligs to describe the movements taking place. Because of the detailed analysis possible from frame-by-frame examination of a film and the detailed description of the therbligs, simo charts are associated with micromotion study and represent one of the most detailed recording technique available in → Method Study.

simplex method

a system of linear programming

that makes solutions possible in algebraic equations where there are more unknowns than equations.

simulation

a technique by means of which models representing real systems may be constructed, for the purpose of analysis and measurement. The most powerful means of simulation now are by use of analogue computers, but simulation is also possible without mechanical aids.

simulcast

simultaneous transmission over television and radio.

sinecure

job which is well-paid but involves very little work.

sinistral

left-handed and left-eyed.

sinking fund

money or other assets put aside for a special purpose, such as to pay off bonds as they become due or to replace worn-out or outdated machinery or buildings.

sit down

strike where the workers stay in their place of work and refuse to work or to leave.

situation

job; situation vacant-section of a newspaper where jobs are advertised; situation wanted = section of a newspaper where workers advertise for jobs or offer services.

sizing

this is a process in paper manufacture where resinous substance is added to the pulp or a coating of resinous substance is given to the paper after it is made. The size holds the fibres together and makes the paper resistant to the penetration of water or ink.

skeleton staff

few staff left to carry on essential work while most of the workforce is away.

skill

ability to do something because of training.

skilled

having learnt certain skills.

skyline

headline across top page over name plate. Also calls over title and over the roof.

slack

lazy or no busy.

slackenoff

to become less busy.

slackness

being lazy.

slant

emphasis given in a story or programme.

slide film (or filmstrip)

a continuous strip of film in which the frames are presented in a fixed sequence, but not simulating motion. Usually accompanied by a recorded sound track that is synchronised with succession of the film frames.

slides

individual film frames that are projected onto a screen to serve as visual accompaniment to an oral presentation.

sliding

which rises in steps.

slow

to go slow = to protest against management by working slowly.

slow down

to stop rising or moving or falling.

slug lines

words placed at the upper left of a story to identify the story during typesetting and make-up of a publication.

small business

a private venture that is limited in its number of employees or sales volume.

small claims court

a special court which handles small cases involving a legislatively amount of money.

small newspapers

a newspaper having a circulation of up to 15,000 copies per day publishes.

social

referring to society in general.

social accounting

a particular concern with the social aspects of a cost benefit analysis.

social class

a major social group, the members of which occupy similar economic status, occupational rank, etc., characterised by a consciousness of class membership.

social control

the control that a group or culture or society exerts upon the individuals who comprise it. This control stems from the process of socialization and is established as conformity pressures towards social norms.

social deviant

one who is willing to go contrary to the mores of those surrounding him.

social distance

the degree of stiffness or formality in a social relationship. Such formality is a recognition of a difference in status between the persons concerned as, for example, between members of different social classes or between superior and subordinate in formal organization. Social distance in superior/subordinate relationships is associated with the use of authority. It is, therefore, particularly a feature of authoritarian organizations, and is commonly manifest in formal rules constraining social interaction: army officers may be forbidden to fraternize with other ranks, the captain of a civil aircraft may be required to stay overnight at a different hotel from that used by crew members. Social distance does not necessarily imply any hostility in the relationship; on the contrary, where the status difference is fully accepted by both persons, the maintenance of social distance will be regarded with mutual satisfaction. However, the existence of social distance militates against the development of free communication between the persons concerned.

social ethic

term used by William H. Whyte. Jr., in The Organisation Man to mean the concept that man is primarily a group member and should subordinate his individuality to the group mores. Used in contradistinction to Weber's Protestant ethic, which emphases individualism.

social insurance

a mechanism for pooling risks by transferring them to an organisation (usually governmental) that is required by law to provide indemnity (cash) or service benefits to or on behalf of covered persons for certain losses.

socialization

the process whereby an individual becomes a social being. Although it is a lifetime process it is particularly important in childhood when society is represented by (and through) a child, parents and the rest of her family.

socially responsible policies and programmes

how can a management group that is sensitive to the changing business environment decide what socially responsible policies and programmes are feasible for their business to adopt? And, whatever policies and programmes may be adopted, how can managers assure their effective and efficient implementation? A chief executive officer who develops on his own initiative an intellectual posture favouring socially responsible performance by his company needs positive support from his board for both the general concept and specific policies and programmes. Alternatively, of course, the initiative may come from within the board. Either way the emerging social pressure favours some kind of representation or the board that might be described as a trustship for the public interest.

social norm

behaviour that is expected of all the members of a society. The norm of social behaviour is therefore one way of defining social normality.

social overheads

municipal services, such as water supplies and public transportation.

social responsibilities, management

management's responsibilities to those other than the owners, e.g., to employees, the local community, or even the national or international economy.

social responsibility of business

awareness and acceptance throughout the free enterprise world, that companies, as well as public corporations, have responsibilities towards parties other than their owners. They owe a duty not merely to shareholders or to the state in case of public corporation—but to their employees, customers, suppliers and the community at large.

social sciences
those branches of learning concerned with the study of man and society. The precise delineation of the boundaries of academic disciplines is not possible but by convention the social sciences are held to include economics, political science, psychology, social psychology, social anthropology and sociology. The claim to scientific status, less disputed now than formerly, rests on the fact that each discipline involves the collation and analysis of data derived from a systematic observation of phenomena or controlled experimentation, and the formulation and constant refinement of general principles.

The subject matter of the different disciplines overlaps and each is distinguished mainly by the nature of the concepts it employs and only partly by the range of phenomena studies. The nature of Economics and Psychology, including social psychology, is discussed in separate entries. Political science is concerned with the forms of power in society, the various bases of power, the manner in which power is exercised institutionally and the ordering of power relationships. The study has increasingly developed an empirical basis and as such has virtually become a branch of sociology (political sociology). Social anthropology, as distinct from physical anthropology, studies approximately the same range of phenomena as sociology but has tended to concentrate on small tribal or village communities in pre-industrial societies and to make almost exclusive use of direct observation and questioning as research techniques.

Sociology seeks to study all those aspects of human behaviour that are socially determined. Including within its focus society as a whole, it necessarily embraces the subject matter of each of the other disciplines discussed above, as well as those features of society that have not yet become the subject of specialist concern. Central to the sociological approach is the concept of the Social System: a complex of interrelated parts. At the societal level the most basic of these parts are social Institutions, which arise in response to the need to regulate the means to satisfy fundamental human requirements. Thus sociologists study the culture and institutions of specific societies, the structure and processes of the organizations to which the institutions give rise and the nature of the relationships between institutions. Such a study encompasses an enormous range of phenomena and it is not surprising that, in common with other sciences, sociology has been subject to a considerable degree of division into specialisms. Such subdivisions tend to follow, in the first place, the main social institutions; there are thus sociologists specializing in the study of the family, education, work and industry, government, science, religion, etc. All these areas, and many more, have received attention from social scientists other than sociologists. What characterizes the sociological approach is that each area is studied in terms of its relationship to other areas in the total system. For example the industrial sociologist will study not only the structure and functioning of specific industrial organizations with a view to formulating and testing of general principles, but also the relationship between various features of industrial organizations and relevant aspects of the wider society, such as the educational system, social class and social status, and societal values.

social status

the position an individual holds within society and the prestige attaching thereto.

social values

in practice a manager often finds himself working with several means and chains. He is trying to choose a course of action that will contribute to several objectives and there will be a mean-end chain for each. Stable employment growth, short-term profit, low risk control are examples of internal objectives.

society and management

no modern management can function for long in isolation and in disregard to the society in which it exists. Management holds itself accountable for the quality of life of the society. It has an obligation to be a real part of the society, not merely in its industrial life but in the other spheres of its life also. Management must develop a deeper commitment to, involvement in, and engagement in the attack on pressing social problems beyond its normal economic activities.

socio-economic

referring to social and economic conditions.

sociology

science of the origin and evolution of society.

socio-technic system

system that studies the interaction of people and machines, in order to improve efficiency.

soft and hard criteria

two types of criteria are used to measure the improvements: (i) soft, and (ii) hard. Soft criteria includes leadership style, enthusiasm of manager, employee satisfaction, harmonious relationships and term spirit. To measure soft criteria observations, personal interviews and prepared formats are used. The latter are printed forms which when filled out supply data to reveal the characteristics of the organization.

soft sell

indirect, subtle effort to persuade without over presentation of arguments on the issue. Motivation by indirect techniques.

software

computer services except hardware and accessories, such as computer programmes, training, and other services in a computer installation.

solemn

solemn and binding agreement = agreement which is not legally binding, but which all parties are supposed to obey.

solidarity

loyalty of members of a group to each other.

solid state

the technology concerned with solid materials that can change or mould the character of an electrical value without the use of moving parts or straight mognetic principles. Solid-sate parts, e.g., transistors produce effects through phenomena taking place within or at the junction of solid materials.

solution

answer to a problem.

solve

to solve a problem = to find an answer to a problem.

solvency

solvency means the capacity or ability of the business to meet its short-term and long-term obligations. The capacity to pay off the current debts of the company is represented by the liquidity ratio. The long-term solvency ratios enable shareholders, debenture-holders and other long-term creditors like financial institutions to analyse the capital structure of the company. They indicate the pattern of financing, whether long-term requirements have been met out of long-term funds or not.

somatic

having to do with the body. The "opposite" of psychogenetic.

sour

to make things become unpleasant.

source

place where something comes from.

spaces

these are pieces of metal blanks. They are lower in height than the types. Hence they do not print. They are used to separate the world in a line, producing white space. They are cast to different thickness. They are sub-divisions of an em.

span of attention

number of letters, parts of words, or words that can be identified at one fixation.

span of control

number of subordinates which a person supervises or administers at the workplace.

span of supervision

it is a step in supervision which is designed to determine the number of subordinates who should report directly to each executive. Narrower the span, taller would be the structure with several levels of management.

spare

extra or not being used.

speaking vocabulary

words that are used and understood in conversation.

specialist

person who deals with one particular type of skill or product or area of study.

specialization or US specialism

study of one particular subject or concentration on one particular type of work.

specialize

to deal with one particular type of skill or product or service.

specialized staff

in contrast to personal staff the specialized staff advises and serves all line and other staff departments in a functional capacity. For instance the staff finance department reporting to the chief executive is available not only to advise and serve him but also to serve other departments that need help in financial matters. The specialized staff thus becomes a reservoir of special knowledge, skills and experience which the entire organization can use.

specification

detailed information about what is needed or about a product to be supplied.

specify

to state clearly what is needed.

speech

speech sounds are produced by the expulsion of air from the lungs past the larynx, which provides the basic sound-producing process, phonation. This primary sound tone is then modulated by means of the vocal organs in the throat, month and nose to produce a wide range of possible speech sounds. The comparatively small number of different symbols used in the written form of a language gives a misleading impression of simplicity compared with the rich variety of the spoken word. Individual speakers exhibit different characteristics in their speech habits. Some of the most important of these characteristics are intensity, pitch, speed and the frequency and duration of pauses. Intensities of speech vary not only between different speakers, but between different elements of the language. The amount of sound energy in certain vowel sounds, for example, may be 700 times greater than the energy in a soft 'the' sound in the same word. Different pitches are attained by the utilization of frequencies ranging between about 300 and 6,000 Hz. Speeds much below 100 words/minute are slow; fast talkers can more than double this speed.

The proportion of **spoken** language that can be

understood by a listener depends upon the type of material and upon its context, as well as upon the quality of the received signal. This is usually measured in terms of the articulation index, which is derived from measurements of both speech and noise levels in each of a number of frequency bands. The extent to which noise will affect reliable speech communication may be expressed in terms of the speech interference level, an index that provides a measure of the required intensity level of speech to overcome noise of a given intensity.

Many communication systems, such as the telephone, bring about selective filtering of speech, such that the very high and very low frequency elements are severely attenuated. Intelligibility of speech can survive a good deal of such distortion, particularly if noise is absent.

Experiments upon the characteristics of good talkers indicate that the most intelligible speech results from long average syllable duration, high syllable intensity, the absence of pauses and some variation in pitch.

speech processing

the capacity of a computer to recognize and react to the spoken word.

speed of comprehension

the speed at which one can read and still understand the import of the test.

spike

to kill a copy.

spin-off

a method by which a company may divest itself of one of its divisions. An entirely new corporation is formed and the stock distributed to the shareholders of the first company.

split depreciation

a device whereby, under current cost accounting, depreciation is split between that attributable to the original cost of the asset, which is charged to the profit and loss account, and that which is attributable to the increase in valuation, which is charged to the revaluation reserve.

split play

treatment of a news event in which one side of an issue is presented prominently first, and the other side not until later. Often results from second party being unprepared or late in issuing its information.

split run

publication in part of the total circulation of a newspaper or magazine.

split screen

two or more images shown simultaneously in TV transmission.

split shift

in shift work practice this term refers to a shift which has been divided into two or more periods of times and/or groups of workers.

sponsor

a radio or television advertiser. In a strict sense, one who pays for programme time as distinguished from an advertiser who pays only for announcement or commercial time.

sponsorship

act of sponsoring.

spontaneous recovery

reappearance of a conditioned response which had been extinguished, after a short rest period.

spot announcement

a short, attention-getting, public service announcement broadcast on radio or television. Spot announcements are designed to stimulate a specific action, such as a donation, a call to volunteer one's assistance, and so forth.

spot news

news obtained first-hand of the spot where it happened, hence fresh and live news.

spot rate

the rate of exchange between one currency and another which applies at the present time. It is to be contrasted with the rate which would be quoted for future delivery of the currency, which is the forward rate.

spot transaction

a transaction for immediate completion at the spot rate.

spouse

husband or wife.

spread

an advertisement, group of related photographs, or copy that occupies two facing pages in a publication usually without separation by 'gutters', and usually printed from a single plate.

spreadsheet

a form of computer program, very widely used in processing financial information, which provides the user with a large grid in which to enter values.

squib

a short story in a newspaper or magazine. Sometimes, a short second heading that tells more about a long story.

staff

experts in techniques who aid the line management to do a better job of reaching corporate objectives.

staff assistants

the staff assistant is also commonly known as the assistant too. He usually serves in a much more restricted fashion than does the line assistant. The staff assistant is differentiated from the line assistant in that he has no authority over other employees except in the case of special assignments. Neither does he take over the department in the absence of his principal.

staff departments

staff departments are not all alike and are generally thought to be of four kinds (1) advisory, (2) control, (3) service, and (4) coordinating. The four categories are not mutually exclusive and in fact it may turn out that many staff departments have duties and responsibilities that fall into all four categories.

staffer

member of the permanent staff.

staff function

analysis, planning, or communications by an organisation's headquarters, as opposed to the execution of tasks by the line or divisional forces.

staff general

staff members who assist an executive with responsibilities he cannot delegate.

staffing

providing workers for a company.

staffing function

staffing function includes those activities essential to man, and keep manned, the positions required in the organization structure. It thus involves defining the human requirements for job to be done and the recruitment, appraisal, and selection of candidates for positions, as well as training and developing both candidates and incumbent to perform well. It also includes the provision of adequate basic inducements to abstract and maintain needed personnel.

staff management

the management of staff in an organization; managers who have a specialist service or advisory support function and are not in the chain of command of the organization's hierarchy.

staff personal

an aide-de-camp or private secretary who helps the manager by making his corporate life easier and more convenient.

staff specialised

executives (and their subordinates) who handle specialised function that contribute indirectly to the attainment of organisation goals. Also those who provide advice on and develop techniques for use in these specialised areas.

staff work, completed

staff work whose end-product is a single recommendation which a line executive may either approve or disapprove without further investigation.

staffing

selecting and hiring managers and employees.

stag

one who subscribes for a new issue of shares with the intention of selling any allotment immediately as opposed to holding it as an investment. Stages are sometimes regarded as a nuisance.

stages in management

(1) planning. A manager is planning when he decides which objectives or goals he will pursue, when they will be achieved and exactly how his resources of manpower equipment and time will be devoted to their achievement.

(2) organising. Organising involves the establishment of an intentional structure of roles by identifying the activities required to achieve the purpose of an enterprise, the grouping of these activities,

the assignment of such groups of activities to a manager, the delegation of authority to carry them out, and provision for coordination of authority and informational relationship horizontally and vertically in the organisation structure.

(3) directing. Directing involves guiding and leading subordinates whether they be managers or non-managers.

(4) controlling. Controlling is the measuring and correcting of activities of subordinates to assure that action conform to plans. Thus, it measures performance against goals and plans, shows where negative deviations exist, and, by putting in motion actions to correct deviations, helps assure accomplishment of plans.

(5) coordination. Many authorities consider coordination as a separate function of the manager. It seems more accurate, however, to regard it as the essence of managership, for the achievement of harmony of individual effort towards the accomplishment of group goals is the purpose of management. Each of the managerial functions is an exercise in coordination.

staggered

(holidays, working hours) arranged so that they do not all begin and end at the same time.

stag payments

payments made under a long-term contract, e.g., for the erection of a building, at defined stages in its completion. This avoids the necessity for the contractor to finance the whole of the work.

stake

a deposit or investment in a particular situation.

stake cheque

a cheque which, whilst otherwise valid, has passed the date by which it should have been presented for payment. A cheque must normally be presented for payment within 6 months of the date on which it was drawn.

stamp

small piece of gummed paper which you buy from post office to pay for national insurance contributions.

stamp duty reserve tax

a charge relating to certain transactions in securities not otherwise subject to stamp duty.

standard batch control

a system of ordering in which the materials and components for products are always ordered in the same standardised batches of product sets, the component requirement quantity for this standard number of products being always ordered to the same special schedule for each product.

standard costing

standard costs may be defined as 'predetermined costs related to carefully planned methods of making and selling a product or, in the case of services, rendering a service. In principle there is no difference between standard costs and budgeted costs; both are based on the principle of predetermination of cost. But there is a difference in scope between a budget system and a system of standard costs. Budgeting includes objectives for all activities of a business during a certain period, whereas standard costs relate to detailed costs of operation' (Cost Accounting And Productivity, OEEC Report, 1952).

A standard-costing system serves as a method of feedback whereby deviations between actual and predetermined costs for a given period are isolated and reported. Costs are accumulated by departments and cost centres covering the direct and overhead costs allocated to them, which are considered to be the direct responsibility of the individual managers (Responsibility Accounting). Each managerial unit is charged with actual costs and credited with output measured in standard-cost terms. The difference between actual and standard cost is known as variance and represents the discrepancy between actual and standard performance. This total variance is generally broken down into component parts; variances for materials and wages are analysed as price (wage rate) and usage variances; overheads as volume, budget and efficiency variances. A cross-classification in terms of controllability and non-controllability is also attempted. The analysis of standard-costing variances gives a point of departure for the investigation of costs, but since the analysis is not in terms of causation, it cannot settle all issues about control and efficiency.

In so far as standard costs are target costs they implicitly contain assumptions about how people are motivated. It is therefore important that the basis for the setting of standards be investigated from a behavioural viewpoint and to ask whether the particular standards set motivate people in the way that best helps the achievement of a firm's objectives regarding production efficiency and cost minimization. However, from a human-relations viewpoint such economic ends are by no means the only 'values' present when considering a control system such as a standard-costing system.

standard deviation

a measure of the dispersion or variability of the scores in a distribution. It is the square root of the mean of the squares of each deviation from the mean. Or, to put it simply it is the average distance of each score from the mean.

standard hour

in work study this term refers to a unit of work rather than time. It is the measure of the performance of a standard operator for a given task over one hour.

standard incentive plan
various incentive plans have been designed from time to time. These plan can be broadly classified as: (i) plans based on output, (ii) plans based on time saved.

standardisation
standardisation is the general term which includes the establishment of standards for products, the inspection of products in order to determine the standards to which they conform, and where necessary the sorting of products in lots confirming the established standards.

standardisation hour
using one type of component, material, or machine for as many purposes as possible.

standardised possessing test
a scientifically constructed measure both reliability and validity.

standing committees
among the standing committees of Lok Sabha, the financial committees, viz., Committee on Public Accounts, Estimates Committees on Public Undertakings, constitute a distinct class and between them keep a vigil over government spending and performance.

stand off
to reduce workers' hours of work because of shortage of work.

standstill
situation where work has stopped.

standstill agreement
a reciprocal understanding between a company's management and an outside party that usually owns a significant minority position in the company. In the agreement, each party gives up certain rights in exchange for corresponding concessions by the other party.

start
beginning of something.

starter
young person who is starting in a job for the first time.

starting
starting date = date on which something starts.

state intervention
the intervention by government, either directly or indirectly, in the working of the economy.

statements and reports
considerable paper work is done in industry and business. A part of this work is standardised in the form of statements and reports. Another part consists of correspondence which varies considerably with the parties concerned and the subject matter. In both types of paper work improvements have been made through redesigning and despatch systems and improved procedures. All these contribute to ensuring relevant information being conveyed to

all the concerned persons on time.

statement of affairs

a document prepared in bankruptcy setting out all of the assets owned by the bankrupt and the claims against him or her.

static electricity

this is a current produced in paper by friction.

statistical analysis

the processing and analysis of data by statistical techniques which are founded upon a body of statistical principles such as the theory of probability, the normal distribution of a phenomenon, etc.

statistical error

an inaccuracy that occurs in actual measurement, sampling, calculation, etc.

statistical methods

statistical tools such as graphs, charts, diagrams and presentation index number etc. make the information impressive and comprehensive. Other tools such as the series regression analysis, sampling technique, etc., are highly useful for planning and forecasting.

statistical process control

the use of statistical techniques to determine the acceptable limits of variation in output on a given process and to correct the process if the output falls outside these limits.

statistical quality control

the use of statistical technique to determine the acceptable limits of variation in quality of a given product, usually involving random sampling of the output.

statistical tests

it is often necessary to compare sets of data to determine if they have certain statistical properties in common. Statisticians have a number of tests that perform these tasks. The most commonly used ones are as follows:

(i) student's 't' test. This test may be used when we wish to compare the means of sets of data. For example, it may be used to determine: (a) whether the mean of a sample of observation differs significantly from the mean of the normal population from which it is drawn; (b) given two independent samples with different means, whether their means differ significantly or whether the two samples may be regarded as drawn from the same normal population.

(ii) 'F' test. This may be used when we wish to compare the variability or variance of sets of data. For example, given two independent samples of different variances, it may be used to determine whether their variances differ significantly or whether the two samples may be regarded as drawn from the same normal population.

statistics

facts or information in the form of figures.

status
importance or position in a group.

status quo
existing structure and procedures in an organization.

statute barred
a matter, usually a debt, which can no longer be the subject of legal action because the time limit decreed by the statute of limitations has been exceeded.

statute of limitation
the period of time provided by law, ordinarily beginning with the wrongful act, during which an injured party may use for recovery of damage arising from the act.

statutory
which is laid down by law.

statutory apportionment
an apportionment of the receipt of a trust between capital and income so that the rights of the beneficiaries of the trust can be preserved.

statutory books
records which are required to be kept by a company under the companies Acts. These include the Register of Members and the Register of Directors interests.

statutory company
a company incorporated by its own special Act of Parliament. It is thus to be distinguished from a registered company which is merely registered under general company legislation, Statutory companies are normally established to provide some public utility such as water supply.

statutory declaration
a written declaration, made at the time that registration of a limited company is sought, that all illegal formalities have been observed.

statutory instrument
a detailed rule or set of rules issued by government under the authority of an Act of Parliament. Many details of legislation which are complex or which need revision from time to time are dealt with in this way.

statutory law
a specific body of law created by statute, and contrasted with law created by court decision or administrative interpretation.

statutory reserve
a reserve in the balance sheet of a company which is required to be created by the Companies Acts. These include the share premium account and the capital redemption reserve.

statutory sick pay
amounts paid to an employee who is absent from work due to sickness prescribed by statute.

stem
a word from which words have been developed by the addition of prefixes, suffixes, and inflectional endings.

step
type of action.

step by step acquisition
the assumption of control of one company by another where

the shareholding giving control is acquired in a number of steps. These may not initially have given full control. The process has implications for the preparation of consolidated accounts.

steps in planning

the various steps in planning are: estimation of opportunity; establishing objectives; premises formulation; determining alternative courses; evaluating alternative courses; making choices among alternatives; formulating derivative plans.

sterling silver

silver of a defined standard of purity. It will bear a hallmark as a guarantee of this.

steward

shop steward = elected union representative of workers, who represents their complaints to the management.

stipend

remuneration for the services of certain types of employee such as the clergy.

stipulate

to demand that a condition be put into a contract.

stipulation

condition in a contract.

stochastic

refers to randomness in operational research and model making. Stochastic models are concerned with chance and incorporate probabilities of events happening.

stock

quantity of goods for sale.

stock audit

a complete enumeration of the stock of goods (or of a selected range of goods) at regular intervals, in a retail outlet.

stockbroker

a member of the stock exchange who buys and sells securities on behalf of clients. Unlike a market maker a stockbroker does not deal on his or her own account. Remuneration comes from the commission which is charged to clients.

stock common

shares in ownership on which the return depends so what the company makes. That return may be nothing or it may be very high.

stock control

Also known as Inventory Control. The techniques used to maintain full knowledge of the level and condition of stocks of goods held, necessary to compute reordering levels and to establish standards for the volume of stocks held.

stock exchange

an organised market in securities. The stock exchange in many companies is governed by a council and imposes rigid rules of conduct on its members. It also imposes reporting requirements on the companies in whose shares it deals.

stockholder

a business which makes its profits by holding stocks of a wide variety of raw materials, e.g. steel. This allows its customers to operate with much smaller stocks.

stock holders, institutional
insurance companies, pension funds, and similar institutions which hold company stock.

stock in transit
stock which at a balance sheet date is in transit from one business to another with the consequence that it is included in the assets of neither.

stock letters (or stores, etc.)
letters prepared at a centre office that are provided to members or others in various areas for their dissemination.

stock options
options granted to executives to purchase stock in the future at a given price approximating the current market price, regardless of its price at the time of purchase. (Sometimes granted to employees as well).

stock preferred
shares in ownership on which dividends are fixed in advance. Preferred stock dividends must be paid in full before common stockholders receive anything.

stock split
the process of reducing the nominal value of the shares of a company by dividing one share into two or more parts. Thus shares of £1 each may be split into ten times the number of shares of 10p each. The object of stock split is to increase the amount of trading in the shares.

stock-taking
the process of making a physical count of the types and amounts of stock on hand at a particular date with the object of determining its total quantity and, ultimately, value. Stock is frequently a large item on the balance sheet and its periodic verification is, therefore, important. It will be a part of an audit that the auditor attends the stock-taking.

stock turnover
a ratio: cost of sales/average inventory. An indication of the velocity with which goods or merchandise moves through a business.

stock warrants
an agreement which entitles but does not require the holder to purchase a certain number of shares at a stated price during specified time periods.

stop
end of an action.

stop loss
an order given to a stockbroker to sell shares on behalf of a client if and when their price descends to a stated level. The object of a stop loss order is to place a limit on the possible loss on an investment if it does not succeed as expected.

stoppage
act of stopping work because of industrial action.

stopped cheque
a cheque which a band has been ordered not to pay by the person drawing the cheque. A cheque can only be stopped before payment has actually been made. The circumstances in which the action is appropriate may be where the cheque has been lost or stolen

or where its issue was induced by misrepresentation.

storage and warehousing
warehousing is a very important function of marketing. It refers to the storage or accumulation of goods from the time of production to the time of consumption. It creates time utility and removes the hindrance of time. It brings about equalisation of demand and supply from time to time and from place to place. Warehousing is essential for commodities having seasonal production but perennial demand.

story "angle" or "peg"
the distinctive interest element that makes a story notable or newsworthy.

story board
sequence of roughs depicting the continuity of television programme contact or commercials.

straight matter
copy without any display lines.

strategic planning
strategic planning does not predict the future but it; assists in coping effectively with future contingencies; provides an early opportunity to correct inevitable mistakes; helps in making decisions about the right things at the right time; and focuses on what action to take in order to shape the future as desired. Strategic planning begins by asking questions regarding the purpose and the operations to which an enterprise is presently devoted.

strategy
plan of future action.

stratification
the division of a population into parts (strata); particularly for the purpose of drawing a sample in which a predetermined proportion of the sample is drawn from each stratum.

stratified sampling
a technique frequently used for mass opinion polling. It involves the division of a population into subgroups or strata and then taking a random sample of each one.

streamline
to make (something) more efficient or more simple.

streamlined
efficient or rapid.

streamlining
making efficient.

street name
securities that are held for the investor by his broker, and not identified with him, are listed on the stock registration in the broker's name. "Street names" may be a shield of secrecy for buying up blocks in seeking to gain control of the company.

stress
nervous tension or worry.

stressful
(situation) which causes stress.

stretch
to pull out or make longer.

strike
organized stopping of work by workers (in order to strengthen their position in bargaining with management or because of lack

of agreement with management or because of orders from a union).

strikebound

not able to work or to move because of a strike.

strikebreaker

worker who goes on working while everyone else is on strike.

strike—forms

(i) constitutional. A strike called only after the procedure for dealing with Industrial Dispute agreed by the union(s) and the employer of the Employers' Association has been exhausted (Grievance Procedure).

(ii) general. A strike supported by all or most of the trade union movement of a country. The only British case is that of the 1926 General Strike in support of the miners. There is some doubt about its legality. In many countries general strikes for political purposes may be a feature of emergent nationhood or opposition to single-party government.

(iii) lighting. A sudden stoppage of work at the workplace, which may be spontaneous, as when tempers flare (known as a 'wildcat' strike in the USA), or planned, as part of a strategy to harass a specific employer or employer in an industry.

(iv) local. A strike involving union members in a small geographical area, usually a workplace, plant or company, but occasionally a town or district. Most workplace and plant strikes are short, unofficial and unconstitutional.

(v) national. A strike involving the whole of a union's membership wherever it may be found, or involving a whole industry and thus all the unions with members employed in it, e.g. a national engineering strike.

(vi) official. A strike sanctioned or ratified by the union(s) whose members are on strike in accordance with the appropriate union rules. National strikes are official, but most local strikes are not. There is no legal distinction between official and unofficial strikes.

(vii) sit-down. A strike where the employees in question do not walk off the premises but stop work and remain at their workplace. Such strikes are unofficial, unconstitutional and illegal.

(viii) sympathetic. A strike by a group of trade unionists not in dispute with their employer(s) in support of and in sympathy with strikers in a trade dispute.

(ix) token. A short stoppage, e.g. a one-day strike, which may be official or unofficial, national or local, to indicate the attitude and strength of trade union members in an industrial dispute. If official, this is an economical form of action, making only a limited call on union funds.

(x) unconstitutional. A strike called without using or exhausting the disputes procedure.

striker
worker who is on strike.
string man
a reporter in a given area who is available on call to cover stories for a medium headquarters elsewhere.
strong campbell interest inventory
the 1974 revised version of the 1927 strong vocational interest blank which takes account of nearly half a century of history in the world of work and the communication vocational and occupational changes.
strong vocational interest bank
a questionnaire about a person's interests which is matched with the reported interests of people in different vocations to assess their suitability for a particular kind of work. This test was first developed in 1927 and revised in 1974 as the Strong-Campbell interest inventory.
structural change
deep-seated changes that affect the very structure of a society, like the industrial revolution.
structural unemployment
unemployment that arises from the changing structure of an industry or society (e.g., in the pattern of demand) that is long-term or even permanent, as opposed to seasonal unemployment or unemployment is a temporary reflection of prevailing economic conditions.
structure
way in which something is organized.
structuring
bringing order into an organization.
study
examination something carefully.
stuffer
a printed piece intended for insertion into pay envelopes, packages delivered to customers, with bills and receipts, or any other item that provides a medium of delivery.
stunt
a created event developed by a press agent to evoke publicity.
style
the design given by manufacturers to their products in an effort to appeal to long-term mass criteria of beauty.
style book
manual setting up standards for handling copy, i.e., spelling, capitalisation, abbreviations, word usage, and so on.
style of the house
rules regarding grammar, punctuation, spelling, compounding, word-division, use of capitals, italics, etc., in a printing press.
style of work
rules regarding style in the use of capitals, type faces and sizes, white spaces, etc., for a particular work.
sub
informal wages paid in advance.
sub-
prefix under or less important.
subcontract
contract between the main

contractor for a whole project and another firm who will do part of the work.

subcontractor

company which has a contract to do work for a main contractor.

subhead

small heading within a news story or article to break up solid type mass and catch reader's eye.

subject to

depending on.

subjective

considered from the point of view of the person involved, and not from any general point of view.

subjective data

data not readily quantified or measured with mathematical or statistical precision; personal opinions, values, concepts, and social relationships rather than objectively derived facts.

subliminal advertising

sensory stimulation below the 'limen' or threshold above which perception becomes conscious. Subliminal advertising would therefore mean that the viewer of a film or television message would not be conscious of seeing it—and therefore, it is argued, not conscious of being persuaded. For this reason such advertising is banned in most countries, although there is no firm evidence that subliminal perception actually has any effect.

submit

to put (something) forward to be examined.

subordinate

person in a lower position in an organization.

sub-sample

a small sample drawn from larger sample; a part of the larger sample.

subsidiary

a company controlled wholly or partially by another through ownership of its stock.

subsidiary company

a company that is controlled by an organisation which owns more than one half of the subsidiary's voting stock.

subsidize

to help by giving money.

substance

weight of given area of paper or board.

substandard

not of the necessary quality or quantity to meet a standard.

substitute

person who takes the place of someone else. To take the place of someone else.

substitution

an attempt to replace one goal with another.

subtopic

a subheading in an outlined exposition.

succeed

to do what was planned.

success

getting a good result or getting the desired result.

successful

having got the desired result.

successfully

well or getting the desired result.

successor
person who takes over from someone.

suggestion
proposal or idea which is put forward.

suffix
one or more syllables added at the end of a word to change the meaning.

suitable
convenient or which fits.

superannuation
pension paid to someone who is too old or ill to work any more.

super calender
this is a process whereby the paper is subjected to a further glaze after its manufacture by running it through a steam bath and then passing it through hot rollers.

super imposition
printing one colour over another colour as in tri-colour printing.

superior
more important person.

supernumary
someone who is surplus to requirements for an organization at a given time and place, e.g., as a result of over manning.

supervise
to direct personally. A supervisor exercises leadership by overseeing the activities of others in person. Supervision implies that the people supervised report directly to the person doing the supervision.

supervision as an instrument of control
every executive below the apex of the hierarchy is subject to supervision from a higher level. Observing a subordinate behaviour under various conditions is sometimes the best way to evaluate his performance or potential. Much of the process is informal and indirect and becomes an aspect of the socio-psychological dynamics of the superior subordinate relationship.

supervision, plan of
the number of people supervised by a manager.

supervisor
person who supervises.

supervisory
as a supervisor.

supplement
thing which is added.

supplementary
in addition to .

supplier
an institution, individual, or agency that furnishes a service; persons or organisations, that furnish equipment or services covered.

supply-side economics
a form of economic policy that emphasizes the importance of supply rather than demand in the working of the economy. It encourages measures like the removal of restrictive positives the reduction of the public sector in favour of the private sector and the cutting of taxation as an incentive to the entrepreneur.

suppression
1. Psychological blocking of vision in one eye. 2. Involuntary

exclusion of anything from awareness.

surcharge
an extra charge or something already charged; a special payment; an overcharge.

surplus
more of something than is needed.

survey
the collection and examination of representative data regarding an aggregate of units, e.g., people, social and/or economic institutions, etc.; usually used of a sample survey in which it is assumed that the findings based on information from the sample may be applied to the whole of population.

survey group
also Experimental Group. The group (sample) upon which the experiment is carried out, e.g., in interviewing, the variables under examination would be changed for this group.

survey research
a technique for gathering data from large numbers of people by the use of questionnaires and using statistical sampling methods.

suspend
to stop (someone) working for a time.

sweated labour
people who work hard for very little money.

sweat shop
factory using sweated labour.

swing shift
a flexible form of shift work practice where a shift has no set hours. The workers have a variable number of hours at work depending on the circumstance in order to ensure the continuity of production.

syllabication
division of word into syllables, usually for purposes of pronunciation.

syllogism
a logical scheme or analysis of a format argument consisting of the major premise, the minor premise, and the conclusion.

sympathy
feeling sorry because someone else has problems.

sympathetic
showing sympathy.

syndicate
a group of individuals or organisations who combine for some common goal which is to their mutual benefit.

syndrome
collection of symptoms which characterise a particular disorder or disease.

synergy
synergy is said to have taken when the combined return on a firm's resources is greater than the sum of its parts. It is sometimes known as the two-plus-two-equals-five effect. When a company adds to its existing activities the new activity will make use of the company's existing resources to a greater or lesser extent: the extent to which it does so is the extent of the synergy arising from this new activity. Where there is no relation at all between the new and existing activities there will be

no synergy, i.e. the return on investment of the company as a whole will simply be the return on the existing activities plus that of the new activity. But where the new activity makes use of existing resources, the return for the company as a whole will be greater than the simple weighted average of the new and existing activities (two plus two equals five).

Synergy can arise from the commonality of resources required by the new and existing activities including not only such physical resources as factories, transport facilities, etc., but also management competence, know-how, research, marketing, operations and starting up economies. In estimating the extent of synergy likely to be obtained from a project, it is possible to prepare a capability profile for the company to determine how far the new activity might mesh with the existing activities. This profile is similar to a list of Strengths and Weaknesses.

synonym

one of two or more words of the same language having the same or nearly the same essential meaning. For example, Little, Small.

synopsis

a summary of the salient points of a study usually incorporated in the final report.

system

arrangement or organization of things which work together.

system analysis

the analysis (usually by computer) of a physical system within an organisation, like its communication or heating, to see how it might be made more efficient.

systems analysis and design

before a computer can be installed in a business application a number of investigations must be performed. These can usefully be grouped into three stages: (1) feasibility study, which determines whether it is feasible on economic and/or technological grounds for a computer to perform the desired task. If it is feasible, this is followed by (2) the system analysis stage, which determines the structure of the existing system into which the proposed computer installation will be introduced, and (3) the system design stage, which is the complete design of the new computer based system.

The individuals who perform the systems investigations, as distinct from the detailed computer programming, are known as systems analysts. However, in some companies the distinction between the two roles is not clear-cut and one individual may perform both tasks in a given project.

The term systems analysis is also used to a limited extent as a synonym for two other activities not necessarily associated with computers: (i)

Operational Research, since OR workers analyse man—machine systems; (ii) systems engineering, a term sometimes used to describe the engineering of new large-scale complex man-machine systems (e.g. a new weapons system, or an intercontinental microwave system).

systematic

contrasted to random. Used of sampling methods or rules, which are systematic if they are not based on probability theory (random sample). Pertaining to some system other than that of random selection.

systematic error

as opposed to random error. An error which is in some way biased, i.e., has a distribution with a mean not a zero.

systems technique of management

the study of management has been made more scientific and useful by the application of systems technique which the managerial scientists are increasingly using year by year. The term system refers to a group or complex of parts (such as people and machines) inter-related in their actions towards some goals. Typically it is the inter-relationship among these system elements, and between them and their environment, that is of most interest in systems design both for human organizations and for purely physical systems. Although these inter-relationship often are difficult to describe fully and precisely for human organizations, we can anticipate that a systems approach provides a useful framework for examining organizational phenomena, and allow us to fill in whatever detail we find appropriate.

system theory

the attempt to formulate general principles that could be applied to any system by a comparative analysis of the structures and functions of as wide a variety of system as possible.

table

a listing of numerical data.

table recorder

machine for recording sound magnetic tape or wire, which can be played back.

tabloid

a newspaper format, smaller than standard size, and usually having five columns per page, each page being slightly more than half the size of a standard paper.

tabulation

summarisation of survey results in the form of statistical tables.

tachistoscope

equipment which permits visual presentation of objects for very short periods of time, i.e., the subjects have time only to glance at the object.

technical vocabulary

words used in specialised fields such as chemistry, engineering, medicine, and agriculture.

tactic
way of doing things so as to be at an advantage.

tactile, Tactual
having to do with touch.

tactual imagery
the mental reconstruction of sensory experiences secured by touch.

take
to receive or to get.

take back
to take back dismissed workers = to allow former workers to join the company again.

take-home pay
amount actually included in the pay check, that is, pay minus deductions for taxes and other purposes, such as contributions to a pension plan.

take over
to start to do something in place of someone else.

take over bid
an effort to assume control of a publicly held company without the approval of the management. This may be through election by stockholders of a controlling number of directors or through purchase of a controlling proportion of the shares.

talent
actors, performers, musicians, models, usually in television or motion pictures.

tall organization
an organization with relatively numerous levels in its hierarchy. The classic examples are the Army and the Civil Service with a dozen levels or more.

tally cards
cards onto which are written the number of times certain responses are given, for the purpose of preparing totals.

tally light
red light on a TV camera indicating its picture is being transmitted.

tangible asset
an asset, either physical or financial in character, e.g., plant, stock, cash receivable, investments.

tardiness
(formal) being late or unpunctual.

tare
the weight of the packaging, wrapping, containers, or other materials used in shipping goods, tare weight plus net weight make up gross weight.

target
something to aim for.

task
work which has to be done.

task analysis
the analysis of a task into its constituent operations for the purpose of identifying the skills involved and the training necessary to improve them.

task force
a group of people who are brought together for a particular task, usually involving a special project or unusual problem. The group is normally disbanded when the task has been successfully completed.

task leader
the individual who may emerge

in a small group as the person who tries to keep the attention of the group focused on its task and who tries to ensure that it gets done.

tax

regular payments made by citizens of a country to the central or local government to pay for government services.

taxable

which can be taxed.

taxable expenditure

an expenditure by a tax-exempt organisation that is in violation of federal tax code rules.

taxation

act of taxing.

tax avoidance

the arrangement of a taxpayer's affairs so that his or her tax liability is legally reduced. An example of tax avoidance is the phasing of the sales of securities over a number of years so as to make maximum use of the exemptions to capital gains tax. Tax avoidance, which is legal, should be contrasted with tax evasion which is not.

tax base

the value of assets or monies on which taxes are levied. Some of the more common tax bases include, individual income, corporate income, real property (real estate), gifts, estates, and other property.

tax cab advertisement

advertising medium consisting of advertisement panels fitted to the nearside cab driver's door.

tax credit

a direct reduction of tax liability for income tax purposes, authorised by law to serve some broad economic, social, or political objective. Tax credits for plant construction or energy expenditures, or for conservation improvements are examples. Tax credits permit all or some percentage of the cost of such items to be deducted from the amount of tax which would otherwise be paid.

tax deductible

which can be deducted from an income before tax is calculated.

tax deferred annuity

an annuity the employee contributes which is not subject to taxes at the time that the contributions are made; the contributions are instead taxed later as they are paid out after retirement, when the annuitant is presumably in a lower tax bracket.

tax efficient

description applied to any procedure for achieving a desired objective which at the same time minimises any tax liability. Use of a personal equity plan, for example, is a tax efficient method of building up an investment in shares.

tax evasion

the escape from the payment of tax which is legally due. Tax evasion usually takes place by a failure to make a full declaration of income. Tax evasion is fraud and, if detected, is punishable as such.

tax-exempt

not required to pay tax (income or goods) which are not subject to tax.

tax exempt bond

a certificate sold by a tax-exempt organisation that pays interest to the bondholder. The bondholder is not required to pay taxes on the interest.

tax expenditures

government revenue losses resulting from tax deductions, tax exemptions, and other tax-related matters. Deductions and exemptions represent negative income or "opportunity costs" to the taxing government unit.

tax free

on which tax does not have to be paid.

tax haven

a country that provides tax advantages for companies incorporated under its laws.

tax liability

an amount which a business or individual has become obliged to pay in taxation, e.g., because an income has been earned, but which has not yet been paid, perhaps because the due date has not arrived.

taxpayer

person or company which has to pay tax.

tax planning

planning financial operations and arrangements so as to take full account of the incidence of taxation. A large aim of tax planning will be to minimise total liability to tax to the extent that this can legally be done.

tax return

a statement of financial circumstances required to be submitted to the Inland Revenue annually by each taxpayer. There is a legal obligation on any individual having taxable income or capital gains to submit a tax return whether or not asked specifically to do so. The return in made on a special form and relates to a period of 1 year. It requires disclosure of the taxpayer's income under a number of separate categories including chargeable capital gains. It also enables tax allowances to be claimed.

Taylor differential piece rate system

Taylor developed this plan in which there is low piece rate for low output below standard and a high rate for output above standard. The worker also receives special bonus on his daily wage rate when the performance exceeds the stipulated quality and quantity.

taylorism

an alternative name for the scientific management approach to the world of work pioneered by F.W. Taylor.

taylor system

a piece – rate method of wage payment where the increment of payment increases as the worker speeds up his rate of working in contrast to the premium-bonus methods of payment under which the increment falls the more quickly the work is completed.

tea break

rest time during work when the workers can drink coffee or tea.

teaching machine

machines (usually specially programmed computers) which can be used to teach skills without an instructor.

team

group of people who work together.

team briefing

the practice of encouraging communication in an organization via the face to face group.

team building

a technique that aims to help work groups by improving the quality of their members' interpersonal relations as well as their skill at solving problems and accomplishing their task. This is usually done with the aid of an external consultancy which will diagnose the way the work group functions, helping member to identify difficulties and suggest improvements.

teamwork

group effort applied to work.

teamwork between staff and line

this teamwork creates an understanding of the basic relationship that company experience indicates. The unit are then designated as line have ultimate responsibility for the successful operation of the company. Therefore line department must be responsible for operating decisions. Staff elements contribute by providing advice and service to the line in accomplishing the objectives of the enterprise. Staff is responsible for providing advice and service to appropriate line elements when requested to do so. However staff also is responsible for proferring advice and service when it is not requested but where the staff believes it is needed.

tearsheet

a page containing an advertisement clipped from a publication and sent to the advertiser for checking purposes.

teaser

material that stimulates interest in forthcoming media content without providing specifies.

technical

referring to scientific methods of production.

technical adjustment

a movement of shares prices which occurs as a reaction to a previous movement which has been overdone than a change in the underlying situation. If the market has been rising strongly for a period there is likely to be a technical adjustment whereby the price rise is temporarily reserved before it resumes.

technical proficiency

in a staff manager implies more than specialised knowledge. It also requires that the specialist has a knowledge of the company and its operations. The more he knows of line problems and operations, and those of other staff specialities, the better he can develop effective recommendations in his own area.

technician

person who is specialized in industrial work.

technique

skilled way of doing a job.

technological change

industrial and social change, leading to change in workplace environment, which can be attributed to the introduction of technology

technological content in management education

great deal of more technological content is needed, necessitating new outlook and mix in the managerial competence. Since public sector enterprises are mainly in heavy and core industries, their level of technology is higher than in traditional private sector industries, not only in terms of intensity but also in terms of complexity.

technologist

a person trained in the study and use of specialised skills, techniques, tools, machines, an electronic and other instruments of applied science and engineering, who specialises in a particular field of application of technology.

technology

applying scientific knowledge to industrial processes.

technology and organisation

the system of machines, equipment and technical methods fundamental to economic performance, together with their associated knowledge, beliefs and values. Technology, surprisingly neglected for so long by students of organisational behaviour, has been recognized in the last decade or so as an extremely important variable. Joan Woodward showed a relationship between technology (in terms of unit, batch, mass or process production) and organisational structure. By so doing, she demonstrated that many of the principles of management formulated by the classical theorists were specific and not universal application.

It is now known, therefore, that a relationship exists between technology and organizational (and hence social) structure and process. However, this is not to say that organisational structure is determined solely by technology: the work of the Tavistock Institute drew attention to the possibility of basing different organizational arrangements on the same technology. Nevertheless, similar technologies are likely to give rise to broadly similar organisational structures and behaviour by limiting the range of structural and behavioural alternatives from which a choice can be made.

techno-marketing synergy

to overcome longer gestation periods in technology and its

effect on marketing the forecasting, technology and marketing are brought together with use of computer to forecast introduction of new products. Uses technique such as Delphic time scaling.

telecommunications
long distance transmission of signals.

teleconference
a discussion of conference where participants are geographically scattered and linked by mean of telecommunication such as audio conferencing or video conferencing.

telephone interviewing
an adoption of the interview technique used in survey research where fact-to-face interviewing is not possible or advisable.

teletype
an electronic system of transmitting information in typewritten form. Used in operation of the various public relations newswires, as well as by the Associated Press and United Press International.

teleworking
working at home with a computer, either linked to a main database, or supplying material on disk.

teletypesetting
setting type from punched tape, enabling one source to provide exact typeset material to many linotype locations.

television research
all research relating to the medium of television.

temping
working as a temporary secretary.

temporal method
a method used for the translated at rates determined by the rate of exchange obtaining at the time of the original transaction underlying them.

temporal relationship
subjects or ideas arranged in a sequence in which time is an essential factor.

temporary
which only lasts a short time.

tenancy
the state of renting of property by one person from another.

tenant
a person or organisation occupying or having rights to a property or real estate.

tender
to offer money or something else of value in payment for goods or services or in payment of a debt; money or something else of value.

tender offer
offer to purchase a designated number of shares of a corporation at a specified price by a specified date. This is often, but not always, intended to acquire enough shares to control the corporation.

tenor
the implication, direction, or tone of a social or business interaction, or of a statement or act; a theme that continues throughout a social, business, or therapeutic interaction, communication, or transaction.

tentative
not certain.

tenure
right to hold a post permanently. Time when a position is held.

term
period of time when something is legally valid.

term debt
a debt due to be paid over a period of time as opposed to be paid entirely at one time in a lumpsum.

terminal
a place in a communication system where information can either leave or enter.

terminal bonus
a bonus paid on maturing policies of life assurance. It is given at the option of the company issuing the policy and is paid out of profits. It is given in addition to any other bonuses which may have accrued to the policy.

terminal loss
a loss made by a business in its last year of trading. A terminal loss has significance in the calculation of the business's liability to tax. It may be set off against the assessment of profits for the previous 3 years, thus reducing the tax due on them.

terminate
to end (something) or to bring (something) to an end.

termination
bringing to an end. End to a contract of employment leaving a job (resigning, retiring, or being fired or made redundant).

term life assurance
an assurance which provides a stated benefit on the death of the assured during a specified period of time. Since the policy becomes valueless at the end of this time the premiums paid are less than they would be on endowment or whole life policies.

test
any procedure for the assessment of a specific ability or aptitude of psychological state.

test data
data introduced by an auditor into an accounting system, particularly a computerised system, to verify that it is working correctly.

test group
a group selected for reaction to or use of a product or an idea.

testimonial
written report about someone's character or ability.

testing
to sample the opinion or acceptance of a carefully selected and well-defined area or group of any particular product, event, or question. Tabulated results frequently serve as the basis for determining the directions of a larger campaign.

test marketing
a form of pilot study on a new product, where it is tried out in a limited area first in order to see whether it would be worth marketing more widely.

tests, projective
psychological tests to which the "right" answers are not

predetermined and which, therefore, require the testee to project himself.

test, thematic apperception
a projective test in which the testee is asked to describe the situations portrayed in a series of rather ambiguous pictures.

test town
also Test Area. The town or geographical area selected for the purposes of controlled testing or products, packaging, advertisements, etc., the population of which is supposed to represent that of the universe being studied.

t-group
a small group of people that meets, with a trainer, for the purpose of improving members' skills in interpersonal behaviour by talking and thinking.

the contract system
this system is also adopted as a method of managing public enterprises. Under this system there is a contract between the government on the one hand and a contractor, may be individual, institution or organization on the other. The government assigns certain services to the contractors and on their completion the contractors are paid their dues.

the industrial development Bank of India (I.D.B.I)
an outstanding feature in the structure of financial institution in India since independence has been the establishment of a number of development banks both at the national and state levels of which the Industrial Development Bank of India is the apex institution.

the public relations function
while no one organizational device will assure effectiveness in discharging social responsibilities, one of the most logical internal structural changes is to build upon the present public relations function. For the most part, public relations officers are not charged simply with "telling the story". Seldom are they in a position to influence decisively the important decisions of business policy and practice. Usually their task focuses on favourable interpretation after the decision is made.

the systems theory
under systems theory organizing is viewed as a system of mutually dependent variables. It is somewhat similar in approach to the systems or school of management thought.

thematic apperception test
projective test which requires the subject to make up stories appropriate to a series of pictures. These themes given an indication of the subject's basic personality structure.

theories of organization
(a) the fusion theory.
(b) the systems theory, and
(c) the quantitative theory.

theory of discrimination
the concept of decision control point is a structural one. It is a useful starting point for weaving

the information network. Unclear organisations with overlapping roles, missing responsibility centres, non coterminus decision-making and control points and the like have to be sorted out as the building up of MIS is undertaken.

theory x

the traditional view of direction and control. It contains three assumptions: that the average human will avoid work if he can, must be coerced and directed, had no ambition and prefers to avoid responsibility. This theory leads to restrictive discipline and close managerial control.

theory y

in the terminology of Douglas Mc Gregor this describes a view of human nature in which people would like to be creative in their work and take more responsibility for it. They would thus be more responsive to democratic management and its enabling function than is suggested by the proponents of theory x.

therapy

treatment intended to cure or alleviate a disordered condition.

thereblig

the smallest discreet human motion that can be identified in the performance of a task.

thin market

a market in which very few transactions take place. The shares of a named company might be said to trade in a thin market on the stock exchange. The consequence of a thin market is that substantial price movement may be triggered by an unusual increase in activity.

third party beneficiary

a person who is not a party to a contract or agreement but who has a legal interest in and who benefits from it. For example, a guardian of an elderly person is a third-party beneficiary to the elderly person's health care insurance benefits.

threshold

a level of price or income at which some provision comes into effect. Income above a certain threshold, for example, will be subject to national insurance contributions.

threshold of consciousness

the point at which a given subject passes out of the mass of unperceived subjects into the awareness of the individual.

throw out

to reject or to refuse to accept.

thumbnail

a rough layout in miniature.

tie-in

a promotional technique used to describe the joint (or combined) activities of two or more organisations on one project.

tight money

a situation in which it is difficult to borrow money, often because government policies are in place to restrict the level of debt in an economy.

time and a half

a common method of calculating the payment of overtime working. The number of hours actually worked is paid for at one and a half times the normal rate.

time band averaging

a technique for ship loading and concurrently providing a reliable estimating base for selling price calculation. The aggregation of different work–pieces in excess of a predetermined minimum quantity, all of which in respect of their floor to floor manufacturing cycles are assessed to fall within the limits of a declared time band (e.g. 15-20 minutes).

time budget

the preparation of a detailed timetable of work activities in order to help improve time management and efficiency.

time card

time clock card = card which is put into a timing machine when a worker clocks in or clocks out, and records the time when he starts and stops work.

time element in planning

one common ingredient of all planning is time, and plans with respect to time can be conveniently expressed as short-range (SR) covering a period of 1 year and less: intermediate – range (IR) over 1 but less than 5 years; and long range (LR) over 5 years.

time horizon

the degree to which the planning of an organization or an individual manager extends into the future.

time in lieu

a period of time off work, usually taken at the employee discretion to make up for time worked over and above normal working hours, i.e., exchange of time for the money that would have been pair for working an overtime rate.

time off

time away from work granted to an employee to attend to private affairs.

time rate

rate for work which is calculated as money per hour or per week, and not money for work completed.

time schedule

an itemised timetable for the whole, and for parts, of the research.

timeshare

a form of shared property ownership whereby the purchaser of the timeshare has the right to occupy the property for a given number of weeks at a prescribed time in each year.

time sharing

the sharing of resources, such as a building, office space, laboratory, or computer, by two or more providers (or other business or professional enterprises) under an agreement.

time span of discretion

a term introduced to the work study area of ergonomics in the 1960s by the British industrial psychologist Elliott

Japues. It is an attempt at equity in setting salary levels and differentials following a job evaluation. What is measured is the length of time during which someone has to exercise discretion, i.e., personal judgement and responsibility in their job before requiring decision from superiors.

time study
a method of determining the time necessary to perform a task. Procedure may involve timing the various elements (e.g., very small components of the task such as picking up material, positioning it, or inserting it in the machine) with a stopwatch, totalling the number of times and adding "allowance" for such things as fatigue and personal time.

time value of money
the difference between the value of money on hand today and that of money to be received in the future. The difference is due to the interest or other return that money available now might be producing in the meantime.

tint
reduction or dilution of a solid colour.

tint block
solid unhatched plate for printing light, flat colour over a sizable area.

tip
a small amount of money given voluntarily to a person who has given a service which is paid for separately.

title
a right of ownership. Thus a landowner is said to have a title to the land.

token
thing which acts as a sign or symbol.

tokenism
an action taken for its symbolic value as opposed to serious attempt at changing a given situation, e.g., appointing a lone woman to an all male board of directors as an end in itself, i.e., to show how open minded and progressive the organization is.

tone
the intensity of colour or strength of a colour in a photograph or picture.

tools and equipment
a fixed asset on which depreciation is often charged on a renewals basis, i.e. the amount charged as depreciation if equal to the amount spent on renewals.

tools of financial analysis
(i) comparative financial statements. (ii) common size statements. (iii) trend percentage or ratios. (iv) ratio analysis. (v) fund flow analysis. (vi) cash flow analysis.

tool subject
school subject thought of as valuable because of service to other subjects or to practical pursuits rather than by itself. Reading, writing, arithmetic and English are considered tool subjects.

topical relationship
subjects or ideas which fit

together to make up a unified whole.

topical sentence

a sentence in a paragraph which provides the subject to be discussed and developed.

total account

an account containing the totals of values which have been posted in details to other accounts. A total account is a form of control account.

totalisator

a mechanism for betting on horses or greyhounds in which the total staked is placed into a pool and then divided, after a deduction to allow a profit, amongst those winning bets.

total quality control

an overall approach to quality which recognises that control is a company-wide activity, beginning with product design and ending only when the product is in the hands of a satisfied customer.

total systems

the complete integration of all major operating and information systems within a company through the medium of data processing.

totten trust

a trust agreement in which a first person puts money into a bank accounts in his or her name as trustee for a second person or a nonprofit organisation. The first person can take the money out at any time, but if he or she does not do so before dying, the money becomes the property of the second person or organisation.

tracking

much of the study of human control performance has taken the form of experiments on tracking; the subject is faced with a moving display and is required to carry out appropriate movements in an attempt to minimize an error function.

There are two basic designs of tracking task. In pursuit tracking subjects see both a target, over which they have no control, and a follower, whose position is determined by them. Their task is to keep the follower upon the target. Such a task might be performed by an anti-aircraft gunner. In compensatory tracking there is only one moving part on the display, the position of which is determined partly by the tracker's control movements and partly by external circumstances. An example of a compensatory task is a motorist attempting to drive at constant speed over undulating country.

Tracking accuracy is a function of such variables as the shape and speed of the independent track, the type of display and control used, in addition to the skill of the individual tracker.

trade advertising

advertising directed at wholesalers or retailers.

trade association

a voluntary organisation of members of the same trade or industry, or sector of a trade or industry, who perform similar functions in relation to industrial or commercial activities.

trade discount

a discount given by one business to another which is making a purchase for resale to an ultimate customer. In effect it is a device for selling at wholesaler rather than retail prices in these circumstances. Trade discount is not normally available to the private consumer.

trade gap

the difference between the value of exports and the value of imports of the country during a specified period of time. The gap may be either favourable or unfavourable.

trade investments

investments owned by an organisation which are not held for sale.

trademark

a brand that is registered under the Federal Trade Mark Law, or otherwise receives legal protection.

trade name

1. The name by which an article or a certain type or grade of an article is known among buyers and seller. 2. The name by which a business is conducted.

trade press

regular publications specialising in news and editorial material relevant to particular trades, industries, professions, or sectors thereof.

trade publications

periodicals dealing with matters of interest to a particular trade or industry.

trade secret

information or technique known only to members of a particular trade or profession public knowledge of which would detract from their standing and income, e.g., how a magician saws a lady in half.

trade union

an organization of workers in a particular trade of industry which furthers the welfare of its members and acts on their behalf in collective bargaining with employers on pay and conditions of employment.

trade union — at law

the Trade Union and Labour Relations Act 1974 defines a trade union as an organization of workers whose principal purposes include the regulation of relations with employers, or a federation of such organizations. The organization may be permanent or temporary. 'Worker' is defined to include employees, independent contractors and Crown servants. A trade union is an 'independent' trade union if it is not employer dominated, nor employer controlled, nor subject to interference by an employer tending towards such control. It is important to know whether a trade union is 'independent' since, while it would be an unfair dismissal if an employee were dismissed for refusing to join or to remain in a non-independent union, it would not be unfair if the union in question were an independent one.

The legal status of trade unions since 1974 is that the union is treated as an unincorporated association but it still enjoy some of the privileges of an incorporated body, e.g. it may sue or be sued in its registered name and it may enter into contracts in that name. This means for example, that a member can sue to prevent officials acting contrary to the union's rule book, which constitutes a contractually binding constitution defining the rights of the union and its members. Consequently no member can be expelled or otherwise disciplined except in accordance with the terms of the rule book. Since 1980 members and would be members have had an additional statutory right to complain of unreasonable exclusion or expulsion by a union operating a closed shop at their place of work. Here reasonableness is not defined exclusively by what the rule book contains.

trade union—government and administration

trade unions each have their individual character. A union's internal organization is a function of the aims, size and diversity of its membership, but a general picture can be drawn that does not do too much injustice to the realities of each separate situation. Typically the union has a pyramidal structure and the main lines of formal communication are expected to extend from the individual member through the branch, possibly via a district committee, to a national executive committee and, periodically, to a national delegate conference.

The branch (know in some unions by other names, e.g. lodge, club, chapel) is the basic organizational unit. Branches in their size, form and content of meetings should encourage the active-co-operation of the membership, but their policy-making power varies from union to union. The branch is usually based on a geographical area and varies greatly in size; the Amalgamated Union of Engineering Workers has set a maximum of 300 members, while the Transport and General Workers' Union has had a branch of 9,000 members. The branch deals with applications for membership and provides for the collection of contributions and distribution of benefits. In a study of a branch in 1952 Joseph Goldstein emphasized membership apathy and showed that attendance at branch meetings could often be as low as 3 percent. Clearly resolutions in the branch meetings need not necessarily represent the views of branch membership. It is often suggested that where numbers permit, unions should base their branches on the workplace, rather than on some wider geographical area, in order to stimulate greater interest and attendance and to tighten the link between the Shop Steward, the local leader at the workplace, and branch officials, who are responsible for formal two-way communication between the branch and the main body of the union. This can work well, as in the Steelworkers' Union, but in other cases, e.g. the National Union of Mineworkers, it has made no apparent contribution towards reducing independent, unofficial action.

District organizations are concerned with the proper functioning of branches in the district and with local negotiations. They are composed of delegates from branches and the secretary may be a lay member or a full-time official. Some have a wide measure of autonomy. The Transport and General Worker' Union also has regional committees, regional trade group (or industrial) committees, and national trade group committees.

The national executive committee is the governing body or top leadership of the union, responsible for its day-to-day operation and subject only to the national delegate conference. It can influence the conference, containing as it does the principal national officers, of who the general secretary (Trade Union-Officers) is normally the most important and who, except in the very small unions, is always a full-time official.

The national delegate conference, which meets annually or at longer intervals, is the supreme authority of the union and is usually composed of delegates from branches or larger units, together with the national executive committee. The committee normally presents to the conference a report on its work over the previous period and this is discussed. Motions and amendments are submitted by branches or district organization. The conference is sometimes responsible for electing the principal lay officers, the full-time officials, the executive committee or part of it.

It is apparent that the study of a trade union as an organization cannot be effected solely by examination of its rule book. Both its formal and informal organization structures are products of more than its legal rules. Nevertheless rule books could often be clearer, and many might be redrafted with advantage, for example with regard to the rights of members.

trading account

an account which determines the gross profit of a business.

trading area

a district whose boundaries are usually determined by the economical buying or selling range for a commodity or group of related commodities from a centre of distribution.

trading down

a seller's practice of handling cheap or low-grade products in order to secure higher volume sales (usually at a low rate of profit with a high stock turn.).

trading up

a seller's practice of handling expensive or high-grade products in order to gain prestige and secure a better class of trade (usually at a high rate of profit with a low stock turn).

traffic department

in an advertising agency, the department that schedules the work of other departments and is responsible for its completion according to schedule. In broadcasting, the department responsible for the scheduling of all programmes and announcements to be aired.

trail and error procedure

securing adjustment by random responses, gradually rejecting those proving unsatisfactory.

training contract

a contract between an accountant in practice and a student whereby the accountant undertakes to provide the student with experience which will fit him or her for membership of a professional body.

training office

an office of a professional chartered accountant which has been approved as being able to provide acceptable training to recruits.

training within industry programmes (TWI)

a series of short training programmes for first-line supervisors developed during World War II.

trait

an enduring characteristic of an individual's personality.

trait theory

any approach to the study of leadership which emphasizes the importance of tryping to identify distinguishing characteristics or traits of personality common to successful leaders.

transaction

a business action or agreement, usually involving a financial consideration; also, a system, process, or procedure resulting in an exchange of information; any mechanical or human interaction.

transcription error

mistakes made in transferring data from the source form to another form of record.

transfer agent

an office, usually a bank or trust, that acts for a corporation in transferring stock from one owner to another.

transfer of training

the process whereby the learning achieved in one situation is transferred to another situation. This can have positive effects (knowing Spanish aids the learning of

Italian) or sometimes negative effects (knowing how to steer a car is detrimental to sterring a boat with a tiller).

transfer prices

prices charged by a division when it sells to another division of the same organisation.

translating economic factors into money

it is hard for any executive to keep in mind all the factors pertinent to a decision and to give each its proper relative weight. One way to reduce the complexity of the job is to translate economic factors into rupees of income expenses or investment. Usually these rupees figures can then be combined into one or two key net amounts which are concise and relatively easy to handle.

transportation

transport is the carriage of goods from places where they are less useful to places where they are more useful. Effecting transport is inevitable for economic progress. There can be no real market other than that of a local nature unless goods can be transported safely and quickly and at a low cost.

treasure trove

valuable items which are found accidentally after having been hidden for many years. They are legally the property of the government although the finger will usually be rewarded by a sum equal to the value of the objects discovered.

trend

a general direction predicted from past movements. Prices on the stock exchange may, for example appear to be following an upward trend because they have been moving upwards for sometimes in the past.

trend forecasting

a method of forecasting using the ratio of the weighted to the unweighted average of a series.

trial and error learning

the step-by-step form of learning over many trials characteristic of most animal learning and much human learning and the basis for conditioning procedures. It is a very laborious process compared to insight learning.

trial balance

an interim financial report used for checking the accuracy of book-keeping system entries before preparing financial statements. A trial balance is created by totalling all credit entries and debit entries, and comparing them for equality.

tribunal

a court constituted for a special purpose, e.g., an industrial dispute.

truck

a method of paying workers in goods rather than cash. In earlier centuries this was popular with employers but was outlawed when it became too widely abused.

trust

a term used in the early twentieth century for combinations of companies that resulted, or were expected to result, in quasi-monopoly.

Also used of funds set up for specific purposes and managed by a group of trustees. For example, a company may set up a pension trust to provide money for the payment of pensions.

trust account

an account established by a depositor or trustee with a trust company. The depositor or trustee controls the trust accounts during his or her lifetime. After the donor's death, the balance of the trust account is payable to the beneficiary (ies).

trust company

a corporation established and operated to perform the functions of a trustee. Most trust companies also engage in other banking and/or financial business.

tum

the difference between an offer price and a bid price for a security.

turnkey system

a complete set of equipment and an installation agreement for it in which the vendor assumes all responsibilities for installation, including analysis of the buyer's needs, selection of the proper components, installation, maintenance, documentation, and training for all users of the hardware and operating software.

turnover

in fiance, the number of times that assets are paid in full over a given time interval. For examples, the turnover for accounts receivable is calculated by dividing the average balance of accounts receivable by the total billings on account for the same interval.

turnover, employee

the percentage of the work force who quit, get fired, or are otherwise separated from the payroll in a given period.

turnover, inventory

the number of times total inventory is used up and replaced in the course of a year.

two-tier offer

a takeover device in corporate acquisitions and mergers in which a relatively high per-share price is paid for a controlling interest in a company targeted for acquisition, and a lesser per-share price is paid for the remaining shares.

type A personality

a set of personality characteristics that have been linked to a particular susceptibility to heart disease. These characteristics include being impatient, always rushing, trying to do too many things at once walking, talking and eating fast being hard, driving at work, having few interests outside work and hiding feelings. Type a personality is always contrasted with type B personality.

type B personality

a set of personality characteristics that are the

opposite of type A personality and therefore considered to be much less suspectible to heart disease. These characteristics include being causal about appointment, being a good listener, never feeling rushed, slow and deliberate in manner and speech, easy-going with many interests outside work and able to express feelings. Both A and B are estreme instances and people would generally fall somewhere between the two.

type high

same height as normal type; 918 of an inch. A plate is type high when mounted to this height for printing.

typist

person whose job is to write letters using a typewriter.

type page

the printed area on a page. The area round type page is the margins. Inside margins, adjacent to the fold, are called gutters.

ultimatum

statement to someone that unless he does something within a period of time, action will be taken against him.

unanimous

where everyone votes in the same way.

unbundling

the breaking up of a large and complex business into clear components each concentrating on a narrow range of activities.

uncleared lodgement

an amount paid into a bank which has not yet been cleared to the account to which it is to be credited. Its accounted significance is that it may be one of the items which has to be taken into account in preparing a bank reconciliation statement.

unconditional

with no conditions or provisions attached.

uncontrollable cost

the cost chargeable to a job or cost centre which cannot be affected by the action of the person who controls the centre.

undated security

a security which has no date for redemption. The presumption may be that it will never be redeemed but that the holders will continue to receive an income at a rate of interest determined when the securities were first issued.

underachiever

person who achieves less than he or she is capable of.

undercapitalised

the condition of having too little capital invested in the business. It will show itself by the frequent short-term cash crises which the business has to meet and by the inability of the management to undertake any investment in profitable opportunities.

underemployment

a situation in which people do not have enough work to do or are not being fully utilized in terms of their skill level.

undermanning

a situation in which there are

fewer people employed by an organization than are necessary for the efficient performance of its work.

underrun

printing trades practice permits an allowance of 10 percent less than the total printing order as completion of an order. Normally, the printer provides for an overrun, but excessive spillage in printing or in binding may cause a slight shortage.

underwriter

a person professionally trained and specialising in the underwriting of insurance.

underwriting

the acceptance of a financial risk in consideration for the payment of a premium or commission. A new issue of shares in a company may be underwritten, the underwriter agrees to take up any shares which are not applied for by the public and thus guarantees the success of the issue.

underwriting profit

that portion of an insurance company's earning that comes from the function of calculating a profit factor during underwriting.

undivided profit

profit which has not yet been distributed to the shareholders.

unearned premium

that portion of a premium for which the protection of an insurance policy has not yet been given.

unemployment benefit

a social security benefit given to persons who, whilst unemployed, are actively seeking employment.

unemployment insurance

a form of social insurance that pays benefits to qualified people who are unemployed. Unemployment insurance is financed through a payroll tax. People qualify for benefits by accumulating covered employment as defined in states' law. Most persons receiving unemployment insurance do not continue to receive any group health insurance coverage they might have had through their most recent employer.

uniform accounting

a system whereby a number of business in a similar line of activity prepare accounts on a uniform basis so as to aid comparison.

uniform capital factor

a uniform percentage added onto all diagnosis-related group prices to cover hospital costs for pricing in prospective payment systems.

uniform costing

a set of common accounting principles and methods used by a member of individual companies within a given industry to enable cost comparisons to be made.

unilateral

on one side only or done by one party only.

unilateral arbitration

a situation in which one side in an industrial dispute decides unilaterally to go to an arbitration body to seek a solution to the problem.

unincorporated business

a business which does not have the status of a corporation. Examples partnerships. An unincorporated business cannot enjoy the benefit of limited liability and its life does not exceed those of its proprietors.

union

trade union or trades unions or US labour union = workers' organisation which represents its members in discussions with management about wages and conditions of work and defend their interest.

unique selling point

in marketing this term refers to the distinctive feature of a product that gives it a competitive advantage.

unit cost

the cost of one unit of production or of a single item. It is found by dividing the total costs by the number of units or items produced.

unite

to join together.

unit trust of India (UTI)

established by the government of India on 1st July, 1964 by an Act of the Parliament, the main objectives of UTI are:

(i) to mobilise the small savings of the public through sale of unit schemes.

(ii) to invest these small savings in a wide range of securities.

(iii) to provide reasonable income with minimum risk and maximum of liquidity of investments to the unit-holders.

(iv) to enable small investors to take advantages of the skill and knowledge of the experts in the field of investments.

(v) to facilitate growth and diversification of the economy through capital formation.

unity of command

only one superior for each person.

unity of direction

one head and one plan for each segment of the organisation.

universal standard data

a type of simplified predetermined motion time system developed from methods time measurement consists of seven tables of date a time standards which can be applied to any type of manual activity with a high degree of accuracy on all but very short cycle operations.

unlimited company

a corporate body, i.e. company, the members of which do not have limited liability. Such bodies are very rarely encountered as trading concerns but their activities are governed, like those of limited companies, by company legislation.

unmanned manufacturing

the technology of operating entire manufacturing facilities without the need for human operators (e.g., with the use of robots).

unpaid work

work carried out within the

household for the benefit of its members, and difficult to assess in terms of a national real income.

unsecured creditor

a creditor whose claim is supported only by the agreement that payment should be made. The position of an unsecured creditor should be distinguished from that of a secured creditor.

unsuccessful

not successful.

unsuitable

not suitable.

unwaged

the unwaged = people with no jobs.

update

bring the information in a story up-to-date.

use-friendly systems

the manufacturers of computer hardware have expertise in electronics; writers of operating systems and applications programs have expertise in software; neither necessarily has any formal understanding of the capabilities and limitations of human performance. As a consequence, accounts of computerized systems that are difficult, or even impossible, to use are by no means rare.

The term 'user-friendly' is applied to those systems in which the needs of the user have, supposedly, been fully taken into account. Ideally the factors involved would include the ergonomics of the hardware, the software and the supporting documentation, such that system users are able to perform their tasks with the maximum efficiency and the minimum stress.

useful economic life

the length of time for which a fixed asset can be used before a deterioration in its condition or developments in technology elsewhere makes this unprofitable. The useful economic life will be an important factor in deciding the rate of depreciation for the asset.

uses of financial statements

different classes of people are interested in the financial statements analysis with a view to assessing the economic and financial position of any business or industrial concern in terms of profitability, liquidity or solvency.

utility

the usefulness or satisfaction to be derived from a product by a potential buyer. Something that performs a useful service, like a public utility.

vacancy

job which is to be filled.

vacation

holiday or period when people are not working.

valid

true or which can be used lawfully.

validity

the extent to which a result is free from bias measured by reference to independent sources. Contrasts with consistency which has to do with the internal agreement of data.

validity analysis

a systematic analysis of each component of a product and of the operations performed on each to determine whether the value contributed by each is good enough to justify the cost.

validity tests

a process for checking the accurance definite proportional values, according to the desired degree of importance of various parts of the results.

value added tax

a tax levied on a product at each stage of manufacture or distribution in proportion to the estimated increase in its ultimate sales value.

value analysis; value engineering

technique developed in America for systematically analysing every component at operation in the making of a product and examining the function and usefulness in relation to cost.

value for money

a term used particularly in the public sector to denote the benefit derived from a particular expenditure for a particular purpose.

values

fundamental beliefs, either generally or personally held, that serve as the criteria by which all social alternatives are appraised. Values always involve an emotional commitment, in that people feel strongly that behaviour in accordance with the value is good whilst behaviour in violation of the value is 'bad'. The value may not be something wholly attainable (e.g., absolute honesty) but may be, nevertheless, something towards which one should constantly strive.

Differences in values underline many of the differences in behaviour that occur in industrial organizations. Thus common managerial values include a belief in the sanctity of authority as an organizational principle and in the importance of personal advancement, whilst shop-floor values may include a belief in the importance of shared power leading to negotiated rules of behaviour governing the relationship between management and workers, and in the importance of collective loyalty through which there can be general advancement. These conflicting values may lead managers to become over-concerned with the maintenance of managerial prerogatives whilst trade unionists assume the right to participate in organizational decision-making, to question orders and, where appropriate, to disobey. Similarly managers may elaborate systems of individual incentive bonuses and merit-rating, whilst trade unionists press for equality of treatment.

Values are acquired by the individual, often during childhood as a result of family influences, but also during adulthood as a result of experience and widening social contacts. Values differ from one society or group to another and will change over time. An individual's values do not change easily, although a process of modification usually takes place continuously during a person's lifetime.

value survey
an instrument used to help an individual identify and clarify the priorities in his or her own value system. A typical value survey lists values and asks the survey taker to rank-order the values based on their importance to him or her.

value to the business
a concept of value which values an asset at the maximum which a business would be prepared to pay in order to retain the asset.

variable cost
the cost which tends to vary in direct proportion to changes in the volume of output or turnover.

variable costing
a from of marginal costing which examines costs at various alternative levels of production.

variable element
element for which the basic time varies in relation to some characteristics of the product, equipment or process, e.g., dimensions, weight, quality etc.

variable factor programming
vfp is based on the principle that it is a function of management to determine what constitutes a fair and reasonable day's work, to assign work and to control its flow.

variable rate
the rate of interest charged on a mortgage or similar loan on terms such that the rate of interest charged will be varied from time to time in line with fluctuations in the market rate of interest.

variety reduction
reducing the range of products manufactured or marketed. Also promoting the increased use of standard parts where possible.

variety store
a store carrying a wide range of relatively inexpensive goods for the household.

vendor rating
classifying of distributors by volume of sales, with preferential trade terms for different grades of vendor.

venture capital
funds which are invested in a business on the basis that the investor receives a share in the outcome of the enterprise rather than an agreed fixed rate of return. It is thus capital which is at risk.

verbal
using spoken words, not writing.

verification
the process of assessing the truth of a statement. An auditor will be concerned with the verification of the information contained in a company's

accounts.

vertical

upright or straight up or down.

vertical communication

a term sometimes applied to downward communication though more usually to upward communication in an organization.

vertical or horizontal delegation

customarily delegation is considered as being from a higher to a lower level but it can also be from a lower to a higher level or between levels on the same plane. In other words delegation can be downward, upward or sidewise. Downward delegation of authority is illustrated by a sales manager to the sales staff, upward delegation by state governments to the federal government.

vestibule training

form of in-service training which takes place in special rooms separate from the actual place of work.

vested right

benefit, such as a retirement pension, that a person is entitled to and that he or she cannot be legally deprived of.

vet

to examine something carefully.

veteran

employee who has been in the same post for may years.

vibration

the most common sources of vibration are transport vehicles, such as ships, aircraft, cars and agricultural vehicles. The effects upon the human body may include discomfort, headaches, nausea, pain and permanent internal damage, in addition to severe decrements in working performance.

The type and severity of these effects depend upon the amplitude, frequency and duration of the vibration as well as the physiological and psychological condition of the individual.

Motion sickness result most commonly from very low frequency vibration. At higher frequencies severe discomfort and fatigue may occur. The natural frequencies of different parts of the body lie in the range 3-9 cycles per second. Within this range resonance resulting in anatomical damage may arise from exposure. Experiments upon animals indicate that injury may result from displacement of the abdomen or from mechanical collisions between lungs and the heart.

Numerous damping devices are available to protect human beings from deleterios effects. Correct posture is of the utmost importance, and appropriate training procedures may help people to cope.

vicarious liability

the liability of an employer for the actions of employees while working under instructions.

vice-president, executive

generally the second in command to the president.

victimization
the persistently unfair treatment of a worker, either by colleagues or employers.

video
the visual television signal.

videophone
combined telephone and television transmission, by which voice and sight of the two parties are received at each end.

videotape
a recording of the video and sound of television subject matter.

vignette
feature, usually a sidebar, providing a humorous, poignant, etc., look at subject.

violate
to break a rule or law or agreement.

visible earnings
the element in the earnings from the international trade of the country which derives from tangible goods.

visual acuity
keenness of vision.

visual defect
an imperfection of vision.

visual display
the part of computer that provides a visual display of its operations on a television-like screen.

visual display terminal (VDT)
displays copy selected from computer memory and allows editing.

visual imagery
a mental reconstruction of sensory experiences secured by means of vision.

visualisation of entirety
the overall comprehension is valuable for it enables the manager to see important relationships gain a fuller understanding of each activity and appreciate the basis upon which managerial actions are supported. Isolation and confusion are reduced. Through planning a constructive identification with the problems and the enterprise as a whole is gained.

visual punch(ed) card
punched card in which the information is retrieved by looking through the holes of a group of cards. Also known as feature cards.

vocational guidance
a branch of occupational psychology which helps people to choose an occupation or a career which will be of mutual benefit to them and their prospective employers. It makes use of the interview technique plus an extensive battery of psychological tests, including tests of ability, aptitude etc.

vocational training
education or training for a business, trade or profession as distinct from general education in the sense of preparation for life and living.

vocabulary test
a sample of the words selected from a complete general dictionary presented for definition; the score is an index of the testee's total vocabulary.

vocalisation

movement of lips, tongue, or vocal apparatus of the throat while reading silently.

voice-over (VO)
in films, a narration with the narrator not visible on the screen.

voidable
description of a contract which can be voided by one party to it but not another. A contract entered into following misrepresentation is voidable by the deceived party.

volatile securities
securities the price of which is liable to frequent substantial movements. A speculator in securities will make use of volatile securities where, in the event of success, of profit is likely to be greatest. There is also the greatest risk of loss.

volition
a state of decision or choice, the end condition of voluntary activity

volume of trading
a measure of how many deals have been concluded in the stock exchange in a given period of time, usually 1 day. The volume of trading is believed by some to be as important a predictor of future performance as is the movement of prices.

volume variance
a variance brought about by deviations of the actual volume of production from the budgeted volume.

voluntary chain
associations of retailers who have agreed to buy exclusively from a certain wholesaler in return for which the retailer obtains additional discount, advice on merchandising and good retail practice and the benefit of group advertising schemes.

volunteer
person who offers to do something.

vote
marking a paper, holding up your hand, etc., to show your opinion or to show who you want to be elected.

voucher
a document providing evidence of some transaction. Many examples exist. Petty cash should be paid out only against a voucher signed by the person claiming the money and bearing an explanation of what it was used for.

vowel
an unconstructed letter sound made with open throat, mouth, teeth, and lips. These are vowels: a, e, i, o, u, and sometimes y.

wage
money paid regularly (usually in cash each week) to a worker for work done.

wage and salary survey
a survey of what other companies are paying for various jobs.

wage assignment
a voluntary transfer of earned wages to a third party to pay debts, but savings bonds, pay unions dues, or execute other fiduciary actions.

wage councils
wages councils were set up in

Britain by the Wages Councils Act, 1945, replacing the earlier trade boards. They provide machinery for an indirect form of statutory wage regulation where no facilities for collective bargaining, or only inadequate ones, exist. Each council has a tripartite membership, consisting of an equal number of persons representing employers' and employees' interests, together with three independent members appointed by the Secretary of State. The function of each council, since 1975, has been to fix not only the remuneration but other terms and conditions of employment of workers in the relevant industry. Before the proposals of the council are implemented in an order they are published in draft form to all affected persons. Employers and employees in the industry are given a fortnight in which to lodge objections with the council.
Once the council has made a wages-regulation order, employers would be guilty of an offence if they paid employees at a rate below that given in order and employees would also be able to recover by civil action from the employer any difference between the statutory wage and that actually paid to them. Special inspectors are appointed by the Secretary of State to ensure observance of the provisions of the Act

wage survey
after evaluation jobs are grouped or classified according to their worth, it is necessary to convert them to monetary values to determine the wages rates. To build up a competitive wage structure it is necessary to know what are the rates prevailing for similar jobs in the same industry in the area.

wants
desires which may not yet be apparent. They may be converted eventually into needs. New wants have to be anticipated by the markeer and satisfied with new products or services.

warn
to say that there is a possible danger.

warning
oral or written message to an employee, threatening punishment or dismissal if performance or behaviour is not improved.

warrant
a document giving some right. A company may issue warrants which give the option to their holder to subscribe for a defined number of shares at a defined price on specified future dates.

warranty services
service of a consumer product carried out free of charge under what is commonly called a guarantee. The total cost of warranty services is an expense of the business which must be recovered in the price charged for the product.

wash drawing
water colour or diluted Indian ink brush drawing that requires

halftone reproduction.

wastage

natural wastage = losing workers because they resign or retire, not because they are made redundant or are sacked.

wasting assets

assets whose economic value decreases as they are used because they cannot particularly be renewed or replaced, e.g., coal-mines or oil–fields.

watchdog body

body which watches something (especially government departments or commercial firms) to see that regulations are not being abused.

watered stock

shares in a company whose nominal value exceeds the actual market value of the underlying assets.

water mark

identification mark left in texture of paper, which can be seen when held up against the light.

waver

an agreement attached to an insurance policy that exempts from coverage certain disabilities or injuries normally covered by the policy.

way leave

the right, and hence the amount paid for the right, to make use of part of a person's land for providing transit for persons or goods.

weak market

one in which there is very little interest in buying so that the price tend to fall and business to be at a low ebb.

weed out

to remove unsuitable candidates or employees.

week

period of seven days (from Monday to Sunday).

weighted average cost of capital

the cost of capital taking into account the various source in use and the proportions in which they are employed.

weighting

the adjustment of data by assigning definite proportional values, according to the desired degree of importance of various parts of the results.

weight of type

the relative blackness of a particular type face.

welfare

public financial assistance to certain categories of poor persons.

wellness programme

a programme that encourages improved health status and a healthful life-style through health education, exercise, nutrition, and health promotion.

well-paid

earning a high salary.

well-qualified

(person) who has good qualifications for a job.

wet printing

in colour printing, the application of one colour before the preceding colour is dry.

white collar crime

crimes committed by business people or office workers (such

as embezzlement, computer fraud, insider dealings).

white collar union
trade union representing white collar worker.

white collar worker
worker in an office, not in a factory.

white knight
a company which volunteers to take over another company to rescue the latter from an unwelcome takeover bid from some third party.

white paper
a document prepared as an argument in behalf of an organisation on a given issue. It may be more argumentative than a position paper.

whole life policy
a form of endowment policy where the proceeds of the policy are paid out at the death of the assured whenever that occurs.

wholesaler
one who, holding stocks and selling goods that are produced by others, generally sells to retail outlets rather than directly to users or consumers, obtaining his revenue from a discount paid to him by the producer.

wholesaling
acting as an intermediary or middleman between the production of goods and their retailing to the general public. It usually involves the stocking of relatively large quantities of goods for onward distribution.

widow
a short line at the end of a paragraph, leaving unprinted "white space". Permissible except when used in first line of column.

width or set
the distance between the side or the width across the shank. This distance varies according to the shape of a letter.

wildcat strike
strike organized suddenly by workers without the approval of the main union office.

windfall profit
an unexpected profit usually arising from matter not directly connected with the activities of the lucky individual or organization, e.g., a bequest or a change in taxation. The original windfall consisted of apples blown off trees.

windowe dressing
applied to financial statements (e.g., balance sheets) which give a false impression of the financial position.

window tax
an obsolete form of taxation in which the payment depended on the number of windows found in a building.

withdraw
to take back (an offer).

without profits policy
a policy of life assurance which gives the holder no right to share in the profits of the company issuing the policy.

witness
one who observes an event and can provide evidence that it actually took place. The signature of certain documents such as a deed or covenant or a

will requires to be witnessed before the document is valid. The witness also signs the document in the presence of the chief signatory to evidence that the signature is that of the person which it purports to be.

word analysis
analysis of an unfamiliar word into known elements for the purpose of identification.

word association test
projective test in which the subject is asked to state words, objects and feelings associated, in his mind, with the given word stimulus.

word processing
the computerised creation, editing, and printing of written text; a component of office automation providing text entry through computers or terminals, and automated assistance in correcting, editing, formating, copying, deleting, storing, retrieving, and printing documents, text records, and correspondence.

work
physical and mental effort.

work climate
essentially psychological and social in character the delegator must have a feeling of confidence that delegation of authority will reward, not penalize her or him. Authority delegation should have the blessing of the top managers as evidenced in such things as a reasonable and satisfactory compensation as impartial means for evaluating a manager's work and a significant part of the executive of development programme.

workday
day when work is done, as opposed to a holiday.

work design
the part of the job design process that is concerned with the actual working operations, as opposed to the personnel management aspects.

worker-director
a representation of the workforce on the board of directors of an organisation. This is sometimes considered the ultimate in industrial democracy. It is extremely rare.

work experience
a period to time spent doing unpaid work in a workplace environment by young people about to leave school, as preparation for future employment.

work factor
a system of predetermined motion time (PMT). Performance times are those of employees working under an incentive scheme.

work flow
the arrangement of jobs in a particular sequence intended to help an organization run smoothly and productively.

working capital
more usually known as net working current assets, meaning current assets minus current liabilities. Also known as circulating capital.

work in progress
materials, components or

products in various stages of completion through the manufacturing processes, including raw material released for initial processing and completely processed material awaiting final inspection and acceptance as finished products.

workload

amount of work which a person has to do.

workman

man who works with his hands.

work measurement

an integral part of the work study process in which a variety of (subjective) methods like work sampling are used to fix a standard time for the acceptable performance of a given task by a trained worker.

workout

he is working out his notice = he is working during the time between resigning and actually leaving the company.

workplace

place where you work.

work sampling

a technique to promote efficiency by determining through observation, continuously or at random intervals, exactly how employees are spending their time.

work sheet

a sheet laying out the effects of particular transactions on a financial position.

work simplification

a process used in organization and methods or workstudy where a system of work is examined to see if unnecessary expenditure of energy can be removed.

work station

the physical environment in which a job is done. It is used most often to refer to the location of a computer operator or work processor operator.

work study

a generic term for those techniques, particularly method study and work measurement, which are used in the examination of human work in all its context and which lead systematically to the investigation of all the factors which effect efficiency and economy of the situation being reviewed in order to effect improvement.

work to rule

working strictly according to the rules agreed between the union and management and therefore very slowly, as a protest.

w.p.m.

the average number of words per minute which a person covers in reading a selection.

write in

written enquiry from outside an organization, asking if there are any jobs available.

write off

the reduction in the book value of an asset to correspond more closely to the fair market value.

writing vocabulary

words used and understood in ordinary writing.